MEDIA AND COMMUNICATION RESEARCH METHODS

D0583054

Media and Communication Research Methods

By
Anders Hansen
Senior Lecturer, Department of Media and Communication,
University of Leicester

David Machin
Professor of Media and Communication, Örebro University

palgrave
macmillan

© Anders Hansen & David Machin 2013

All rights reserved. No reproduction, copy or transmission of this
publication may be made without written permission.

No portion of this publication may be reproduced, copied or transmitted
save with written permission or in accordance with the provisions of the
Copyright, Designs and Patents Act 1988, or under the terms of any licence
permitting limited copying issued by the Copyright Licensing Agency,
Saffron House, 6–10 Kirby Street, London EC1N 8TS.

Any person who does any unauthorized act in relation to this publication
may be liable to criminal prosecution and civil claims for damages.

The authors have asserted their rights to be identified as the authors of
this work in accordance with the Copyright, Designs and Patents Act 1988.

First published 2013 by
PALGRAVE MACMILLAN

Palgrave Macmillan in the UK is an imprint of Macmillan Publishers Limited,
registered in England, company number 785998, of Houndmills, Basingstoke,
Hampshire RG21 6XS.

Palgrave Macmillan in the US is a division of St Martin's Press LLC,
175 Fifth Avenue, New York, NY 10010.

Palgrave Macmillan is the global academic imprint of the above companies
and has companies and representatives throughout the world.

Palgrave® and Macmillan® are registered trademarks in the United States,
the United Kingdom, Europe and other countries

ISBN: 978–0–230–00006–3 hardback
ISBN: 978–0–230–00007–0 paperback

This book is printed on paper suitable for recycling and made from fully
managed and sustained forest sources. Logging, pulping and manufacturing
processes are expected to conform to the environmental regulations of the
country of origin.

A catalogue record for this book is available from the British Library.

A catalog record for this book is available from the Library of Congress.

UNIVERSITY
OF SHEFFIELD
LIBRARY

Contents

Acknowledgements

This publication has come to fruition with encouragement, guidance and gentle steering from our Palgrave/Macmillan editors, initially Emily Salz and subsequently Rebecca Barden. We gratefully acknowledge their editorial direction, encouragement and support.

The authors and publishers would like to thank the following for granting permission to reproduce material in this work:

We are grateful to Sage Publications Ltd for permission to use an adapted version of Anders Hansen's Editor's Introduction from Hansen, A. (ed.) (2009). *Mass Communication Research Methods* (Vol. 1, pp. xxiii–xxxiii). London: Sage. ISBN 978-1-4129-3004-8) in Chapter 1.

We gratefully acknowledge Professor Jenny Kitzinger's kind permission to reproduce as Figure 10.2 an excerpt from the report Hughes, E., Kitzinger, J., and Murdock, G. (2008). *Media Discourses and Framing of Risk: Social Contexts and Responses to Risk Network* (SCARR) Working Paper 27. Available at http://www.cardiff.ac.uk/jomec/resources/KitzingerWkPaper27.pdf.

We are grateful to R. J. C Watt for his kind permission to reproduce as Figure 11.1 a screenshot from the text analysis and concordancing software *Concordance*. Version 3.3 (2009). Available at http://www.concordance software.co.uk/.

We are grateful to International Business Machines Corporation (IBM®) for permission to reproduce screen images from SPSS® (© SPSS, Inc., an IBM Company) as follows: Table 11.1 (p. 266) and Figures 11.1–11.9 (pp. 258, 259, 261, 263, 264, 266, 267, 268). Reprint Courtesy of International Business Machines Corporation, © SPSS, Inc., an IBM Company.

We are grateful to Getty Images for the following:

p. 176: Two women with a laptop. Per Magnus Persson/Johner Images/Getty Images. © 2012 Getty Images. All rights reserved.

p. 178: Young businesswoman standing on desk, portrait. Tim Robberts/The Image Bank/Getty Images. © 2012 Getty Images. All rights reserved.

p. 180: Portrait of an assertive female CEO standing with two businessmen. Rayman/Digital Vision/Getty Images. © 2012 Getty Images. All rights reserved.

p. 181: Young woman in white dress dancing in meadow. Mike Timo/Photographer's Choice/Getty Images. © 2012 Getty Images. All rights reserved.

List of tables and figures

CHAPTER 1

Introduction to *Media and Communication Research Methods*

Research methods do not, and never should, exist in isolation from theory. Media and communication research methods are no exception, but the point is possibly more important to make for the field of media and communication research than for some other and longer-established fields or disciplines. The simple reason for this is that media and communication research, rather than being a well-defined discipline, is a sprawling and multidisciplinary field of research approaches and theories, drawing inspiration from a wide range of disciplines in the humanities, the social sciences and even from some sciences. Far from being a weakness, this has in fact proved to be one of its major strengths: a productive impetus to continuous development and adaptation to what have historically been rapid changes in the nature and application of media technologies as well as political and social concerns with 'the media'.

The aim of this book is to provide an introduction to selected key research methods, approaches and tools for the study of media and communication. We introduce methods which we have found to be the most productive, appropriate and coherent for addressing core questions about the role of media and communications within wider social, political and cultural contexts. Our perspective is principally sociological, although – as will be evident throughout the book – the methods and approaches introduced here draw inspiration from a broad range of disciplines in both the humanities and the social sciences.

The emphasis throughout is to provide the reader with a 'how to' guide to addressing research questions in media and communication research, although we also seek, where appropriate, to give examples of how each method has been used and how it fits into the wider historical context and development of the field. Each of the methods introduced in the book can be used on its own, but a common theme throughout is also to emphasise the potential gains from combining two or sometimes more research methods. Thus, as we shall see, many of the most successful and prominent models of media and communication have been based on research

combining methods for analysing media content with methods for studying media audiences.

Mapping the field of media and communication research

Even a cursory glance at introductions to media and communication
research will quickly reveal that there are many approaches that can be taken,
and many principles that can be used, to categorise and map this broad field
of inquiry. Some approach this from a strictly *method-driven* perspective,
often making a broad distinction between qualitative and quantitative methods and with the individual method as their starting point and organising
principle. Others approach it from a *theory-driven* perspective, discussing the
particular (and often multiple) methods that have been applied in research
guided by each specific theory. Still others take a *media-driven* approach,
focusing in turn on the methods and theories which have been used in
research on each individual medium (film, television, newspapers, radio,
advertising, etc.). Many – not always entirely successfully – use a mixture of
these organising perspectives, and furthermore attempt to place their discussion of methods and approaches in chronological and historical context.

   As the late James Halloran – one of the pioneers of communication
research in the UK – insisted throughout his long career (see e.g. Halloran,
1998), research methods cannot and should not be discussed or understood
in isolation from the theories, models and socio-political concerns which
have guided media and communication research. Likewise, neither method
nor theory can be understood in isolation from the technological and
economic possibilities and arrangements, or from the social and political
struggles and concerns which characterise different historical periods. A
sense of the wider historical, disciplinary and political context of media and
communication research thus helps in appreciating that just as each method
has its own history, so too is its use, application, development and career very
much a result of historical conditions and changes.

   While much variation exists in how scholars characterise, categorise and
describe the field of media and communication research – which in itself of
course is symptomatic of its multidisciplinary nature – prominent media
scholar Karl Erik Rosengren (1983) argues that four key paradigms inform
the field. Paraphrasing McQuail (2004: 14–15), Rosengren's four paradigms
can be summarised as follows: 1) a *functionalist* paradigm which stresses the
media's contribution to the functioning and maintenance of the existing
social order and favours quantitative research; 2) an *interpretive* paradigm
favouring qualitative methods for describing and investigating cultural issues
of meaning and content in relation to communication processes; 3) a *radical-*

humanist paradigm, which, like the interpretive paradigm, favours qualitative methods but with a clear sense that the goal of research is to expose the 'hegemonic' role of the media and to effect radical change in society; and 4) the *radical-structural* paradigm, which 'looks at the media as a material, especially political-economic, force in society that has to be investigated in its concrete manifestations (i.e. with reference to patterns of ownership and control, market power, political connections) and by objective methods of analysis applied to reliable data' (McQuail, 2004: 15).

Another helpful taxonomy is offered by Oliver Boyd-Barrett (2002), who groups media and communication research under the main headings of *effects research*, *cultural studies* and *political economy*. Recognising the (neat) simplicity of this categorisation, Boyd-Barrett proceeds to expand each of these headings considerably in an overview that plots *theoretical models of society*, *concepts of media power* and *types of communications process* with *prevailing focus* (i.e. individual or social), *tone* (positive/negative) and *characteristic method of inquiry*, against a *timeline* that broadly indicates the predominance of each paradigm by decade(s) from the 1930s onwards. The historical purview is important, because it enables us to appreciate that different approaches and methods exist on a timeline: although they may be ever-present, they originate in particular historical circumstances and they wax and wane in response to social, political, historical and, of course, academic/scholarly pressures, factors and endeavours.

Perhaps the key influences on the development of the media and communications research field then can be identified and summarised as:

1) *Technological* – every new medium brings with it new communications possibilities, new formats and types of communication, new ways of relating to producers, audiences or consumers, new types of integration with other media technologies, and hence new research questions about their social and political roles in society.

2) *Disciplinary* – the nature of communications inquiry, including not only the questions asked but also the theories and methods used, has depended to a large extent on whether the informing disciplines – sociology, psychology, social psychology, linguistics, philosophy, literary studies, anthropology, ethnography, etc. – were social sciences or humanities/humanistic sciences (we should, of course, not forget the influence of science disciplines such as mathematics, computing, cybernetics, engineering, etc., but their major influence dates back to the early days of media and communication research and has been much less pronounced in the later developments of communications research); related to the question of disciplinary home, albeit not mapping on to disciplines in a simple straightforward manner, is the question of

whether communications inquiry is executed with predominantly quantitative or predominantly qualitative methods, whether predominantly about 'measurement' or predominantly about 'interpretation'.

3) *Political* – by which we wish to signal the classic division between administrative and critical communication research (a distinction first introduced in a now classic article by one of the founders of modern communication research, Paul Lazarsfeld (1941)), between research that is driven by commercial or administrative interests in functionality, efficiency and profit-maximisation, and research that is formulated from a socially and politically critical perspective with a view to informing critical social understanding and policy. 'Critical' in this context has nothing to do with being 'negative', but is about research designed and conducted from a socially conscientious perspective for the 'common good' and not as a means to furthering particular economic or political interests. The importance of political-historical context for understanding the development and focus of media and communication research has been noted by many, but is particularly succinctly expressed by British media scholar Graham Murdock (2002). He notes that while media and communications research was a key beneficiary of the tremendous growth in the 1930s to the 1960s in social scientific research, 'it was also profoundly shaped by the political climate created by the onset of the Cold War'. This climate and ideological conflict dominated the intellectual landscape and provided a fertile ground for the prevailing model of the social order during that period, 'structural functionalism', and its concerns with 'maintaining social stability and cementing consensus' – a task in which media and communications systems were seen as playing a key 'gluing-together' role (Murdock, 2002: 54–5).

On theory and methods – and asking the right questions

Appreciating the *political* context of the development of communications theory, research and methods links directly to the continuing debate in media and communication research about whether the right questions are being asked (Halloran, 1998). This is a debate that raises questions about method and focus (*media-centric* or *socio-centric*), but most significantly it points to the key argument that research should always be theory and policy driven, not method driven: 'methods are but a means to an end, important though they are, they are not an end in themselves, nor should they be used, as they have been, to determine the end or define the nature of the problems to be investigated' (Halloran, 1998: 10–11). Halloran thus criticises communications research, particularly in its early history, for being unduly dominated by the 'administrative' (in Lazarsfeld's terminology) needs of the media and the market place. This resulted, Halloran argues, in the favouring of a positivistic orientation leading to a concentration on methods which produce accurate and 'scientific' information on simple, narrow and, in sociological terms, relatively uninteresting phenomena. Essentially, his critique is that if much of the accumulated evidence from a long history of communications research appears both contradictory and inconclusive, then it is to a large extent because the wrong questions have been asked. That is, if communications research has failed to come up with clear answers, it is because much of it has been asking narrow and media-centric questions, using methods more concerned with what could be easily measured and counted than with whether that which was measured actually helped answer key questions about the social and political roles of media and communication processes.

Halloran's critique was in large part directed at the body of mainly and originally American communications research generally referred to as 'the dominant paradigm' (Gitlin, 1978). However, it is perhaps evidence of the persistence of this paradigm that prominent media scholars continue to echo the call for research questions which consider media and communication processes in their social, political and historical context and which critically address the core classical sociological concerns about power, organisation and control in society. Philo and Miller thus seek to issue a challenge to social scientists by asking 'why much of social science and in particular media and cultural studies can now communicate little that is critical or relevant to its own society' (2000: 831).

Murdock is similarly clear that the research questions addressed by media and communication research must be anchored by their social relevance and historical awareness, and must deal in a social scientific and critical way with questions of power, structure and change in society. Few have succeeded in bringing together the imperatives of critical inquiry, social relevance and historical awareness as eloquently and succinctly as Murdock:

illuminating the exercise of power and structural constraints and exploring the possibilities for change remain the central aims of a critical social-scientific approach to media and communication ... in pursuing this task, we have a rich stock of concepts and methods to draw upon. Their originators are not distant figures to be consigned to dusty back rooms in the museum of ideas. They remain our contemporaries. We still confront the central questions they grappled with, and their search for answers still has much to teach us. We are part of a continuing conversation about the structure and meaning of modern times and the ways they are changing. They stand at our shoulder, advising, carping, urging us on. To refuse their invitation to debate is to condemn ourselves to regularly reinventing the wheel. (2002: 57)

Quantitative and qualitative methods – and convergence

When considering the historical development of media and communication research and the various paradigms that have dominated during different periods, one is continuously confronted with the relationship between, on the one hand, researchers' theoretical conceptions of society and of the associated role of media and communications therein, and, on the other hand, their choices of research methods, data quarries and modes of data collection. This relationship is, of course, core in a book such as this, which has as its principal focus 'methods' for the study of media and communications processes. Because of the priority that the book gives to 'methods', it is even more important to emphasise, in Halloran's words, that 'methods are but a means to an end' (1998: 10–11).

All research, in other words, must start by 'asking the right questions', duly informed by existing research, knowledge and theory, and *only then* consider which method or methods might be most suitable for addressing the issue or problem at hand. Never should research start by choosing a method before considering what research questions to ask and what theoretical frameworks to draw on. Research is not principally about gathering data that lend themselves to easy collection or analysis, but rather about using/choosing the right methodological tools for addressing 'relevant' questions. There are of course many criteria of 'relevance' that could be applied, but principal amongst these should, we would argue, be considerations about the social, political and policy relevance of research.

There are two main reasons for highlighting these points: *first*, to re-emphasise that there is no single 'best' method for media and communication research, and, *second*, to encourage an eclectic approach that keeps an open mind on which methods – quantitative or qualitative – are most suitable for the research problem at hand, *and* which appreciates that a combination of several methods can often achieve more and better illumination of a research problem than a single method applied in isolation.

The plea for methodological open-mindedness is spurred on by the long history of both real, and perhaps more often 'perceived', ostracism and entrenchment between quantitative and qualitative approaches to media and communication research (a divide which itself parallels, but is not synonymous with, a positivist social scientific approach versus a humanistic 'interpretive' approach to media and communications processes). Jensen (2002: 254), making the case for convergence between and complementarity of qualitative and quantitative methodologies, aptly describes how the 'perception of fundamental difference has generated various kinds of response – from "imperialism", seeking to subordinate or delegitimate other approaches, to "apartheid", protecting one's own worldview through insulation from those of others'.

Much of the intellectual debate from the 1960s through the 1980s was taken up with sometimes bitter entrenchment into quantitative and qualitative camps, and while 'convergence' has been on the agenda for several decades, that Jensen and others writing in the first decade of the twenty-first century continue to see the need to address and bridge this chasm is perhaps symptomatic of the fact that much still needs to done. As in other manifestations of imperialism and apartheid, the unhelpful rhetorical devices of caricature and stereotyping come into play in the separation of quantitative and qualitative camps in media research. As Murdock's (2002) historical perspective on communications research makes clear, many of those, like Lazarsfeld, who have come to be remembered for their quantitative methods, and who have often been dismissed as crude empiricists, were in fact pioneers of multi-method research, whose 'choices were always dictated by the issue to be addressed, and there was no question of one method being suitable for all questions' (Murdock, 2002, referencing Morrison, 1998: 140).

Jensen (2002: 258) argues that it 'is at the level of *methodology*, defined as a theoretically informed plan of action in relation to an empirical field, that the distinction between qualitative and quantitative research becomes most apparent' and he goes on to discuss a number of binaries and differences of perspective, which are helpful for thinking about the differences and complementarity of quantitative and qualitative approaches. These include the *inductive* and *deductive* epistemological models underpinning research, and the different perspectives on *reliability* and *validity* in quantitative and qualitative research.

> The realist framework is of special interest in a convergence perspective. It indicates that while different empirical procedures (e.g. experiments or depth interviews) document and, in a sense, privilege particular kinds of events (the recall or decoding of media content), they may nevertheless bear witness to related mechanisms. Instead of engaging in conflict over a singular definition of the empirical domain, a realist strategy thus proposes to take advantage of several methodologies in order to document various aspects of mediated communication. It is the overriding task of research to inquire into the actuality of the phenomena as documented, and to explore whether they may be subsumed under similar explanatory mechanisms. (Jensen, 2002: 269–70)

Jensen concludes by pointing to three approaches to convergence between qualitative and quantitative methods: 1) *facilitation* – quantitative and qualitative approaches are used at separate stages of the research process, one informing the other; 2) *triangulation* – increasing reliability and validity of findings by using several methods to illuminate the same phenomenon; and 3) *complementarity* – different methodologies are used to examine different aspects of a research question, and not necessarily in the same concrete empirical domain.

Structure and contents of the book

We intend this book to be used as a reference handbook for the media and communications student or researcher who wishes to learn about how to use and apply a selected method or methods for studying media and communications phenomena and processes. Together with the contents list, this section then offers an overview that should enable the reader to select and go directly to the appropriate method or tools. We start with a brief outline of the book's structure and then proceed to provide one-paragraph overviews of what is covered in each chapter.

In brief outline, the structure of this book is as follows: we start with an introduction to the key steps in the research process. This is followed by introductions to the core methods for each of the three major domains of the communication process and of media and communication research: 1) *Institutions/Organisations/Production*; 2) *Content/Representation*; and 3) *Audiences/Consumption*. We round off with a final chapter that discusses tools and approaches for managing and analysing communications research data.

Chapter 2 is aimed primarily at students or novice researchers embarking on one of their first research projects and adventures. The chapter aims to take some of the intimidating complexity out of 'the research process', by offering an accessible step-by-step guide to the key stages of any media and communications research project. It charts the process from formulation of a research question/topic, through literature review, conceptualisation, choice of method(s), to data collection, management of data, analysis and write-up/presentation of results. The emphasis is on giving the student or novice researcher a recipe for how to get going on a piece of research, and on demonstrating that, with the right ingredients and the right procedures, success is perfectly achievable.

Chapters 3 and 4 introduce ways of researching media organisations and media professionals. Chapter 3 introduces the study of the political economy of the media, that is how to investigate the nature of media ownership, how they are financed, the organisation of production and how this is regulated by governments and international governing bodies. Researching ownership and control is important on the one hand simply to understand the nature of media organisations and processes. On the other it is at this level of analysis that we can begin to find out why media content is the way it is. We can ask whether the nature of the content of news on a webpage or an article in a magazine is down to the individual choices of the writer, journalist or photographer or to institutionally established processes and corporate strategies. Such things cannot be understood at the level of textual analysis alone.

Chapter 4 introduces ethnography and observational methods, which have been used widely in media research to study both production and consumption of the media. On the one hand these methods are associated with actually watching or sharing in what media professionals or media audiences are doing and saying. But on the other hand these methods, ethnography in particular, should be seen as a way of approaching the data that we collect and it can incorporate many different kinds of research methodologies. Traditionally, observational methods in particular have been used predominantly for studying media professionals and the production of media content. Much of the classic research of this type has focused particularly on news organisations and the practices of journalists, editors and other media professionals involved in the production of news. What is special to observational and ethnographic approaches is that they are used to understand social phenomena such as media use, effects and production, by viewing them as one part of people's lives and the culture they inhabit. It is this culture which provides them with the ideas and values through which they think about and share the world, and something like media consumption or any work practice must be seen in the context of wider cultural influences. So if we wish to understand what someone feels about, or how someone is affected by, say, a particular news report, we need to know more about this person in particular, the kinds of social values and ideas they normally live by and share with the people around them. We need to know how they behave more generally. If we wish to understand the production processes behind the creation of that news report then we may not simply be able to ask a journalist what they did, although this would be one important source of data. We would also need to look at what kinds of values and ideas the journalist has about what they do, the journalistic culture in which they have emerged and work, and also the processes and practices they used to produce the news report. In this chapter we show how these approaches are simple to use.

Chapters 5, 6, 7 and 8 focus on different – but also overlapping – approaches to researching media content. We start in Chapter 5 with the technique of content analysis, which continues to be one of the most frequently used methods in media and communication research. The chapter begins with a brief review of the history and development of the method since it first came to prominence in communications research in the 1950s. It discusses some of the key issues which have underpinned and circumscribed the use of this research technique, including questions regarding the analysis of manifest and latent meaning, quantitative versus qualitative emphases, reliability and validity, social and cultural indicators, trend analysis, performance monitoring, etc. The key strengths and weaknesses of the method as an approach to studying media content and textual data more generally are examined as is the relationship between content analysis data and other types of data in communication research. Drawing on examples from published content analysis studies, this is followed by a detailed step-by-step guide to the process of doing content analysis, from the selection and sampling of media material to the preparation and analysis of the data produced by content analysis.

Chapter 6 extends and elaborates the previous chapter's discussion of ways of analysing media content and meaning by focusing on the analysis of discourse. It looks at the particular set of tools for analysing texts and spoken language known as Critical Discourse Analysis (CDA), an approach founded in linguistics. Guided by linguistic expertise Critical Discourse Analysis focuses on two core dimensions of language, namely lexis (the choice of words in a text) and syntax (the way that sentences and texts are constructed or organised). CDA allows us to reveal more precisely how speakers and authors use language and grammatical features to create meaning, to persuade people to think about events in a particular way, sometimes even seek to manipulate people while at the same time concealing their intentions. Critical Discourse Analysis offers the promise of showing exactly what features of language, what language choices, have been used to accomplish particular kinds of communicative aims. In this chapter, we introduce the key components and tools of Critical Discourse Analysis and demonstrate how these can be applied to reveal how meaning is constructed and manipulated in media texts.

Chapter 7 introduces narrative and structural analysis as approaches to examining media content. While narrative and structural analysis have long had a prominent place in the study of literature and film, their application to the examination of news, documentary, drama, advertising and other media genres is more recent. It is perhaps symptomatic of the origins in literary and film analysis that such attempts have tended to focus on television drama, particularly soap opera, rather more than on other genres. This chapter argues that narrative and structural analysis offer valuable tools for the study of a broad range of media genres. The chapter traces the origins and key dimensions of narrative and structural approaches, and it demonstrates how and when these approaches can be used productively either on their own or in combination with some of the other approaches to media content discussed in the book. We look at how to research the narrative structure or 'discourse schema' of texts or other media representations. Such analysis allows us to break down what appear to be quite complex stories and texts to reveal very basic messages about the kinds of values and identities, concerns and social boundaries that underpin them.

Chapter 8 brings together a number of approaches from traditional semiotics and linguistics-based Multimodal Critical Discourse Analysis in order to show how we can produce much more systematic analyses of photographs. The chapter gives a set of guidelines for how in the first place we can *describe* what we see in photographs. Often this level of investigation is what is overlooked as the analyst jumps immediately to *interpretation*. But description is a vital level of analysis in the case of photographs and this chapter thus offers a guide to how to really 'see' what we are looking at. The methods described in this chapter are to some extent qualitative and are intended for detailed analysis of a smaller number of cases. Yet also, since they draw on linguistic forms of analysis, they have a quantitative aspect as we describe actual concrete features of photographs. So some of the tools in this chapter can lend themselves to quantitative research and can be aligned to content analysis as described in Chapter 5. At the end of the chapter we discuss specifically what a research project using this approach would look like. As with other chapters in this book it should become clear just how this approach should be used by the way the examples are dealt with and the models applied.

Chapters 9 and 10 deal with core methods for analysing media audiences, although – like those discussed in Chapters 3 and 4 – these methods can of course be applied in any study of human subjects, whether classed as 'media audiences', 'media producers' or otherwise. Chapter 9 introduces survey methodology, a method of data collection that has been at the centre of many of the studies which during the comparatively brief history of communication research have come to be seen as classics with a formative influence on the development of the field. While the emphasis in critical audience research has in more recent time shifted towards the more qualitative approaches of group interviewing, participant observation and audience ethnography, the survey method continues to be of central importance in communication research. The survey thus continues to be an essential tool for the regular monitoring of audience attitudes, opinion and media-related behaviour per se, while also, perhaps equally significantly, increasingly being used in conjunction with observational methods and audience ethnographies. The chapter starts by briefly charting the history of survey studies in communication research. It proceeds to discuss the strengths and weaknesses of survey research compared with other approaches to the study of media audiences, and it outlines the major types of survey research. A detailed outline of the key steps involved in carrying out a survey is provided, including sampling considerations, strategies for planning and managing the survey process, questionnaire design, direct interviewing versus self-completion questionnaires, interviewer training, coding of closed and open-ended questions, and analysis and interpretation of the data collected. The chapter considers the implications of the internet and new advances in computer-assisted analysis for the execution and administration of survey research.

Chapter 10 introduces the focus group interview as a method that is more suited than survey research to discovering *how* audiences make sense of media messages. Focus group methods thus lend themselves to a more in-depth examination than is possible in survey research of what experiential knowledge and frames of interpretation audiences bring to bear in their use and understanding of media content. While the individual in-depth interview and the focused group interview produce similar data in many respects, our reasons for concentrating on the group interview are twofold: first and foremost, focused group interviews allow the researcher to observe how audiences make sense of mediated communication *through conversation* and interaction with each other in a way that is closer, although clearly not identical, to how we form opinions and understandings in our everyday lives. Second, group interviews are more cost-efficient than individual interviews – a wider range of people can be interviewed within the same limitations of time, resources and research money. The chapter outlines the steps involved in focus group research: selecting groups, arranging and convening group interviews, preparing an interview structure or menu, strategies for coping with group-dynamics, and the use of visual material and other prompting for stimulating and focusing group discussion. The chapter further discusses ways of managing, analysing and interpreting the data produced through group interviews.

In the final chapter, Chapter 11, we introduce ways and tools for managing and analysing quantitative and qualitative communications research data. In the first section, we introduce the analysis of quantitative data using one of the most powerful and widely used statistical analysis programs in the social sciences, namely SPSS® (Statistical analysis Program for the Social Sciences).[1] In the second section, we consider computer-assisted management and analysis of qualitative data, and we introduce some of the ways of using qualitative analysis programs in the study of qualitative communication research data. This section discusses the organisation, management and analysis of 'qualitative' textual data, be they in the form of participant observation field-notes, interview transcripts or electronic newspaper text. We introduce readers to the significant gains of flexibility, efficiency and reliability which computer-assisted handling of qualitative data offers over more traditional manual methods, and we outline some of the types of analysis which can productively be used in research on qualitative textual data.

---

[1]   SPSS, Inc., an IBM Company. SPSS® was acquired by IBM® in October, 2009. IBM, the IBM logo, ibm.com, and SPSS are trademarks of International Business Machines Corp., registered in many jurisdictions worldwide. Other product and service names might be trademarks of IBM or other companies. A current list of IBM trademarks is available on the Web at 'IBM Copyright and trademark information' at www.ibm.com/legal/copytrade.shtml.

CHAPTER 2

The research process

This chapter aims to take some of the intimidating complexity out of 'the research process', by offering an accessible step-by-step guide to the key stages of any media and communications research project. It charts the process from formulation of a research question/topic through to the write-up, presentation and publication of research. The emphasis is on giving the student or novice researcher a recipe for how to get going on a piece of research, and on demonstrating that, with the right ingredients and the right procedures, success is perfectly achievable.

To 'research' means literally to 'search' 'again' (re-), but the common uses of the word imply a 'careful' or 'systematic' investigation, as indicated in the two following excerpts from the Oxford English Dictionary Online (2011):

1 The act of searching carefully for or pursuing a specified thing or person [...].
2 a. Systematic investigation or inquiry aimed at contributing to knowledge of a theory, topic, etc., by careful consideration, observation, or study of a subject. In later use also: original critical or scientific investigation carried out under the auspices of an academic or other institution [...].

The word 'research' is often used in everyday English conversation to signify, it seems, any looking up or gathering of information, no matter how trivial or casual this may be. For our purposes it is useful to distinguish between this more casual use, on the one hand, and, on the other, the meanings stressed in the second dictionary definition above. It is particularly the emphasis on the 'critical' and 'systematic' gathering of facts and information, through 'careful consideration, observation, or study of a subject' that provide important pointers to how social science/communication 'research' is more than the casual looking for information that is implied in everyday uses of the word 'research'.

We define media and communication research then as the planned, critical, systematic and transparent investigation into or gathering of information about media and/or communication processes.

'Critical' in this context should be taken to mean simply undogmatic and free of preconceived assumptions or prejudices about the nature of the object of investigation. 'Planned', 'systematic' and 'transparent' are inter-related defining characteristics of scholarly research, as planned and systematic both help to ensure that the research is neither haphazard nor subjectively selective (i.e. only picking out information which confirms or supports preconceived assumptions or prejudices). Transparency is of the utmost importance in scholarly research, as only through transparency can other researchers and the scholarly community as a whole determine whether the research and its findings are sound, genuine and valid.

Our aim in this chapter is to introduce students and novice researchers to the stages involved in 'research', that is to introduce the research process, from deciding on what to do research on, through planning the research, collecting data or information, to writing up and presenting/publishing the research. This process can often seem both daunting and intimidating. Here, we hope to show that – as with many other things in life – it helps to have a mental road-map of what the constituent parts of the process are and it helps to make a good plan, complete with a timetable.

What to research

All scholarly research starts with choosing a topic, that is with a decision about what to research. As a media and communication scholar or student, one would expect the topic to be some phenomenon or aspect relevant to media and communication. This may seem obvious, but given the very wide range of technical, social, cultural, political, interpersonal, etc. dimensions pertaining to media and communication it may not always be as self-evident as it sounds. For the student looking for a topic to research, it is imperative to start by ascertaining what the formal requirements of their university or other organisation are with regard to acceptable topics, areas or fields for a research project (which may be for a research assignment, a dissertation or a thesis). For all researchers, it is relevant – even at this early point – to consider how a potential topic relates to 'media and communication', why it is interesting to research, whether it has been researched before (i.e. what other research has addressed this or similar topics), whether you (the researcher) have the skills and knowledge required (and, if not, what sort of training would be needed), whether the relevant data/information can be accessed and collected, etc.

Ideas about what to research can come from a broad variety of sources, but probably arise from two main categories: 1) everyday observation, curiosity and inquisitiveness, and 2) familiarity with scholarly debates, theory and research in a particular field (including general awareness of the kinds of study, research and data collection which get funded in a particular field).

Everyday observation can be anything from the personal (what media we use, media content we consume, how we as individuals communicate with our friends, etc.) to much wider questions about social, political and cultural phenomena in our everyday lives (e.g. what role social media play in political uprisings or in the breakdown of law and order in society). But the two categories inevitably also overlap, because we always of course draw on whatever knowledge system (religion, science, philosophy, scholarly research, etc.) is most readily available or familiar to us to 'make sense of' or 'construct meaning out of' what we see around us.

The steps of the research process

Table 2.1 Steps of the research process (adapted from Giddens, 1989: 663; and from Wimmer and Dominick, 2011: 16)

Step/Task	... involves:
1. Selection of research problem/topic	Select a topic for research

2. Review of relevant literature
  2.1. Searching for relevant literature
  2.2. Retrieving, managing and 'processing' relevant references with a bibliographic database
	Familiarise yourself with existing theory and research relevant to the chosen topic

3. Statement of research question or hypothesis	On the basis of the review of relevant literature, formulate a focused research question (or a hypothesis) to address some aspect(s) of the selected research problem. What do you intend to find out about? Which variables or dimensions are involved?

4. Determination of appropriate methodology and research design
  4.1. What method(s)?
  4.2. Population and sample
  4.3. Research instruments and variables
  4.4. Research ethics considerations
  4.5. Piloting
	Determine how data will be collected/gathered (methods), from which sources or population (sampling), using which instruments of data collection

5. Data collection	Collect, record and organise your data
6. Analysis and interpretation of data	
7. Presentation/publication	Write up a full account of your research in the format required for scholarly presentation (e.g. conference presentation) and publication
[8. Replication/further research]	

1.   Selection of research topic/problem

In the previous section we indicated where ideas or inspiration about 'what to research' may come from. For students as well as researchers of media and communication, the main source of inspiration will most likely be derived from a general surveying of and familiarisation with traditions and trends in communication theory and research. As we study and learn about particular trends, approaches and theories of media and communication, we also become aware of what key questions have been addressed in past research, what has attracted research attention and what has not, and what researchers have said about 'further research that needs to be done'.

As students of media and communication, we are also – one would assume – generally interested in finding out about and understanding the roles that media and communication processes play in the society, culture and politics around us. As communication and media are all-pervasive, the problem rarely is to find a media/communication 'dimension' to potential research questions. The main problem is often one of deciding which type of communication theory, approach or tradition is most suitable for the topic at hand, and indeed of deciding how the issue or topic is best researched. This is where the next step in the research process – the review of relevant literature – comes in. Before attempting to refine the focus and objective of a research project, and most definitely before even considering methodology (including the choice of population/sample and method(s)), it is imperative to examine and to gain an overview of what research relevant to the topic has already been carried out or published.

2.   Review of relevant literature

Identifying and reviewing the relevant literature is possibly the single most important step in any research. Why? Because only by gaining a good overview of what has already been researched and published in relation to our chosen topic, can we: a) be sure that the questions we wish to research and find answers to have not already been researched and answered; b) be sure that we focus our research on questions that are relevant, of interest and indeed researchable; c) be sure that we don't waste time on 'reinventing the wheel', when we can build on research designs, methods and instruments that have already been (successfully) tried and proved to yield data and findings of relevance.

On a more pragmatic note, we have often seen students who have chosen a fashionable-sounding research topic (e.g. product promotion/marketing through new/social media) for their dissertation getting very frustrated when they find that they have little or no idea about how to design a research project (assuming maybe that all research consists of or requires a 'survey') or that they are unable to find a relevant theoretical framework or any other research/studies relevant to their topic. The best way to avoid such confusion and frustration is to move quickly and directly from the selection of a general topic to the second step in the research process: identifying and reviewing relevant literature. As we have said, but wish to stress again, this should be done before attempting to narrow down and focus the research question, and particularly before considering, let alone deciding on, the most appropriate research design and methodology.

While identifying and reviewing 'relevant literature' can be one of the most challenging parts of the research process, it is also undoubtedly one of the most exciting aspects, as it combines the thrills of 'detective' work (following leads, trails, clues – that lead to more trails etc.) and the excitement of discovery ('wow, look at all this stuff that's already known about this topic!').

At the end of this chapter, in the Further Reading section, we refer the reader to a couple of the many excellent book-length introductions to conducting literature reviews, but here we wish to provide a brief introduction to the key components. While it is perfectly possible (and sometimes tempting) to just throw yourself into searching for relevant literature by typing a few keywords into Google or similar search engines, it pays – as with the research itself – to adopt a planned and systematic approach. The literature search and review process comprises the following two principal tasks:

1) Searching for, identifying and selecting relevant literature (including deciding on what sources, databases, etc. to consult, and on what search terms or search strategies to use).
2) Retrieving, managing and 'processing' relevant references (i.e. skim-reading, indexing, extracting key points, annotating relevant studies in preparation for the writing of your literature review) with a bibliographic database.

It is essential to keep a record or log of all searches in order to ensure that this is done systematically and to avoid wasting time (e.g. by inadvertently repeating searches that have already been done). Likewise, it is essential to organise, index and perhaps even go so far as to start annotating retrieved references for their use in the literature review. This type of record keeping, managing and indexing is best and most efficiently done with a bibliographic database, as we will explain further under 'retrieving, managing and processing' below.

2.1. Searching for relevant literature
Potential starting points for a relevant literature search include course reading lists, textbooks and the increasing number of subject or topic area *handbooks*

published by major publishers. Library books are generally catalogued by subject/topic area, so perusing the relevant sections or aisles in your university library can also be a potentially productive way to get started on gaining an overview of the type of research that has been done relevant to your area of interest. By far the most efficient, reliable (in terms of making sure that as wide a range of potentially relevant sources as possible have been checked or consulted), discerning (in terms of distinguishing 'good' from potentially less reliable or good research) and dynamic way to search for relevant literature is to use the scholarly databases that any university or equivalent major library offers. There are many high-quality indexes and databases to choose from, and a key consideration before starting is to determine what period of time and what range of publication types (e.g. books, journal articles, conference papers, theses, dissertations) or media types (print, audio-recordings, film and other visual media content, etc.) are included. It is also relevant to check which disciplines or broader fields are covered, for example is the database primarily aimed at psychology, education, social sciences, the humanities, etc.

For media and communication researchers we suggest that a literature search could usefully start with a relevant periodicals database, then proceed to looking for book publications in a comprehensive database of books in print, and only then to potentially cast a much wider net using internet search engines such as Google in order to identify reports, organisations or websites that may be of relevance. The reason for leaving this till last is that it is much more difficult to assess the quality of information and to narrow down searches to ensure that only the most relevant material is identified. The reason for starting with periodicals databases is that journal/periodical articles are likely, due to the shorter publication cycle, to be more up to date than book publications; they are generally subject to rigorous peer-review; they are generally more comprehensively and systematically indexed than books; they are fully abstracted; and the full journal articles (depending on library subscriptions) are often available for direct download.

For media and communication research(ers), we recommend that the search for relevant literature be focused on the following sources, in the order that they are listed:

1)   Web of Knowledge/Web of Science
2)   WorldCat
3)   Google or Google Scholar

The first step is to familiarise yourself with the search conventions of the individual database or search engine, particularly the conventions that apply when narrowing and refining searches (e.g. by time period, publication, search-word combination), how to search for specific strings of terms or how to use Boolean operators (and, or, not) and wildcards (e.g. 'scienti*' would find occurrences of words starting with this string, such as scientific, scientist, scientists, scientism).

Once a search has been done, and assuming that the search terms have been refined sufficiently to narrow the number of hits down to a manageable number (i.e. if a search produces several hundreds, or indeed thousands, of hits, then that is a clear sign that the search terms need to be refined/restricted further), then look through the resulting list and on the basis of the title or the accompanying abstract select (normally by ticking a tick-box next to the individual title) those that appear to be relevant.

2.2. Retrieving, managing and 'processing' relevant references with a bibliographic database

The relevant (ticked) references should then be exported or downloaded to a suitable bibliographic database. A bibliographic database is one of the most useful and important tools for any researcher, as it is essentially key to building up and keeping track of literature that is or could potentially be relevant to your research. Thus, it is also a key tool in the process of building an overview of relevant literature and is essential for managing and reviewing that literature. It is also a huge time-saver in the simple sense that the bibliography which will eventually appear in the research report, thesis or other publication resulting from the research can be created in the required format without any laborious and error-prone manual typing of individual references.

Increasingly, leading bibliographic databases, such as EndNote, interface seamlessly with major publishers' lists and key publications databases. This means that all you need to do to 'capture' a reference to your personal bibliographic database is to press the relevant export-to-bibliographic-database button (e.g. the button labelled EndNote, RefWorks or simply 'bibliographic database') on the website of the publications database on which you have performed your search.

The importance of using a bibliographic database for managing and organising relevant and potentially relevant literature derives from more than simply the gains made in speed and accuracy by not having to manually re-type references. It also helps in keeping track of the many searches (often over an extended period of time) necessary to ensure a comprehensive overview. Thus, the bibliographic database is key to what we listed above as 'Record keeping/keeping a detailed log of searches and results' because it enables you to keep track of *what searches* (using what search terms) have been performed, *when* (particularly important if engaging in long-term research where the field may 'move on' at pace even in the course of a few months, and most certainly if the research stretches over more than a year), using what sources or databases, and with what results (i.e. how many references were selected/deemed relevant out of the total number of 'hits' resulting from a search).

But, most significantly, using a bibliographic database is essential for the process of systematically digesting, processing and reviewing relevant and potentially relevant literature. This should be done by further indexing (e.g. by adding to any *keywords* that may have already been downloaded with the reference), using terms that are directly relevant to the research project at hand and further categorising (e.g. by creating relevant subject or topic subgroups within your bibliographic database – which may of course contain references relevant to a number of different projects that you are working on). But perhaps one of the most productive ways of using a bibliographic database is for summarising in your own words what the relevance and contribution of the individual reference is to the field of research that you are reviewing; how it fits thematically, theoretically or methodologically into the field that is being reviewed; how and to what extent the methods, variables and research instruments used can be built on or deployed in your own research; and, of course, your initial assessment of the quality and contribution of the research. In this respect the bibliographic database becomes the main tool in the first stage of processing or reviewing the relevant literature, and it helps ensure that the literature review itself – that is the review that will eventually form a key section or chapter in the research report or publication – becomes a critical synthesis and review, not a simple listing, of the relevant research.

A good literature review then should be much more than an annotated study-by-study listing of relevant research; in fact, such a listing would not qualify as a literature *review* at all. The term *reviewing* the literature crucially implies notions of comprehensiveness, thoroughness, being systematic and objective (or at least open-minded and non-prejudiced) and critical (in terms of assessing the assumptions, frameworks, methods and contributions of relevant research to the topic at hand).

3.   Statement of research question or hypothesis

Having established an overview of literature and research relevant to the originally formulated research topic or area, and having synthesised and critically reviewed this, it is now possible to narrow down and focus the research. Narrowing down and focusing are important to ensure that the research to be planned and done is set in its proper context (theoretically and methodologically), is relevant (i.e. will further our understanding of the particular field) and is doable given the time, tools and resources available for the project. Narrowing down is also about specifying the type of media, communication or people that are to be researched or studied (see also under Step 4 below).

The research objective can be formulated as a hypothesis – a statement about the relationship between two or more variables, phenomena or dimensions – to be tested by the proposed research. Or it can be formulated as a research question, which – like the hypothesis – should indicate what the key variables or dimensions to be examined are.

Stating the research objective in the form of one or more hypotheses is a good strategy if very specific relationships between variables are the subject of examination, for example, as in the communication research tradition known as cultivation analysis, the relationship between amount of television viewing and viewers' beliefs about selected specified aspects of social reality. Hypotheses can, however, easily end up being unduly narrow and potentially even unduly trivial, so unless the review of literature has suggested some clear hypotheses used effectively in previous relevant research, we would suggest that the formulation of research objectives as one or more research questions offers a better starting point.

The research question should indicate what key areas or variables of investigation are involved, but, unlike the hypothesis, it does not propose a specific testable relationship. Thus, the objective (in research question form) might be to examine how specific broadcast news organisations differ in their coverage of (specified) political issues. As a hypothesis this might have been formulated with reference to how ownership or known political leanings of the selected broadcast organisations skew or bias (according to the hypothesis) the coverage of the specified political issues.

4.   Determination of appropriate methodology and research design

The main objective of this book is to introduce and show what kind of research methods and approaches are commonly used and most appropriate for investigating what research questions, what media and what communication processes. In broad terms, choosing an appropriate methodology thus starts by having some idea about what is available and what has worked well in previous comparable research. We emphasise again, as we did at the beginning of this chapter, that the formulation of the research objective should always, as indicated by the sequence of the research process in Table 2.1, precede the choice of method and research design. For example, don't start by assuming that a particular problem always requires or is done with 'survey methodology' or 'content analysis'.

The key to choosing an appropriate research methodology is, again, the literature review. The literature review will have shown what kinds of approaches and methods have been used effectively and productively in previous research addressing similar or comparable questions, issues or topics. The review of literature may of course show that the topic at hand has been addressed in a number of different ways, using a range of frameworks and approaches, so one of the key objectives of the literature review is to assess critically which of these approaches (and associated methods) look most promising, effective and doable. The choice of an appropriate approach and method then should ideally emerge out of the review of the relevant existing research literature, but this is not confined simply to determining whether focus groups, a survey, a content analysis or other major methods are most appropriate for the investigation. It also – importantly for the considerations, choices and planning in this step of the research process – refers to sampling strategy and to the design of research instruments such as a questionnaire or a content analysis code-book.

This step in the research process then details what method is to be used; what (population) is to be investigated and how relevant and representative cases/data will be sampled; and what research instruments will be used to collect information on what dimensions or variables.

4.1. What method(s)

At the most general level, the choice of method depends broadly on whether the research is primarily aimed at investigating communications/media content (text or documents in the widest sense of these words) *or* people and their beliefs, actions and behaviour. Suitable methods for investigating communications/media content include content analysis, semiotics, discourse analysis, corpus linguistics, narrative analysis, genre analysis. Suitable methods for investigating people include surveys, individual interviews, focus group interviewing, (participant) observation, ethnography. However, methods for analysing communication content (such as the communication content produced by individual or focus group interviews) may also be an important part of research that is primarily concerned with studying people. In addition, a research design may call for a combination of both categories of method. Prominent communication research traditions, such as cultivation analysis and agenda-setting research for example, frequently (although not always) call for a combination of content analysis (to establish what is or is not prominent in the media) and survey methodology (to establish what and how much media content people 'consume' and to establish what beliefs people hold about the issues under investigation).

4.2. Population and sample

Regardless of the type of research – whether qualitative or quantitative, whether focused on media/communications content or focused on people –

it is essential to be clear about what 'population' (i.e. the general body/ collection) of media, communications or people the planned research aims to investigate and, eventually, to be able to describe. Terms like the 'mass media', 'the media', 'film', 'advertising' and even terms like 'news media' or 'new media' are too general and all-encompassing to be of much help in focusing a research project. Recognising the key differences and variations in characteristics which exist even within such slightly more specific labels as 'broadcast news media', 'action-adventure films' or 'magazine advertising', it is therefore useful to be as specific as possible about the population of media or people to be studied.

Even when the population has been defined relatively narrowly and specifically, it is still highly unusual – and indeed unnecessary – for research to study every individual case in that population. Instead, a strategy is devised to obtain a manageable (given the time and resources available for the research) and representative sample. A representative sample is a smaller version of the population, containing the same key characteristics and in the same proportions as they are present in the population. Strategies for obtaining a sample divide broadly into those that are based on and conform to the requirements of statistical probability and those that do not (non-probability sampling).

We discuss the various sampling strategies appropriate to media and communication research in more detail in Chapters 5 (content analysis) and 9 (surveys). Here we simply wish to stress that the most important aspect of defining the population and sample in any research is to transparently account for the way in which these are selected and the justification behind their selection. Selection and sampling criteria can be many and varied, but it must always be clear what they are and why they were seen/chosen as the most relevant criteria for specifying the population and sample.

4.3. Research instruments and variables

The collection of data, regardless of the method used, must always be focused on what is relevant or necessary in order to address and answer the objectives or questions posed for the research. This may seem self-evident, but, surprisingly, we have often come across the assumption that there is always a standard set of data collection categories associated with each method. In surveys, this assumption tends to relate to demographic variables of survey respondents. In content analyses, the assumption is often that variables such as duration, word length, type of news item or programme must always be coded. While such dimensions are indeed often relevant, they – like other variables – should only be included if they are relevant to the research objectives. In other words, there is no point in collecting information on dimensions or variables that would appear (either from the literature review or from the researcher's general familiarity with the topic being researched) to have little or no bearing on the research questions or to have little or nothing to contribute to understanding the issues or phenomena under investigation.

Consequently, the design of the research instrument and the identification of the dimensions on which information/data are to be collected are a matter – as with sampling – of transparently explaining the rationale behind focusing on the selected variables. How do they relate to the overall objectives of the research, and in what sense is it anticipated that they will provide information relevant to testing the research hypotheses or to answering the research questions posed in the third step of the research process? This step is then essentially about translating the research questions or hypotheses into variables for data collection, and into variables or dimensions that can be coded, measured or about which information can be collected.

In practical terms, the research instrument and definition of variables for data collection will differ depending on the method used (see under each method discussed in the following chapters) but in very general terms the research instrument is the researcher's menu of questions/variables and manual of how to collect the information. In a content analysis, this is the code-book that specifies what content dimensions are to be coded and how; in a survey, it is the questionnaire and any associated instructions to interviewers/respondents; in a focus group study, it is the script indicating the moderator's role, speech and menu of questions/topics to be discussed, as well as directions for any prompts or stimuli that are to be used; in an observational study, it is the plan for who will be observed where, what dimensions will be observed, what questions will be asked, how answers and observations will be recorded, etc.

4.4.   Research ethics and approval

Just as academic research must always be transparent in terms of design, framework, methods and procedures used, so too must it always be ethical. This is especially important where people are the subjects of research or in other ways involved as informants/respondents. Indeed it is increasingly a requirement by all recognised academic institutions as well as professional and scholarly bodies that researchers demonstrate their adherence to their institution's or professional body's code of practice regarding ethics, and that their research design is subjected to formal review and approval by the institution's relevant ethics committee or equivalent board, before any data collection is embarked upon.

Different institutions and professional bodies operate different ethics requirements or codes of practice, but they generally revolve around core principles regarding consent, confidentiality, privacy, coercion/freedom, deception or harm to individuals. First and foremost, participants must give their informed consent, must be assured of the confidentiality of the information obtained from them (i.e. that the information will not be used to identify the individual respondent, unless they have expressly given their consent to this), must be aware that they are under no coercion or obligation to participate, and that they can opt out at any point in the course of the research if they wish. The research must not involve procedures that could cause either physical or psychological harm to the participants, nor should it involve the deliberate deception of individuals. These considerations are important and increasingly required in any research involving people, but they are absolutely essential where children or teenagers under the age of 18 are involved.

The requirement to ensure that research is ethical should not be seen as some red-tape bureaucratic obstacle. Rather, in addition to being a requirement, it offers the researcher a useful 'check' on whether the research design is asking the right questions in the most appropriate, acceptable and efficient way. Careful consideration should thus always be given to ensure that the language, terms and phrases used in questioning are sufficiently sensitive to the actual or potential sensibilities of respondents, so as not to cause undue offence or in other ways risk biasing the response. Likewise, the researcher needs to ensure that the process of conducting research does not in itself unduly intrude on or cause offence to the people whose activities, institutions or practices are being observed or studied (e.g. by unacceptable intrusion into what they may regard as sacred, private or in other ways 'off-limits' to outsiders). The internet (including fan-sites, social networking, blogging, etc.) has brought with it massively increased opportunities for observing, studying and analysing human behaviour and communication practices, but also new questions about ethical conduct in research: see the website of the Association of Internet Researchers (http://aoir.org/documents/ethics-guide/) for a full discussion of the particular ethics questions and issues applicable in internet research.

In practical terms, the researcher needs – at this or an earlier stage in the research process – to establish what their institution's or professional association's requirements are regarding ethics approval (these can generally be found on the institution's or association's website) and the procedure for obtaining formal approval to go ahead with the research, which will normally consist of submitting an application to the relevant committee or body for formal approval. Under no circumstances should any data collection involving human subjects commence – not even for the piloting of research instruments – until the required approval has been granted by the relevant body.

4.5. Piloting
In both qualitative and quantitative research, it is important, once the research design and instruments have been finalised, to apply them consistently to all

cases or subjects in the research. In other words, new content analysis variables or interview questions should not be added halfway through the data collection process, nor should the way in which content variables are coded or the way in which interview questions are asked be changed during the data collection period. Such changes or additions may be tempting, as one learns more about the nature of the topic being investigated or the type of responses that people give. However, such changes or additions will potentially invalidate the research, as not all of the sample will have been subjected to the same 'conditions' (i.e. the same coding, questions or measurement) and it will consequently be impossible to account for what causes the trends or differences that might be found in the analysis. Because of this, it is necessary and desirable to make sure that the research design (including instruments, sample and variables for data collection) 'works' before embarking on the full-scale collection of what can in many cases be a large amount of data and a time- and resource-intensive endeavour.

It is therefore highly advisable to do a small-scale pilot study before embarking on the full data collection. A pilot study consists of simply testing the research instrument on a small sample of cases to see whether the codes or questions can be readily applied without misinterpretation, and whether they succeed in capturing the kind of information that will be relevant to answering the research questions. The piloting of an interview schedule or questionnaire will show up any questions that are either not understood by the respondent in the way that was intended by the researcher, or questions that are insufficiently precise and thus result in unacceptable diversity in the type of answers given; the piloting of a content analysis coding schedule will show up categories that are difficult or impossible to code/apply consistently and will show whether the coding schedule succeeds in capturing the type of information that is relevant to answering the research questions.

5. Data collection

An important key to successful data collection is careful and realistic time-planning and timetabling. Issues to do with availability of and access to relevant research sites, documents and respondents have already been considered under Steps 3 and 4, and indeed some attention will also have been given to the length of time estimated as required for the collection of data. However, at the very start of this step, a more detailed timetable complete with actual target dates, taking into consideration public holiday closures etc., needs to be drawn up. Virtually all research (whether externally funded academic research, research theses or taught-course dissertations) is conducted to specified deadlines. Given that a range of research sites, researchers and assistants, and respondents may be involved it is essential to construct a realistic timetable which specifies who is doing what, where and when. The data collection itself consists of accessing the research sites (e.g. a news organisation or news room), media content or other documents or respondents, to apply the research instruments or procedures and collect the data in the form of coding/classification, answers or observations. In the following chapters we indicate the type of 'data' that are collected with different methods and we indicate ways of organising, managing and preparing collected data for analysis.

While the steps in the research process are broadly sequential, we strongly advise that some analysis (Step 6) should commence as soon as a small amount of data has been collected – rather than waiting till all the data have been collected – and that some degree of analysis can usefully continue throughout the data collection period. This is to help maintain an overview of the research data and to help develop a sense of key trends in the data that can then be subjected to rigorous analysis and testing, when all the data have successfully been collected.

6. Analysis and interpretation of data

Although the researcher will already have had some glimpses of what the research will find and how it will be able to answer the research questions, Step 6 is where it all begins to 'come together' and where important parts of the jigsaw puzzle that research is finally fall into place to reveal new insights into and understanding of the topic being researched. Step 6 is thus undoubtedly the most exciting and potentially exhilarating part of the research process.

Regardless of whether the research is primarily quantitative or qualitative, or indeed a combination of the two, data analysis is essentially about identifying and summarising key trends, patterns and relationships in the data. What trends do the data show and what is related to what in the data? Quantitative data are subjected, at this stage, to statistical analysis showing both the distribution of individual variables and testing the strength of relationship between variables. Qualitative data is coded, classified or tagged and explored in terms of who says what, using what lexical terms, and focusing on what themes, subjects and discourses, or in terms of its structural arrangements (e.g. narratives, binary oppositions or core juxtapositions). We explore the specific nature of analysis and interpretation relevant to individual methods in the following chapters of this book.

7. Presentation/publication

The final step in the research process is to write up the full research for presentation or publication. Presentation may in the first instance be in the form of a research report to the funding body or a lecture or conference presentation.

```
• Introduction
• Review of literature and framework
• Method and sample
• Analysis and results
• Conclusion
• References
```

Figure 2.1 The core structure of the research write-up/academic publication

Ultimately, however, the objective of all academic research is and should be to make it available to the wider academic community, and indeed beyond to a wider public. Whether the research is written up for an undergraduate or postgraduate dissertation, for a PhD thesis, for a scholarly journal article or for book publication, the main ingredients and structure are very similar. The main reason for this comes back to the scholarly principle of 'transparency', meaning in this context that it is just as crucial, possibly more so in fact, to the way that academic and scholarly research advances that those who read the research are able to follow the process of the research – that is how the problem was defined and how the data were collected and analysed – as it is for them to learn what the results, findings or conclusions were.

The core structure of the write-up of academic research – mirroring key steps in the research process itself – is illustrated in Figure 2.1.

We describe each of these core components in a little more detail in the following, but first we note that different format and style requirements may apply depending on the type of publication and/or publisher. Different academic journals and publishers thus each have their particular format or style requirements, and different universities have different style/format requirements for dissertations and theses (including specific requirements for the cover page, abstract, provision of key words, contents pages, etc.). Early on in the process, and certainly in good time before finalising and submitting the write-up, it is important to check what the institutional or publisher requirements are regarding structure, style and format.

Introduction
The introduction states briefly and succinctly how the research topic was chosen or identified, why it is of interest (and potentially to whom), what it is about and what research questions, topics or issues it aims to address. Although generally not feasible or done for the shorter and restrictive format of a journal article, the introduction may also give a brief overview of what follows in each of the subsequent chapters.

Review of literature and framework

This is the first major substantive section or chapter in the write-up. This section or chapter surveys the relevant theoretical and research context, and it critically discusses and reviews existing research and literature relevant to the topic under investigation. 'Critically reviewing' includes identifying, comparing and assessing the types of research questions asked by previous research, the types of analytical and theoretical frameworks deployed in previous studies, and the types of populations/samples and variables studied and methods used for collecting data/information on these. As we have indicated previously, this chapter must be much more than a summary listing and description of selected key studies: it must critically compare and assess relevant studies and, on the basis of discussion of these, ideally it must arrive at conclusions about what seems to have worked best in previous research. It must then build on these conclusions to outline how they inform the choice of sample, methods and variables to be described in detail in the following chapter.

Method and sample

This chapter details the rationale for the choice of sampling strategy and sample, the choice of method(s) and the selection of variables to be analysed. It needs to offer sufficient detail for other researchers to be able to a) assess the robustness of the research presented in the report and b), if they wish, to replicate the study. The key to the whole of this chapter is justification/explanation, that is nothing should appear as if it just 'fell out of the sky' and no assumptions should be made about the naturalness or rightness of why these particular populations, samples, methods or variables were selected. If people with particular demographic characteristics are selected, or if particular media, media content and periods are selected for analysis, then the reasons behind and justifications for these choices must be explained. The variables chosen for analysis must likewise be justified in relation to the objectives and questions set out for the research. The chapter should also account for the research procedures used, for any piloting carried out and adjustments made on the basis of it, and for measures used to check on the reliability and validity of the research. It is not, however, normal practice to include the full questionnaire, code-book/coding schedule or other research instruments in this section or chapter; instead these may be included in an appendix.

Analysis and results

Analysis and results are presented, supported by relevant tables, graphs or quotes, depending on the type of method(s) used and the nature of data collected. It is worth remembering that the purpose of using tables and or graphs is to offer a succinct, 'at a glance' overview of key trends and findings, but that they cannot and should not be left to 'speak for themselves'. It is thus the responsibility and task of the researcher to provide a narrative account of what was analysed, which key trends were identified and what relationships were examined and seem to be relevant or significant. The narrative thus, rather than repeating in prose what is shown in tables or graphs, should pinpoint their key highlights and provide interpretation of what the findings mean. Likewise, selected direct quotation from respondents or from media content is used to illustrate and support key trends or findings discussed in the analytical narrative, but the narrative itself must show how these trends or findings emerge from the analysis through the use of the method(s) described in the previous chapter of the report.

Conclusion

The conclusion should ideally offer two things: a summary of the key results or findings of the research, and critical reflection on the research leading to recommendations for future research. Critical reflection includes asking – with the benefit of hindsight – whether the research showed what we expected it to show, whether the theoretical framework and methods used were the most appropriate for the topic, whether the sample was appropriate or could have been improved upon, what specific problems arose in the course of the research and how they could be addressed in future research. Combined with the key findings or conclusions of the research, the critical reflection should ideally then lead to brief but succinct suggestions about how the research can be built upon, expanded and potentially improved in future research.

References

It is essential – in all academic research, writing and publishing – to ensure that all sources are clearly identified and referenced. The references section must therefore list the full bibliographic details of every source, work or citation used and referred to in the text body of the write-up. References that may have been consulted during the development or execution of the research, but are not mentioned in the text body of the write-up should *not* be included in the references section. The format of references/referencing may vary by publisher/publication type, and it is therefore essential always to check what the requirements are before finalising the write-up.

8.   Replication/further research

As we have indicated, the aim of academic research is to contribute to the development and advancement of knowledge and understanding in the relevant field of inquiry, in our case, media and communication. Knowledge and understanding are advanced through building on what is already known or has already been researched, and to elaborate on this in ways that will add further insights into the processes and phenomena under investigation. Essentially therefore the final step in the research process – the dissemination or publication of the research – then has as its key purpose to kick off the next iteration of the research process or cycle, that is to serve as inspiration for further research development and/or the replication of this research but applied to a different time period or a different population/sample.

Further reading and resources

Publications databases

Web of Knowledge/Web of Science: the premier periodicals database for social science research.
WorldCat: the premier database for books worldwide.

Search engines

Google and Google Scholar

Bibliographic referencing software

EndNote: http://www.endnote.com/
RefWorks: http://www.refworks.com/

Further reading

Berger, A. A. (2011). *Media and Communication Research: An Introduction to Qualitative and Quantitative Approaches* (2nd edn.). London: Sage.
Berger provides a delightfully accessible and amusing introduction to research (1. What is Research? pp.11–28), literature searches/reviewing (2. Library Searches, pp.29–43) and a 'Putting it All Together' section which includes a chapter (16) on 'Writing Research Reports' (pp.293–308).

Wimmer, R. D., and Dominick, J. R. (2011). *Mass Media Research: An Introduction (International Edition)* (9th revised edn.). Belmont, CA: Wadsworth.
The whole of Part One (pp.1–113) is devoted to the research process, and comprises four chapters as follows: 1. Science and Research; 2. Elements of Research; 3. Research Ethics; and 4. Sampling.

Fink, A. (2009). *Conducting Research Literature Reviews: From the Internet to Paper* (3rd edn.). London: Sage.
Accessible, clear, comprehensive and well-structured introduction to how to do literature reviews. See also: Jesson, J., and Matheson, L. (2011). *Doing Your Literature Review*. London: Sage.

CHAPTER 3

Researching ownership and media policy

While other chapters in this book describe methods for studying the content of the media and how to measure the way audiences take up and use this content, this chapter is concerned with how we study the political economy of the media. This means investigating the nature of media ownership, how it is financed, the organisation of production and how this is regulated by governments and international governing bodies. This is important on the one hand simply to understand the nature of these organisations and processes, to know who controls our media. On the other it is at this level of analysis that we can find out why the content is the way it is. We can ask whether the nature of the content of news on a webpage or an article in a magazine is down to the individual choices of the writer, journalist or photographer or to institutionally established processes and corporate strategies. Such things cannot be understood at the level of textual analysis.

Most of us are familiar with the accusation that media owners have used their power for their own ends. In Europe the typical cases over the years have been Silvio Berlusconi and Rupert Murdoch. It is important to emphasise, however, that media ownership for the most part leads to a kind of control over content that is 'soft' rather than 'hard'. In other words content can be influenced by the way a particular ownership structure manages and organises its companies rather than through direct and open instruction to disseminate specific political viewpoints. And the nature of making profit, of organising production for economy of scale, of seeking out advertisers, can all influence what kind of content we find in the media as much, if not more, than the need of owners to promote their own point of view and agenda. It is, as we show, not difficult to find out who owns a particular newspaper, magazine or radio station, but it is less obvious how we use this information to help us to understand and explain particular kinds of news, web or broadcast content.

This political economic focus has its origins for the most part in Marxist economic sociology. From the 1980s in particular a number of scholars became dissatisfied with the effects studies of the media which they felt were missing the true nature of its power. Curran et al. (1987) looked at the role of media ownership, media concentration and the role of advertising driving the nature of content. McQuail (1994) had been interested in the commodification of audiences as private media chased maximum profits. He asked, to what extent the real plurality of voices offered by the media was challenged by increased privatisation. Golding and Murdock (2000) argued that we should not think only about media effects but also the way that the media have immense control over the cultural forms available to us. And these forms can be traced to specific kinds of commercial interest and the processes that they foster. Writers like McChesney (2003) have been interested in the way that commercialisation of news has lead to a rise in particular kinds of journalism.

In this chapter we look at two examples of how researching ownership and regulation can help us to understand much more about a particular media product. In the first place we look at the content of a local newspaper and in the second the contents of different national editions of a global lifestyle magazine. Each case begins with examples of texts. While it would be possible to say much about each example through content analysis or linguistic analysis, much can be learned through information about the company that produced the text, the organisation of that particular content producer and also about the way the wider industry is structured.

The practical methods of research used in this chapter are archive research and interviews. In the first case, the main sources are annual reports, company websites and government documents. Annual reports give information about company structure, development, strategies and revenue and relationships to other companies. These can be obtained on request by post and are generally available for download from websites. Government documents relating to regulation and policy are also available online. In the second case, interviews with company employees such as journalists and editors, along with regulators themselves can reveal important practical information about working and production procedures. In this case, we only give a limited number of interview examples, but the point is to show how we can use such data, what they can tell us and how we should present them. How each of these sources of information can help us to understand the nature of media content will become clear through the two case studies.

Ownership and news gathering

We begin with an example from a regional newspaper, the *Western Mail*, which is based in South Wales, UK. This case study shows that it is only possible to explain what we find in its pages through coming to understand the changing structure of newspaper ownership in Britain from the 1990s and the effect that this has had on everyday news gathering techniques. In certain research strands such as Critical Discourse Analysis (Chapter 6) texts are analysed for their ideological content. But what such analysis misses are the social practices that lead to specific kinds of content. Therefore certain kinds of content cannot be explained so much by ideology or journalistic bias, or even the powerful voice of ownership, but rather by established practical procedures of news production often based around meeting changing financial constraints and market context.

Below is an extract from a news item from the *Western Mail* 3 November 2005 taken from Machin and Niblock (2006: 86–87). The text was collected during a research project that investigated the changing nature of journalistic practice (see Machin and Niblock, 2006).

How does your life sit with the sofa habits revealed about our nation?

(There is a photograph of a designer sofa and another of Laurence Llewelyn-Bowen.)

The comfort zone is more important than ever before.

Welsh people are spending more of their time sitting on sofas than ever before.

Where once people left the house to socialise or do chores such as shopping, modern technology has made it quicker and cheaper for people to spend their out-of-hours time in the comfort of their own sitting room, and according to a new survey, that's exactly what they're choosing to do.

According to a survey out today, commissioned by Intel, the most popular activities for Welsh families at home are watching television, listening to music, surfing the internet and playing games, all of which can be done from the sofa.

And with so much time spent sitting on them it's no surprise the average household has £23 in loose change down the back of them.

Furniture designer and former *Western Mail* Welsh woman of the year, Angela Gidden, described the trend as 'the migration to the sofa' and said because people now spend more time on them, people have become more concerned about what kind they buy.

She said yesterday, 'There's a lot of people who are watching their pennies and are quite happy to stay at home but it means they're more conscious of what they're living with and so they'll make a more considered choice when it comes to upholstery'.

'People want a sofa which suits their needs and aspirations'.

She added, 'There's also more of a trend towards entertaining at home and less emphasis on going out to bars and restaurants and so living space is becoming more important'.

But Wales' relationship with the sofa is not a new one. For the better part of the last century the centre of the UK's upholstery manufacturing industry was based in South Wales.

In the last few years cheap imports and a downturn in spending have taken their toll.

Christie Tyler, Wales' first major sofa manufacturer which was set up after the Second World War and employed around 1,000 people in Wales, went into receivership earlier this year. The decline of the company credited with creating the first widely available three-piece suites, resulted in factory closures and job losses.

The text goes on to look at a number of sofa retailers in South Wales and some comments on sofa fashions by Laurence Llewelyn-Bowen. This item, according to journalists we interviewed in South Wales, is typical of contemporary local news reporting.

What we draw attention to here is the kind of reporting done to produce this news item and how this can be explained in terms of a particular pattern of ownership that has become increasingly characteristic of newspapers around the world; this has itself been a response to changes in the way the media industry is regulated.

In this particular case what kind of investigation and informing has the journalist done? The item is in fact based on a press release for a survey by Intel. The journalist has drawn out the Welsh angle in order to create news worthiness for the local market. The rest of the text appears to be based on promotional material for sofa manufacturing and sales in South Wales. So what kind of informing is this? Is it really 'news'?

In fact in this text there has been no actual 'investigation' for the news item and the information has been gathered through email and the internet. This text is evidence of the way that journalism has changed since the 1990s and is typical of how the content of much of our news has changed. To understand these changes in content, we need to know much more about the changing nature of news production and regulation.

The commonly held view of the purpose of local news is that it is the way we find out about what is going on in our local community or region. In such a view of the news media, journalists are the eyes and ears of the public. They find out if our local MPs are doing their jobs. Are services being run properly? Are there any concealed issues that should be brought to our attention so that we can approach those in authority and demand answers? Is our local health service run properly? Ordinary citizens do not have the time or resources to find these things out so we rely on journalists to do it for us.

In 1949 the Royal Commission on the Press pointed directly to the role of the press in a democratic society:

> The democratic form of society demands of its members an active and intelligent participation in the affairs of their community, whether local or national. It assumes that they are sufficiently well-informed about the issues of the day to be

able to form the broad judgments required by an election, and to maintain, between elections, the vigilance necessary in those whose governors are their servants and not their masters.

In the ideal scenario where a journalist acts as the eyes and ears of a local community we would imagine that they would detect the most important, relevant events to the community served by the news outlet. This would mean that they would have regular everyday contact with that community and understand its problems and needs. They would be able to identify what kind of people can provide them with further information about those events in order for them to be fully understood from every angle. For example, a reporter might hear about a rise in crime rates in their community from local police figures. They would then seek out those people who could verify this information. They might interview people in the affected area. More experienced journalists often speak of how they would formerly maintain a sense of what was going on in a community by simply spending time in cafes. They may then contextualise this in a picture of a community living with high unemployment, digging out local government information that revealed the true picture. In the piece all points of view would therefore be covered. As a result, the readers are informed about issues that deeply affect and shape the community around them.

In fact this kind of scenario has never actually been the case as regards local reporting. Journalists cannot simply hang out in pubs and cafes as this would seldom throw up interesting stories. Historically, journalists have developed solutions to the problem of ensuring steady predictable supplies of news stories by establishing *beats*. These beats, which might see them given responsibility for particular kinds of stories, such as crime, would take them into regular contact with sources such as police, courts, councils and other bureaucratic organisations. These settings process the kinds of events that are newsworthy on a daily basis at a pace that is predictable. So, rather than eavesdropping on conversations in bars and cafes, community reporters can access files and reports produced by these organisations. Of course this means that what becomes news is defined by the interests of these organisations. Sociologists of journalism have been critical of the way that journalists therefore tend to reproduce the definitions of crime, for example, in accord with the interests of the police and courts.

Defending the beat system

Many journalists would defend the beat system and point out that these official sources can throw up stories that could then be investigated further. The problem is that changes in the industry and changes in regulation and ownership have made this less and less a component of everyday reporting practice thus resulting in the kind of public-relations-based news items of which the 'Sofa' story is an example.

In the following we can see an example of this former kind of reporting in an extract from the *Western Mail* (17.10.78) taken from Machin and Niblock (2006: 80–81). *Western Mail* journalist Colin Hughes, who lamented the changes in journalistic practice leading to 'email and internet news gathering', told us that this is an example of a story where there was time for investigation and where he was engaged with issues important to the community, drawing on his contacts from within that community.

Rugby Club that plays on a 'gold' mine *Western Mail* (17.10.78)
The turf of Blaenau Rugby Club's ground … in West Wales is even more hallowed than that of Cardiff Arms Park.

It may not have the same lush, green appearance but for all that it is regarded with reverence by the locals.

The reason? Beneath the grass of the Blaenau club lie rich deposits of best quality anthracite coal.

It is coal the National Coal Board would love to get their hands on – but stand no chance of doing so.

A member of the village welfare committee who own the Blaenau ground told me. 'The NCB tried to move heaven and earth to buy the land.

'They offered us an alternative ground in Llandybie with all the facilities thrown in. But we said no. It would have been a betrayal of the village if we had agreed because the Rugby Club is the only recreational entertainment left here now.'

The coal board's opencast operation at Glynglas, near Blaenau, was one of the last to go through the public enquiry procedure. It was bitterly opposed by villagers and on environmental grounds by Dyfed county and Dinefwr borough councils.

The board wanted to extract 700,000 tons of anthracite from the 422-acre site. They even wanted to include the rugby ground in their proposals.

But the enquiry result – in July 1976 – although giving the go-ahead to the NCB added certain restrictions. The size of the site was ordered to be cut by 15 acres to exclude the rugby ground and the Inquiry inspector ruled that no excavation work should be permitted within 100 yards of properties in Pennygroes Road, the main road leading through Blaenau.

But the two years that have elapsed have transformed the surrounding countryside into a hive of industrial activity.

Today excavation work has turned once rolling hills into huge craters burrowed out of the ground by giant earth-moving machines.

Dozens of lorries and machines are on the move all day. The noise and dust for the villagers of Blaenau are often intolerable and sometimes plain unbearable.

But that is the way it has to be, I suppose if the 'national interest' is to benefit to the extent of 700,000 tons of anthracite over the next five years. For the once peaceful village of Blaenau, though, it is all like a bad dream.

The story goes on to ask local people their opinions on the matter. This story is based on knowledge of the community and contacts that come from spending time amongst its inhabitants. It draws on information from local people with whom the journalist has a relationship. Colin said that this trust was important as it meant that they would come to him with issues. A person might have heard of a particular problem or event and Colin would know just the kind of person likely to help with his investigation. He would then dedicate some time to developing stories that had particular importance.

Colin said that since the 1990s this kind of reporting had become impossible. There had been huge cutbacks in staffing and marketing arms of the parent company had told them how to write for niche markets in order to address the needs of advertisers and increase revenue. To understand such changes we need to take a step back and look more carefully at ownership of the news media and how this has changed since the 1990s and why. This will give some clues as to the steps we need to take to explore such issues.

Changing media ownership

Media ownership as a means to control what people read about, to promote particular views of the world, is not a new thing. At the turn of the twentieth century the 'press barons', such as Pulitzer and Hearst in the US and Northcliffe and Beaverbrook in the UK, had used newspapers to promote their own political views. Their aim was to promote their business interests and to criticise those who disagreed with them (Curran and Seaton, 1977; Tunstall and Palmer, 1991). Until the 1970s most countries had fairly strict restrictions on media ownership to protect the public from the possibility of single owners expanding their interests to have immense control over what people read, saw and heard. But since the 1970s with the rise of conservative free-market capitalism there have been waves of deregulation. Right-wing thinkers argued that private ownership of the media facilitates a free press and is good for democracy. The logic goes that the free press will be owned by a range of voices who may indeed seek to promote their own interests, but if these voices do not reflect the interests of the public then they will simply go out of business. The idea is that a number of private voices will keep the state and government in check. This led to successive waves of deregulation in the US, UK and then Europe – although the lobbying power of media corporations in these changes should not be underestimated (Tunstall and Machin, 1999).

In 1980s and 1990s there were many big changes in the ownership and structure of news organisations. This was part of a more general bulking up facilitated by changes in broadcasting regulation. The US Telecommunications Act 1996 was the catalyst for speeding up mergers and buyouts, leading to a spread in relaxation of media ownership around the planet. The details of this Act can be found at the Federal Communication Commission website (http://www.fcc.gov/telecom.html). Examples of the wording of the Act are:

> The Commission shall modify section 73.3555 of its regulations (47 C.F.R. 73.3555) by eliminating any provisions limiting the number of AM or FM broadcast stations which may be owned or controlled by one entity nationally.

And

> eliminating the restrictions on the number of television stations that a person or entity may directly or indirectly own, operate, or control, or have a cognizable interest in.

The Act encouraged competition with the assumption that this would drag down prices of news products. But in practice it has meant that more could be owned and companies could get bigger. It also meant that companies could own across different kinds of media. So a company could own newspapers, radio stations, television stations and cinema outlets. The same kinds of deregulation are present in the UK Broadcasting Act 1996, which can be found at the UK Office of Public Sector Information website and also at the Ofcom (Office of Communications, the independent regulator and competition authority for the media in the UK, http://www.legislation. gov.uk/) website (http://www.ofcom.org.uk/), and in other European acts such as the German 1996 Broadcasting Act No. 223 and the French 1994 Broadcasting Law, although in France some control over cross-media ownership has remained. The *Western Mail* with its stories based closely on public relations material is an example of a newspaper that has fallen into the hands of a massive media conglomerate, Trinity Mirror. The nature of the texts found in it can be seen as a direct effect of the drive to maximise profits.

In Britain, the 1995 Broadcasting Bill allowed regional newspapers to take stakes in local radio and for newspaper groups to take stakes in television. The Conservative government's 1995 Green Paper on cross-media ownership allowed local newspapers to control circulations of 50,000 before referral to the Monopolies and Mergers Commission. This vastly expanded the control companies could have over individual cities.

After deregulation in the US all the major news networks were bought up by media conglomerates – ABC by Disney, CBS by Viacom and NBC by General Electric – a pattern of bulking up that was soon to sweep across Europe (Tunstall and Machin, 1999). Such information can be easily obtained from the network websites, which usually carry annual reports providing detailed information about owners. This meant that Viacom, as well as owning CBS News, had control of 40 television stations including the cable stations MTV, Nickelodeon, the Movie Channel, Sundance Channel; 176 radio stations across the US including New York, Dallas, Seattle, Los Angeles, Denver, Philadelphia; a Hollywood film studio, Paramount Pictures, makers of movies such as *War of the Worlds*; an international film distribution company, UIP; the global chain of UCI cinemas; Blockbuster video; and international book publisher Simon & Schuster. Therefore audiences of CBS News are watching news items generated by a billion-dollar-a-year transnational media conglomerate. Websites such as http://www.theyrule.net, which catalogues up-to-date ownership and members of boards of directors, show links between Viacom and other large corporations such as airlines, and petroleum and pharmaceutical companies.

This kind of bulking up enables cost-effective control of multiple stages of the media process – production, distribution and exhibition. It also has the advantage of synergy, meaning that corporations can cross-advertise and self-promote. They can also use material across different media, which brings about massive economy of scale; the larger the corporation's output and the more parts of the process it controls, the more that it can get a return on productions through multiple outlets, the cheaper the product.

Since they are tied into a global corporate network – some critics argue – such corporations are unlikely to be critical of the corporate world in general. Media researchers point out that many of the major shareholders and investors in media corporations are investment banks and other large institutions that have interests across a range of other industries (Wasko, 1982; Herman and Chomsky, 1988). This can easily be checked, again by consulting the annual reports of the companies and then accessing the annual reports of shareholders. For example, Goldman Sachs Asset Management is listed as one shareholder of Viacom/CBS News. We can then see the nature of this company as a global trading bank from its own reports.

Some writers (Hollingsworth, 1986; Herman and Chomsky, 1988; and Kellner, 1990) see this as a process whereby media corporations will tend to support conservative policies, and will be uncritical of neo-capitalism, seeing it as a natural state of affairs. In fact, McChesney (2004) has shown that media corporations are themselves amongst the biggest companies in the world. In 2002, McChesney shows, *Forbes* magazine calculated that over a third of the 50 wealthiest Americans generated the bulk of their fortunes through the media and related industries (2004: 21). He argues: 'our media, then, far from being on the sidelines of the capitalist system, are amongst its greatest beneficiaries' (2004: 2).

Since the mid 1990s in Britain the newspaper industry has been a part of these changes whereby companies have bulked up. In January 2005 the Newspaper Society (http://www.newspapersoc.org.uk/) stated:

Over £7.0 billion has been spent on regional press acquisitions and mergers since October 1995. The top 20 publishers now account for 86% of all regional and local newspaper titles in the UK, and 95% of the total weekly audited circulation.

At the time, there were 1,286 regional and local, daily and weekly titles in Britain. Ownership was dominated by three big press groups: Trinity Mirror plc, Newsquest Media Group and Northcliffe Newspapers Group Ltd. Trinity Mirror, for example, the owner of the *Western Mail*, had 274 titles at the time of writing.

One of the effects of the deregulation of ownership and the forming of a handful of big companies has been the slimming down of the news production process. Increases in commercial competition enabled the larger newspaper chains and conglomerates to use production cost-cutting as a way to maximise profits (Hallin, 1996; Bourdieu, 1998). The reduction in reporters has meant that some beats no longer exist and it has reduced the reporter's ability to go out into the community. Where one reporter now covers an area formerly covered by eight, there is no time for nosing around, for verification, and especially for developing a story as in the case of Colin Hughes' piece about the rugby club. Instead there has been an increased dependence on secondary sources such as press releases as we saw in the 'Welsh Sofa' story. Story development now involves telephone calls to official organisations, press offices or visits to websites rather than finding sources who can best verify a story or provide different angles. Many of the organisations that provide these releases will be staffed by the journalists who formerly worked for the newspaper before the waves of redundancies. A local council may employ ten public relations officers, who feed press releases to two local newspapers where at each of which they deal with only one lone local reporter. Verification of stories may also increasingly involve calls to the kinds of celebrity lifestyle/culture experts that now dominate the mass media.

Trinity Mirror

Trinity Mirror, the company that owns the *Western Mail*, controlled over 274 local and regional titles and five nationals in Britain in 2009 with an annual profit of around £200 million (information easily accessible from annual reports normally available through the company website). This gave the company complete dominance over local news in a number of cities. In Birmingham for example it controlled two former rival titles, the *Birmingham Evening Mail* and the *Birmingham Post*. In South Wales as well as the *Western Mail* Trinity controlled its former rival title the *South Wales Echo*, as well as the *Cardiff Post*, the *Rhondda Leader* and *Wales on Sunday*. Of course, this means that the plurality that might help to voice a range of world views is

UNIVERSITY
OF SHEFFIELD
LIBRARY

removed. This multiple ownership of titles means practically that many titles can be produced by the same teams and facilities, material can be syndicated, and integrated advertising deals can be made. Trinity claimed that in one week it can reach around 80 per cent of the adult population in South Wales and 72 per cent in the Midlands.

The company's annual report (2007), available on their website, lays out their strategy:

> Our strategic goal is to build a growing multiplatform media business, by developing and sustaining strong positions across print and digital, with products and services which meet the needs of our customers, both readers and advertisers.
>
> We will achieve this by both launch and acquisition, and by layering and segmenting our portfolio both geographically and by advertiser or content segment, thereby deepening our penetration and reach across markets. (Trinity Mirror plc, 2007: 13)

It is this strategy that helps us to understand why reporting has moved away from actual engagement with the community, from investigation and checking of facts, to a reliance on press releases.

Working for Trinity Mirror

Colin Hughes worked for many years at the *Western Mail*. Colin spoke of the massive changes experienced by reporters working for the title. These had included huge cutbacks in staffing. Colin worked from the Swansea office for around 40 years. He said that until the 1990s there were around seven reporters working in the Swansea area. The newspaper covered a number of towns over South Wales, each of which had its own office and reporters. Until the 1990s Colin worked a beat which included police stations and local villages, where he would attend meetings and sit in cafes and local bars. Here he developed a link with communities and a network of contacts. This was a beat in the traditional sense and brought him into contact with everyday life in the community. Through this he would learn about issues that had an important impact on the everyday lives of the local people. It was from 1990 that the *Western Mail* started to cut back on staff and close down local offices outside Swansea. At the time of writing there was only one reporter working in Swansea and he worked from home. But now he also had responsibility for the whole of Wales to the west of the city due to other office closures. This meant that there was no longer time to work a beat. There was no time to visit police stations and certainly no possibility to spend time in the community.

Colin spoke of the huge changes that took place in news gathering, where reporters were being made redundant and those left had to cover the same areas. This meant that there was an increasing tendency to take press releases. Colin said

> We would be accepting stories that we wouldn't have before. And we wouldn't really have the time to check them.... On the front cover of the paper you would get the impression that it contained investigative reporting, but inside it was all press releases, official reports and internet. Reporters might make a couple of telephone calls, but you wouldn't have the time to do any background research, any checking. In many cases you wouldn't have to even make any calls to show that you have sources as the press releases would come complete even with these. It would just mean cut and paste.

He spoke of the increased tendency to use the internet to get extra material for stories:

> The internet means that you can get background material quickly. This is important as it is no longer possible to call people, to go and interview people. But this means that we are dependent on the information that organisations put onto sites. But since there have been massive reductions in staffing this is the only way to collect information. And the internet allows journalists to search other news sites to get information as news is not copyrighted. But again this is not the same as investigation.

Two other local South Wales journalists, both former employees of the *Western Mail*, Mary and Malcolm Rees, now working freelance, also spoke of former times where they would have developed stories from a beat which took them out into the local villages. This was before local offices closed and staff cutbacks. Malcolm said:

> I used to write a weekly column which was based on interviews with people who lived in the villages. They would talk about their concerns. This could be money or benefits or work. Now you would not find the voices of real people in the newspapers. You might get vox pops where people are asked what they think of a comment by a US celebrity reporter that Catherine Zeta-Jones has got a big bottom. As reporters you are now told to go out and get these. But previously there was the chance to bring in stories connected to people's real lives.

Mary spoke of the reliance on press releases which had resulted from staffing cuts. She herself was working freelance preparing business supplements. She said:

> where you would previously have a business editor who would write stories drawn from contacts, about local business people and business issues, they will now base a whole business supplement on hand-outs which will be put together by a non-specialist.

Malcolm also spoke of the same lack of digging around due to dependence on press releases and telephone. He mentioned a story he had worked on which involved going through receipts from council expenditure and finding that the tax payer was funding private transport costs for certain council members. This story also relied on information and help from trusted sources. 'All this,' he said, 'has now gone, so much happens and no one is there to keep and eye out. The eyes of the public have been closed'.

The influence of media regulation on content

The content and nature of the news item 'How does your life sit with the sofa habits revealed about our nation?' should now be easy to understand. A textual analysis might lead to a conclusion that the journalist is promoting national identity, or consumer behaviour. This too is an important observation. But we need to understand changes in media regulation, resulting ownership patterns and news gathering procedures to realise that this text has been produced by a journalist of high professional standard, who simply has no time to actually investigate anything happening in South Wales. So an angle is found on a press release to give the impression of local relevance. Of course, press releases will be oriented to the business and commercial interests of those who produce them and who employ many of the journalists who formerly worked for the newspapers, as noted above.

What this section has shown is that in order to understand content we need to know something about production practices, ownership and regulation – in other words how media companies are allowed to behave. Such information, as we have seen, is available through financial reports, the websites of regulators and through interviews with employees. Here we have only given the accounts of several journalists and more would be interviewed for a complete piece of research. But here we have shown how we can use interviews to find out particular kinds of information and also how this information can be presented.

What is in-depth interviewing?

It simply means interviewing persons to gain their own perspective on and insights into a particular issue. For example, we may ask a journalist about how they gather information for publication on websites. Or we might interview individual readers of news to find out where they get their information from or what they think of particular stories. Such interviews may be structured through a list of key themes and issues which the researcher has pre-prepared, although they tend to be 'open-ended', allowing the discussion to develop along any interesting lines. This means that unexpected issues and information may arise which, if of interest, will be discussed further during the interview and/or used to consider further interviews. In-depth interviews can be conducted face to face, which is good for developing trust, over the telephone if a person is very busy or far away, or even by email, or online messenger feeds, such as Skype or MSN. Some of these non-face-to-face methods are useful where people wish to retain anonymity. They also help to reduce travel costs and massively expand geographical access.

When should in-depth interviews be used?

In-depth interviews are used to get personal accounts of behaviours, opinions and experiences. They are often used to support or explore other kinds of data. For example, if we find that there are changing ownership patterns in newspapers along with publicised reductions in staffing we can interview journalists about their daily work experiences to find out how they have been affected. We might carry out a survey of news readership patterns and then carry out in-depth interviews to explore some of the issues further. In-depth interviews may be preferred over focus groups as they allow the interviewer to develop issues that appear of relevance and explore matters in an uninterrupted way. They may be used to gather information that interviewees may be less keen to provide in the context of a focus group. They also allow the interviewer to explore and bring in other aspects of the interviewees' personal characteristics if relevant. For example, if we are interviewing a journalist about their work producing online news we can find out about their own experience, training and broader professional concerns.

How is an in-depth interview done?

First the researcher establishes what kind of information is required. For example, we may need to learn more about the way journalists gather material to place on websites.

We ask who can best supply this information. This might be from a range of perspectives. So we might interview journalists and editors who work at different kinds of news outlets.

We contact these interviewees requesting an interview. In the case of a media practitioner or regulator this is best done first through a very short letter that says in simple terms who you are and what kind of information you require. Busy people tend not to attend to longer letters that are not of immediate importance to them. This can then be followed up with emails and telephone calls. Media practitioners are often busy but can be very responsive when they see you are interested and can even respect persistence.

We should be fully prepared for the interview. If it is a media practitioner we should be familiar with their work or with their own outlet and the broader context where possible. Interviewees respond much better when they see you are well informed, prepared and have taken a specific and genuine interest in them and their work. It is a good idea to have about ten questions ready to ask. Often in such interviews you will not get through these questions, but you may forget what you really wanted to ask once the conversation gets going and they can be used to begin discussions that may then move off in other interesting directions. And each interviewee may provide you with fresh information to carry to the next interview.

We decide how we will gather the data from the interview. Will we take notes or record the interview? One of the authors, who has carried out many hundreds of interviews, prefers to take notes and then write these up once they return home, although they have also used tape-recordings.

We should get consent to use the interview material. If we are quoting people, or naming people, for ethical purposes we should ask their permission.

What are the advantages of in-depth interviews?

They give greater freedom to the interviewer to explore issues. While surveys tend to ask predefined questions that generate limited responses, in-depth interviews can therefore be used to supplement surveys because they provide greater detail of information and further explore any issues that arise. In-depth interviews are very good at throwing up unexpected or unforeseen issues that can then be explored using other methodologies. If we want, for example, to understand the way media regulation is influencing how radio stations are run then we find that carrying out 30 interviews across different kinds of stations, with operators, syndicator and news producers, along with the regulators, enables us to build up a surprising picture of what is happening.

What are the disadvantages of in-depth interviews?

They are time-consuming, in terms of planning, contacting interviewees and possibly travelling to meet them. There is then the time taken to conduct the interview, which may be around an hour or more, and the time required to transcribe it if it is tape-recorded.

In-depth interviews are subjective. Data gathered are the point of view of one person. So if we interview a journalist about their experience of producing online news, this is simply their own opinion. Of course, more interviews should be carried out and in our experience it is through this process that a clear picture of a situation can be built up. In this particular chapter, comments are provided from a smaller number of interviewees in order to demonstrate, in a case study fashion, how such information can be useful. But in practice a study of this nature might involve ten or 40 interviewees depending on timescale and resources. The in-depth interview is also subjective as results may depend very much on the personality and behaviour of the interviewer.

How do you present in-depth interview data?

In this chapter we have shown that sometimes quotes or themes from individual interviews can be selected as part of your explanation of a changing situation. As has also been done in this chapter, it is often useful to provide some background information on the interviewee.

Researching a global magazine

The next example of political economy research shows how we can look at the operation of a media corporation to help us understand smaller details of the content itself, but this time we are dealing with an international publication. Of interest here is the way content is managed across territories to adapt to local markets, but also to maintain the global brand message. Again this involves issues of organisation, staffing, regulation and finance.

In 2001–6 one of the authors was involved in a project investigating a study into the way that media corporations adapt products for different national markets (Machin and van Leeuwen, 2007). One case study was the women's lifestyle magazine *Cosmopolitan*, which was produced in different versions for 50 countries. Often with such magazines, many readers are unaware of the processes that go into creating such texts. On the one hand we my find them trivial and superficial. But on the other hand the global *Cosmopolitan* magazine and other titles like it are successful products that have been cleverly designed and consequently have been able to take large shares in growing national markets around the world. Looking behind the scenes of these magazines helps us to understand this.

In the first place, copies of all the 50 editions were collected by writing to Hearst, the US-based company that owns and controls *Cosmopolitan* around the planet, who sent two of each free of charge. A content analysis was then carried out on each of these editions using discourse analysis and multimodal semiotic analysis. This was done in order to establish how the international versions differed in terms of contents. The analysis revealed that there was some attention to local culture but that also the *Cosmopolitan* brand remained strong across all the versions. But we wanted to understand, how are these versions produced, at what levels are decisions made about contents and localisation and how is this accomplished? How is a global magazine managed? The primary aim of *Cosmopolitan* as with all international lifestyle magazines is to maintain a global brand that is appealing to both (mainly) international and local advertisers, which are the source of their revenue. To do this there must be a strong coherent global identity, but also enough local inflections so as to appeal to national markets. So how is this identity managed in 50 different countries?

Some of these questions were answered by reference to annual reports and financial/circulation information obtained from the owners Hearst Corporation. Often a company will readily provide information on the basis that they wish to attract investors and push up the value of shares. They may also be keen to be seen to be supporting academic research as this too can in itself help to promote the corporate image. When making contact with companies it is important to have a clear letter which, while being brief, also lays out the aims of the research in terms which make it obvious that the researchers are well informed about the company. Often this in itself can engage those you wish to interview. This means that letters should state simple aims that will be recognisable to media personnel rather than abstract theoretical interests.

Most of the information about the organisation of the different versions of the magazine came from interviews with editors, senior staff and writers. Again, these people were contacted via short, concise letters that indicated that background research had been done and which summarised the key areas we would hope to discuss. These were then followed up after one week with telephone calls. Again the aim here is not to show how all the interviews were used but to indicate what kinds of issues can be raised, how they can provide useful data and how this should be presented.

The local versions of *Cosmopolitan*

First, we take a closer look at the kinds of similarities and differences found between the various national versions. This is important as it allows us to see what kinds of questions need answering at the broader production, political economic level.

In the textual analysis of the different versions we found that items across these have much in common. There is a very limited range of topics covered (Machin and van Leeuwen, 2003). These are work, relationships, sex and fashion. No real surprises here for those familiar with the magazine. But what we found was that in all cases women always act alone and strategically, whether this is to find a perfect date, to negotiate with an awkward colleague, or have wonderful sex. All of these realms are treated as mini-management projects. But the different versions also had local inflections. The following examples are from the October 2001 versions of the magazine. These show some of the differences that can be found between the Indian, Greek and Dutch versions. Here we compare articles from the careers pages.

Indian Version (October 2001):

Can Your Colleague Be Your Friend?

Ayesha Wahi was only 21 when she landed her first job. Though she was anxious about her new workplace, her fears were quickly put to rest when she met newcomer Shalini Gupta. 'Being friends with her came easy, as she was relaxed and lots of fun', she says. But what started as casual female bonding grew into vile professional jealousy when Wahi was promoted over Gupta. Her jealous co-worker started bad-mouthing her and spreading so many nasty rumours that Wahi eventually quit her job. Today, many years later, she is a very successful vice president of a media company, but Wahi still regrets her friendship with Gupta. 'When my best pal started playing games with me, I just didn't think the job was worth holding on to,' she adds.

What is it that makes us behave like warriors at work? It's a dog-eat-dog battlefield where you have to be sharp about telling friend from foe. 'Friendship at work hinders professionalism as there is an emotional involvement with your so-called friend,' says corporate training consultant Renu Mattoo. Get wise about work mates with our genius work plan.

As in all the *Cosmopolitan* versions, it is never specified what kind of work is done, although it is always some kind of office work, never factory work, for example. What is unique to the Indian version is that women are often highly successful at work, becoming company directors. Also distinctive to the Indian version is that there tends to be a lack of trust in other people until they prove themselves. We see below a different kind of work environment in the Greek version.

Greek Version (October 2001):

All of us have to 'lick'/creep to our boss. At least let us do it with style....

Listen carefully: It is important to listen to your boss carefully and to take notice of certain key expressions that they use. Later on, you can repeat them saying: 'and as our fantastic boss says …'. Besides, the biggest complaint of bosses is that employees are not good listeners.

The wise and me: Don't hesitate to ask his advice, showing that you appreciate his knowledge, experience and wisdom. Try to express your admiration and to repeat how helpful his assistance was.

Something for the hunger: Find out which is your boss's favourite snack/sweet and try to supply him with it. While he is enjoying it, you can gently start talking about work.

Be grateful: Next time you finish a project, or the company gets a new one, remember to show your gratitude to your boss for giving you the chance he gave you to be a part of it. The enthusiasm always flatters the employers.

In the Greek version we find the woman engaged in trivial and largely humiliating tasks – she finds out what kinds of sweets her boss likes. Such a text, with a clear relationship of subordination to men would not be suitable for other markets such as the US. As with the Indian version, and all others, however, the woman still acts alone and strategically and in a professional/business environment.

Dutch Version (November 2001):

Work with emotions: A nurse needs a warm heart

Maarit Virtanen, 23, works in a dermatology and allergy hospital, HYKS. She counsels patients with allergies and asthma, especially those with allergies who are undergoing desensitisation treatment and for whom taking shots on a regular basis lasts between three and five years. Maarit's work also includes a project treating smoking addiction in which quitters are given nicotine substitution therapy and support.

Maarit is often thanked for really engaging with her patients; she thinks of people as more than simply objects that need to be dealt with.

'I feel good when I can give something extra to a customer. I always try to remember the patient by their earlier visits so that they can be more than just a routine case', says Maarit.

The young woman's career choice was surprising in the sense that when she was little she was afraid of injections. Since then Maarit has realised that a nurse does a lot more than that.

'When I was in high school a person who was close to me died of cancer of the pancreas and I felt like I wanted to get involved in developing treatment for cancer patients. Nowadays I'm in a position that fits me well, in which I could imagine staying for the rest of my life'.

As for the well being of nurses, a good working environment is very important. The way nurses treat each other is reflected onto the patients and affects the professional's credibility. Fortunately work-related issues don't follow her home and Maarit is not afraid of tying herself up in her work even though as a devoted employee she belongs to a high risk group. A stable relationship and spending time with friends help her to switch off.

Sometimes a customer's problems touch upon the nurse's own life but Maarit thinks that a nurse's private matters are never the patient's responsibility.

'Even though things are affecting you deeply, they have to be kept outside of nursing situations. The main focus should not be moved off the patient'.

No one really wants to become a nurse because of the pay. Extra money for shift work usually makes up a significant part of the income except in the case of Maarit, who only works the day shift. Nursing does not suit everyone.

'A nurse must have a warm heart, genuine interest in people and a good attitude towards colleagues. Mastery of technical tricks is not enough. A nurse needs both emotional intelligence and brains.'

Here the woman has a personal relationship with her work, in keeping with the *Cosmopolitan* philosophy, but there is no manager telling her what to do, or to fear, as in the Greek version. In the Dutch version, unlike the Indian version, women tend not to be company directors. Work is more about fulfilment. The Dutch version's approach to work is one of almost religious devotion and the sense of seeking a higher truth through it.

What we can clearly see here is that while the topics are the same, there is some attention to local culture. But in all versions women act alone and strategically to take control over their lives, however trivial the activities involved might be.

There was a further interesting observation in terms of the style of the different versions. Our translators often commented to us that the language style they found was slightly unusual. This suggested that the kind of language style used in the US version was being maintained in the local versions. Language style is able to connote identities and attitudes. For example, all versions tended to use a direct form of address seen here in the Spanish version (October 2001):

> Aprovecha para exfoliar tu piel y recuperar su luz
> (*Take* the chance to exfoliate *your* skin and give it back its glow)

This is a linguistic device that can be used to give a sense of confidence and of agency. Rather than 'why not take advantage' or 'try to take advantage', the imperative form gives a sense of immediacy and 'no messing'. There was also the frequent use of adjectives as can be seen in the US version (October 2001):

> Dramatic, passion-inspiring purple is the season's hottest hue. To instantly make any outfit feel more 'fall 2002' just add a taste of plum.

The use of adjectives increases the sensory experience of what is depicted and is often used in advertising. Also we found the use of poetic devices such as rhyming and alliteration. We see this here in the Indian version (October 2001):

> Flaunt that gorgeous body: A sure shot way of upping your sinister sister image is showing off that bold bod – the right way.

Here we see both these in the case of 'sinister sister' and 'bold bod'. Poetic devices can make writing more entertaining and pleasurable than, say, technical descriptions of products and processes. Here the pleasure, as is often the case in advertising, is not communicated through descriptions but the language style itself. In this case while there is clearly attention to localisation through translation we find that the values of the magazine are nevertheless communicated via the language style (see Machin and van Leeuwen, 2005b).

From such observations we begin to get a sense of the different levels to which a corporation must adapt its product for different markets while also maintaining brand identity. But the question remains, how does the corporation, based in the US, manage this process? How does it make sure that the brand identity is maintained while at the same time having this sensitivity to the local market? And, crucially, how is this managed in terms of costs in order to maximise profits? To answer this we needed to understand more about the way the Hearst Corporation operates and how a global magazine is managed and coordinated.

Hearst Corporation

The Hearst Corporation, as is clear from its website and annual reports, has interests across a range of media: in magazines, newspapers, business publishing, cable networks, television, radio, internet business, TV production and distribution and real estate. It has a news service which syndicates material from its 12 newspaper dailies in US cities. It has 27 TV stations, which reach 17.5 per cent of US households. It has production and syndication partnerships with NBC's 24-hour network. It owns the ESPN sports network, which reaches over 80 million homes around the world. ESPN has 19 international networks reaching over 140 countries in 9 languages. Hearst also owns the History Channel, which reaches 64 million homes around the world, and claims, reasonably, to be the world's largest publisher of magazines (see below). Hearst is clearly a large global media corporation. Like many such conglomerates it has global ambitions and has been taking advantage of expanding international markets, particularly as countries such as Taiwan and China have become members of the World Trade Organization.

Hearst Magazines International oversees the publication of Hearst's magazines around the world. This includes 152 titles in 36 languages, which are distributed in over 100 countries. Titles include *Cosmopolitan, Good Housekeeping, Harper's Bazaar, Esquire, Marie Claire* and *Country Living*. Having this raft of publications brings many advantages such as economy of scale and the ability to offer advertisers deals across titles and platforms.

Cosmopolitan itself is the largest magazine franchise in the world. The title began in the 1880s but was relaunched in the US by Helen Gurley Brown in 1965 and at the turn of the new millennium was No. 1 on the news stand in the US.[1] Since the 1970s the magazine has introduced international editions

---

1   Such information can be found in trade publications for the advertising industry such as *Advertising Age* or at websites such as http://adage.com.

and now has 50 versions in Europe, Latin America, Asia and Africa, selling about 3 million copies monthly (*Advertising Age*, 13.05.08). Hearst has pioneered the expansion of markets for magazines.

Therefore, when we open *Cosmopolitan* magazine in any of these 50 countries we should be mindful that however much it has the appearance of 'localness' it is part of a large powerful corporation with global ambitions.

Interviews with editors of different national editions revealed that most are joint ventures or partnerships which involve a licensing agreement between a local publisher and Hearst. Hearst company representatives travel round the world making contacts with existing dominant national publishers to plan possible launches of the magazine with suitable partners and to monitor editorial content – to make sure that the brand identity is maintained. These national publishers will be those that already have the infrastructure to easily add further titles to their portfolios. This infrastructure will involve printing facilities, writers, editorial and other production staff. These national publishers will normally have partnership arrangements with a raft of other titles from global publishers. Economy of scale will mean these local publishers are extremely powerful, increasing their dominance of their local market. And ownership of a range of leading international titles will also bring the possibility of cross-advertising deals.

In 1995 when the World Trade Organization replaced GATT – the organisation regulating many global trade tariffs on behalf of powerful nations – telecommunication and the mass media were added to its remit. This has meant that countries wishing to participate in the WTO have had to open up their media industries to foreign investment. Companies like Hearst have been at the forefront of pioneering new territories, for example by setting up three different language editions of *Cosmopolitan* in China. This is having a transforming effect on local media, and with its existing portfolio, advertising links and economy of scale, Hearst will be able to set new standards of quality (Machin and van Leeuwen, 2007).

The different national editions of *Cosmo*, depending upon the agreement between Hearst and the local publisher, will contain varying amounts of material taken from the other international editions and will generate some of their own material that will then itself be available for syndication, meaning that all other national versions will be able to use it. Hearst, a number of editors revealed, encourages local editions to use as much existing material as possible to keep costs down. Collections of stories and images are pooled by the different versions and are available online and also distributed to editors on CD-ROM. So, for example, problem pages and 'confessions' can be downloaded, translated and modified for the local market. In the case of careers pages, as we saw above, this might involve slightly foregrounding or backgrounding the role of the boss, for example.

Local editors and senior staff attend meetings with Hearst staff in order to discuss the brand image and development of the magazine. Also, where new editions are developed, Hearst give training in writing for the brand style. Here we can see how staff learn the language style and genres of *Cosmo* writing that were observed above. It is in the brand message of the 'Fun, Fearless Female' that the lone woman acting strategically against the world, mainly concerned with relationships and seduction, is to be found. Historically women have been tied to family and the domestic environment and have not been encouraged to celebrate their sexual desires. Editors told us that in the 1960s Helen Gurley Brown challenged this model by promoting an alternative in which women could have sexual desires and live for themselves rather than their family. The Fun, Fearless Female is this legacy. So in the examples above we find the woman not dependent on anyone, acting to take control of her life. In fact our analysis showed (Machin and van Leeuwen, 2007) that *Cosmo* women mainly take control over relatively trivial matters and that much of the power exists in the kind of language used rather than what the women actually accomplish. But the aim of the magazine, in the words of one of the editors, was 'to create a sense of women having fun and being in control'. The word 'sense' here is crucial. In many of the versions of *Cosmo* it is the act of sex that creates a sense of 'naughtiness' and in which the women behave with most agency.

Adapting to different cultures

From what we have considered so far we can begin to get a clear sense that *Cosmopolitan* is part of a media corporation with global ambitions. We see that changes in global media regulation have opened up markets to the likes of Hearst to search new territories for partners through which they can begin to establish their brand. This means that powerful local publishers can become stronger through links with these global media corporations thus creating pressures on those that do not make these partnerships. What we have yet to explain fully is exactly how local editions work with the brand concept and at the same time adapt this for local markets. Interviews with editors, designers and writers in the Spanish, South African and Finnish versions can help us to understand some of this process.

Cosmo Spain appeared in 1989 after Hearst approached Bertelsmann, a European media conglomerate which has dominated publishing in Spain since the 1980s. Bertelsmann has 23 TV channels in Europe and has the largest media distribution network outside of the US. It is this pattern of making alliances with dominant local media that creates powerful interconnections between large conglomerates around the planet, often making it difficult for new publishers to gain a foothold.

The Spanish editor, Sarah Glattstein Franco, explained some of the differences between the Spanish and other versions. Her main observation was that the position of women in Spain was not the same as in Northern European countries and the US. She said that the women who read *Cosmo* in Spain are not financially powerful and are unlikely to have positions of responsibility at work, if they work at all. This means that in the magazine work would mostly be referred to in abstract terms as in 'when at work', 'your job', 'your boss'. It was important, nevertheless, to include work as it was a powerful symbol of the liberated woman. She said that unlike in the UK and the Netherlands, for example, Spanish women live in a society very much controlled by men. For this reason, rather than using the brand slogan of other versions, the 'Fun, Fearless Female', the Spanish version used 'For the woman who is changing the world'. Other versions could show independence as something already achieved, whereas this would simply not be accepted by a Spanish reader. There was therefore something more measured compared to the go-getting of other international versions. For this reason genuine career and education advice is included as well as other more abstract career items.

Glattstein Franco said that the brand was maintained through the use of the 'hot-tips' items, the 'fun' and 'lively' writing style and through clean modern-looking images. At first when *Cosmo* was introduced into the Spanish market Glattstein Franco said that she reduced the amount of sex compared with other versions, although soon afterwards this became much more like the other versions. Initially she used the US covers but cut the images so that there were no breasts. Gradually she left more in until eventually the covers were used without changes. She also said that stories translated from some of the other European versions on the topic of sex would be changed, not necessarily to make them less explicit but to emphasise sex with boyfriends rather than strangers. She said that in the UK version sex with strangers could be used as a routine symbol of independence and power. 'It's not that the readers themselves would actually want to do this, but it helps to communicate that the magazine is about fearlessness and rejecting certain traditional social pressures'. In contrast in Spain she said that raising the issue of women's sexual needs within established relationships could itself signify assertiveness. It would appear odd if women were to have sex with strangers, and this would instead carry connotations of being used and lack of intimacy. In Spain demanding intimacy in sex was in itself a breakthrough.

The South African and Finnish versions have slightly different publishing arrangements. In South Africa the magazine was started in 1982. Jane Raphaely, the mother of the current editor Vanessa Raphaely, who we interviewed, having read the British version of the magazine felt that it could be

made successful in her own country. She set this up in partnership with
distributor and publisher Media 24. In South Africa the magazine industry
is extremely monopolistic with only two publishing houses dominating the
market. Media 24, Africa's largest publishing group, controls about 60 per
cent of the country's magazine circulation with over 30 titles. It also has four
daily newspapers and 37 community newspapers. It is owned by the multi-
national media group Naspers, which has interests in pay TV, book publishing and internet in Asia and Southern Europe.

Raphaely said that they used the New York office for much of their content
and design such as cover styling and page layouts. She herself had a staff of
15 although there were 160 in the wider company who were able to share
production tasks with other magazines. There had been no training for the
writers but they were told to follow the *Cosmo* format, which she described
as being direct and feeling good.

The readership addressed by *Cosmopolitan* in South Africa was described
as more upmarket than in the UK or Spain, with the readership having high
income and mainly in work. *Cosmo* South Africa, Raphaely said, does not
have the same amount of sex or material on men. This was because, she
suggested, there was far less 'laddish' culture than in the UK. She explained
this as being due to the fact that women were more emotionally and politically developed due to in-your-face social issues. Although she said that in
other ways, for example as regards sex, they were much 'less worldly'.

Due to the size of the market, much of the material in this edition of *Cosmo*
is in fact syndicated material. This also meant that apart from story selection
and the use of English-language material there was less need for staff to be
so carefully trained in the *Cosmo* writing style. Raphaely said that she also
bought in a lot of material from other places, such as from story banks. These
are syndication agencies where journalists and writers place material that can
be bought by publishers from around the world.

The licence for the South African version was based on royalties, on
percentage of profit, therefore giving an incentive to use as much of the material from other international versions as possible. Profit was generated from
the 100 pages of advertising in each copy. All of the cover price would be
used on production, printing and distribution. Raphaely said that Hearst
were always pushing her to use more existing material in order to further cut
costs, but she felt that this would mean that the magazine would lose its
market position.

The licence for the Finnish version is held by Sanoma Magazines and it
was launched entirely with a Finnish editorial team. Most were recruited in-
house from existing titles. The whole staff received training by Hearst in
order to get to grips with the English terminology that was to be emulated in
Finnish. They were all familiarised with the tone of '*Cosmo*-speak', which is

the editor's way of describing the language style we described above. In Finland *Cosmopolitan* is now the leading women's magazine. Based on the licence agreement the Finnish *Cosmo* is able to use up to 80 per cent of all the material, including the cover, from the US parent magazine. But generally, we were told, the local office produces up to 75 per cent. A content analysis of a number of the Finnish versions, however, suggested that this figure is an overestimate. Local editors are sensitive to criticisms of the magazine being highly generic and lacking in hard content. Much of the core material in the Finnish version was that which appears in all of the international versions. The cover, horoscopes, Irma Kurtz's problems column, the sex and relationships features and also often the celebrity interviews are published in many versions. There was a combination of international and local fashion content, which would be generated through promotional relationships with national boutiques and department stores. Typically, local material would be cheaply put together from local street interviews and reader polls but would be assembled in terms of layout and language style in line with the *Cosmo* brand values. All of this material was to be used to signify confidence and directness.

What this section on *Cosmopolitan* magazine has shown us is that on the one hand our content analysis allowed us to establish that the publication has some core values of 'fun' and 'fearlessness' that are communicated not through women actually doing things in the world but through language styles, genres and images that are able to signify these values even though what women are depicted as doing is largely trivial. The magazine works by encouraging women to align with these values through acts of consumption rather than by acting in society. This is achieved by always depicting women as acting alone for their own ends with no broader connections to society. But on the other hand we have been able to understand a little more of the way that this is achieved on a practical level. The aim is to maintain a global brand that is able to carry both high-status global and local advertising while also being attentive to the needs of local readers. Huge economy of scale, pooling of content, and the ability to offer international advertising packages allow national publishers to grow stronger, often equipped with a portfolio of other international titles, therefore excluding other local publishers. Machin and van Leeuwen (2007) showed the effect of this process on other more local genres of magazine that did represent real women involved in the community through concrete actions. Simply put, titles had to adapt or disappear when confronted with the new confident, highly stylised world of '*Cosmo*-land'. Yet patterns of global deregulation increasingly open up new markets to the likes of Hearst and other media corporations with international ambitions. The jury is still out on what effects all this will have.

Doing a research project with political economic analysis

The point of political economic analysis is to look at the nature of media ownership and organisation with a view to investigating how this influences the kinds of content and output that we find. Fundamentally, this kind of investigation is driven by concerns about fairness of representation, who and what processes lead to the kinds of content that we find.

This form of analysis can draw on a range of methods. In this chapter we have used archive research and interviews. But we could have carried out an ethnographic/observational study where we spent time in production environments to see how news and magazines are put together, speaking with managers and even owners and regulators. We could have composed a survey and sent this to news and magazine workers. But importantly in political economic analysis we need to place our topic in historical context. This means we need to find out how the market is regulated and how this has changed. We need to find out how a particular company operates. Can content be explained partly, for example, as arising from the need to create material for cross-media platforms, or with an eye to suitability for international markets? For instance, some news producers, such as Bloomberg, create news that is intended to have international accessibility. Writers are trained in a kind of 'neutral' language that avoids local inflections. A textual analysis of their output would be problematic unless carried out with an understanding of the nature of the product. And this is the point of much political economic analysis.

How much data are required for such a study will depend on various factors. The number of archive documents required will very much depend on the specific situation and case study but the aim should be to provide a comprehensive account of the state of and changes in that context so that current operating practices are understood. The number of interviews required will depend for the most part on time and resources and may range from five, for example, if the aim were to provide evidence into design decisions on local newspapers, to 200 if the aim were to claim to have understood broader media changes in the context of new regulation.

Summary

- Political economic analysis reveals the importance of looking behind the texts themselves and how the kinds of content offered to audiences can be a result of a number of processes based on the way that media organisations are operated, regulated and funded.

- The kinds of cultural forms produced by the media and how these are influenced by factors like commercial imperatives are the fundamental concern of political economic analysis.
- Political economic analysis is concerned with the kinds of plurality of voices offered to society by the media. At issue here is the role the media plays in our democracies.
- This kind of analysis is carried out either through interviews and/or the study of annual reports, financial reports and government reports, which allows the researcher to find out the nature and form of a media organisation and what it controls. Political economic analysis also allows the researcher to explain the extent to which commercial imperatives govern an organisation's practices and what kinds of regulation either limit or foster these.

CHAPTER 4

Inside the producers' domain: ethnography and observational methods

Ethnography and observational methods have been used in media research to study both production and consumption of the media. These methods are associated with actually watching or participating in what media audiences or media practitioners are doing and saying, on the assumption that this is the best way to study and understand what they think. Ethnography, in particular, should be seen as a way of approaching the data that we collect and it can incorporate many different kinds of research methodologies as well as long periods of observation. But in this chapter we focus specifically on the observation part of this kind of research.

What is special to these approaches is that they are used to understand social phenomena, such as media use, effects and production, by viewing them as one part of people's lives and the culture they inhabit. It is this culture which provides them with the ideas and values through which they think about and share the world, and something like media consumption or any work practice must be seen in the context of wider cultural influences. So if we wish to understand what someone feels about, or how they are affected by, say, a particular news report, we need to know more about this person in particular, the kinds of social values and ideas they normally live by and share with the people around them. We need to know how they behave more generally. If we wish to understand the production processes behind the creation of that news report then we may not simply be able to ask a journalist what they did, although this would be one important source of data. We would also need to look at what kinds of values and ideas the journalist has about what they do, the journalistic culture in which they have emerged and work, and also the processes and practices they use to produce the news report.

In the case both of the news receiver and the news producer, researchers who use these methods would see them as a powerful way to reveal and understand instances of human behaviour by placing them in cultural context and particularly as a way to draw out values and beliefs that otherwise often remain tacit, and therefore undetectable by other methods. In other words they allow us to find out what people actually do rather than what they say they do, and also to understand and research human behaviour in a way that is sensitive to the broader context of people's lives.

In this chapter we show how these methods or this approach are simple to use. We provide a specific example of a case study of media consumption that examines the way that young women from different countries read and understand the international women's lifestyle magazine *Cosmopolitan* with its core brand image of the 'Fun, Fearless Female'. We show that it is not so much that we can use these methods to identify media effects but rather to explore the way that certain ideas, values and identities are present and drawn upon by both the magazine and the readers. What is evident from this case study is that no other research method could have yielded the same quality of information.

Placing data in social processes

Ethnography and observational methods have often been contrasted to more scientific research approaches with which we measure opinions, beliefs and values, etc. through questionnaires. However, in fact, in ethnographic and observational research, such data as those generated by a questionnaire would themselves be permissible and could be used to find out basic measurable facts such as how many rooms a family house has or how many computers the family owns. A questionnaire could also be used to see what opinions people express about particular media products. But the difference is that ethnography would not see such data as producing social facts but rather as evidence of one particular kind of human behaviour which must be understood by further observation and research. Ethnographers would argue that broader social behaviour is far too complex to understand by simple questionnaires alone. Let us give an example to illustrate.

Recently one of the authors was talking to some of the regulars in his local bar. At the time a current issue in the news media debated whether a contestant in a reality show had been behaving in a racist manner. One regular local asked two other regulars what they thought of it. Both announced that they didn't watch, nor were interested in, such rubbish. Yet about an hour later the same regulars were heard chatting about the topic, clearly revealing the kind of knowledge that indicated that they had been watching the programme and were fully attentive, although the conversation was not so much about the programme itself but was a general complaint about the excessive amounts of political correctness found in present-day society.

It is this kind of instance that indicates some of the problems for researchers wishing to measure and describe the way people use and respond to the media. Had we entered the bar with a questionnaire to assess how many people watched reality shows and to record the opinions they had about them, what would we have found? Had we not remained in the bar to hear the later conversation we may have recorded only that people did not watch reality shows and that they considered them to be of extremely low quality. But this would not have been a faithful representation of the case. Clearly there is value in observing people where they act in everyday life. A questionnaire could be seen as a simple snapshot of one moment in time, one response, although what it is a snapshot of is difficult to assess without further contextual knowledge.

With this example we begin to indicate how observation and ethnography can be used as research tools and how they allow us to understand more about people's responses. Of course, as noted above, their use by no means prevents us from also using questionnaires or other kinds of more quantitative methods, but it helps us to place and contextualise the data these yield.

In the first place it is how we think about the kinds of social interaction we saw in the bar that is the key to doing good ethnography and observation. How, for example, might we characterise the behaviour of these bar regulars who state they do not watch a programme but then later reveal that they do? Are they simply lying? Of course people may not want to admit to certain kinds of behaviour or beliefs, for example if we were researching the kinds of pornography people used, or whether people considered themselves to be racist. In such cases the way that people respond will be influenced by their concern with the way they come across as social actors. Importantly, the same can be said about the way the locals behave as they dismiss the reality show as rubbish and then later go on to talk about it. They are not lying but rather are speaking with an intricate knowledge of what others know and think. And they speak always with a vivid awareness of the way others around them are responding. In other words they are aware of the kinds of opinions others might hold about reality TV as lowbrow entertainment. So in the first case they show that they are not the kind of people who watch such rubbish, of which they are clearly quite proud in that given moment. Then later in the evening they are able to use their knowledge of the programme to show that they are against political correctness. In fact many of the nightly conversations in the bar were general complaints about the world out there, most often with a fairly conservative perspective, heavy, for example, on anti-immigration, critical of liberalism, tough on youth crime, favouring a return to national military service to instil discipline. The conversations about the reality show should be seen as being part of this social context.

The conversations heard in the bar allow the men to demonstrate their wisdom and air their sense of anger and bitterness with the world. This is something that can bring no small amount of pleasure. And crucially, as social anthropologists and psychologists have shown, such conversations facilitate a sense of community and belonging (Bauman, 1986). Of course, these men may speak differently outside of the bar and even complain about each other.

The same requirement to look at how people behave over different contexts is found in production observation studies. For example, if we want to know about the production of a particular kind of media text, such as a women's lifestyle magazine, the practitioners may want to emphasise certain roles they carry out in their jobs. It is of course crucial to take very seriously what these practitioners tell us. If the researcher has never worked in the media production environment, they may have a tendency to impose quite wild interpretations on what they study. This can lead to practitioners becoming frustrated with academic work. But on the other hand any practitioner who has become embedded in a particular way of working, with its established procedures and culture, may have become so immersed that they are less able to reflect on some of the assumptions they make.

One of the authors interviewed editors and writers of women's lifestyle magazines. These practitioners tended to talk about the way the stories they wrote were about empowering women. Yet an analysis of the texts shows something very different. Observing the process of production revealed a series of training, marketing, targeting of consumer groups and localisation processes that tended towards a particular way of writing about the world. To understand what the practitioners mean by 'empowering women' we must understand them in the context of production.

What we must remember is that while observations gathered in settings in this manner can shed light on general processes of human interaction and culture, for the most part they tell us about that particular setting at that particular time. However, they do provide us with components that along with further observations can help us to build up a much more complete picture. In sum, as Hills (2002: 65) suggests in the context of studying fan cultures, all justifications offered by those whose opinions and attitudes we wish to understand should not be treated as 'social facts' but should be subjected to further analysis. He emphasises that an ethnographic approach that simply 'asks the audience' is potentially highly reductive.

In what follows we see that what lies at the heart of observation and ethnography is not so much a precise set of procedures but a particular way of viewing human behaviour that thinks slightly differently about what people are doing when they talk. By looking at some of the origins of ethnography in anthropology and of observational methods in sociology we show exactly what this means in terms of doing research and using these methods to answer research questions.

Ethnography in anthropology

Ethnography as a research process has its origins in anthropology. Many people think of anthropology as the study of 'exotic' cultures and small-scale societies. To some extent this has indeed been the case and the field's history is very much connected to colonialism and the Victorian adventurer. But anthropology itself, in fact, challenged the idea of the 'primitive' or 'exotic' that was predominant in Victorian intellectual thinking where the people of Africa or Polynesia, for example, had been seen, through an evolutionary model, as being evidence of primitive versions of Europeans and European societies such as in James Frazer's classic work *The Golden Bough* (1922). In this earlier view the ways of life and beliefs of these people, such as magic and witchcraft, had been seen as evidence of primitive thought in contrast to the rational thinking characteristic of European culture. Anthropologists, first in the work of Franz Boas (1921) and later through that of Bronislaw Malinowski (1922) and Edward Evans-Pritchard (1937), amongst others, rejected such ethnocentric assumptions and argued that cultures should be studied in their own right. For these writers this meant coming to see the world through the eyes of the people being studied. Like the regulars in the bar, given in our opening example, we need to understand what these people say and do, what they seem to believe, as part of a particular culture at a particular time. As we saw this means that behaviour that in the first place might appear as irrational can come to seem reasonable and comprehensible. In order to see the world through the eyes of the native people, anthropologists spend many years living within the societies they study, experiencing every part of their social lives.

Malinowski, through his studies of the people who inhabited the Trobriand Islands in Melanesia, made a crucial point about the way we can gather data about what people think and why they do things. He emphasised that we cannot simply ask people why they do things, such as why they believe in, and act in accordance with, magic and witchcraft, as they would only be able to give idealised or 'official' reasons. This is important as it means we have to look much more carefully into different aspects of a social context. For example, if we were to ask a person in the UK why they drink a particular brand of beer, they might say simply that they like the taste. Of course this may be true. But advertisers have shown that it is possible to transform an ailing product through rebranding. A cider drink can be relaunched to give it associations of Celtic authenticity and cosmopolitanism. The drink's identity is changed and if the rebranding is successful it allows the consumer a differ-ent experience of the drink. Yet when we ask the person why they favour this drink they will not provide this as part of their explanation. For Malinowski this is because we generally do not have access to why we do things. Therefore we need to think about what people do and say in the context of broader information about their particular culture and society.

Evans-Pritchard (1937) in his fascinating book *Witchcraft, Oracles and Magic among the Azande* gives an example that allows us to see the limitations of a subject's ability to understand their own knowledge and behaviours and therefore of our need to understand broader social context. He was fasci-nated by the way that the Zande used an oracle to answer questions, for example, to solve a dispute or to establish blame or guilt. The oracle worked by giving a poison called *benge* to a chicken along with the casting of a number of spells. Before administering the poison it would be decided what the chicken's death or survival would mean. It might mean a certain person was guilty of something, for example. The oracle could also be used for many purposes such as to predict the weather. Evans-Pritchard was particularly drawn by the fact that faith in the oracle was maintained in the face of evidence that he would see as indicating its inadequacy. Even where the oracle was unsuccessful this would be explained through reference to proba-ble inadequacy in the procedure, spells or other rites, or to the presence of other magic. He noted that the Zande were not able to stand outside their own beliefs as these form part of an interpretive framework.

On the one hand we could see this as evidence of a primitive way of think-ing. No Western person would think that they could establish guilt or ascer-tain whether it would rain or not through using such an oracle, since we use scientific knowledge based on the facts of meteorology. On the other hand Evans-Pritchard saw many similarities between the two world views. Our acceptance of science, he said, has nothing to do with superior thinking, logic or intelligence. In fact most of us have little knowledge about the physical processes that affect weather and certainly we do not base our belief in it on any kind of observations of our own. Rather we simply accept the established view in our society which existed long before we were born into it.

Most of us have never seen with our own eyes that rainfall involves water molecules that gain energy and then invisibly rise up in the air where they seem to know how to gather together at an agreed height, and for a while somehow don't fall back down, but cluster into clouds, and then at some point make the collective decision to reform as water and then fall to earth. Scientific names are given to this process such as evaporation and precipita-tion. We accept that all this must be true but not because we have observed it ourselves, but because our culture holds this as true. Further, most of us have had the experience of wrapping up warm ready for rain and cold predicted on a weather bulletin and then cursed as we have carried our sweater and waterproof in the warm sun. But this still does not make us question this interpretive system. This is not to suggest that science does not bring powerful analytical possibilities, only that the way we relate to science is much the same as the way people relate to witchcraft. Evans-Pritchard wrote: 'They reason excellently in the idiom of their beliefs, but they cannot reason outside, or against, their beliefs because they have no other idiom in which to express their thoughts' (1937: 338). He was referring to Zande belief but could equally be speaking of European thought.

The example of Zande belief illustrates a number of things that are important to bear in mind when carrying out ethnographic research:

1)   People may not be aware of why they do what they do or of the nature of their own values, beliefs and knowledge of how the world works. Their system of belief simply appears natural to them.
2)   When we encounter people talking, we can think about them as using a set of ideas which have become established in their society. To an outsider they may appear odd and arbitrary, but from within, as simply the way things are.
3)   What people believe and say should be understood as part of their sensitivity to others. We all have an intricate and delicate knowledge of what everyone else knows and thinks. This is in the sense of us living in a more or less shared social reality with common-sense assumptions about how the world works even if these are erroneous.

In the context of these three points it appears natural that we should study things like media effects and uses through ethnography and observation. We can only understand why a person might drink a particular beer if we understand a whole range of factors associated with gender, with definitions of friendship and pleasure, all which may be exploited, or constructed, by advertisers. Of course we can simply record what people say and do in one particular moment, such as when the bar regulars claim to take no interest in reality shows. But we need to take a next step and reconnect this observation to its meaning in the flow of everyday life.

We must, of course, be careful with how we understand the kind of statement made by anthropologists that people may not be aware of the reasons why they behave in a particular way. This should be taken strictly not in the sense that they are naïve but that all human behaviour tends to be placed in the context of beliefs and values to which individuals may not have conscious access.

One question we haven't yet dealt with is how such data should be collected and recorded. We will look at a specific example of how this can be done later in the chapter. But for Malinowski and Evans-Pritchard, collecting ethnographic data meant making as many notes as possible. These would be notes about settings, procedures, conversations and interactions. In fact Malinowski suggested that just about anything could be used to grasp the native's vision of their world: 'statistical documentation of concrete evidence ... the imponderabilia of everyday life (and) ethnographic statements, characteristic narratives, typical utterances ... documents of native mentality' (1922: 24–5).

More recently anthropologists have added recording of conversations, video-recording and photographs. We will show how recorded conversations can be presented in analysis and then thought about alongside wider contextual information later in the chapter. In the case of the men speaking in the local bar above, we can see that the more information we have on them as individuals, the more contexts in which we observe them behave and speak, the better we can understand the way they think and relate to the media. But what is important in ethnography is not so much the *kind* of data we use and how we collect it but *how* we view it. Any data is valuable providing we consider it in the light of the three principles above.

Participant observation in sociology

Before moving on to examples specifically from media research we look at another case of the use of participant observation, this time in an urban setting. Importantly this helps us to further develop our sense of looking for the way that particular instances of behaviour are to be located in, and explained by, broader cultural connections.

Here we look at the work of the Chicago School of Sociology from early in the twentieth century. These are wonderful studies and possibly the best examples of the use of participant observation; they give fascinating insights into certain human behaviours. At the root of the Chicago view, like Malinowski's, was seeing the world, specifically in their case, social problems, from the native's point of view. So issues such as drug use, violence, crime and vandalism were to be viewed not simply as the behaviour of malevolent people, but also through the way such behaviours are meaningful to those who do these things. Only through such understanding, they believed, was there to be any chance of changing such behaviour.

In the Chicago School during the 1920s Herbert Blumer became dissatisfied with statistical methods, which he felt failed to increase our understanding of the social world. Influenced by the view of the psychologist G. H. Mead (1934) that humans define their environment in terms of their needs, the aim of the School became to understand the way that the kinds of people associated with social problems defined their environments.

One excellent example of this kind of work was Thrasher's *The Gang: A Study of 1,313 Gangs in Chicago* (1927). The methodology used, like that of anthropologists such as Malinowski and Evans-Pritchard, was for the researcher to immerse themselves in the everyday lives and experience of the people who they were to study. So Thrasher spent seven years investigating the lives of gang members. He carried out interviews, took life histories of respondents and observed routine social interactions. When he was with the gangs themselves this was in a covert manner, not letting on that he was a researcher. His writings tell of a fascinating world of gang life with raids, fights, stabbings and robbery. However, in the name of social reform he urges readers to see the gang members not as deviants or a social problem to be dealt with – a disease which infects an otherwise healthy society – but as people who have no access to the wider society and who simply try to live in a way that makes them feel worthwhile and good about themselves. He gives much detail on the formation and organisation of gangs and their politics and interactions.

Thrasher's book shows above all that the boys who formed gangs in Chicago did so to generate a sense of self-worth, belonging, status and purpose. Boys from the slum neighbourhoods of the city had no opportunity to enter the same kinds of status networks as boys from wealthier areas. They experienced poor education and had little possibility for other than mundane jobs or unemployment. Therefore these boys sought prestige in other ways. Instead of valuing academic achievement they valued characteristics such as toughness, excitement and streetwise credibility. Through fights they could have status; through crime, a sense of excitement and influence on the world. The loyalty required by gang members brought a sense of having a moral code. He goes as far as saying that the gang members lived by a very similar set of values as the middle-class boys – the need for individual status, achievement, excitement, but denied access to the broader society, these were realised in a different fashion. Thrasher concludes that this kind of criminal behaviour then needs to be understood in social context.

We can ask, how else could Thrasher have made these discoveries other than through participant observation? Could it have been possible to gain such an understanding through questionnaires, for example? As in the case of Evans-Pritchard's understanding of witchcraft and science, how could this have allowed us access to the kinds of tacit knowledge and cultural values, possibly not consciously available to the gang members themselves?

Media use and observational methods

Ethnography and observational methods have been used effectively in media research mainly to investigate media use and media production, the latter especially in the case of news. As regards media use Tufte (2000) researched the way that women used soap operas in Brazil. By spending time in the homes of the women he was able to make comments on the way that they used the soaps to understand issues of gender behaviour, personal problems and issues of citizenship and responsibility. In an investigation of the uses of television Lull (1978) had his researchers spend time in the houses of 200 families and observe viewing behaviour. One of his interesting conclusions was that much television viewing was for companionship or for avoidance of talking or alternatively to facilitate chat. In all cases, how people reacted to what was being broadcast seemed to be anything other than simply watching.

Miller and Slater (2000) used ethnography to study the way that people in and from Trinidad used the internet. They produced many fascinating observations on the way that people manipulated servers to get free accounts. But mainly they showed its importance in maintaining family ties in a dispersed community.

In terms of production ethnographies there was a wave of influential studies of news production in the 1970s and 1980s (Tuchman, 1978; Warner, 1973; Schlessinger, 1978; Gans, 1979; Fishman, 1988). In Fishman's classic study, for example, he was able to show the extent to which journalists were dependent for their definitions of news on official sources and bureaucratic organisations. As with all good ethnographic work he was able to reveal processes of which journalists were on one level unaware, or tended to background in their own accounts of their work, as these to some degree clashed with their broader sense of their professional identity. While studies of texts could show ideological qualities of news, these production studies revealed the way that things like 'objectivity' and 'neutrality' were simply misleading myths that should be better thought of as strategic rituals of journalism.

Much later other researchers have continued this tradition of news production studies. Van Hout and Jacobs (2008), Paterson and Domingo (2008) and Fenton (2009) have been interested in the way that new technologies have changed news production. Hasty (2006) looked at the way journalists in Ghana drew on Western notions of objectivity even though the news organisations for which they worked were of a completely different nature to their Western counterparts. Wahl-Jorgensen (2007) has looked at the way that local news editors use readers' letters to show good relations with the community. Schwenkel (2010) has shown how the lives of photojournalists in Vietnam must be taken into account in order to understand their professional practices and the work that they produce.

Ethnographic research and consumption of women's lifestyle magazines

We now take a more detailed look at using ethnographic and observational methods to answer a specific research question: how do women relate to the models of the world presented in the international women's lifestyle magazine *Cosmopolitan*? The data here were collected between 2001 and 2005 for a project investigating the way that the magazine *Cosmopolitan* is localised in its different versions for various national markets, being adapted in each case yet also maintaining its basic brand identity captured by its moniker the 'Fun, Fearless Female'. There were several levels on which this was investigated. We looked at content, production and ownership, which is dealt with in Chapter 3 of this book, and additionally at the way that women readers associated with the values communicated by the magazine.

A textual and visual analysis of the different versions of the magazine revealed that women depicted in the magazine, in features, problem pages and quizzes, did very little apart from seducing men, finding ways to have perfect sex and dressing up. They always acted alone and strategically, having no families, children or social connections. Visually they were seen sitting and standing in modernist spaces with much light and with minimalistic furnishings, and wearing clothes associated with traditional forms of seduction. They still did very little, although they were often depicted with arms raised in the air in excitement. The magazine was dominated by a 'problem–solution' format, in which all parts of life can be managed with simple easy steps often labelled as '*Cosmo* hot tips'. A linguistic analysis of the language style revealed a heavy use of directives giving a sense of confidence along with use of poetic devices and alliteration bringing a sense of playfulness. In sum, this is a world where control and power are signified, although not really articulated apart from in the case of sex or other more abstract forms of 'getting ahead'.

Our research question was therefore, if this is the world as represented in the magazine how do readers relate to and use these representations? Do they see that women do little in its pages? Do they take on its values? Research has suggested a number of possibilities. Caldas Coulthard (1996) has argued that women may get a sense that sex is daring and roguish from these magazines. Hermes (1995) suggests that women may get very little from the magazines, simply using them for titillation, although Machin and Thornborrow (2003) suggest that just because we laugh at something or see it as ironic does not remove the possibility of us learning something from it. But in this case we wanted to find out specifically what women thought.

The aim of the participant observation we carried out was to spend time with women and get a sense not so much of their opinions of magazines like

Cosmopolitan but to find out about what those who had read the magazine thought of themselves, work, relationships and their place in the world. Were these in harmony with the world view served up by *Cosmo*? As we have established already in this chapter, asking such questions directly to women is unlikely to yield useful insights. Six researchers spent time with women who read *Cosmopolitan*. They made notes and recorded relevant conversations, interactions and behaviours. Research was carried out in six different countries: UK, US, Mexico, India, Taiwan and the Netherlands.

To show how we can use the data that were collected we begin with one example of two women talking about relationships. In this case there is not the space to describe everything that this study revealed. But we can show what observational and ethnographic methods can reveal as regards a specific question.

Here is an extract from a discussion with two 37-year-old women in the UK (names have been changed). While this is a conversation started by one of the researchers, we will see that it is how we deal with this information and how we see it in broader context, in the fashion of the Chicago School research, or the ethnography of Malinowski, that is the key. Here the women were asked to describe their identity to a male interviewer, and they did so confidently. As one of them said: 'I know who I am and what I want.'

Extract 1

Sandy: I am a confident person. I think that this is difficult for men.
Researcher: What do you mean by confident?
Sandy: Well, me and my friends, we are just confident and independent. I guess we just really know ourselves. We are independent. Men don't know what to do with this.
Researcher: What do you mean?
Sandy: Well my friends just do anything they want, when they want.
Researcher: Like what?
Sandy: Well anything. They go to parties, they like dancing. I really like cars.
Linda: They have whatever boyfriends they want. The men have been doing it for years and now we can do exactly the same. I have a friend who just picks guys up. She knows just what she wants.
Researcher: Are they independent in terms of political thinking?
Sandy: I just don't bother with politics; you have to get on with life, not be so heavy. Live a bit. You have to get out some.
Linda: Well I think it's about really knowing yourself. You have to know who you are. I think my boyfriend has difficulty with that. I just say to him I am independent and I am proud of that. I just know who I am and what I want.

As a first step in analysing this conversation, we can consider exactly what they say as regards identity. First of all they talk in terms of gender, of female identity, which they positively contrast to male identity. Being a woman is fundamental to their view of who they are. Secondly, they use identity traits that are 'psychological' and individual rather than social, 'personality traits' such as 'confident' and 'independent'. And thirdly they describe themselves by mentioning their preferred leisure-time activities such as 'going to parties', 'picking up guys' and consumer goods such as cars. What is crucial here is that there are many other potential aspects of identity that they do *not* mention, for instance nationality, race, class background, family relationships (being someone's daughter, wife, mother, aunt, etc.), job, income level, education, religion, political convictions.

These two women told the interviewer that they do like to read *Cosmopolitan*, although they said that it was a light read, for relaxing and certainly not to be taken seriously. While we could not conclude that these women directly take their ideas about how women should behave and what they should believe about themselves from the magazine, what we can consider is how much they have in common with the values found in it. The women who are depicted in the features, stories, confessions and problem pages of *Cosmopolitan* do not have political or religious beliefs. They are part of no community and seem to have no solidarity with anyone, always acting alone and strategically. Their main preoccupations are romantic and sexual pleasures, health and beauty, and, importantly, their acquisition of consumer goods. Clearly there are similarities between this model and the way the women in the interview described their identity to us.

However, this is only one conversation. As with our conversation in the bar where the locals spoke of their opinions on reality television, we need to understand more about the women and this particular conversation.

The researcher had met the two women for six months previously and therefore much was known of their life situation. Both women worked in a children's nursery. Their income was low, and neither had job security, working on short contracts without paid holidays. Both lived in rented accommodation and wished they could buy their own houses. But in the interview they do not choose to see that as part of 'who they are'. In this particular context they choose not to mention these factors, or race or family position, etc. It is important to remember that in other times and places these would be the identity factors chosen by speakers. There was a time in Britain when social class would have been high on the agenda of who a person was, particularly for working-class women such as these, and also possibly being a wife, mother and daughter. In Jane Austen novels we find that people identify themselves through family connections. Anthropologists have shown the vast array of ways in which people talk about who they are. And the concepts used connect to forms of social organisation and power. Importantly, these linguistic categories are informed by, and inform, practices that have material consequences; how people are categorised in society, how they are allowed to categorise themselves, such as 'citizen', 'British', 'British Asian', can have material consequences.

These are two women who are finding life a struggle in economic terms and who experience much self-doubt in certain respects. So why do they talk about themselves in terms of 'independence'? Who and what are they independent from? Are they independent in thought? As we saw when the researcher raised this, ideas and opinions are not so important in themselves. The term 'independence', and the other patterns of identity revealed in this snippet of talk, were repeated throughout conversations recorded by all the researchers on the project. So what is this about? Why not use terms like 'responsible', for example? Here is another snippet of conversation between the researcher and the women from later in the evening. They had been talking about casual versus long-term relationships.

Extract 2

Researcher: So you are happy to have casual relationships?
Sandy: I would like to fall in love and have a family. I haven't met the right guy.
Linda: It's hard in the clubs and pubs. Most guys are just after a shag [sex] really.
Sandy: Or they are just boring. You want someone who can have a laugh but is also pretty sensitive. Lots of guys are scared of us I think.
Linda: We just end up having a laugh together. We have a drink, take the piss out of some guys.

In this example there is a sense that the women are not quite so happy with their lot. In the first extract the women suggest that they are taking up a role that has been characteristic of men – the freedom to sleep around [have promiscuous sex] – whereas in the second they see the men's desire to do this as a problem. But running through both extracts is a sense that men are afraid of them, which they were keen to express in many conversations, although after dates where men had not later called them, this would quickly change. Imagine if a man were keen to express that women were afraid of him. This would seem very odd. Clearly, while the two women wanted to express their independence, which seemed to mean from men, much of their time and energy was spent on men. On the one hand this independence could be seen as a rejection of women's prior dependence on patriarchal practices where women were subordinate to men, receiving unequal pay, unequal access to professions, etc. On the other hand rather than having any concrete political or social strategy to describe this independence they use it as an 'attitude' embodied in consumer goods such as cars, and lived out in leisure-time activities such as clubbing and having casual affairs, exactly as in the *Cosmopolitan* discourse of the 'Fun, Fearless Female'. Although as we saw in the second extract the identification with this kind of independence, with the devaluation of identities that are relational to men such as 'wife' and 'mother', is not expressed in all of their interactions. We can see that the women therefore live through certain contradictions in how they present identity, for instance the contradiction between identifying with the idea of 'independence' and yet also longing for 'Mr Right' and for 'having a family'.

How then has this kind of ethnographic/observational approach helped us so far to think about how *Cosmopolitan* affects its readers? Perhaps a better way to phrase this, as an anthropologist might put it, is: what is the relationship between the two sets of ideas and what do they allow us to understand as regards the world view, ideas and values that they represent?

What *Cosmopolitan* sells to its readers is not so much a magazine, as a brand. In this sense what it sells is independence, power and fun in the way that beers are marketed to sell, friendship, or Celtic authenticity. In the pages of the magazine women are oriented towards social interaction rather than technical, creative or intellectual skills and they act always alone, as noted, advancing through pleasing or manipulating others, and mainly through the power of their sexuality. It is this that defines women's independence in *Cosmo*. And for the most part the magazine presents the world as consisting of playful fantasies. In *Cosmo* the only real things are the products themselves. Women are then able to align themselves with the *Cosmo* brand values of the 'Fun, Fearless Female' not through social action but through the clothes they wear, the cafes they visit, the way they dance. Capitalism can sell us signifiers of power, independence and fun.

What we can see from this case is the way that the heritage of feminism becomes intertwined with consumerism. Luce Irigaray (1985) lamented the fact that the mass media had hijacked feminism in order to sell products where the discourse of women's power has been harnessed to consumerist lifestyle ideology. This power can be signified through consumer choices and lifestyle products, by seduction, which of course requires all the right fashion and beauty accessories. If women come to act upon the world through consumption and their sexuality, is this really 'independence'?

It is, of course, no bad thing that women are more able to talk about their desires and move away from the traditional relative dependence relationship to men, but consumerism has meant that rather than therefore seeking to reorganise society, to change their positions in it, they may simply signify power through codes of dress, and lifestyle drawn from consumer culture. It may be true that 'people use lifestyles', but it is easy to forget that lifestyles also use people. They are created and propagated to serve the interests and needs of powerful social institutions, in this case large corporations. These corporations monitor our identities through market research, credit and loyalty card use, so that they can offer us new lifestyle signifiers. In this sense *Cosmopolitan*, and the way these women talk, can be understood as part of this regime of lifestyle consumerism under which we live. Formerly, identities were defined and policed for the purposes and interests of the nation state but this now exists alongside a very different regime. Through this clever harnessing of women's challenge against dependency one cannot help but note the sheer power and adaptability of capitalism.

Of course we shouldn't imagine that all women will talk in this manner. As part of our study we also carried out ethnographic research across age, socio-economic and national groups. This showed that media are of course read differently in different cultural contexts. However, we found that the agenda the magazines set is the same everywhere. In the Netherlands, we interviewed middle-aged (45–51) and young (22–5) women. Both groups distanced themselves from *Cosmopolitan*. They described the magazine as superficial. But in other ways their descriptions of the values and priorities of the younger generation were in complete harmony with *Cosmo*. Here is an extract from a conversation between the middle-aged Netherlands women.

Extract 3

Anja: Well, they are not my values, but I don't think there's anything wrong with it, enjoying your freedom a little bit …
Olga: Yes, if I were that age, I would do it myself.
Joke: Yes, there's nothing wrong with it.

The younger women were more critical of the magazine. They said that the women portrayed in *Cosmopolitan* were perfect and 'too' glamorous. The Dutch often pride themselves on their pragmatic, down-to-earth attitude. Interviews with the editor of the Dutch version of the magazine, Viola Robbemondt, pointed out that this was something she had to bear in mind regarding material she could include in the magazine (Fernhout, 2004: 33). When the young women were asked about their own values, they nominated those such as 'honesty', 'love', 'social contacts', 'equality' and 'tolerance'. But when asked about the values of young Dutch women generally, they used terms like 'independence', 'equality', 'having different experiences' and 'enjoying life', very much like *Cosmopolitan*'s 'Fun, Fearless Female', and they admitted they would like to have lives like those found in the magazine.

Extract 4

Saskia: I would like to be smart, and enterprising, and sexy.
Heidi: A bit of everything [laughs].
Saskia: Yes, well, I think so.
Yvon: I think so.
Marieke: Yes.
Saskia: There's nothing I don't want to have but it is all so enormous. I'd like to be cool in real life.

Of course we would need to say more about these women, about the way that they speak and act in different settings and at different times, knowing more about the way they plan their lives and view the world. Why is it, for example, that the middle-aged women are in some ways very positive about the magazine? Is it because their lives have been characterised more by the dependency relationship to men? By considering this material in the Dutch context we can begin to see what more we would need to know in order to expand our understanding of the kinds of values found in the Dutch version of *Cosmopolitan*.

In contrast, in the following extract from a conversation about *Cosmopolitan* between four Spanish women in their late twenties there was a completely positive evaluation of the magazine and no comments made on its superficial nature. This was more akin to that of the middle-aged Dutch women in Extract 3. In the extract below we find an exchange between two of these women.

Extract 5

Raquel: I would like to be like this – have my own business and look great all the time.
Maria: When I read I go to the horoscope, which I don't believe. Then I go to the sex. And I love those articles on work when they say go tell your boss where to go.
Raquel: When you read *Hola* you know it is another world. But with *Cosmo* they offer you solutions in real life.
Maria: l would like to be a strong woman like in *Cosmo*.

Even the British women, whose talk about identity reflected the *Cosmo* values, when asked, said that the magazine itself was both superficial and silly. But an ethnographic study would tell us more about the cultural context of such talk. In Spain gender equality has made much less progress than in the UK and the Netherlands. This was something stressed by the *Cosmo*

Spain editor when we interviewed her (see Chapter 3). To simply have women represented in non-dependency roles is seen as positive. It did not occur to these young women, who lived in subordinated roles within their families, and in relation to their husbands, that these representations should be criticised. Would further ethnographic and observational research reveal that these women had more in common in some senses with the middle-aged Dutch women, in terms of their sense of power and relationship to men?

In other cultural contexts, in contrast, we found that women spoke in a way that completely rejected the values of *Cosmopolitan*. Here is an extract from a conversation with two Taiwanese women in their mid twenties:

Extract 6

Pei-Fen: You can see it from the way they look. They all have jobs and are very beautiful.

Researcher: Is this something you would like to be?

Tsai-Yun: I don't think it's real. The women in *Cosmo* have everything. Real women cannot be so confident. You can't become like that. Not in real life.

Researcher: But you might like it?

Pei-Fen: No, it's not possible.

Tsai-Yun: In Taiwan we respect our partner. We want to work together. We are not interested in sex in this way.

Researcher: You think younger women these days are not interested in sex in this way then. They want to wait for the right partner?

Pei-Fen: No, some of the students have sex now. They don't want to wait. They want to have boyfriends. This is from the influence of Western images.

Researcher: Is it a bad thing?

Tsai-Yun: Yes, it is bad for relationships as there is no respect. It is all superficial. I think we want to find a man where there can be respect and where there can be a family. *Cosmopolitan* is always about sex.

The young women here, from one point of view, could be seen to be using identities that are part of the traditional dependency relationship to men. But using this methodology we would want to know more about these women. We would also need to find out why such talk might make sense in the Taiwanese cultural context. Why are these women not so keen to celebrate the demise of traditional dependency roles in the same way as the Spanish women, for example? Also an ethnographic study would include the students who, one of them says, are influenced by Western images. What is it that marks the difference between the two groups?

One of the women here talks about 'respect' as being an important value in a relationship with a man. In fact this term cropped up often in the talk of Taiwanese women, yet was absent from that of the British women. Does respect in this case mean on men's terms? The problem is, as ethnographers themselves have considered, that the research itself here may be based on a set of assumptions that are culturally relative. This is one of the criticisms of the kind of research that is based on these methods, although equally the same could be made of any research. In the next section we assess the strengths and weaknesses of ethnographic and observational methods.

The problems with ethnography and the role of the researcher

The strength of the methods described and applied in this chapter lies in the validity of the data. When we ask if the data we have collected are valid or not we are asking whether they actually show what we think they show. If we designed a questionnaire to find out what women think of the contents of *Cosmopolitan* magazine and 100 per cent of the women answered 'yes' to the question 'is this magazine silly?', what would this really tell us about their relationship to the magazine and the ideas, values and identities that it contains? Such an item of data would have low validity as we wouldn't really know if this were entirely true. It may be true that respondents all wish to express this opinion, but it tells us much less about what they actually think and do. Ethnography and observation are therefore good at checking validity of data and being more certain about someone's actual feelings/opinions. If someone says they never read *Cosmopolitan*, by simply spending more time with them the researcher can find out whether or not this is true.

Ethnography and observational methods have been criticised on the basis of three other terms used to evaluate research methods: representativeness, reliability and transparency. Representativeness is the extent to which the sample used in a piece of research is representative of people in general or of a specific group such as women aged between 20 and 25, or even more specifically of women of this age who are single parents and on low income. A questionnaire might be used in a survey about opinions on local news coverage carried out on 1,000 people who are randomly chosen in a city centre. The results might then be claimed to be representative of the opinions of people in the city. But what kind of representativeness can be claimed for the case studies of the women talking about identity and magazines that we have presented in this chapter? Many of the women were chosen as they were contacts already known to the researchers or made opportunistically as the project moved along. This is one common approach in ethnography. Another might be to advertise, if a specialist group is required, where again a relatively small number of people would be selected. This level of detailed research is time-consuming and larger numbers are simply not practical. To what extent then can these women be said to have been chosen systematically or with any degree of objectivity? And with such small numbers, to what extent are they representative of the wider population rather than being individual peculiar instances? One counter to this criticism is that these smaller samples do give us valid data and therefore allow us to understand more about how people really relate to the media. What would be the point in having massive samples if the data produced were not valid in the manner offered by ethnography?

Reliability is the extent to which a piece of research is repeatable. Research is said to be reliable if a different researcher could come along and, using the same methodology, produce the same findings. For social surveys this is crucial where individual researchers are carefully trained to make sure the same questions are asked in the same way. The same level of continuity will also be sought in content analysis research where coders will be trained to code in the same way, and where the decisions behind this will be made known as part of the methodology. In ethnography and participant observation there is no actual systematic research process. For the collection of the extracts given above the researchers were told to find groups of women who they could become or were already familiar with and make notes and recordings about how they talk about themselves and behave. They were also told to gather information to allow us to understand the lives of the women. So the data produced consisted of notes on conversations, interviews, group discussions, information about families and jobs and also accounts, for example, of an evening out on a 'hen night' where a group of women dressed as schoolgirls with very short skirts and stockings and went around 'intimidating' men. But how could such research be repeated to produce the same result? Ethnography in this sense is, as the anthropologist Michael Carrithers (1992) puts it, more akin to 'hanging out'. Of course this lack of reliability means that there is no way to check the data. And this leads to what has been the gravest criticism of this kind of research. If this is not open to verification and if it is the findings of one person as they are hanging out, to what extent are the data they gathered for the most part down to the interpretations of the researcher, or what they thought relevant to record? To a certain extent ethnographers have given as much attention to this problem as they have to using the method to learn about social life.

During the 1980s a number of anthropologists (Clifford and Marcus, 1986) began to challenge the idea that ethnographers can simply reproduce what is going on in the world transparently through observation and then produce this in their writing. What they argued was that we must understand how such an observer is very much a part of the research process, the data produced, and what gets written up in terms of findings. In particular they were critical of the idea of white upper-class male anthropologists going out into an exoticised, primitive field in order to bring back accounts of the thought processes and cultures of the 'other'. They argued that the ethnographer always enters the field with extensive cultural baggage of their own. Writers like Asad (1986) questioned whether cultural concepts could be so easily translated and rendered intelligible to the researcher's culture. The understanding and interpretation is additionally done through a particular academic paradigm which shapes how we write things up. In other words this research process should be seen as just another kind of writing. This lead to the increase of 'autobiography' in the writing up of field work (Okeley, 1992). This meant that researchers, rather than pretending to view the world objectively, included their own feelings and reactions in their reports. Jahner et al. in a volume called *Lakota Belief and Ritual* (1991) about Native American Culture took a different approach and moderated the voice of the anthropologist by including the voices and opinions of the indigenous people themselves.

This reflexive approach has been taken up in more recent ethnographic research. Gillespie (1995) reflects on her role as a white woman in her study of Punjabis in London and how this affected what she witnessed. And media ethnographers have also suggested that reflexivity can serve to enrich our research. Mayer (2005) suggests that who we are and our processes of discovery in the field can contribute to our knowledge of our own culture. Of course we might think that this could defeat the object of doing research, if we spend so much time talking about who we are. Hills (2002) argues that this does not necessarily have to be the case so long as we are cautious of 'endless self interrogation' and narcissism (2002: 73). He reminds us that it is important that the researcher must be aware of the way that questioning people about their lives does not transparently reveal the true nature of their lives but causes them to 'cut into the flow of their experience and produce some kind of discursive "justification"' (2002: 66), as in the case of how women relate to the values carried by *Cosmopolitan* magazine. In other words we must be aware of the way the kinds of research questions we formulate can help to create an artificial set of accounts. Geertz (1973) was concerned to remind us that ethnography can be used productively and that we can learn to be good ethnographers. Ethnographies may be interpretations but this does not mean that they are false.

Carrithers (1992) offers a slightly different suggestion. For him the capacities used by the ethnographer are very much like those used to engage with everyday life. But he says ethnography is a kind of scientific knowledge and can be done in a rigorous and systematic way. Students who study social anthropology, who understand how it works best, can become good ethnographers themselves and produce work of a nature that reflects a social world that could then be recognised by subsequent researchers. Carrithers says that it is because ethnography is both like scientific knowledge and the knowledge used to engage with everyday life then it is the best way to investigate human social life. It is the best way to examine the finer details of everyday life because it is both sensitive to how humans actually behave, which allows us to look at social life as it happens, and it is a process that a person can learn to do well. It is useful because it is able to deal with the ambiguity and flow in social life, as we saw in the cases of our bar regulars and the two British women talking about identity, which other methodologies have to suppress or ignore.

Many writers (Polanyi 1958; Ziman, 1978; Hacking, 1983; and, most famously of all, Kuhn, 1962, in his classic work *The Structure of Scientific Revolutions*) have shown that the idea of objective knowledge independent from social and historical moments is a myth. Knowledge is always embedded in the social world. In this sense there seems no reason that ethnography should be criticised above other methods which strive to claim to produce a form of knowledge that is indeed free-floating and independent from the social world.

Carrying out ethnographic and observational research

As we have seen throughout this chapter, ethnography and observational methods are not governed by large samples in the fashion of quantitative methods. These kinds of methods can be very time-consuming. On the one hand these methods are a way of viewing our data. Some of the data in the case study of women talking about *Cosmopolitan* were collected through focus groups, which are the topic of Chapter 10 of this book. Viewing these ethnographically means that we see them as one moment in people's lives as they are involved in specific interactions. We look not for what the women believe as much as the kinds of ideas and models of the world that they use in talk and how these relate to how they talk in different contexts. But what we do need to know is something more about who these women are. In terms of ethnography, the more we know about them, the more we are able to understand their relationship to media. On the other hand some of the data were gathered from friends and associates, through observing and noting their opinions and reactions on a range of issues. Views on media such as women's lifestyle magazines can then be placed in this context. This is more akin to the research carried out by the early anthropologists and Chicago Sociologists.

Deciding on an area for investigation

Since these kinds of methods are time-consuming, scale is an issue here. A project might be able to look at the way a small number of young women related to a particular television programme, such as *The Apprentice*. We could look at how they discuss the programme in different settings. We could look for how they think about and evaluate business, corporate activity and ambition in general. We could ask how this fits with their attitudes to other parts of their lives. But the aim would be not to generalise about all women, but to say something about these particular women at this particular time. For a student project an in-depth study of five people could generate ample data. Importantly, in such a study, we could use any data that appeared relevant. The ethnographic studies by Fishman (1988), Miller and Slater (2000) and Bjorkvall and Engblom (2010) all used a mixture of observation and interviews. And all also combine this with things like textual and production analysis.

For student projects, production studies may be more difficult although many of our own students have done such studies during work experience, internships or where they have a part-time job. These students have been able to shed light on topics such as assumptions and processes that lie behind writing promotional news items for local councils, public relations practices and advertising products. In each case the student had a research question relating to investigation of production practices of certain media texts that they had shown through textual analysis were ideological. The aim of the research was to find out to what extent the practitioners were conscious of this and to locate the origins of this ideology in the production process.

Asking a research question

This is an important part of these kinds of research projects for a particular reason. When choosing an area for investigation we might come up with a theory about what is taking place and then go out and test it. This is called the deductive approach. If we wanted to look at how young women respond to a women's magazine we might hypothesise that they will be positive about the stronger representations of women. This would be called the hypothetico-deductive approach. But in ethnographic research we would tend not to have a hypothesis. Rather we would explore what kinds of themes arise when we get women to talk around some important issues. So the research would more likely lay out its intention to explore a particular area, for example, the way journalists use the concept of objectivity, or the way that women relate to the world as represented in a magazine.

Finding respondents

The problem here is gaining access to the places where we wish to research. This may be easier if you want to research how your friends talk about a particular news story. But it will be more difficult if you wish to look at the kinds of practices and understandings of the people who create the magazine. In this case you will need to write to these people or take a job that takes you close to them. Recently one student researched workers in social media campaigns to market alcohol to students. To gain access she worked leafleting for one company and then developed contacts.

Recording data

One of the key tools for anthropologists was the note book. We can use tape-recordings or videos where possible, but this may not always be an option if we seek to use naturally occurring events, such as the example of the men talking about a reality show mentioned earlier. In such cases it is important to take notes as soon as possible to record topics of conversation and if possible the exact language. But ethnographic research asks us to think more broadly about the nature of our data. You might want to make a collection of editions of a particular magazine which are first analysed in the sense of what kinds of representations they contain before then looking at the way that these representations resonate in the lives of readers.

Presentation of data

You should consider the main themes that came out of the data analysis which can be presented through what anthropologists call a 'substantive thesis'. This means you present what is intriguing about your data, such as in the above examples showing the different ways that the young women relate to a particular set of ideas depending on cultural context. You will then present the data in a way that provides evidence for this claim such as including quotes or sections of conversation. You will at all times show how the different themes answer your overall question, which is to investigate a particular issue – such as how women relate to representations in magazines.

Ethical issues

This kind of research can be done overtly, so that you tell people that you are doing research, or covertly where you do not. Currently universities tend to require that permission is gained from all respondents and/or that the resulting material is anonymised. In the case of the locals in the bar mentioned earlier in the chapter, their talk has been used here as data although of course they were not aware that it would be considered as such. But this is completely anonymised. The *Cosmopolitan* study involved overt data gathering with the consent of the women in all cases. We would advise that the latter approach is taken and that university regulations are followed closely.

Summary

- These methods are associated with actually watching or sharing in what media audiences or media practitioners are doing and saying. The assumption is that the best way to study and understand what they think and do is to watch them, or participate in what they are doing.
- These methods, ethnography in particular, should be seen as a way of approaching the data that we collect and they can incorporate many different kinds of research methodologies.
- These methods place all data into the flow of social life. In other words any idea a person expresses must be understood in the context of life and culture. If a young magazine reader says she values 'independence' we must understand why her culture currently places value on such a concept as opposed to, say, 'responsibility'. We must also understand more about what this woman means by this term.
- People may not be aware of why they do what they do or of the nature of their own values, beliefs and knowledge of how the world works. Our system of belief simply appears natural to us. The job of the researcher is to place these things into the cultural context.
- This kind of research method may not involve making a hypothesis but simply expressing a desire to understand a particular thing, such as how women relate to a magazine's message, or how journalists use the concept of objectivity.
- Ethnography and observational methods are time-consuming and generally used for small samples, such as a group of news room workers, several groups of television viewers or a group of friends.
- Samples may be fixed, such as a number of friends or family, or may simply 'snowball' as any case of social interaction can be viewed as potential data if the aim is to increase understanding of particular phenomena rather than a particular group of people.
- In this kind of method we will present evidence from this data according to themes.
- These methods produce data that have high validity but which are low on reliability.

CHAPTER 5

Measuring output: content analysis

Content analysis is one of the most efficient and most widely used research methods for the systematic and quantitative analysis of media output/content. Since first becoming firmly established as one of the core methods in media and communications research in the middle of the twentieth century, it has enjoyed tremendous popularity both in this field and across many other disciplines (see Franzosi, 2007, for a comprehensive discussion of the history and uses of content analysis). Its popularity no doubt derives from a combination of characteristics, including that it is systematic, quantitative, highly flexible and adaptable, easy to use (although also equally easy to abuse) and particularly well suited for revealing trends and patterns in the large quantities of communications and symbolic content characteristic of modern societies. It is also a method that lends itself well to integration with other (quantitative as well as qualitative) methods in media and communication research, and, indeed, as such it is core to some of the major models in communications research and theory. While the method has certainly, over its long history, had its fair share of criticism (including of its foundations in positivist science, its claims to objectivity, its fragmentation of textual wholes and its lack of a theory of meaning), it continues to play a key role in communications. If anything, it has enjoyed something of a renaissance with the rise of new digital media and associated computer-assisted forms of analysis.

This chapter starts by examining briefly the origins and evolution of content analysis, as a formal method of inquiry in the social sciences and humanities. We then proceed to discuss some of the main problems and criticisms associated with this method. Drawing on examples from published content analysis studies, this is followed by a detailed step-by-step guide to the process of doing content analysis, from the selection and sampling of media material to the preparation and analysis of the data produced by it.

A brief history

Content analysis is notable as a communications research method for its relatively long history of use. Krippendorff (2004) cites an eighteenth-century Swedish study of 90 hymns of unknown authorship as one of the earliest documented cases of quantitative analysis of printed texts. During the twentieth century, some of the most spectacular early uses of content analysis were in propaganda studies. Through the systematic analysis of German radio broadcasts, Allied intelligence was able to monitor, and in some cases predict, troop movements, the launch and location of new military campaigns, and the development and deployment of new weapons. While these studies used content analysis for finding out about the intentions of the originator of messages, the aim of content analysis in media research has more often been that of examining how news, drama, advertising and entertainment output reflect social and cultural issues, values and phenomena.

Indeed, from an early stage, sociologists, political scientists and others interested in the social and political roles of the media saw the potential of content analysis for monitoring the 'cultural temperature' of society, as a method for the regular and systematic production of the social/cultural equivalent of the economic indicators used for monitoring the state of the economy. In the 1930s Harold Lasswell proposed a 'continuing survey of "world attention" – as reflected in trends in media coverage of various social issues – to show the elements involved in the formation of public opinion' (Beniger, 1978: 438). A couple of decades earlier, in 1910, Max Weber had similarly proposed an ambitious long-term systematic study of press coverage of social and political issues to be carried out together with the monitoring of public opinion responses and changes (see Neuman, 1989). Weber's proposal, however, was not realised. One reason for this was undoubtedly the very considerable cost of sustained collection and analysis of media coverage. Another reason was that neither survey research nor content analysis had been developed into fully fledged methods at the time.

The development of content analysis as a formal method of social science inquiry took place in the years between the two World Wars, as well as in the major research programmes of Lasswell and his associates around and during the Second World War. Krippendorff (2004) argues that developments in the method were spurred on by concerns about the contribution of the mass media to social upheaval and international conflict, a concern with the new electronic medium of radio, and the desire to make social inquiry 'scientific' in a manner comparable to the controlled, systematic, objective and supposedly predictive methods of the natural sciences.

From being used in its early days mainly for keeping inventories of the contents of American newspapers and for journalistic studies (Holsti, 1969:

21), content analysis gradually became part of larger and theoretically much richer projects of social and political analysis. The method was increasingly integrated into larger research efforts involving, not just the analysis of media content, but also other types of data and other methods of inquiry (surveys, experiments, participant observation, qualitative and ethnographic audience research).

A prominent and influential programme of research, which skillfully integrated content analysis with survey research in the analysis of media roles in the cultivation of public consciousness, was George Gerbner's cultural indicators programme. Originally outlined in 1969, Gerbner's cultural indicators programme proposed the use of content analysis for the systematic monitoring of trends and developments in the symbolic environment of American television (Gerbner, 1995). Combining detailed content analysis of television entertainment programming with surveys of public beliefs and attitudes, the cultural indicators research (e.g. Gerbner et al., 1994; see also Shanahan and Morgan, 1999, and Morgan and Shanahan, 2010) aimed to examine how far television 'cultivates' certain world views in its audiences. In this respect, the cultural indicators/cultivation studies are typical of a considerable body of research which has used content analysis together with various types of studies of audiences to examine media influence on public beliefs, attitudes, opinion and behaviour. Another prominent strand in this general area of research is represented by agenda-setting studies (McCombs, 2004; McCombs and Reynolds, 2009; Dearing and Rogers, 1996). Agenda-setting studies explore how far the issues which dominate the media agenda (as established through content analysis of media coverage) also come to dominate and influence what the public 'think about' or regard as the most important issues of the day (as established through surveys of public beliefs and opinion).

As well as being used for mapping changing cultural and socio-political trends in the media – and the relationship between such trends and changes in public opinion and beliefs (Janowitz, 1976; Neuman, 1989; Danielson and Lasorsa, 1997) – content analysis became integrated into studies of media organisations, media professionals, sources of media information and, generally, the production of news and other media content. Several of the classic studies of news production combine observational methods (in news organisations) and interviews (with media professionals and sources) with content analysis of the 'product': the news (e.g. Gans, 1979; Fishman, 1980; and Ericson, Baranek and Chan, 1987, 1989, 1991).

More recent trends have seen a resurgence of content analysis, as this has, since the 1990s, become a prominent component of much framing research (Tewksbury and Reynolds, 2009; Tankard, 2001). It is particularly interesting how many of the ambitions of early sociologists, such as Weber and Lasswell in the first half of the twentieth century, have been realised with the

rise of digital media and the concomitant rise of analytical software for
continuous monitoring of both media content and public interest and opinion. A particularly excellent example of this type of continuing monitoring
is the work of the Pew Research Center's Project for Excellence in
Journalism (2011a), whose *News Coverage Index* monitors, using content
analysis, the news coverage of major newspaper, television, radio and online
news outlets.

Content analysis: definitions and problems

The classic and much quoted definition of content analysis comes from the
first major review of the method – Bernard Berelson's *Content Analysis in
Communication Research*, published in 1952: 'Content analysis is a research
technique for the objective, systematic, and quantitative description of the
manifest content of communication' (1952: 18). Much of the controversy
over content analysis has focused on the notion that it must be 'objective'.
Critics of positivist science have argued that objectivity in content analysis,
as in any other kind of scientific research, is an impossible ideal serving only
to cosmetically cover and mystify the values, interests and means of knowledge production which underpin such research. Content analysis, of course,
could never be objective in a 'value-free' sense of the word: content analysis
does not analyse everything there is to analyse in a text (no method could,
nor would there be any purpose in trying). Instead the content analyst starts
by delineating certain dimensions or aspects of text for analysis, and in doing
so, they are also making a subjective choice (albeit one generally informed by
the theoretical framework and ideas which circumscribe the research), indicating that the dimensions chosen for analysis are more important than
others not chosen. The criticism of positivist 'objectivity' criteria is by now
both well rehearsed and generally accepted, and it is indeed possible that a
strictly positivist 'value-free' notion of objectivity was never what was
intended in the first place in definitions of the requirements of content analysis. Thus, it is perhaps symptomatic that later definitions of content analysis
have omitted references to 'objectivity', requiring simply that content analysis be 'systematic' (Holsti, 1969) or 'replicable' (Krippendorff, 2004).[1] A
recent definition by Riffe et al. captures the essence of content analysis
methodology very well, while at the same time avoiding earlier definitions'

---

[1]   Holsti (1969: 14) defines content analysis as: 'Any technique for making inferences by systemat-
      ically identifying specified characteristics of messages', while Krippendorf (2004: 18) defines it
      as: 'A research technique for making replicable and valid inferences from texts (or other mean-
      ingful matter) to the contexts of their use'.

reference to 'objectivity' or the problematic distinction between 'manifest' and 'latent' content:

> Quantitative content analysis is the systematic and replicable examination of symbols of communication, which have been assigned numeric values according to valid measurement rules and the analysis of relationships involving those values using statistical methods, to describe the communication, draw inferences about its meaning, or infer from the communication to its context, both of production and consumption. (Riffe, Lacy and Fico, 2005: 25)

Content analysis is per definition a quantitative method. The purpose of the method is to identify and count the occurrence of specified characteristics or dimensions of texts, and, through this, to be able to say something about the messages, images, representations of such texts and their wider social significance. The problem, however, is how far quantification is taken in content analysis and to what degree the quantitative indicators that this technique offers are read or interpreted in relation to questions about the intensity of meaning in texts, the social impact of texts or the relationship between media texts and the realities which they reflect.

As noted by Holsti, early 'definitions of content analysis required that inferences from content data be derived strictly from the *frequency* with which symbols or themes appear in the text' (1969: 6). More than half a century of communication research has, however, made it plainly clear that there is no such simple relationship between media content and its reception and social implications. Content analysis can help provide some indication of relative prominences and absences of key characteristics in media texts, but the inferences that can be drawn from such indications must be firmly anchored in a theory that articulates the relationship between media and their social contexts.

Thus, it would clearly be naïve to assume that a television serial showing ten incidents of cigarette smoking in every hour of programming is ten times more likely to influence viewers to smoke than a television serial showing only one incident of cigarette smoking in every hour. The relationship between the frequency with which some activity or phenomenon is portrayed and its wider social impact is, as long recognised in communication research, far more complex than this, but this recognition is not in itself an indictment against the practice of quantitative analysis; rather it points to the need for placing what is counted in content analysis within a theoretical framework which articulates, in the form of a model of communication influence, the social significance and meaning of what is being counted.

On the question of quantification, we might similarly ask: is the over-representation of certain occupations, types of (anti-)social behaviour, ethnic groups, etc. a case of media misrepresentation, distortion and bias? Or, could the highly selective emphases of media images of reality be seen as an accurate *symbolic* reflection and perpetuation of dominant social values (see Gerbner, 1972)?

The point arising from these two questions is again that it is not the practice of counting and quantifying as such that needs to be questioned, but rather the 'meaning'/interpretation which is attached to the quantitative indicators provided by content analysis. There are two dimensions to this problem. The first concerns the practice of counting the frequency of symbols; the second concerns what is seen as the fragmentation of meaning arising from the practice of singling out countable dimensions of texts for analysis. On the first aspect, critics of content analysis have thus argued:

> It is not the significance of repetition that is important but rather the repetition of significance. In which case the first question to answer concerns significance and perhaps then there can be some counting. But content analysis has no theory of significance. It merely assumes the significant existence (or existence-as-significance) of what it counts. It may be counting illusions or a fragmentary part of a real significance, but without a theory of significance it would not *know*: its concept of the significance of repetition gives it no knowledge of the significance of what is being repeated. (Sumner, 1979: 69)

There can be little disagreement that counting the insignificant has little purpose. Nor need we quarrel with the argument that the meaning or interpretation associated with certain symbols does not become any more 'right' or 'accurate' by counting the number of times they appear. Thomas makes this point very lucidly:

> In recent years, the fuss over interpretational pluralism has pushed claims of indeterminate meaning to such extremes that we may have lost sight of the important difference between coding and interpretation.
> … [However] it is not at the level of coding at which the so-called reception problems reside. For instance, if there is a count of words or a coding of characters' hair color, or even noting violent acts (as explicitly defined), few would argue that these measurements alone are sites of contested meaning. The astute critic of content analysis would more likely say that the problem resides either in the unitizing (e.g., 'it's not that I can't identify a punch, it's that I question whether you should be counting punches') or in interpreting the data after they are collected (e.g., 'It's not that I can't identify a punch, it's that I don't agree that the distribution of punches signifies what you suggest it does'). (Thomas, 1994: 693)

The second line of criticism concerns the argument that in counting individual units and their frequency of occurrence, content analysis fails to capture the way in which meaning arises from the complex interaction of symbols in texts. In the words of Burgelin:

answer to P3

above all there is no reason to assume that the item which recurs most frequently is the most important or the most significant, for a text is, clearly, a *structured* whole, and the place occupied by the different elements is more important than the number of times they recur. (Burgelin, 1972: 319)

True to his argument for a semiotic approach to the analysis of texts, Burgelin goes on to state:

the meaning of what is frequent is only revealed by opposition to what is rare. In other words, the meaning of a frequently-recurring item is not essentially linked to the fact that it occurs ten times rather than twenty times, but it is essentially linked to the fact that it is placed in opposition to another item which occurs rarely (or which is sometimes even absent).... Structural analysis provides a way of approaching this problem, which traditional content analysis does not. (1972: 319)

Clearly, a content analysis which confines itself to counting the number of times a violent act is committed, or the number of dark-haired characters, or the number of times the word 'fundamentalism', appears will fail singularly to capture the meaning or significance of these symbols in the texts analysed. But then again very few content analyses confine themselves to such 'meaningless' counting. Content analyses count occurrences of specified dimensions and they analyse the relationships between these dimensions. Although content analysis initially fragments texts down into constituent parts which can be counted, it reassembles these constituent parts at the analysis and interpretation stage to examine which ones co-occur in which contexts, for what purposes and with what implications. Moreover, and in contrast to many 'qualitative' or 'interpretive' approaches, content analysis, because it follows clearly articulated rules and procedures, lays open to scrutiny the means by which textual meaning is dissected and examined (Thomas, 1994).

In summary then, it is argued here that much of the criticism which has been directed at content analysis touches on problems more to do with the potential and actual (mis-)uses and abuses of the method, than to do with any inherent weaknesses of this as a method of data collection.

Doing content analysis: key steps

The process of content analysis can be broken down into eight consecutive steps:

1) Define the research problem
2) Review relevant literature and research

3)   Select media and sample
4)   Define analytical categories
5)   Construct a coding schedule and protocol
6)   Pilot the coding schedule and check reliability
7)   Data preparation and analysis
8)   Report findings and conclusions

Define the research problem

The first step in content analysis, and one which logically precedes even the decision to use this method, is to define the research problem; what do we hope to be able to say something about by analysing a body of media texts? What aspect of communication, media roles, social phenomena, textual characteristics does the proposed research aim to throw some light on?

Content analysis is a method for examining communications content. It is not a theory. As a method, it does not in and of itself provide any pointers to what aspects of communications content should be examined, or how those dimensions should be interpreted. Such pointers have to come from a theoretical framework, which would include a clear conceptualisation of the nature and social context of the type of communications content which is to be examined. In relation to the analysis of media content this may concern questions about its production (e.g. the influence of ownership, commercial interests, editorial policies, journalistic practices, news sources) and/or its consumption (e.g. the role of news coverage in relation to social, political, ideological and economic processes, or in relation to individual audience/readership phenomena).

Content analysis is not and should not be carried out simply for the purpose of counting what can be counted in media content (see the earlier discussion of problems associated with this method). Any number of dimensions could potentially be categorised and counted, but it is only by making a clear statement about the objective of the research that the researcher can ensure that the analysis focuses specifically on those aspects of content which are actually relevant to the research. It is not uncommon, for example, to see a great deal of time and effort being spent in content analyses on measuring the column inches of newspaper articles or the duration of news items in television news. These dimensions are easily, if laboriously, measured and counted. Yet, unless such space/time dimensions are particularly articulated as an important aspect of the research problem under investigation (i.e. the research statement specifically hypothesises about the significance of the overall volume of coverage), they generally yield only relatively shallow pointers to the nature of the content being analysed.

Review relevant literature and research ○

A clear conceptualisation of the research problem – and the subsequent definition of what aspects and categories of content should be analysed – should always be anchored in a review of relevant literature and related research or studies. This is partly a question of not reinventing the wheel unnecessarily: reviewing previous content analysis studies on similar or comparable media, types of communication, issues, events or phenomena will help in terms of discovering what kinds of theoretical frameworks have been used to good effect previously, and in deciding on both a relevant sampling strategy and analytical categories to focus on in the actual content analysis.

Identifying and reviewing relevant previous research is also a question of taking advantage of comparisons, where possible, with previous analyses in order to identify, for example, national or cultural differences in media coverage (e.g. Scott, 2009; Mody, 2010) or changes over time in media portrayal (see e.g. Weigel et al., 1995, on racial stereotyping in television content; Smith, 1994, and Davis, 2003, on gender stereotyping in advertising during television programming aimed at children; or Gunter, Hansen and Touri, 2010, on trends in the portrayal of alcohol and drinking in television entertainment, as identified in content analyses using similar coding definitions from the early 1980s through to the present century).

Select media and sample

It is rarely either possible or desirable to analyse absolutely all media coverage of a subject, area or issue. At the same time, it is precisely one of the major advantages of content analysis over, for example, semiotic analysis that it lends itself to the examination of large bodies of media content. Nevertheless, one characteristic of modern media and communications is the sheer enormity of the volume of text, sound and images produced. For conceptual and, more specifically, for practical reasons therefore content analysis must start with the selection and narrowing down of the type of coverage to be analysed. First, it is necessary to define clearly what body of media or communications content ('population' in sampling language) will be analysed, described and characterised. Next, it is often desirable and necessary to choose a representative sample from this body of media content. In practice the process of defining the media (the population) and sampling comprises, as Berelson indicated in 1952, the following steps: a) the selection of media or titles; b) the sampling of issues or dates; c) the sampling of relevant content.

The selection of media or titles

The term 'media coverage' is all-encompassing and could refer to anything from newspapers, television and radio to magazines, cinema, bill-board advertising or news websites on the internet. In practice, any content analysis of 'media coverage' would start by specifying more particularly which media (radio, television, press, websites, etc.), and which channels or particular titles within these media, were to be analysed. In general, of course, the choice of media and titles to be analysed would depend on the nature of the research problem or subject.

The choice of media and titles involves considerations which may include one or more of the following: geographical reach (e.g. global, national or regional); audience size (e.g. mass versus minority); audience type (e.g. as defined by age, social class, profession, ethnic origin, gender); format/content characteristics of media (e.g. 'popular' versus 'quality'); political stance (e.g. liberal versus conservative) and, last, but in practice often one of the most decisive factors, accessibility and availability of research material. Accessibility and availability are decisive factors particularly where a retrospective analysis is contemplated.

In general, content analysis studies tend – for both practical and conceptual reasons – to focus on one particular medium, although larger-scale research projects may indeed comprise analysis of several media types; Ericson and his colleagues (1991), for example, sampled news coverage from newspapers, television and radio; Mody's (2010) study of international news comprised both print news and selected online news sites; and, as mentioned earlier, the Pew Research Center's *News Coverage Index* (2011a) monitors the news coverage of major newspaper, television, radio and online news outlets.

The sampling of issues or dates

Once the medium or media have been selected, the next step is to choose issues, dates or periods to be analysed. The choice of dates or periods depends essentially on whether the subject of analysis relates to a specific time-limited event or whether it concerns the mapping of some general dimension of coverage such as the portrayal of women, immigrants, minority groups, violence, crime, science, environmental issues, health, alcohol consumption, risk, terrorism, foreign countries, etc. In the former type, the period to be analysed is 'naturally' defined by the time and dates of the event concerned. Thus the Gulf/Iraq Wars of 1991 and 2003 both had relatively clearly defined start and end dates. This has similarly been the case with many other military conflicts of the past, although in other cases – particularly where armed conflict extends over prolonged periods of time (e.g. the Vietnam War, the war(s) in Afghanistan, or armed conflict in Chechnya or the former Yugoslavia) – other considerations may need to be taken into account when deciding on a suitable period of media coverage to analyse.

It is important to bear in mind, however, that while event-specific coverage may be clearly defined by the dates of an event, understanding the role and nature of media coverage would often necessitate analysis of coverage both before and after the dates or period of a specific event. In their classic study of an anti-Vietnam War demonstration in London in 1968, Halloran and his colleagues (1970), for example, noted that the media's emphasis on violence in their coverage of an essentially non-violent demonstration could be explained largely as a self-fulfilling prophecy: media coverage in the period leading up to the actual demonstration had put great emphasis on the expectation that the demonstration would lead to violent clashes. Consequently this became the main frame for the coverage of the demonstration itself. Similarly, many of the major frames influencing the nature and focus of media coverage of the Iraq War of 2003 were inevitably being rehearsed and put into place months, if not years, before the actual commencement of armed conflict.

The point of these examples is to emphasise that even where a content analysis focuses on the coverage of a specific event, clearly delimited by start and end dates, it may still be useful to sample coverage from both before and after the dates of the specific event. Likewise, and depending of course on the rationale and aims of the research, a helpful strategy for profiling and understanding the media coverage of a specific event may also include the sampling and analysis of coverage of a comparable event or events. This strategy, for example, is a fundamental aspect of the 'Propaganda Framework' approach advocated by Herman and Chomsky (Herman, 1985; Herman and Chomsky, 1988), who have analysed US media coverage of political events which are similar in most respects but differ principally in terms of whether they appear in places regarded by the US government as 'enemy' or 'friendly' countries.

In the analysis of more general types of coverage – not specifically tied to certain dates or periods – there are numerous, more or less systematic, ways of obtaining what we may call a 'reasonably representative' sample of material. 'Reasonably representative' here is taken to mean a sample which is not skewed or biased by the personal preferences or hunches of the researcher, by the desire to 'prove' a particular preconceived point, or by insufficient knowledge of the media and their social context. It is thus important, when deciding on a sampling plan, to be aware of the cycles and seasonal variations which characterise much media coverage.

Television schedules in many countries, for example, vary according to special holidays, seasons and diary events (e.g. major events in the sporting calendar). The summer is generally known in news terms as the 'silly season' in which the 'man bites dog' variety of news has a higher likelihood of receiving coverage because of the lack of activity in the political, legislatory and decision-making institutions of society. Television news casts during weekends are normally much shorter than those Monday–Friday. Many types of advertising, across all media, are also seasonal to varying degrees.

While care should be taken to avoid relying on short sample periods which coincide with seasonal variations or other events affecting the nature of coverage, choosing a sample essentially amounts to combining good knowledge of the media and their cycles with straightforward common sense. Thus, a study purporting to offer an analysis of the extent and nature of alcohol advertising on television should clearly not confine itself to, say, the second week of December, given that in countries which celebrate Christmas the level of alcohol advertising is particularly heavy in this period. Likewise, an analysis seeking to examine the extent and nature of British or American press coverage of China would clearly end up with some potentially unrepresentative conclusions if the period of analysis coincided narrowly with the 2008 Olympic Games in Beijing or with major political events or natural disasters in China.

A strategy often used for obtaining a representative sample of television coverage is that of one continuous week – Monday to Sunday – followed by a 'rolling' or composite week – Monday of one week, Tuesday of the following week, Wednesday of the following week, etc. (see e.g. Riffe, Aust and Lacy, 1993, for discussion and evaluation of this type of sampling; see also Riffe et al., 2005). Another strategy used for both broadcast and newspaper sampling is systematic random sampling: a start date is randomly selected, and then every n'th day (the sampling interval) after that is selected throughout the chosen period. It is clearly important that the sampling interval should not coincide with any 'natural' media cycle – for example seven or any multiple thereof would yield a sample consisting entirely of media output from the same weekday and would thus not reflect the variation in media content across different days of the week.

The sampling of relevant content

Once the medium/media, issues and dates have been selected, there still remains the task of sampling relevant content. The definition of 'relevant content' should be derived principally from the stated research objective and the theoretical framework of the study, but will also often involve more practical considerations, that is how to limit the amount of material selected for analysis without compromising the requirement that it be 'representative'.

Some studies have thus looked at the portrayal of certain phenomena or issues across all types of television programmes – fiction and factual – broadcast during peak viewing hours (Shanahan and McComas, 1999); others have focused on specific genres such as television news (Philo and Berry, 2011), popular television series (Russell and Russell, 2009; Hether and Murphy, 2010), sports programming (Christopherson, Janning and McConnell, 2002), television advertising (Paek, Nelson and Vilela, 2011), or music videos (Wallis, 2011). In numerous content analyses of television news, the sampling has been confined further to include only the main evening news programmes rather than breakfast news, lunchtime news or early evening news. Such sampling choices can generally be defended on the grounds of audience reach: which news programmes attract the largest audiences? During which parts of the television day do most people watch (the 'peak' viewing hours)? Sampling choice may also be based on the 'status' assigned to programmes either by the television organisations themselves or by audiences.

Similarly, the sampling in print media may be restricted to specific types or genres of content. Thus, general analyses of newspaper coverage of certain issues or phenomena tend to exclude advertising content, weather forecasts, stock-market and related financial listings, sports pages, cartoons and perhaps more specialist newspaper sections, such as reviews of the arts, or education or holiday supplements. For studies which are principally interested in the operation of news values and factors governing the production of news, such exclusions are reasonable on the grounds that these types of coverage are generally less directly driven by the news values and journalistic practices which apply in the main news sections of newspapers (although such boundaries are not always clear in relation to, for example, sports pages). As emphasised earlier, the selection of types of content must depend fundamentally on the rationale and objectives of the study.

Having chosen the medium/media to be analysed, sampled titles or channels from these, sampled issues and dates, and sampled types or genres of content, there still remains the task of identifying the articles, reports, programmes which are actually 'about' the subject or issue under scrutiny. Should a newspaper court case report, in which reference is made to DNA analysis of hair samples found on a murder victim's clothing, be included in a study of 'science' coverage? At what point can a television news item be said to be 'about' race, or to convey images of race? A classic question to have exercised a very large body of communications research is, 'how do we define "violence" on television?' These questions illustrate the need to define clear selection criteria and rules for the inclusion/exclusion of media reports, articles and programmes in the analysis.

Related to this is the definition of the 'unit of analysis'. The 'unit of analysis', that which is counted, can be the individual word, the sentence, the paragraph, the article, the news programme, the news item, an individual character, actor or source, the programme, the scene, the 'incident' (e.g. a violent incident, the consumption of alcohol), etc. As a quantitative technique, content analysis is about reporting how often different textual dimensions occur, what their prominence is relative to other aspects or dimensions (or compared with text-external indicators, e.g. the relative prominence of the elderly in television drama compared with their proportional representation in the population). For such quantitative indicators to be at all meaningful it is therefore crucial to have clearly defined exactly what is being counted. Units of analysis and their definition are equally important when comparing different content analyses over time, for instance in order to establish whether media portrayals of selected activities (e.g. smoking, drinking, drug-taking) have become more or less prevalent (see Gunter et al., 2010, on content analyses of alcohol and drinking in television entertainment programming).

Define analytical categories

The 'task' of content analysis is to examine a sample of media or communications output and to classify the content according to a number of predetermined dimensions. In conceptual terms, the most taxing aspect of any content analysis is to define the dimensions or characteristics which should be analysed. While any number of communications content characteristics could be categorised, counted and quantified, coding and analysis should focus solely on characteristics which are relevant to the theoretical framework, questions and objectives stated for the research.

In an analysis of press coverage, it is tempting, for example, to measure and code the area (e.g. column inches) of each newspaper article simply because this is easily done, if time-consuming. But unless the sizes of newspaper articles have (or are expected to have) a direct bearing on the research questions asked, time would be far better spent analysing and counting more substantive text characteristics. As a measure of relative prominence, it is, in most cases, entirely adequate and sufficient to use a simple count of the number of articles (irrespective of size).

Likewise, it is not uncommon to see researchers spend a great deal of time logging the number, size and contents of photographs included in newspaper reports, only to ignore these data when it comes to interpreting and presenting the research results. Because the cataloguing or categorising of communications content is a time-consuming, laborious and even potentially tedious task, it is important to include for analysis only those dimensions or characteristics of texts which can reasonably be expected to yield 'useful' information relevant to the research objectives/questions.

What categories then should be included in a content analysis? In general terms, there is no single or simple answer to this question as the analytical categories will, and always should, depend on the specific aims, objectives and focus of the research, on the theoretical framework and questions stated as part of the formulation of the research problem. There are, however, a number of categories which will tend to be standard in any content analysis, namely 'identifier' categories such as medium (which newspaper, magazine, television channel, etc. does the content appear in?), date (day, month, year), position within the medium (e.g. 'page' in print media, or 'schedule time' in broadcast media), size/length/duration of item (although, as indicated above, careful consideration needs to be given to the question of whether the analytical use of this dimension warrants the time and effort invested in the coding). Another descriptive identifier category often included in analyses of media content is a type/genre classification. Thus, newspaper content is often categorised along the lines of 'news report', 'editorial', 'letter to the editor', 'feature article', etc.; broadcast programmes are categorised in terms of their genre: 'news', 'current affairs magazine', 'documentary', 'quiz show', 'talk show', 'drama serial', 'film', 'advertisement', etc.

Although at one level, type/genre typologies can be regarded as basic identifier categories for general classification and comparison of media output, it is important to recognise that these also have much more far-reaching analytical potential. Thus, different media formats, types or genres set different limits for what can be articulated, by whom, through which format or context (Altheide and Snow, 1979).

In addition to being informed by the general theoretical frameworks and research questions guiding one's research project, there is at least one further principle which should be borne in mind when constructing coding categories for a content analysis: a content analysis should never be merely a fishing expedition applying a preconceived category-set to an 'unknown' body of text. Thinking up appropriate content analysis categories is as much a question of immersing oneself in the textual material to get a general 'feel' for its content and structure prior to the construction of categories, as it is a case of deriving category ideas from the theoretical framework and questions which guide the research project. In other words, the researcher needs some familiarity with the content/structure and general nature of the material to be analysed in order to be able to set up categories that will be sufficiently sensitive to capture the relevant nuances of the content.

Going beyond these basic identifier categories there is inevitably considerable variation in the kinds of dimensions that different content analyses have examined and counted, reflecting the many and varied research purposes for which quantitative analysis of texts have been used. In the following, we describe some of the most commonly analysed dimensions or categories in media and communication research based broadly in a political science or sociology oriented framework.

Actors, sources and primary definers – and their attributes

The analysis of characters, actors or sources is important both from a straightforward narrative/literary perspective, and from a more sociologically articulated theory of media representations and media roles. Whether informed by a hegemony framework, a constructivist perspective, social learning and modelling theory, or a social representations framework, the analysis of who is portrayed as saying and doing what to whom, and with what key attributes, is essential to an understanding of media roles in social representation and power relationships in society. Studies working broadly within a hegemony framework have successfully used content analysis techniques to show that public issues are defined in the mass media and for public consumption overwhelmingly by representatives of powerful institutions, agencies and interests in society, and that 'alternative' voices, critical of the status quo, are much less likely to gain access to the mainstream media. Deviance, social disturbances, terrorism, race, crime, etc. are defined in large measure by the law enforcement agencies, the judiciary and the parties of formal politics.

In their comprehensive analysis of the representation of crime, law and justice in broadcast and print news, Ericson and his colleagues (1991) undertook a very detailed coding of the knowledge providers/sources who, through the media, came to create the public definitions of these areas of coverage. Ericson et al. analysed:

1) the number of sources used or represented in each news item;
2) the types of sources (including 'journalists' themselves, but also 'government sources', 'private sector sources', 'individuals' not representing agencies or institutions, and 'unspecified sources' referenced through non-specific terms such as ' "analysts", "reports", "observers", "intelligence sources", "authorities", "experts" ' (Ericson et al., 1991: 199);
3) source contexts (e.g. interview, official meeting, press release, drama/actual event, etc.);
4) types of knowledge provided by sources, categorised into primary (factual, asking 'What happened?'), secondary (explanatory, asking 'Why did it happen?'), tertiary (descriptive, asking 'What was it like to be involved in what happened?'), evaluative (moral, asking 'Was what happened good or bad?'), and recommendations (asking 'What should be done about what happened?') (Ericson et al., 1991: 204).

Ericson and his colleagues also looked at visuals and sound used in the representation of different sources. Amongst other things this enabled them to show that some types of sources were far more likely (relative to their overall prominence) to be pictured than others in the newspapers analysed, and that the use of photographs of sources varied considerably across the different newspapers in their sample.

While analysing and quantifying the types of actors and sources quoted or referred to in media coverage goes a long way towards showing how social power is expressed through and with the mass media, many content analysts have rightly pointed out that the analysis of actors/sources needs to go further to examine the differential uses to which various 'voices' are being put in the media. In other words, how are the voices of those sources – often official, institutional sources – who initially define events and issues (the so-called 'primary definers') being used, elaborated and framed by the media? Cottle (1993: 155–7), in his analysis of regional television news coverage, for example, points to the ways in which the different presentational formats of news create a hierarchy of opportunities for primary definers to articulate their views. Thus, the 'restricted' format of the news reader delivering a news desk presentation gives virtual monopoly to the news reader's account, 'with the minimum of direct reference to outside voices, viewpoints and visuals' (Cottle, 1993: 155). At the other end of the hierarchy of access for news sources is the 'expansive' format, which 'entails either live or full interview inclusion in which the interviewee is allowed to develop his or her point of view at some length, perhaps in engaged debate with an opposing voice' (Cottle, 1993: 156).

While quantitative analyses of the different 'voices' represented in the media form a useful starting point, the traditional notion of primary definition (Hall et al., 1978) suffers from several problems. Most notably, this type of analysis does not normally distinguish between the potentially very different messages that may emerge from within the same group of primary definers, nor does it indicate the varying degrees of 'legitimacy' accorded different sources/voices by the media. In their analysis of television coverage of the Three Mile Island nuclear power plant accident, Nimmo and Combs (1985), for example, discovered that while 'average citizens' were generally prominently represented, the narrative uses of 'average citizens' were very different from network to network: 'The CBS citizen interview normally involved persons expressing confidence in how things would turn out (for example, expressing appreciation for President Carter's visit to Middletown). ABC's average citizen interviews focused instead upon personal fears and anxieties' Nimmo and Combs, 1985: 81). Similarly, we suggest that in order to understand the relative 'weight' carried by different types of primary definers, it is necessary to take into consideration the 'news-making scenarios' or 'fora' through which such primary definers become news worthy and through which they articulate their claims (Hansen, 1991). When, for example, environmental pressure groups appear as primary definers in media coverage of environmental issues, they may do so mainly through the forum of 'demonstration or public protest action' – a forum which carries considerably less legitimacy in Western democracies, than the forum of 'formal political activity/Parliament' or the forum of 'Science'.

Scientific, technical, medical and environmental controversies are defined largely by the 'authoritative' institutions of establishment scientific and medical communities, by politicians and by expert authorities, while the views of dissident scientists and experts are effectively sidelined. Despite this prevailing authority orientation, it is, however, also worth noting that in some areas of scientific controversy the 'majority' view may be under-represented in media coverage, to the extent that a very different view of the consensus opinion emerges. In relation to controversy about nuclear energy, content analysis has thus been used to support the argument that the media give a disproportionate amount of space and time to a small but highly vocal body of anti-nuclear scientists/experts who are not representative of the views of the scientific community as such (Rothman and Lichter, 1987). More recently, similar work on media coverage of climate change debates and controversy has argued – with the help of content analysis – that the journalistic objective of 'balanced' reporting results effectively in coverage which is biased because it gives undue prominence to so-called climate change sceptics; in other words, coverage ends up being biased in the sense that it misrepresents the degree of consensus opinion amongst climate scientists about the existence and causes of global climate change (Boykoff and Boykoff, 2004).

Social constructivists are particularly interested in coding actors to see who successfully makes claims about social problems and they thus help 'construct' and elevate new or low-profile issues to centre public stage. Not only does this kind of analysis tell us about source–communicator relationships, but also about source-power and power in public space (Hansen, 2010). In their classic content analysis of media reporting on an oil spill, Molotch and Lester showed that while an unexpected and unplanned news event such as an oil spill provided temporary access for groups who would not normally be given media coverage, over time 'the fact of the spill ... tended to be brought under control as the definition of its character increasingly fell into the hands of those news promoters with routine access to media' (1975: 258).

Social stereotyping, misrepresentation and what Gerbner (1972) has termed the 'symbolic annihilation' (through under-representation or non-representation) of different groups and types of people in society have been central concerns of content analysts since the early days of media and communication research. In his study of radio daytime serials (soaps) Arnheim (1944) found, for example, that working-class people were numerically under-represented. In addition, the kinds of problems people had ... were almost always interpersonal, while problems that might have been regarded as institutional were defined as individual and private. Change, if it occurred at all, was not brought about by planned collective efforts, but by chance, or a sudden, unexpected, and unexplained transformation of character, a moral conversion. In general, then, these daytime serials diverted attention away from the larger social institutions and failed to offer their fans any fresh insight or self-knowledge. (Quoted in McCormack, 1982: 157)

DeFleur's (1964) study of the portrayal of occupational roles in television serials came to similar conclusions, showing that certain occupations were heavily over-represented while others were virtually absent. Numerous content analyses have been carried out to examine further the highly selective representation of occupations, the sexes, race and ethnicity in both news/factual media content, drama/entertainment fare and advertising.

Studies working within a cultivation approach or social modelling approach are concerned about the characteristics of those who are portrayed as the perpetrators of socially unacceptable behaviour, or of those who may serve as role models for media audiences. Content analyses have been used for meticulously mapping not just the overall demography of television characters (in terms of sex, race, social class, age, etc.) but also the attributes and behaviours of characters along such lines as sexual conduct, moral values, drinking, smoking, drug-taking and dietary habits.

Subjects, themes and issues ✓

A key objective of many, perhaps even most, content analyses is to determine how a general area/domain of coverage sub-divides into a range of specific subjects, themes or issues, and to determine the relative prominence or importance of each of these in the overall coverage analysed. Thus, Ericson and his colleagues, while generally concerned with the representation of 'deviance and crime' in the news media, sub-categorised 'deviant activities into five general types for analysis: violence, economic, political, ideological/cultural, and diversionary' (Ericson et al., 1991: 243–4).

Frequently, much more detailed classifications are used. Thus, Hartmann and his colleagues, in their pioneering analysis of British press coverage of 'race' in the period 1963–70, aimed to see 'whether any central defining themes could be identified that might be taken as indicating the meaning and significance given to race in the newspapers' (Hartmann, Husband and Clark, 1974). To this end, they arrived at a list of 23 categories of subject matter, including such subjects as housing, education, health, discrimination, crime, cultural differences, etc.

The classification of what topics, themes or issues are covered within a general area is a common starting point for studies of media content for the simple reason that most studies would wish to establish which themes or issues are given prominence, and which are sidelined or marginalised in media coverage. In other words, how (by emphasising/marginalising certain themes, topics, issues) do different media contribute to the public/political definition of any number of – often controversial – issues? Thus, studies of political conflict would want to examine the relative prominence of individual topics, which together make up the media 'discourse' on a particular conflict, for example the Palestinian intifada in the Middle East (Wolfsfeld, 1997). Studies of news media roles in political integration in Europe would want to examine the relative prominence and thematic emphases of 'European' news across member countries of the European Union (Peter, Semetko and de Vreese, 2003). Studies of media and terrorism would want to know what kinds or types of terrorism are covered, and, indeed, what kinds of activities are defined by the media as 'terrorist' activities. Studies of war coverage would want to examine what aspects receive most attention (e.g. technology/weaponry, political negotiations, dissent, troop morale, strategy and military progress, civilian suffering). Studies of health and medical coverage would often start by establishing what kinds of health issues, medicine or diseases receive coverage (Entwistle and Hancock-Beaulieu, 1992; Weitkamp, 2003). Studies of coverage of science and technology or of environmental issues would similarly often start with a classification of the types of science, technology, environmental issues which receive prominence in media coverage (Hansen and Dickinson, 1992; Clayton, Hancock-Beaulieu and Meadows, 1993). Studies of international news flows would start by mapping and classifying types of news coverage (Stevenson, 1995; see also the classic study of news values by Galtung and Ruge, 1965). And studies of crime reporting would often aim to show, amongst other things, the relative prominence given to different types of crime (Schlesinger and Tumber, 1994).

Vocabulary or lexical choice

Since the very early days of content analysis, considerable interest has focused on the vocabulary or lexical choice in the texts studied. Indeed, some of the very first documented uses of content analysis were studies which focused on the occurrence of specific words/symbols in texts (Krippendorff, 2004). In his pioneering work on quantitative semantics, Lasswell was essentially also interested in vocabulary and in the symbolic meaning of words. Much of his concern focused on the quantitative analysis of key symbols (such as 'liberty', 'freedom', 'authority') and he aimed to construct a dictionary of symbols and their uses in texts. The idea, that dictionaries of symbol/word use could be created for coding and content analysis purposes, has also been central to developments in computer-assisted, electronic approaches to the analysis of texts since these were first formalised in the 1960s by Philip Stone and his colleagues through their General Inquirer programme (Stone, Dunphy, Smith and Ogilvie, 1966; see also Hansen, 1995).

The analysis of vocabulary/lexical choice continues to be a central component of many content analyses, often also drawing on a wider linguistic and discourse analytic framework. Van Dijk, for example, commences his discourse analytic study of press reporting of race with a lexical content analysis of headlines:

> Words manifest the underlying semantic concepts used in the definition of the situation. Lexicalization of semantic content, however, is never neutral: the choice of one word rather than another to express more or less the same meaning, or to denote the same referent, may signal the opinions, emotions, or social position of a speaker.... To describe the civil disturbances in Britain in 1985, the headlines may use such words as *riots*, *disturbances* or *disorders* among many other words.... Not only do they [words in newspaper headlines] express the definition of the situation, but they also signal the social or political opinions of the newspaper about the events. That is, headlines not only globally define or summarize an event, they also evaluate it. Hence, the lexical style of headlines has ideological implications.
> (1991: 53)

In a similar vein, Picard and Adams (1991) used content analysis to examine the characterisations of acts of political violence through such words as 'hijacker', 'bombing', 'shooting', 'seizure', 'assassination'. Picard and Adams distinguished between 'nominal characterisations', 'words that label or describe the acts in a manner that merely indicates what happened' (1991: 12), and 'descriptive characterisations', words that 'contain judgments about the acts or perpetrators within their denotative and connotative meanings' (1991: 12). Stahl (1995) used a lexical content analysis of *Time* magazine over a ten-year period to examine the use of explicitly magical and religious language in coverage of computers and related technologies. Fan (1988) and others (e.g. Druschel, 1991; Einsiedel and Coughlan, 1993; Andsager, 2000; Hart, 2000; Bengston et al., 2009) have also used vocabulary-focused computer-assisted content analyses for examining media coverage of a diverse range of topics and issues such as political campaign messages, anti-abortion pressure groups, AIDS, drug abuse and the environment. Altheide's (2002) longitudinal analyses of a discourse of 'fear' in media content offer a particularly instructive example of the considerable potential – realised by the increasing availability of electronic news text – of analyses focused around particular key words in their relevant contexts.

Value dimensions and stance

A general category dimension which often forms part of content analyses is an attempt at classifying coverage in terms of value judgements, or assessment of the ideological stance, accuracy or informativeness of coverage. In her analysis of Canadian press coverage of science and technology, Einsiedel (1992) analysed and coded the tone of stories in terms of whether they were predominantly 'positive', 'negative', 'neutral' or 'mixed':

> Coders were instructed to read the story as they normally would and to indicate the 'overall impression' they got from the story. This impression could result from information conveyed in a number of ways including: what was highlighted in the lead, the balance (or imbalance) of consequences described, and the type of information or description included. For example, if a new treatment was presented in terms of being a 'landmark discovery', or compared favourably with current methods but at lower cost, these elements would result in a positive evaluation. A story coded as 'mixed' in tone was one which had both types of consequences described but neither as dominant in the lead, in the range of consequences described or in the descriptors applied. (Einsiedel, 1992: 93)

Numerous studies have focused on assessing the positive/negative or favourable/unfavourable stance of media reporting on anything from party politics, international relations and wider political issues to specific professions, public organisations or public services. Logan and colleagues (2000), in a study of science and biomedical news in the *Los Angeles Times* and *The Washington Post* from 1989 to 1995, for example, examined whether the key social actors in such coverage were portrayed in a generally favourable or unfavourable light.

Semetko (1989), in a study of television news coverage of the 1983 general election campaign in Britain, used a number of evaluative categories, including an evaluation of whether TV reporters' commentaries on politicians' campaign activities were predominantly 'reinforcing' (positive), 'deflating' (negative), 'straight' (descriptive) or 'mixed'. This coding sought to analyse and evaluate reporters' contextualising comments to determine whether: 'in describing the scene they appeared to reinforce or deflate the activities or statements of politicians; the reporter appeared to correct what a politician said; and whether there appeared to be any disdain in reporter comment' (Semetko, 1989: 465). Classifying media coverage as 'positive' or 'negative' has also been important in many agenda-setting studies which attempt to establish whether public attitudes or opinions are swayed one way or the other accordingly (e.g. Wanta, Golan and Lee, 2004).

Although evaluative categories in content analysis are often a variation on the relatively fundamental dichotomies of favourable–unfavourable, positive–negative, accurate–inaccurate, critical–uncritical, there are clearly many more possibilities, including the incorporation into more complex concepts such as framing (see below). Perhaps the main problem with evaluative categories is that they generally require a considerable degree of interpretation by the coder – they can rarely be deduced on the basis of single words or sentences, but require the coder to consider the 'overall tone' of a newspaper article or broadcast item. Unless very clear interpretation guidelines are laid down, content analysts often find it difficult to achieve a high degree of coder agreement in the coding of evaluative categories.

Frames and framing analysis

Increasingly, the relatively crude classification of value dimensions or stance into simple variations on positive/negative in content analysis studies has tended to assimilate the notion of stance into the more comprehensive and flexible concept of 'framing' (Entman, 1993; Reese, Gandy and Grant, 2001). Nisbet and Lewenstein (2002: 359), in a comprehensive content analysis of biotechnology coverage in the American press, thus show that 'The character of biotechnology-related coverage has been overwhelmingly *positive* [emphasis added], with heavy emphasis on the frames of scientific progress and economic prospect.' A similar move towards incorporating stance under a framing typology can be seen in content analyses of political communication and the coverage of politics; compare, for example, Semetko's 1989 study referred to above, with Semetko and Valkenburg's (2000) more nuanced study a decade later on the framing of European politics. While some of the same difficulties and subjectivities mentioned above in relation to the coding of value dimensions or stance in media content also apply in framing analysis (e.g. subjectivity in determining core frames, difficulties in determining where one frame ends and another begins, overlap between frames), researchers have increasingly found ways of addressing some of these weaknesses (Matthes and Kohring, 2008; Entman, 2009) and framing analysis within the framework of content analysis has become widely used in recent years.

Construct a coding schedule and protocol

Defining the categories which are to be analysed, and constructing a formal coding schedule for the analysis and coding/classification of content are two dimensions of the same 'step' in content analysis. Once the categories have been chosen and defined, they need to be set out in a codeable form on a coding schedule. A content analysis protocol, also frequently referred to as the code-book, which sets out clear guidelines and definitions for the coding practice also needs to be written before the content analyst can proceed.

Traditionally, a content coding schedule has looked very similar to a survey questionnaire – that is a printed sheet listing the variables which are to be coded for each programme, article or other case-unit of analysis. Increasingly, however, the development in content analysis has been towards dispensing with the printed coding sheets and instead coding directly to computer, in other words entering the relevant codes directly into a statistical analysis program listing the variables of the content analysis and their associated values (see the example coding schedule in Figure 5.1).

The content analysis protocol, on the other hand, is still essential. It sets out not only what variables are to be coded, and their associated values, but equally importantly it gives clear instructions about how the coding is to be done. It thus provides definitions, where appropriate, of the variables and their values, and it helps ensure that most fundamental aspect of content analysis, namely that it must be 'replicable'. Replicable means that other researchers or coders applying the same rules and procedures to the same communications content should arrive at the same or very similar results) If they do, then the content analysis is not only replicable, but its results also meet the scientific criterion of reliability. The content analysis protocol then, in short, is the 'manual' that coders refer to when they code.[2]

Pilot the coding schedule and check reliability

Before embarking on a full-scale content analysis it is crucial to 'try out' the coding schedule on a small sub-sample. 'Piloting' and 'fine-tuning' the coding schedule are important in content analysis, just as it is important to pilot one's research instruments, strategy or data collection tools in any other type of sociological analysis. Test coding of a small sub-sample often helps to reveal inadequacies and/or inconsistencies in the category systems of the coding schedule. Four types of problems are fairly typical: different levels of classification are mixed, when categories need to adhere to a single level of classification; a category system may be insufficiently and inadequately differentiated; a coding schedule may set out a large and highly differentiated list of actors, primary definers or sources to be coded; there is confusion of different units of analysis.

Examples of mixing different levels of classification include: confusing macro-categories and sub-categories within a single coding category, for example types of product advertising on television (cars, cosmetics, food, drinks, beer – 'beer' is of course a sub-category under 'drinks'); confusing race and religion (Caucasian, Afro-Caribbean, Asian, Christian – any person belonging to one of these races can of course be 'Christian') or age and sex (male, female, children).

---

2   Good examples of content analysis protocols or code-books can be found in the content analysis textbooks by Neuendorf (2002a: 121–3; see also the associated web resources at http://academic.csuohio.edu/kneuendorf/content/index.htm) and by Riffe et al. (2005: 131–4). Other examples include Mody's (2010: 363–8) comprehensive content analysis code-book for the study of international news coverage. A search on 'content analysis codebook' on Google also locates numerous readily accessible code-book examples on the internet.

Where a category system may be insufficiently and inadequately differentiated, resulting perhaps in a large part of the coverage falling into just a single category, the results of a content analysis will offer few or no analytical pointers to the nuances of the coverage, and are consequently of little use to understanding the nature of the coverage. The solution is to make sure that categories are developed from and anchored in some familiarity with the content, and to redraw categories in a way that will usefully accommodate or capture the nuances of the coverage.

A coding schedule may set out a large and highly differentiated list of actors, primary definers or sources to be coded. In practice it might turn out that only a very small proportion of these ever appear in the media content analysed. Rather than spending unnecessary time and effort on putting zeros (i.e. 'no occurrence') in coding boxes, the coding schedule should be changed to include only those actors likely to appear in the coverage. Of course, it is impossible to know in advance of doing the actual analysis precisely who will appear and who won't, but a general familiarity (see also the argument above, that such familiarity is a prerequisite for the construction of sensible and text-sensitive coding categories in the first place) with the body of texts to be analysed should enable the researcher to narrow down types of actors, subjects, contexts, issues, etc. that are likely to occur in the texts. Moreover, it is perfectly feasible – and indeed often desirable – to simply add new values to a variable such as 'actors/sources quoted' as the coding progresses and as new actors/sources appear.

Confusing different units of analysis results in loss of ability to relate different categories and dimensions to each other. A mistake which is commonly made when researchers first set out to construct a coding schedule, particularly for the analysis of advertisements, is to confuse the *advertisement* as a unit of analysis with the *character(s)* appearing in the advertisement as the unit of analysis. If coding categories are constructed along the lines of subject of advertisement, scheduling time of advertisement, number of male and/or female characters, age of characters, race/ethnic origin of characters, dress code of characters, etc., the problem is that although the analysis would provide data on the distribution of male/female characters, young/old characters, etc. it would not be possible to say whether the young ones were predominantly smartly dressed black male characters, the older ones predominantly white, conservatively dressed, female characters, etc.; in other words, this coding strategy would not facilitate cross-referencing of the actor characteristics.

Piloting should also include some checks on how reliable the coding process is. Reliability in content analysis is essentially about consistency: consistency between different coders (inter-coder reliability), and consistency of the individual coder's coding practice over time (intra-coder reliability). If checks on reliability reveal considerable divergence in how the same material is being categorised by different coders, or by the same coder over time, then it is necessary to tighten up on the coding guidelines, to make the coding instructions and definitions clearer. There are several different ways of checking or measuring reliability in content analysis, from a simple check on the percentage of coding decisions on which coders agree, to more complex formulae which take into account the degree to which a certain level of agreement would occur simply by chance in a set number of coding decisions. Scott (1955) offers one such statistical test (referred to as Scott's Pi statistic), which is relatively easy to apply (Scott, 1955; see also the helpful discussion of reliability testing in Chapter 7 of Neuendorf, 2002a).

Data preparation and analysis

While content data can be coded by hand on printed coding sheets, and then later typed into a computer data analysis programme, it is preferable to enter content analysis coding data straight into an appropriate data analysis programme. Not only does this save on paper and printing, but it is also faster (cutting out the laborious process of transferring data from handwritten sheets to computer) and much less prone to error, as codes are entered directly to computer and don't have to be retyped.

Suitable programmes for managing and analysing content analysis data include the powerful statistical analysis program SPSS (Statistical analysis Package for the Social Sciences) as well as the widely available Microsoft Excel and similar. Most of these programs have a very similar-looking spreadsheet layout, which displays each case as the row and each variable as the column. Content analysis coding is then a matter of entering, case by case and following the instructions set out in the content analysis protocol/code-book, the coding values relevant to each variable. Figure 5.1 shows a content coding schedule set up directly in the spreadsheet format of programs such as SPSS or Excel, with the first three rows/cases of the analysis and the first few variables (date, newspaper, etc.) to be coded. The relevant codes, as described in the content analysis protocol, are then entered into the blank boxes, and we eventually – when the coding has been

Case number	Date dd/mm/yy	Newspaper	Article type	Reporter type	Topic	Actor 1	Actor 2	Actor 3	Stance
1									
2									
3									

Figure 5.1   Example of a coding schedule/coding spreadsheet

completed – end up with a spreadsheet of numbers that refer to the values outlined in the content analysis protocol.

In an SPSS data file or Excel spreadsheet, each column corresponds to the individual variables analysed (date, newspaper, type of article, length of article, main actor, main theme, etc.) and every row corresponds to an individual 'item' (e.g. a newspaper article, an advertisement, etc.).

How should the data be analysed? There is no single answer to this question, just as there was no single or simple answer to the question 'which categories or dimensions of content should be coded?' Fundamentally, the data analysis needs to address the questions or hypotheses set out in the statement of research objectives, the definition of the research problem. The statement of research objectives should, for example, make it clear what kind of comparisons (across different variables) will be examined. These may include: comparisons of different television channels, radio channels or types of newspapers ('quality' versus 'popular', 'liberal' versus 'conservative', 'independent' versus 'government controlled'); comparisons of coverage during different time periods; comparisons of the media content of different countries; comparisons of UK media coverage of other countries; etc.

While the definition of the research problem should indeed give a good indication of what kind of analyses need to be done, it is also important to be flexible and open-minded in the process of analysing the data. In other words, it is quite possible that while examining basic trends in the coded categories, it becomes apparent that some dimensions seem to co-occur, or that some dimensions only appear in certain parts of the coverage. Such discoveries, in turn, call for further analyses, perhaps with a different grouping of dimensions, or with different axes of comparison.

A good starting point for any content analysis is to establish simply the distribution or frequencies for each of the main categories analysed (e.g. types of newspapers, actors, topics, types of reporters) before moving on to conduct more complex crosstabulation analyses comparing two or more dimensions with each other.

Report findings and conclusions

As in all academic research, the final objective is to publish the research or to make it publicly available in some other form. The write-up of the research needs to be fully transparent about its own method and approach: it must be clear to the reader what the theoretical framework is, what the sampling rationale was, what sample was analysed, how the content coding schedule was constructed and how the variables included relate to the overall objectives of the research, how the coding schedule was pilot-tested, what the coder reliability was (and how it was calculated), what analyses were carried out and what was found. The presentation of content analysis results is best done either with tables or graphs. Finally, the conclusion should summarise the key findings, relate these to the problem/questions articulated at the beginning of the report, and should include critical reflection on how well the analytical approach succeeded in answering the objectives, as well as critical reflection on what was learned about the appropriateness of the method and the appropriateness of the theoretical framework for this type of analysis.

Conclusion

Content analysis is a flexible research technique for analysing large bodies of text. It follows a clearly defined set of steps, one of its attractive features, but is also vulnerable to abuse. Fundamentally, those choosing to use content analysis for the study of media content should recognise that content analysis is little more than a set of guidelines about how to analyse and quantify media content in a systematic and reliable fashion. What it does not – and cannot – tell us is what dimensions (categories) of content to analyse, or how to interpret the wider social significance or meaning of the quantitative indicators generated by content analysis. Both of these aspects need to be drawn and developed from the theoretical framework circumscribing one's study, a framework which, amongst other things, must articulate the relationship of the texts analysed to their wider context of production and/or consumption.

Summary

- Content analysis is a method for the systematic and quantitative analysis of communications content.
- Content analysis is well suited for analysing and mapping key characteristics of large bodies of text, and it lends itself well to the systematic charting of long-term changes and trends in media coverage.
- While early uses of content analysis aimed principally at finding out about the intentions of the originators of media messages, the aim of content analysis in media research has more often been that of examining how news, drama, advertising and entertainment output reflect social and cultural issues, values and phenomena. Content analysis is well suited to integration into larger research efforts which also involve a range of other methods of inquiry (surveys, experiments, participant observation, qualitative and ethnographic audience research).
- Although content analysis initially fragments texts into constituent parts which can be counted, it reassembles these constituent parts at the

analysis and interpretation stage to examine which ones co-occur in which contexts, for what purposes and with what implications. Moreover, and in contrast to many 'qualitative' or 'interpretive' approaches, content analysis, because it follows clearly articulated rules and procedures, lays open to scrutiny the means by which textual meaning is dissected and examined.

- The process of content analysis can be broken down into eight consecutive steps: 1) define the research problem; 2) review relevant literature and research; 3) select media and sample; 4) define analytical categories; 5) construct a coding schedule and protocol; 6) pilot the coding schedule and check reliability; 7) data preparation and analysis; 8) report findings and conclusions.

- In conceptual terms, the most taxing aspect of any content analysis is to define the dimensions or characteristics which should be analysed. While any number of communications content characteristics could be categorised, counted and quantified, only categories and characteristics that relate directly to the overall research questions or hypotheses of the research should be coded and analysed.

- While the categories singled out for analysis will depend on the purpose and objectives of one's research, content analyses in mass communication research have often included, in addition to basic 'identifier categories', one or more of the following substantive dimensions: a) actors, sources, primary definers and their attributes; b) subjects, themes, issues; c) vocabulary/lexical choice; d) value dimensions and/or ideological/political stance; and e) frames.

- The method of content analysis offers a set of guidelines about how to analyse and quantify media content in a systematic and reliable fashion. What it does not, and cannot, tell us is what dimensions (categories) of content to analyse, or how to interpret the wider social significance or meaning of the quantitative indicators generated by content analysis. Both of these aspects need to be drawn and developed from the theoretical framework circumscribing one's study, a framework which amongst other things must articulate the relationship of the communications content analysed to its wider context of production and/or consumption.

Further reading and resources

Selected web resources

The Pew Research Center's Project for Excellence in Journalism produces the prestigious annual report 'The State of the News Media – An Annual Report on American Journalism'. A major component of this is drawn from Pew's continuous monitoring and content analysis of a wide range of media. See this website for a detailed account of the content analysis methodology used, including details about sampling, units of analysis, coding and reliability testing:

http://stateofthemedia.org/2011/methodologies/#a-year-in-the-news

The Content Analysis Guidebook Online is a website accompanying Kimberly Neuendorf's (2002) *The Content Analysis Guidebook*: http://academic.csuohio.edu/kneuendorf/content/. Although now a little dated, this website continues to offer useful archives, insights and guides, including examples of code-books and advice on reliability testing.

Further reading

Krippendorff, K. (2004). *Content Analysis: An Introduction to its Methodology* (2nd edn.). London: Sage.
Originally published in 1980 and now available in an expanded and revised second edition, Krippendorff's introduction to content analysis continues to be one of the most excellent, comprehensive and rigorous accounts of this method.

Krippendorff, K., and Bock, M. A. (Eds.). (2008). *The Content Analysis Reader*. London: Sage.
Accompanying Krippendorff's (2004) book *Content Analysis*, this reader offers a fine and comprehensive collection of original publications thematically organised to address key dimensions, including the history and conception of content analysis, unitising and sampling, coders and coding, reliability and validity, and computer-aided content analysis.

For detailed, accessible and comprehensive introductions to the method and application of content analysis, we also recommend the following two:

Neuendorf, K. A. (2002). *The Content Analysis Guidebook*. London: Sage.
Riffe, D., Lacy, S., and Fico, F. (2005). *Analyzing Media Messages: Using Quantitative Content Analysis in Research* (2nd edn.). Mahwah, NJ: Lawrence Erlbaum.

CHAPTER 6

Text and talk: Critical Discourse Analysis

In media and cultural studies there has been a growing interest in the particular set of tools for analysing texts and spoken language that is called Critical Discourse Analysis (CDA), an approach founded in linguistics, associated for the most part with a number of key authors (Kress, 1985; Fairclough, 1989; Wodak, 1989; Van Dijk, 1991; Van Leeuwen, 1996; Caldas Coulthard, 1997). One reason for this interest is the fact that CDA allows us to carry out a more systematic analysis of texts and language. Guided by linguistic expertise CDA can allow us to reveal more precisely how speakers and authors use language and grammatical features to create meaning, to persuade people to think about events in a particular way, sometimes even seek to manipulate these people them while at the same time concealing their own intentions.

Critical Discourse Analysis offers the promise of showing exactly what features of language, what language choices, have been used to accomplish particular kinds of communicative aims. Key here is the notion of 'language choices'. CDA draws on a form of linguistics inspired by the work of Halliday (1978) initially developed by critical linguists such as Kress (1989) and Fowler (1987). Halliday was interested in the way that when we code events in language this involves choices amongst options which are available in grammar. These choices shape the way that reality is represented. For example, it is important which terms we use to describe people. Why might we want to emphasise that a soldier is a 'father' and 'husband' but not do the same for the enemy? How does this coding of events in language shape how the world appears? Consider these two hypothetical news headlines:

Young people attack buildings

Youths attack family homes

Both of these describe the same event. But different language choices have been made to represent the attackers and the places they attack. In the second, 'youths' sounds much worse than 'young people'. 'Youths' brings connotations of anti-social behaviour whereas 'young people' sounds more positive and would be unlikely to be used in this case. In the second headline the use of 'family homes' also brings certain connotations. Here 'family' suggests something moral and cherished, something sacred. In fact families can be dysfunctional, violent and themselves criminal and provoking. But we often find 'family' used in the news media to connote something that should be protected, something that suggests love and humanity.

In the same way, mentioning a soldier as a 'father' or 'husband' can bring the same set of associations. It therefore humanises him. It suggests that he is an ordinary decent person. In contrast the enemy will not be called such things but rather will be anonymised. It is language choices amongst available options that allow us to foreground certain aspects of identities and background others. Doing CDA we look closely at language and grammar to show how such processes are able to shape our understandings of events and persons.

CDA offers a number of tools to reveal the ideas, values and opinions in texts and speech that may not necessarily be obvious on first reading, or hearing. Some of these tools will be presented in this chapter. Often these meanings are 'buried' in the texts as their producers seek to conceal or evade making them obvious, for example in political rhetoric where politicians harness language for the purposes of persuasion. But this process of using language to persuade and influence is by no means confined to such official talk and is characteristic of everyday conversation, news and other media texts.

CDA takes an overtly critical stance towards language and to society in general. Much linguistic inquiry takes the form of describing language features, of creating inventories of the nature of language or processes of language use. CDA seeks in the first place to be critical of the way that language is used for particular purposes. It is through such criticism, its proponents believe, that we can bring about social change. Hodge and Kress (1993) argued that this view of language is a political project (1993). Of course, this motivated view of research may sound 'unscientific' since it lacks the necessary objective stance to what we study that is normally required by academic ideals. But those who carry out such research would argue that this overt acknowledgement of its agenda is in fact its advantage, since researchers generally conceal exactly why they are carrying out research (Kress, 1989: 85).

In fact, there is no neutral way to represent the world through language as all the words we use are motivated and are laden with certain kinds of meanings and values. Even if a person says 'it's a sweltering day', they have clearly chosen an adjective that is subjective and evaluates. Yet the untrained ear or eye may not be able to detect exactly how this process works in the language they encounter everyday, even though we may often get the sense that we are being encouraged to think in a particular way. In such cases, we may be aware *what* speakers or text producers are doing but not exactly *how* they do it. It is how language can be used to subtly convey ideas and values that CDA can draw out. And through this we can get a much clearer idea of what is actually being conveyed. In this chapter we move through a number of tools for the critical analysis of language, each of which helps us to make more precise observations about what is going on in language. We begin with some of the main theoretical concepts that are used in CDA, such as 'discourse' and 'ideology', which relate to the broader ideas and values expressed through language. We then move on to look at some simple ways of analysing language choices as well as more specific cases of how people and actions are represented – in ways that are able to communicate broader ideas, or discourses, that are not necessarily overtly specified. We then deal with a number of other features such as *nominalisation*, where actions can be concealed by turning them into things, *presupposition*, where highly contestable things are presented as given and as common sense, and finally the use of *modality* in language, which is how speakers and writers express levels of commitment to what they say. All of these help us to show precisely *how* a text communicates in a way that may remain hidden to the casual observer.

The meaning of discourse

The term 'discourse' is central to CDA. In CDA the broader ideas communicated by a text are referred to as discourses (Van Dijk, 1993; Fairclough, 2000; Wodak, 2000). These discourses can be thought of as models of the world, in the sense described by Foucault (1972). The process of doing CDA involves looking at choices of words and grammar in texts in order to discover the underlying discourse. One example of such a discourse is that 'immigrants are a threat to a national culture'. This is a model of events associated with the notion that there is a unified nation and an identifiable national identity and culture. Normally this discourse encompasses a mythical proud history and authentic traditions. A different discourse framing the same topic is 'immigrants enrich the existing culture'.

We can see the first more negative discourse in an editorial from the *Daily Mail* (25.10.07) titled 'Britain will be scarcely recognisable in 50 years if the immigration deluge continues'. The item goes on to discuss how 'we' need to 'defend' our 'indigenous culture'. Who 'we' are remains unspecified, as does the nature of our 'indigenous culture'. In the context of Britain's evolving multicultural make-up and the diversity of ways of life and cultural values that have long been present based around social class, regional and other groupings, how can we pin such factors down? In the headline, immigration is described using the term 'deluge', a metaphor that draws on the idea of torrential rainfall that creates floods and damage. While the author of the text is keen to point out that they are not racist, much of what they say could be construed as such. Of course, in this case it is clear that this *Daily Mail* text is anti-immigration and has the potential to be interpreted as racist. But by looking at the word choices in the text we can pinpoint exactly why this is so, which is equally important in text where the discourse is less obvious.

There are other discourses for thinking about nation and national identity. A sociologist or historian would tell us that what we think of as nation and national identity are for the most part invented, with only a relatively short history (Gellner, 1983; Hobsbawm, 1984). Here the proud history and indigenous culture under threat by the immigrants, as described in the *Daily Mail* article, are themselves not factual at all, but simply a discourse that has come to be established in the interests of particular parties. Marxist thinkers would point to such an emphasis on difference based on national identity as concealing actual divisions in society between the rich and the exploited and poor. It therefore serves the interests of the powerful. We can thus see that CDA allows us to reveal just what these interests are even if at the surface level such views are denied.

Van Leeuwen and Wodak (1999) suggest that we should think about discourses as including, or being comprised of, kinds of participants, behaviours, goals, values and locations. We see this in our example from the *Daily Mail*. This discourse involves participants: real British people and immigrants. It involves values or an 'indigenous culture'. It specifies that 'we' must 'defend' this culture. This discourse represents a 'we' who should not see incomers as an opportunity for change and growth, or as fundamentally the same as ourselves on many levels, but as a threat to be repelled and something that will change 'us'.

What we can see from the *Daily Mail* example of the national 'we' versus the deluge of immigrants is that discourses do not simply mirror reality but, as Fairclough and Wodak point out, bring into being 'situations, objects of knowledge, and the social identities of and relations between people and groups of people' (1997: 258).

Fairclough (2000) explains that these discourses, such as of national unity or racial or cultural superiority, project certain social values and ideas and in turn contribute to the (re)production of social life. In other words, it is through language that we constitute the social world, or, put simply, how we talk about the world influences the society we create, the knowledge we celebrate and despise and the institutions we build. For example, if in a society the discourse that dominates our understanding of crime is that it is simply wrongdoing which requires retribution, then we build prisons and lock people away. Yet, it is the case that most people who end up in prisons are from poor or more vulnerable sections of the population. Sociologists and criminologists will tell us that if we are born black in countries like Britain or America then our life position will mean that we are much more likely to end up in prison. This is because of the complex relationship of poverty, race and inequality. Yet we do not organise our societies on the assumption that crime is associated with such factors. Nor do we tend to associate crime with what global corporations provoke in Third World countries or the acts of our governments when they go to war or reorganise society in the interests of the wealthy. It is our dominant discourse of crime that means we build prisons, use the police in the way that we do, take particular crime prevention measures and vote for political parties that will be tough on crime, rather than creating societies where it is less likely to take place. In this sense we can see that discourses represent the interests of specific groups. In the case of crime it will be in the interests of those who have wealth and power to conceal its relationship to factors such as race and poverty.

Power and ideology

The question of power has been at the core of the CDA project. The aim is to reveal what kinds of social relations of power are present in texts both explicitly and implicitly (Van Dijk, 1993: 249). Since language can (re)produce social life, what kind of world is being created by texts and what kinds of inequalities and interests might this seek to perpetuate, generate or legitimate? Here language is not simply a neutral vehicle of communication but a means of social construction. Therefore, discourse does not merely reflect social processes and structures but is itself seen to contribute to the production and reproduction of these processes and structures. As Fairclough and Wodak state, 'the discursive event is shaped by situations, institutions and social structures, but it also shapes them' (1997: 258).

Along with the idea of discourse, writers like Fairclough (1995) speak of 'ideology'. This is a term that is derived from the work of Marx and Gramsci which, like 'discourse', is used to capture the way that we share broader ideas about how the world works. Ideology here is used to describe the way that the ideas and values that make up these views reflect particular interests. The aim of CDA is to draw out the ideologies, showing where they might be buried in texts. Drawing on Gramsci (1971a) Fairclough (2003) argues that, while many institutions and forms of social organisation clearly reflect ideological interests, one place where we can observe exactly how these interests operate is in language. This is simply because language is a common social behaviour which involves us sharing our views of how the world works, what is natural and common sense. It is through language that we share the idea of things like 'British culture', nationalism and what immigrants are like. People and institutions then draw on this language as it appears to be neutral and common sense.

Ideology characterises the way that certain discourses become accepted and this therefore obscures the way they help to sustain power relations. Ideology obscures the nature of our unequal society and prevents us from seeing alternatives. It limits what can be seen and what we think we can do. In present common sense we take for granted that 'business' should be at the heart of everything, that it is the lifeblood of our societies and of human existence. Such is the power of this view that alternatives are ridiculed. Ideologies can be found across whole areas of social life, in ideas, knowledge, institutional practices. In the case of 'business' this ideology comes to dominate everything in society, even how we run schools and hospitals. Halliday (1978) believed that language can create dispositions within us. Writers like Fairclough, following from Foucault, believe that one way to put this is that language constitutes us as subjects (Foucault, 1994: 318). This is because the person who comes to think through the discourses of business is thinking of themselves, their identity, their possibilities through this discourse.

We can summarise what CDA is and what it does using this quote from Ruth Wodak, one of its pioneers:

> CDA may be defined as fundamentally concerned with analysing opaque as well as transparent structural relationships of dominance, discrimination, power and control as manifested in language. In other words, CDA aims to investigate critically social inequalities as it is expressed, signalled, constituted, legitimised and so on by language use (or in discourse). (Meyer and Wodak, 2001: 2)

Analysing texts and discovering discourses

In CDA texts are analysed in terms of the details of the linguistic choices they contain as these allow the analyst to reveal the broader discourses that are realised. What follows is a description of tools drawn from CDA that allow us to ask particular questions about the lexical and grammatical choices found in written and spoken texts. Not all of these have to be used every time we carry out an analysis, but rather only those that are useful in each particular case. For each, we give examples to illustrate the point.

Lexical analysis

To begin with, following Kress (1989) and Fairclough (2000), we can analyse the basic choice of words used by the text producer, referred to as simple lexical analysis. We ask what kinds of words are used. Is there a predominance of particular kinds of words, for example? Below there are two short texts. The first is an international news agency feed received by a news organisation, Independent Radio News. The second is the text after they had reworked it for broadcast for one of their clients, based on knowledge of their client listeners.

Associated Press Television News (APTN) feed as received by IRN 18 September 2003:

> One of the few suspects to express remorse over his alleged involvement in last year's bombings on Indonesia's Bali island arrived at court on Thursday to hear his sentence. Ali Imran is facing a possible death penalty, but prosecutors have asked that he receive 20 years in prison because he has shown regret and cooperated with investigators. Imran's older brother Amrozi bin Nurhasyim, and another key defendant, Imam Samudra, already have been sentenced to face firing squads for their roles in the attack, which killed 202 people – mostly foreign tourists.

IRN rewrite:

> A man's been jailed for life for helping to plan and carry out the Bali bombings. Twenty-six Britons were among more than two hundred people killed in the attack in October last year. Ali Imran was spared the death sentence handed down to other suspects because he expressed remorse and co-operated with the Indonesian authorities.

IRN has of course simplified the story in order to reduce ambiguity. Such stories have to be delivered in very short bursts. But it is revealing to look at how it has been changed. This has been done in a number of ways, but for the present purposes we can attend specifically to a number of important lexical changes or omissions. In the original text we find many legal terms such as 'alleged', 'prosecutors', 'defendant'. These have been removed from the rewrite. In fact, the original text has been generated from a court report as is standard in news gathering of crime. But the rewrite has omitted all legal reference. The journalist had believed that listeners to this particular radio programme would not be interested in legal information. But the effect is that we are no longer required to think about whose court or under whose jurisdiction this event is taking place. This becomes one more story in the fight against terror, where the journalist has inserted information about the number of Britons killed – a story about evil-doers being caught. Clearly, on the one hand this could be explained through the needs for simplicity and for ease of understanding. But on the other it is nevertheless important and revealing to ask what has been left out or added and what ideological work this does.

This next example is taken from an East Midlands Development Agency (EMDA) document. EMDA is one of a number of regional organisations set up in Britain by the New Labour government to 'regenerate' parts of the country that suffer from a number of problems such as poverty, unemployment, urban decay and inter-racial tensions. Again we can look at the kinds of words that we find in the text and ask what kind of discourse these realise, what kind of world they constitute and what kinds of interests they serve. Here is some text taken out of the EMDA 'mission statement'.

> The vision is for the East Midlands to become a fast growing, dynamic economy based on innovative, knowledge based companies competing successfully in the global economy.
>
> East Midlands Innovation launched its Regional Innovation Strategy and action plan in November 2006. This sets out how we will use the knowledge, skills and creativity of organisations and individuals to build an innovation led economy.
>
> Our primary role to deliver our mission is to be the strategic driver of economic development in the East Midlands, working with partners to deliver the goals of the Regional Economic Strategy, which *emda* produces on behalf of the region.
>
> I am committed to ensuring that these strategic priorities act as guiding principles for *emda* as we work with our partners in the region and beyond to achieve the region's ambition to be a Top 20 Region by 2010 and a flourishing region by 2020.

In fact when reports by these developmental agencies are read it is rather difficult to get any concrete sense of what they actually do. A lexical analysis of the text reveals a predominance of words like 'dynamic', 'innovation', 'competing', 'creativity', 'strategic', 'ambition', 'challenges', 'goals' and 'strengths'. When discussing what seems like a simple matter of unemployment or poverty such terms are used and those involved – the poor and the local council workers and businesses that are to deal with them – become 'partners' and 'stakeholders'.

These kinds of terms, Chiapello and Fairclough (2002) point out, come from the language of business rhetoric, and they describe them as the empty rhetoric of corporate-speak. The result of referring to things such as poverty as a 'challenge', the poor as 'stakeholders' and solutions in terms of 'creativity' and 'innovation' can conceal what the actual problem is and therefore what the solution should be. For Fairclough (2000) this process serves to conceal where the actual responsibility lies – that is with the government – and the fundamental nature of social organisation. Poverty and unemployment in the East Midlands are in actual fact due to changes in economic policies pushing Britain into the global economy thus allowing industries that formerly created employment to shift to other parts of the world where labour is cheaper (Levitas, 2005). So in certain areas whole sections of the population live where there have been no workers in the family for often as many as three generations. While terms like 'creativity', 'innovation' and 'knowledge economy' sound exciting and active, they will not help us to deal with fundamental structural issues. And calling local people, along with the local councillors and businesses who are to provide solutions, 'stakeholders' further obscures power relations. It hides who actually needs help and who might be able to provide this. Of course, as Fairclough (2000) explains, this is precisely the point as we are distracted from real causes and necessary solutions.

Over-lexicalisation

Over-lexicalisation is where there is an abundance of particular words and their synonyms or where there is evidence of over-description. This is normally evidence that something is problematic or ideologically contentious. In the EMDA document above we have an over-lexicalisation of words that convey energy and power: 'dynamic', 'innovation', 'competing', 'creativity', 'strategic', 'ambition', 'challenges', 'goals' and 'strengths'. In this case we have to ask what is problematic here? Of course such words are used precisely to conceal actual actions.

Another simple example of over-lexicalisation is:

Male nurse

Female doctor

Why do these job titles require further elaboration in terms of gender? While things have changed in society as regards accepted gender roles and who should do what kind of job, these terms reflect a previous time where men were doctors and women were nurses. They therefore signal a time when this represented a deviation from social convention or expectation. Achugar (2007) gives a further example of where titles require excessive elaboration. Here an enemy is over-lexicalised:

Certainly our Armed Forces victorious in the battle against the unpatriotic forces of Marxist subversion were accused of supposed violations to human rights. (El Soldado, April 1989)

Here the use of 'the unpatriotic forces of Marxist subversion' is a case of over-lexicalisation. It displays some anxiety about the need to persuade. And this use also suggests something about the contentious nature of the claim being made.

Teo (2000) carried out an analysis of the representation of drug dealers in the press. He found that there was an over-lexicalisation of words for youth:

'looks and sounds like he is about 13', 'The 16 year old', 'five other youths', 'two young Asian gang members', 'some as young as 12', 'these kids', 'their leader at 13', 'had beaten two murder charges by 17', 'at least two of the accomplices were of the same age (13 and 14)'

Of course, such facts about age would be expected as the basic information of reporting. But why this excessive use of such terms? Emphasising youth in this way could be seen as one way to get sympathy. But Teo rejects that being young is being used as a mitigating factor here. Rather, in his view, this adds to the moral panic. 'The kids are out of control'. 'What is society coming to?' 'We need greater discipline, law and order in this society'. All of these are common news themes that of course distract from broader social changes and the causes of what we call criminal behaviour.

Teo points out that there is also over-lexicalisation of terms of disfavour:

'The cult of extreme violence', 'Extreme youth and extreme violence', 'Hacked and stabbed 11 times with machetes'

That we are continually told it is extreme must be for a reason. Why can we not be left to judge this ourselves?

Dunmire (2005: 481–513) studied the speeches of former American President George W. Bush. Here is one of his examples:

The threat comes from Iraq. We resolved then and we resolved today to confront every threat from any source that could bring sudden terror and suffering to America.

While there are many dangers in the world, the threat from Iraq stands alone because it gathers the most serious dangers of our age in one place. Knowing these realities America must not ignore the threat gathering against us. Today in Iraq we see a threat whose outlines are more clearly defined and whose consequences are far more deadly.

Here there is over-lexicalisation of 'the threat'. In fact at the time in 2002 no actual threat had been made against the US. But this overuse of the term suggests a point of anxiety, of contention and immediately should signal cause of concern as to the nature of what we are being told and why. The strategy in this case is of course to create an imagined global threat of terror.

Naming and reference

Kress (1989) and Fairclough (2003) have shown that the way that people are named in a text or speech can have significant impact on how they are viewed. We have a range of naming choices that we can make when we wish to refer to a person. These allow us to place people in the social world, to highlight certain aspects we wish to draw attention to and to silence others.

For example, take the following sentence:

Muslim man arrested for fraudulently claiming benefits

In fact there were many other possibilities that could have been used to characterise the man: an Asian man, a British man, a Midlands man, a local office worker, a Manchester United supporter, a father of two young daughters, a man named Mazar Hussein. Each of these can serve psychological, social and political purposes for the writer and reader (Meyer and Wodak, 2001: 47).

This is shown in the following:

Father of two daughters arrested for fraudulently claiming benefits

In this second case the meaning is different. In the first case the headline locates the story in a news frame emphasising his 'otherness' and the man as part of something that is problematic. Since 2005 Muslims have been represented through news frames that emphasised their threat to the wider society and resistance to wider cultural values (Poole and Richardson, 2006). Since the man was born in Britain the headline, as already noted, could equally have said that he was a British man. But this would have appeared odd and would have suggested 'one of us'. Crime reporting usually involves creating moral others, so that the perpetrator is not like us. In the second headline, in contrast, referring to the man in the first place as a father humanises him and has the opposite effect – that possibly the fraud was justified.

Van Dijk (1993) has shown that how the news aligns us alongside or against people can be thought of as what he calls 'ideological squaring'. He shows how texts often use referential choices to create opposites, to make events and issues appear simplified and often in order to control their meaning. For example, phenomena can be associated with old or new, future and past, etc. Van Dijk specifically gives the examples of sexual assaults in the press. Where the man is considered guilty he will be referred to as a 'sex fiend', 'monster' or 'pervert'. In this case he will *attack* innocent women who will be referred to as 'mother', 'daughter', 'worker'. However, where the man is considered innocent the referential strategy will be different. In this case the woman will be referred to as 'divorcee' or through physical features such as 'busty'. In this case she will *provoke* an innocent man referred to as 'hubby', 'father of four', 'worker'. In this way the referential strategy becomes part of the way we perceive people and their actions. As in the case of the Muslim man the actions of the man or woman become part of the broader social problems caused by this category of person.

Classification of social actors

To help us to be more systematic when describing referential choices van Leeuwen (1996) offers a comprehensive inventory of the ways in which we can classify people and the ideological effect that these have.

Personalised/impersonalised

We can ask to what extent the participant is personalised or impersonalised. This can be seen in the following two sentences:

> *Prof John Smith requires academic staff to give notification of strike action*
>
> *The University requires academic staff to give notification of strike action*

In the second case impersonalisation is used to give extra weight to a particular statement. It is not just a particular person but a whole institution that requires something. It is simply not personal. Of course, this conceals certain issues. We could argue that the staff, along with the students, *are* the University. But here this has been phrased to give a sense that giving notification may be in the interests of the University as a whole. We often come across the same process where politicians say 'Our nation believes ...' or 'Britain will not be held responsible ...'. This serves to conceal who actually believes it and who is actually responsible in each case. In the EMDA example above we read of 'the goals of the Regional Economic Strategy'. But these goals have their origins in a particular political organisation. Describing them in this way conceals who created them.

Individuals or collectivised

It is also useful to consider how participants are described as individuals or as part of a collectivity, as is shown in the following sentences:

> *Two soldiers, privates John Smith, and Jim Jones, were killed today by a car bomb*
>
> *Militants were killed today by a car bomb*

In the first case these soldiers are actual people. The details individualise them and therefore allow us to associate with them as real people. In the second case the militants are simply a generic group. In the following we can see how additional referential information individualises the participants further:

> *Two soldiers, privates John Smith, and Jim Jones, both fathers of two daughters, were killed today by a car bomb*

In the following example, the same addition of personal details appears odd. We are not normally given personal details of participants classified in this way as it tends to humanise them:

Terror suspects, both fathers of two daughters, were killed today by a car bomb

It is useful in analysis of a text to ask which kinds of participants are individualised and which are collectivised. In this way, we reveal which group is humanised.

Specific or generic

We can also look at whether participants are represented as specific individuals or as a generic type. In our earlier example, we saw that the person accused of benefit fraud could either be named or identified as a type. For example, in the following:

A man, Mazar Hussein, challenged police today

A Muslim man challenged police today

In the second case the man who challenged the police is represented as a type. This is used here to place the story in a particular news frame. In this case the generic category of Muslim can locate this story into a news frame where Muslims are a contemporary problem in Britain, either through extremism or complaining about their situation. In fact the man may not have been a practising Muslim. It could be like saying 'Christian John Smith challenged police today'. It is the use of such generic terms that can give a racist angle on a story even while the newspaper takes a stance that it is not racist.

Nominalised or functionalised

Participants can be nominalised in terms of who they are or functionalised by being depicted in terms of what they do. For example:

George Bush said that democracy would win

The American President said that democracy would win

This can have different effects. Use of functionalisation can sound more official, and nominalising can sound more personal. Functionalisation can also reduce people to their role, which may in fact be assigned by the writer or be generic. For example:

The demonstrator was injured outside the embassy

The defendant was warned by Judge Peter Smithely-Smigely

In these cases the demonstrator and defendant are partially dehumanised by referring to them with functionalisations that highlight only their roles.

Functionalisation can also connote legitimacy. Machin and Mayr (2007) in an analysis of a regional newspaper showed that functionalisation, in the form of 'shop owner' and 'office workers', served to positively evaluate speakers represented as legitimate, decent members of a local community. Those who were not legitimate were represented only in terms of what they said.

Of course, functionalisation can itself be an attempt to define what someone actually does. In the *Daily Mail* anti-immigration story above we find the following line:

A teenage scribbler in a liberal Sunday newspaper, who normally seems to write reasonable sense, virtually accused me of being a neo-Nazi.

The author of the text does not name the journalist who has criticised him but uses a pejorative functionalisation of 'teenage scribbler'. There is also a feature of the language in this text that van Dijk (1991) would characterise as one technique for the process of denial. This follows a pattern where a person first states that they have no general problem with something in order to make the case that the instance in hand is an exception only. Here he finds that the 'teenage scribbler' normally writes 'sense'. Therefore his criticism is not personal and there is a sense that normally the author of the text is open minded.

Anonymised
Participants can often be anonymised.

A source said today that the government would be focusing on environmental issues

Some people believe that globalisation is a bad thing

The first case is common in newspapers. We rely on journalists to have legitimate sources, but in fact this conceals the way that certain social groups and organisations are able to feed information to journalists. In the second case we can see how politicians, here Tony Blair, can use such representations to avoid specification and developing detailed arguments. It allows us to conveniently summon up kinds of arguments that are easy to then dismiss. Such anonymisation can also be used to create a sense of obligation where there may in fact be none. For example:

It is expected that parents will accompany children in the pool

Does this mean that parents *have* to accompany children? And who is expecting this? Is it the management? Often, such anonymisation can be used to hide the fact that there is no actual power to be wielded.

In other cases it can be used to hide responsibility:

It is expected that students will pay fees before the beginning of teaching

Here we can see why this might be used instead of 'The University expects ...' as this allows the institution to distance itself from the financial transaction.

Aggregated
Here participants are quantified and treated as 'statistics':

Many thousands of immigrants are arriving in ...

Scores of Muslim inmates at a high security prison are set to launch a multi-million pound claim for compensation after they were offered ham sandwiches during the holy month of Ramadan. (Daily Mail, 26.10.07)

Van Dijk (1991) shows that this kind of use of statistics can give the impression of research, of scientific credibility, when in fact we are not told specific figures. Is 'many thousands' 3,000 or 100,000, for example? And what are 'scores'? In the news agency feed received by the IRN above we find the following line:

One of the few suspects to express remorse over his alleged involvement in last year's bombings on Indonesia's Bali island arrived at court on Thursday

In this case how many is a few? Exactly how many have shown remorse and how many have not? And if we are not told, then why not? What is clear from this particular text is the depoliticisation. We are not told about the political aims of those who planted the bombs. They become generic terrorists and part of the news frame of the war on terror. What kind of remorse is not clear either. Does this mean they now no longer believe in their political aims?

Pronoun/noun: the 'us' and 'them' division
Concepts like 'us', 'we' and 'them' are used to align us alongside or against particular ideas. Text producers can evoke their own ideas as being our ideas and create a collective other that is in opposition to these shared ideas:

We live in a democracy of which we are proud

They shall not be allowed to threaten our democracies and freedom

We have to decide to be strong and fight this global terrorism to the end

Fairclough (2000: 152) has pointed out that the concept of 'we' is slippery. This fact can be used by text producers. 'We' can mean 'the political party', then in the next sentence can be used to mean 'the people of Britain', and in the next an unspecified group of nations. In the last example above, does it mean 'we' the people who are proud of democracy, or a collection of superpowers? This means that who the 'we' is, who actually has the power or responsibility, can be hidden.

We can see this vague use of 'we' in the *Daily Mail* anti-immigration story above. In this case it is used to evoke a British 'we' who share the indigenous culture, although how this is so and the exact composition of this 'we' is not overtly explained in the text. This can be illustrated as follows:

Britain has an indigenous culture

We must fight the deluge of immigrants

These two sentences imply what is said in the following without actually saying it:

We of the indigenous British culture must fight the deluge of immigrants

Put in this way, the othering discourse becomes much more direct. Splitting the information into two sentences helps the writer to conceal this.

Suppression

We can also look at what is missing from a text. Such absences are a clue to what the author wished to hide from us or distract us from (Fairclough, 2003) as in the following examples:

Globalisation is now affecting all national economies

Market-based economics are establishing themselves in all areas of life

In these cases the agent is missing. Globalisation is not a thing that has power to change other things but is a process or phenomena that is caused by particular agents. It is driven by capitalism and world economic institutions such as the World Trade Organization and World Bank. In the second case market-based economics are not agents themselves but are a result of a particular political ideology. This sentence gives the impression that like a species of plant they are simply self-cultivating and appearing in new places without human help. The fact that they have become established is through specific political decisions and the waves of privatisation that have followed. The result of these two sentences is that both globalisation and market-based economies appear natural and inevitable, something that must be responded to rather than something that is being created through specific decisions and politics.

Passivated verbs without agents

One important quality of the examples showing suppression is that this is one way to obscure who acts and who has responsibility (Fairclough, 2000: 163). One way that this can be accomplished is through passive verb structures. For example:

> *The civilians were killed during a bombing raid*

> *The government found itself facing allegations of spin this week following the release of some confusing crime statistics*

In all of these sentences who carried out the action is missing. But passive verb structures can be used with agents. For example:

> *The civilians were protected by the soldiers*

But this in itself can be ideological. We can ask which kinds of participants are described in passive verb sentences and which are not. Van Dijk (1991) has shown, for example, that ethnic minorities are only presented as active agents when they do something bad. Where they are associated with anything positive they are represented in a passive role and things are done for or to them.

Nominalisation

Richardson (2007) shows how active agent deletion through the use of passivated verbs can be moved a stage further into nominalisation. This is the transformation of a process into a noun construction, which creates further ambiguity. For example:

> *The civilians were killed during a bombing raid*

> *The death of civilians during a bombing raid*

In this case all sense of agency is removed. Another example could be:

The global economy was changed

The changed global economy

While the first of these uses a passivated verb to conceal the agent of the change, the second presents it as a noun, as a thing. In fact 'globalisation' is often used as a noun when in fact it is a process. This itself can make it appear simply like a thing rather than the result of political decisions. Globalisation is not in itself an agent capable of bringing about change – as noted above, it is process brought about by other agents.

Fairclough points out that in such constructions there is 'no specification of who or what is changing, a backgrounding of the processes of change themselves and a foregrounding of their effects. In backgrounding the processes themselves, nominalisation also backgrounds questions of agency and causality, of who or what causes change' (2000: 26). We can see how this process of turning verbs into nouns, works in the following example:

The student lost their course work and was rather upset

The student was upset about the loss of their course work

The actual act of losing the course work, how it happened and who might be to blame have been removed. We can see this again here:

I am sorry I have failed to return my library book on time

I am sorry about the failure to return my library book on time

By turning an action (to lose) into a thing (a loss) a sense of the action is retained, but as a noun we can now point to it, describe its physical qualities, classify it and qualify it. So then we can talk about the failure as a thing:

The regretful failure to return my library book on time ...

Nominalisations can be important ideologically. The use of nominalisations in the following means that the Prime Minister is not confronted with processes to which he must react or by specific agents. Nor is it clear where he has acted. Therefore nominalisation can be used to create ambiguity and also to distract the reader.

The Prime Minister rejected a call to carry out an inquiry into allegations of corruption. He announced that the tightening of sanctions was a decision that had been made through all the legal channels.

Here nominalisations are 'a call', 'the tightening of sanctions', 'a decision'. These are all processes that have been transformed to remove agency. Also, importantly, here we can see that nominalisations are not marked for tense so they are outside of time. This has the effect of avoiding when and how likely something is, which is necessary with verbs. When did someone call for an inquiry? Who made the allegations or tightened the sanctions? When and by whom was the decision made?

Presupposition

Often the authors of texts use concepts without actually saying what they mean specifically and frequently use these in a way that assumes they are taken for granted when in fact they are not. We can analyse texts for such features, which are called presuppositions. Presupposition relates to what kinds of things are assumed as given in a text. In fact it is impossible not to use presuppositions when we speak or produce a text and they are part of the structure of language. Even the sentence 'the bag is heavy' involves the assumption that you know what a bag is and what heavy is. This is presupposition, a sort of background belief. Of course much of this is subconscious. We aren't continually monitoring whether we know what people mean, although in some contexts we may come to be aware that someone is using a slightly different meaning than we normally would for something. And when we speak we can't forever be saying exactly what we mean by things, so we have to rely on shared presuppositions. But as we have been showing in this chapter, CDA has demonstrated that language is continually used to highlight, silence and shape qualities of people, the world and events. Therefore looking at what is assumed in a text can be revealing. What is a text setting out as 'the known'? We can see an example of this in the EMDA mission statement analysed for lexical content above:

> *The vision is for the East Midlands to become a fast growing, dynamic economy based on innovative, knowledge based companies competing successfully in the global economy.*

This presupposes that there is indeed a global economy and that this is a taken-for-granted identifiable thing despite the fact that many analysts see global economic processes as far from equal around the planet and as characterised by particular relations of power and driven by certain interests (Fairclough, 2003: 163). There is much theoretical debate about whether or not there is any such thing. We see the same in a sentence such as:

> *British culture is under threat by immigration*

This assumes that there is such a thing as 'British culture'. Research in social anthropology and cultural studies has shown that this idea of monolithic, what they call 'essentialised' culture, is incorrect and hides massive variation and change within. Yet such concepts can be used for particular interests and ideologies.

Presupposition can be used in order to build a basis for what sounds like a logical argument as above. If we accept that there is such a thing as an established, identifiable British culture, it is easier to accept that it could be changed and that therefore immigration could bring this about. In the following sentences we can see how speakers don't actually say explicitly what they mean and that this creates the basis of what they can then go on to say:

> *This new model of organisation* [suggests that there was an old one]
>
> *Militants launched a new wave of attacks today* [assumes that there was an old wave distinctive from this one]
>
> *The real issue is ...* [suggests that there are other issues but that they are not so important]
>
> *Have you stopped smoking?* [assumes that you were smoking]
>
> *We should take this opportunity* [assumes that it is an opportunity]

All of these examples show how text producers can establish what is known and shared. Fairclough discusses the way that language can reconstitute the social world. If the fact that there is a global economy becomes accepted as a given, as it has for the most part in the Western news media, then we sideline the fact that it is open for contestation, that it is part of political decisions and choices that are being made right now.

Modals

Hodge and Kress (1993) and Fairclough (2003) discuss a characteristic of language that tells us about people's commitments to what they say and also about their own sense of perceived status. These are modals. Modals express degrees of certainty. These are verbs such as 'may', 'will' and 'must' and adjectives such as 'possible', 'probable' and 'certain'. We use them all the time when we speak. For example, as in 'I will have a beer tonight', as opposed to, 'I may have a beer tonight'. Modality can also be associated with hedging terms (see below) such as 'I think' or 'kind of/sort of'. What modals do is set up a relationship between the author and the author's representations – in other words what we commit ourselves to in terms of truth. This is clear in the difference between 'This is the correct procedure' and 'I think this might be the correct procedure'. They also indicate a sense of the author's identity. Some people feel they are in a position to be so certain. If we read a document from our employers saying we 'will' do something rather than we 'should' or they 'think we should do it', these will give us a very different sense of the power that they believe they have over us.

Modals expressing high degrees of certainty might be used in order to convince people. We can see this in an excerpt from a speech on multiculturalism by British Conservative leader David Cameron (26.02.08)[1]:

> *We must not fall for the illusion that the problems of community cohesion can be solved simply through top-down, quick-fix state action. State action is certainly necessary today, but it is not sufficient. But it must also be the right kind of action, expressed in a calm, thoughtful and reasonable way.*

Here he uses the modal 'must' frequently, thus asserting his certainty and confidence. Imagine if he said in the last sentence: 'It should be the right kind of action' or 'It might be the right kind of action'. On the other hand he does not say 'We will not fall …'. In this case too much certainty is expressed, which was clearly not Cameron's intention. Where we find texts filled with uncertainty and lack of commitment we are dealing with an author who feels much less confident. Later in the speech we do find lower commitment:

> *But I don't believe this should mean any abandonment of the fundamental principle of one people under one law. Religious freedom is a cardinal principle of the British liberal tradition. But liberalism also means this: that there is a limit to the role of religion in public life.*

Here while there is certainty about what liberalism means he slightly reduces his commitment with 'I don't believe'. But this is clearly not the same as saying 'I think' as it shows much more of a commitment. And clearly it is important for the opposition leader to talk about beliefs where possible. But we can still look at where and how he uses them. In this case it allows him not to appear too much like he is laying out commandments. In this sentence he could have just said, 'This does not mean any abandonment …'. But the words he does choose show commitment without commanding, with the added advantage that it appears that he is speaking from his own convictions.

Finally, we can see how Cameron attributes less certainty and commitment to others:

---

[1] www.conservatives.com/News/Speeches/2008/02/David_Cameron_Extremism_individual_rights_and_the_rule_of_law_in_Britain.aspx.

Some say the risk is inflation. Others say it's recession. So some think there should be more intervention by the Government in the financial markets. Some say there should be less.

He does not specify who the some are, anonymising them, but they are not described as 'knowing' or even 'believing' there should be more intervention by government but only 'think' it. This is a technique often used to detract from what others hold to be the case.

Murray (2002) gives an example of speech that shows a lack in confidence through use of modals. This is from a nurse:

Yeah. I think it, sort of, provided very holistic care for the elderly lady coming through the unit, who actually gained more benefits than simply having a wound dressed on 'er leg. Erm, I think that had it, had she 'a' been seen in an ordinary unit without nurse practitioner cover, the chances are that the, er, medical staff there would've dealt with 'er leg ...[2]

Such use of modals, 'I think', would not be found, for example, in the speech of a doctor even though the doctor may have no more knowledge than the nurse.

The analysis of modals is also important as they express an ambiguity over power. For example, 'She may talk' can be interpreted as either giving permission or to suggest a possibility. This can be seen if we provide some context:

She may talk; I have now finished speaking

She may talk, although she is often too shy

A speaker can use this ambiguity to build up a sense of power where it can always be denied. So coercion can be masked in surface forms of rationality. In some cases there is no ambiguity but this is rare. This suggests that the ambiguity is highly functional.

You cannot swim here

You may do any of the essay questions

The first might be legal, for safety, or placed there by an annoyed neighbour. The second suggests both a sense of having an option but also that you are being *allowed* to do so. We can see the same ambiguity in a political speech:

We must take globalization as an opportunity ...

Again, we have the sense of rationality against an order.

---

[2]   www.peter-murray.net/msc/dissch6.htm.

We cannot avoid the fact that we are now part of a global economic order ...

Does 'cannot' here mean that since national economies are now subordinate to the WTO and World Bank there are legal reasons that we cannot? Or does it mean that it would not be reasonable? In the following we can see descending order of power by the speaker:

You will come with me

You must come with me

The authorities order you must come with me

In the first the speaker has the power. In the second they appeal to some unmentioned power. In the last their own power is so weak that they have to name the authority. We often hear children use this last one when they say 'You've got to come' to a sibling – the answer is 'No, I won't', so they appeal to the higher authority with 'Mummy says you've got to'.

We often find that pop psychologists and style gurus on TV and in lifestyle magazines use modals like 'will' and 'is' to create a sense of their own authority over knowledge.

People who are successful in life are those who can adapt quickly. I call these 'adaptors'. The next category are those that worry ...

Importantly, modal auxiliaries are ambiguous regarding temporality.

We must adapt to changes in global markets through building a knowledge-based economy that is dynamic and versatile

Is this referring to the future? Is it a statement about what will happen or is this a general law that applies right now? This indeterminacy is useful for speakers who have the contradictory task of portraying a specific issue to give a sense of addressing it, without actually making clear what they will in fact do.

Of course and finally we can use modals to protect our utterances from criticism:

Teacher: Do you understand this process?
Student: Yes, I think I can. I'm sort of realising it's perhaps the key part of the course.

Hedging

As well as modality, authors can use hedging in order to create a strategic ambiguity within their claims (Wood and Kroger, 2000). Hedging refers to the use of words to soften what is being said, to distance oneself from a word's meaning or to avoid being specific. For example, we have already seen sentences such as:

Some people believe that globalisation is a bad thing

And

Some say the risk is inflation

In these cases exactly who is it that says these things? Such vagueness can be used as a way of then moving on to provide a counter-argument that can avoid addressing specific issues. In contrast a speaker might specify who said these things such as:

British economists believe that globalisation is a bad thing

Such a statement would mean that the response would have to specifically address economic matters and it opens up the possibility of further specification as to which economists these might be.

The *Daily Mail* anti-immigration article stated

Some people say that multiculturalism is outmoded, but, in fact, it is still orthodox thinking.

These all allow avoidance of being specific and in this case appear to be setting up a kind of 'straw man' who can then be knocked down. And in fact it is often many people who work in multicultural policy-making itself who now view it as problematic for very specific and important reasons. In the same article we find hedging in the form of the words 'sometimes' and 'quite often':

These incomers sometimes expect everyone to speak to them in their own language, and they quite often make little attempt to integrate themselves into French society or culture.

How often exactly is 'sometimes' or 'quite often'? These are what can be called 'approximators' and are useful for concealing exactly what kind of evidence you have in order to then go on and make your case. So a student might argue the following:

There were quite a few assignment deadlines around the same time of the month that meant I just found it difficult to get this one in on time

So how may deadlines were there and exactly how closely together did they fall?

Sunoo (1998: 16, cited in Faber, 2003) gives the following example:

> Corporate universities come in many shapes and sizes. *Some,* such as Motorola University, have campus locations around the globe. *Others,* such as Dell University, SunU and Verifone University, have no campus at all. *Many* have committed to the virtual university model to express their learning philosophy and commitment to continuous learning.

Here the author aims to justify the virtual university model but does so through rather vague evidence. Exactly how many universities have committed to this and how many universities have no campus at all?

Tusting and colleagues (2002: 656) give examples of the way that exchange students distance themselves from cultural stereotypes through hedging. Here the hedging is highlighted in bold:

> *Um, apart from **I don't know if it's true but** I got the impression that French men are most sexist.*

> ***I don't know if it's just because he's French and likely to be more blatant, or because I'm foreign and seem more like an object than a person** because I can't always express myself, or I'm just different. **I'm sure it's something to do with my situation that he behaved like that.***

Politicians of course are masters of hedging. Here are some examples from Resche (2004):

> The American economy, **like all advanced capitalist economies,** is continually in the process of **what Joseph Schumpeter, a number of decades ago, called** 'creative destruction'. **Capital equipment, production processes, financial and labor market infrastructure, and the whole panoply of private institutions that make up a market economy** are always in a state of flux – **in almost all cases evolving into more efficient regimes.**

This could be shortened to,

> *Though many sectors are being thoroughly affected by creative destruction, our economy will be stronger and more competitive in the end*

All of the text in bold is hedging and in fact completely unnecessary in terms of actual communication of his basic idea. But the hedging is used as it is important for the speaker for two reasons: 1) it allows the statements to be softened and also conceals them, burying what is actually said in words; 2) it in fact gives the impression of explanation and clarification.

Hedging can also be done simply by the addition of extra details and defi-nitions of terms. This is often used by politicians to give the impression of precision and provision of information where in fact they are doing the very opposite. We can see this in the following example:

> *Essay submission deadlines, **that point at which learners are tested on curricula contents**, have been placed close together this semester, **what we might want to call 'heavy clustering'**. This has made it harder to finish work on time, **meaning that date and time specifically documented in individual course material supplied by tutors**.*

Here the hedging sections have been underlined. But their use can bring a sense of informing, precision and even authority.

Quoting verbs

Extremely revealing in any text are the words chosen to represent how a participant has spoken (Caldas Coulthard, 1994). Consider the difference between the following:

> *The management announced that striking workers would be punished*

> *The workers grumbled about problems with conditions*

In the first case the management announce while in the second the workers grumble. Yet there would have been nothing inherent in how each group spoke that warranted these word choices. The word 'said' could have served in both cases:

> *The management said that striking workers would be punished*

> *The workers said there were problems with conditions*

We can see from this that the first examples help to define the roles of the two sets of participants. 'Announcing' sounds more official, formal, and is the stuff of official groups. 'Grumblings' are not necessarily well formulated, coherent nor official and indicate lack of power. In the following example, we also see the power of choice of verbs of saying:

> *Minority community leaders claimed that they have suffered increased levels of abuse*

Here we can see the effect of 'claim'. Claims are not factual but can be contested and the use of this word invites doubt. The word 'felt' would have

and

> *The frenzied bloody attack*

When representing 'our side' in the to describe this last example as

> *A strategic frontal assault*

In the fashion of van Dijk's ideolo enemies carry out frenzied bloody at gic operations. A favoured demon unfavoured one is a 'mob rampage'. bole in texts and think about what it evaluate persons, places and events.

Metaphor
This is where we find objects, peop other things. For example:

> *Banks have said that we must not let*

> *The housing market bubble has burst*

> *The situation in Afghanistan has over*

Here we find the state of the econor that has remained still for too long. a bubble suggests that it was always metaphor of cooking. In each case has actually happened and can c metaphors can also make things an or negative.

   In the EMDA example we find th

> *work with our partners in the region a be a Top 20 Region by 2010 and a fl*

'Flourishing' generally refers to pla here is not clear. This is typical of the solutions and outcomes are all con done is not specified so no one is in metaphor in such documents is wh 'lay foundations', 'cement' parts to

So how may deadlines were there and exactly how closely together did they fall?

Sunoo (1998: 16, cited in Faber, 2003) gives the following example:

> Corporate universities come in many shapes and sizes. *Some,* such as Motorola University, have campus locations around the globe. *Others,* such as Dell University, SunU and Verifone University, have no campus at all. *Many* have committed to the virtual university model to express their learning philosophy and commitment to continuous learning.

Here the author aims to justify the virtual university model but does so through rather vague evidence. Exactly how many universities have committed to this and how many universities have no campus at all?

Tusting and colleagues (2002: 656) give examples of the way that exchange students distance themselves from cultural stereotypes through hedging. Here the hedging is highlighted in bold:

> *Um, apart from **I don't know if it's true but** I got the impression that French men are most sexist.*

> *I don't know if it's just because he's French and likely to be more blatant, or because I'm foreign and seem more like an object than a person because I can't always express myself, or I'm just different. I'm sure it's something to do with my situation that he behaved like that.*

Politicians of course are masters of hedging. Here are some examples from Resche (2004):

> The American economy, **like all advanced capitalist economies,** is continually in the process of **what Joseph Schumpeter, a number of decades ago, called** 'creative destruction'. **Capital equipment, production processes, financial and labor market infrastructure, and the whole panoply of private institutions that make up a market economy** are always in a state of flux – **in almost all cases evolving into more efficient regimes.**

This could be shortened to,

> *Though many sectors are being thoroughly affected by creative destruction, our economy will be stronger and more competitive in the end*

All of the text in bold is hedging and in fact completely unnecessary in terms of actual communication of his basic idea. But the hedging is used as it is important for the speaker for two reasons: 1) it allows the statements to be softened and also conceals them, burying what is actually said in words; 2) it in fact gives the impression of explanation and clarification.

Hedging can also be done simply by the addition of extra details and definitions of terms. This is often used by politicians to give the impression of precision and provision of information where in fact they are doing the very opposite. We can see this in the following example:

> *Essay submission deadlines,* **that point at which learners are tested on curricula contents,** *have been placed close together this semester,* **what we might want to call 'heavy clustering'.** *This has made it harder to finish work on time,* **meaning that date and time specifically documented in individual course material supplied by tutors.**

Here the hedging sections have been underlined. But their use can bring a sense of informing, precision and even authority.

Quoting verbs

Extremely revealing in any text are the words chosen to represent how a participant has spoken (Caldas Coulthard, 1994). Consider the difference between the following:

> *The management announced that striking workers would be punished*
>
> *The workers grumbled about problems with conditions*

In the first case the management announce while in the second the workers grumble. Yet there would have been nothing inherent in how each group spoke that warranted these word choices. The word 'said' could have served in both cases:

> *The management said that striking workers would be punished*
>
> *The workers said there were problems with conditions*

We can see from this that the first examples help to define the roles of the two sets of participants. 'Announcing' sounds more official, formal, and is the stuff of official groups. 'Grumblings' are not necessarily well formulated, coherent nor official and indicate lack of power. In the following example, we also see the power of choice of verbs of saying:

> *Minority community leaders claimed that they have suffered increased levels of abuse*

Here we can see the effect of 'claim'. Claims are not factual but can be contested and the use of this word invites doubt. The word 'felt' would have a similar meaning. Feelings are subjective and not necessarily based in fact. But in the following case the use of the word 'explain' changes the meaning:

Minority community leaders explained that they have suffered increased levels of abuse

Of course this also influences the way that we perceive the participants and it can be seen as another part of the way that social actors are categorised. We see this clearly in the following two sentences:

Minority community leaders shouted that they have suffered increased levels of abuse

Minority community leaders remarked that they have suffered increased levels of abuse

In the second case the leaders appear reserved and official, but in the first, emotional and perhaps threatening. Often we can find in news reports that journalists can use more emotional verbs of saying where they wish to draw our attention to the drama of a situation. This can make such speakers more personalised for the reader in positive as well as negative ways. More neutral words such as 'said' tend to background the speaker behind the actual content of their utterances. It is always revealing to carry out a comparison of how different groups or persons are represented as speaking.

Rhetorical tropes

Rhetorical tropes include hyperbole, metaphor, metonym and puns. All of these are typical of political rhetoric and are used to shape understanding of a situation rather than describe it in concrete terms. In any text we can look for the use of these, which are always indications of attempts at persuasion and abstraction. Here we look at hyperbole and metaphor, objectification/ personification, metonymy and synecdoche.

Hyperbole

This is simply where there is exaggeration such as:

I felt ten feet tall

We all died laughing

But we might find it in news texts for example in sentences like,

The demonstration was a mob rampage

and

The frenzied bloody attack

When representing 'our side' in the conflict a journalist might instead want to describe this last example as

A strategic frontal assault

In the fashion of van Dijk's ideological squaring we could imagine that enemies carry out frenzied bloody attacks whereas friendlies carry out strategic operations. A favoured demonstration is a 'human tide' whereas an unfavoured one is a 'mob rampage'. We can always look for the use of hyperbole in texts and think about what it is used to conceal and how it is used to evaluate persons, places and events.

Metaphor

This is where we find objects, people and events described by reference to other things. For example:

Banks have said that we must not let the economy stagnate

The housing market bubble has burst

The situation in Afghanistan has overheated

Here we find the state of the economy described through reference to water that has remained still for too long. The housing market being compared to a bubble suggests that it was always fragile, and 'overheating' draws on the metaphor of cooking. In each case the use of the metaphor obscures what has actually happened and can dramatically simplify. Of course, such metaphors can also make things and processes sound much more positive or negative.

In the EMDA example we find the organisation will

work with our partners in the region and beyond to achieve the region's ambition to be a Top 20 Region by 2010 and a flourishing region by 2020

'Flourishing' generally refers to plant or animal life. What it exactly means here is not clear. This is typical of the way that in such documents, problems, solutions and outcomes are all concealed in rhetoric. What exactly will be done is not specified so no one is in fact held accountable. Another popular metaphor in such documents is where we collectively 'build' our future. We 'lay foundations', 'cement' parts together, 'lay cornerstones'. The building metaphor allows the author to avoid specifying just what they will do, while at the same time summoning up a sense of progress and collaboration.

Objectification/personification

This is simply where human qualities or abilities are assigned to abstractions or inanimate objects. Again, these can obscure actual agents and processes.

The theory explained to me how it worked

This fact proves the point

His religion tells him he can't drink alcohol

Cancer finally got him

Democracy will not stand by while this happens

Terrorism is the enemy of free people the world over

The credit crunch has made all of us rethink

Metonymy

This is the substitution of one thing for a second thing with which it is closely associated.

The top brass [to mean senior personnel]

The suits [to mean officials]

The Kremlin said today ... [to mean the Russian government]

The Redtops all carried the story of ... [to mean tabloid newspapers]

Synecdoche

This is where the part represents the whole, or vice versa. This also has an important function of allowing the speaker to avoid being specific.

We need a few bodies to fill the room

There are a few good heads in the department

I want a new set of wheels

Want a few glasses tonight?

We need some new blood here

There are few new faces here

The country won't stand for it

In the last case a politician saying 'the country won't stand for it' may in fact mean that they themselves won't stand for it. But expressions like this allow such distinctions to be avoided.

When British PM Tony Blair was once asked about the solution to poverty he replied that it was mainly a matter of 'banging a few heads together'. Here these heads represent those placed in positions to implement policy. But through this utterance he avoids saying exactly who he means, and avoids saying exactly what he will do to make sure policy is implemented. In fact Blair's party were often credited as having good ideas but with being terrible at actually realising them.

Representation of social action

Earlier in this chapter we have looked at how the representation of participants in texts and speech can shape our perception, portraying them in ways that tend to align us alongside or against them without overtly stating the case. But how we perceive people can also be shaped by the representation of what they are depicted as doing, or what linguists call 'transitivity'. This too can help to promote certain discourses and ideologies.

The study of transitivity allows us to reveal who plays an important role in a particular clause and who bears the consequences of that action. It shows us who is mainly given a subject (agent/participant) or object (affected/patient) position. In other words who acts and how, and who does not. Simply, it is asking who does what to whom. Transitivity is an analytical component that allows us to sort the huge variety of goings on in the world into a small number of categories. But of course speakers and authors often seek to conceal, obscure or confuse who is subject or object. They might also wish to give a sense that other participants are doing more than they in fact are.

Categories of verb processes

Linguists have explored the lexical choices available for representing actions and found that verbs can be grouped into categories of 'process types' (Halliday, 1978). These can be used to detect the kind of agency attributed to an actor. Here we have glossed Halliday's (1978) six processes:

- *Material*: This is simply doing something in the world that has a material result or consequence. For example, 'the woman built the house'.
- *Behavioural*: This is where we act without material outcome. For example, 'the boy jumped'.
- *Mental*: This is where a person thinks, evaluates or senses. For example, 'the boy saw the dog'.

- *Verbal*: This is where a person is represented as simply saying something. For example, 'the man talked about democracy'.
- *Relational*: This is where people are represented as being like, or different to, something else. For example, 'the militia had crude weapons' (in contrast to the US soldiers), or simply 'the boy was taller'.
- *Existential*: This is where people are represented simply in a state of existing and appearing. For example, 'he sat in the chair'.

We can apply these categories to any text and observe the patterns in transitivity choices. The following sentences allow us to think about how this works:

The pilot bombed the village

The civilians were in the street

The soldier protected the civilian

The mother worried

The militants were a ragtag mob

The politician said it was time to act

At the most basic level we can see that some of these processes are 'transitive' – in other words a transaction is involved such as 'The pilot bombed the village' – and others are non-transitive, where there is no direct outcome such as in 'The civilians were in the street'. This in itself can give us a sense of who is represented as the agent in a text. In this case it appears that the pilot and soldiers are the doers in the text while the civilians remain passive. This passivity can be used by an author of a text where armed forces are occupying an area to give a sense that the soldiers are therefore required in order to defend the vulnerable.

Another way of thinking about this is in terms of how participants in a clause, social actors, can be *activated* or *passivated*. Activated, social actors are represented as 'the active, dynamic forces in an activity' (van Leeuwen, 1996: 43–4), the ones who do things and make things happen. Being activated, in this view, is an important and generally positive aspect of representation. An activated actor's capacity for 'action, for making things happen, for controlling others and so forth, is accentuated' (Fairclough, 2003: 150). Action processes foreground agency, contributing to representations of power (Fairclough, 2003: 113).

Other kinds of verb processes can also play an important role in shaping how we perceive participants. It is often the case that participants who are made the subjects of mental processes are constructed as the 'focalisers' or 'reflectors' of action. These actors are allowed an internal view of themselves. This can be one device through which listeners and readers can be encouraged to have empathy with that person. For example:

The mother had worried since her son's regiment had moved into the region

Here the reader is encouraged to empathise with the mother through being informed of her worrying. In turn this carries over to the soldier himself. Indirectly we are told that he has a mother who worries about him. He is therefore just essentially an ordinary young man from an ordinary family. This serves to help humanise the occupying forces and can be seen as an important part of the humanitarian discourse of war. We might find that accounts of other participants in texts contain no corresponding details on their mental processes. So we learn nothing of the mental processes of the militants nor the concerns of their mothers.

Mental processes can also be one way that these participants appear very busy even though they don't engage in any material transactions. They are busily worrying, thinking, regretting and recalling but do nothing concrete. Additionally, if these mental verbs are mainly about sensing and reacting this can also convey passivity. So, for example, if someone is surprised or feels threatened or jealous, they are reacting as opposed to acting.

In the sentences above the mother is the only person allowed an internal view of herself. In this case we might tend to align with her thoughts. But she still remains passive in the sense that her actions are non-transitive. Were we given access to the fears and worries of the soldier, such as in the following sentence, we would likewise tend to align with his concerns:

The soldier worried as he protected the civilians

We can see from the above list that it would be a simple matter to identify what kinds of actions a participant in a text is engaged in and what this says about their role in the social world represented in the text. Machin and Thornborrow (2006), for example, use this model to show how in women's magazines women are highly active but in non-material processes, in other words those that have no outcome. So the women might be busy 'hoping', 'worrying', 'walking', 'watching', 'reading', which are mainly behavioural and mental processes rather than material ones that actually bring about change in the world. This is even though the magazine is branded as being for the 'Fun, Fearless Female'.

Van Leeuwen (1995: 90) uses the same analytical framework to describe the way that children are represented textually in contrast to teachers. He analyses the texts for 'transitivity', in other words, actions that have an outcome. The analysis reveals that children, in contrast to teachers, are rarely represented as having an effect on the world. He concludes: 'clearly the ability to "transit" requires a certain power, and the greater that power, the greater the range of "goals" that may be affected by the actor's actions' (1995: 90). There is a theoretical assumption here, therefore, that levels of actor agency are directly correlated to material process types and that individuals or groups not involved in such processes are represented as being weak agents.

Unspecified reactions

Another category of reactions are those that are not defined. Such as:

The policeman reacted

The soldiers responded

These are often used to conceal certain kinds of actions. Again we can see how these might be useful in van Dijk's ideological square where the opposing soldiers commenced a vicious and bloody attack whereas our soldiers 'responded'. Where actions are represented as reactions or responses it also helps to legitimise them. One of the authors took part in industrial strikes where continual provocation and aggression by the police were reported in the national press as 'a response', which in fact resulted in the hospitalisation of several family members.

Grammatical positioning of actions: prepositional phrases and subordinate clauses

A further strategy for manipulating how social action is represented is through the way that verbs are placed within a sentence or clause. This can either highlight or conceal this action. Van Dijk says:

> Events may be strategically played down by the syntactic structure of the sentences, for example, by referring to the event in a lower (later, less prominent) embedded clause, or conversely by putting it in the first position when the events need extra prominence. (1991: 216)

Richardson argues that prepositional or subordinate phrases are used to provide context for dominant clauses (2007: 207). When analysing newspaper headlines Richardson points to the way that placing actions in subordinate or prepositional clauses rather than dominant clauses can be used to conceal responsibility for the action and make this part of the information seem less important. Normally actions are provided in the dominant clause and the time, place and manner of this action placed in the subordinate clauses. For example:

The boy ate the sweets in the shop

The way this grammatical feature can be manipulated can be seen in the example of the headline:

Children killed in US assault (Guardian, 02.04.03)

Here 'Children killed' is the emphasis of the sentence. The dominant clause, and 'in US assault' is de-emphasised in the prepositional phrase. Richardson suggests the editor could have written the same information as:

US kill children in assault

In this case 'US kill children' is the dominant clause and the children are passivated in the prepositional phrase that provides details and context. When analysing the representation of social action we can, as well as carrying out a transitivity analysis, look for grammatical positioning and concealment.

Criticisms of CDA

In this chapter we have shown that CDA can provide an excellent way to increase our ability to examine what it is that makes texts work in the way that they do. Nevertheless there are a number of criticisms that should be taken seriously and which for the most part suggest that CDA does not form any kind of coherent methodology, that excessive analysis and use of concepts often yields what might be fairly obvious to the casual reader and that it should be used in unison with other methods such as political economic research and ethnography, as described in this volume.

In the first place Widdowson (1998) has been highly critical of the nature of CDA as a consistent coherent approach. He argues that CDA is not so much an application of a broader theory, of Halliday on whom its proponents draw. It is, he argues, 'a rather less rigorous operation, in effect a kind of ad hoc bricolage which takes from theory whatever concept names come usefully to hand' (1998: 137). For Widdowson there is no broader theoretical model of language that justifies all the bits and pieces that CDA brings together. In his first editorial for the journal *Discourse and Society*, editor Teun van Dijk did appear to be aware of such possible criticisms, where he points to the need for 'explicit and systematic analysis' based on 'serious methods and theories' (1990: 14). However, Widdowson, analysing van Dijk's own work, suggests that for the most part there is little consistency in what analysis constitutes and that often it appears that concepts are used to justify observations rather than in fact to discover or reveal what is buried in a text, and further that aspects of texts that do not fit the argument being made are ignored and suppressed. What more able students, seeking to understand CDA, also tend to notice is that across the leading proponents of CDA there are often competing concepts that appear to describe more or less the same thing. This of course is not a problem in itself, but the use of these concepts often merges and this feature certainly supports Widdowson's observations about there being a lack of broader coherent theory.

A number of writers are also concerned with the way that in CDA there is a tendency to make huge assertions about ideology based only on textual analysis. This is something that we feel is the most serious criticism of CDA. In media studies of the press it has been shown how much of the content we find in news and other texts often subject to CDA analysis can be explained through the nature of production processes, institutional values and simple cost issues as much as ideology. In fact as Widdowson (1998: 142) points out, the leading CDA proponents themselves continually say that it is not possible to read significance straight from texts but that we need to look at their production. But none of them actually ever does this and at the same time they persist with their text-based analyses (Widdowson, 1998: 142). No attempt is ever made to ask what writers meant by a text or how it was put together. An analysis using CDA might reveal the suppression of a particular social actor in a news text due to their lexical under-representation. But a reliance only on textual analysis misses how this could have been a result of production processes, for example due to the way a journalist's sources presented the information. In a news industry where there is currently a great shortage of staffing due to commercial pressures, sources who are in a position to provide news material that is ready to use are highly likely to have their material used directly by journalists. These journalists may not even have the time to leave their office and only be able to verify stories through reference to the internet and the odd phone call to already established sources. The journalist may also be required to write specifically for a particular group of readers identified by market research. In such a case what does a text-based criticism actually tell us about these issues and the current nature of the news media?

Philo (2007) was also concerned with the lack of attention to production factors, but additionally was critical of the lack of engagement with how those who read and hear texts receive them. What is the public understanding of the texts that CDA proponents deal with? And do all of the texts, such as political documents and speeches, actually have the natural effect on social practice that CDA proponents appear to suggest? Research within the news industry itself suggests that the public have lost confidence in journalism and this is certainly supported by plummeting circulations. Does this in part mean that readers have also been sharing in some of the same concerns raised by textual analysis using CDA? One journalist colleague recently joked that there would come a point soon when the only people reading newspapers would be academics doing Critical Discourse Analysis and making claims about the way that language makes societies.

Finally, one criticism of CDA, which some of its practitioners seem to in some ways enjoy, is that they are themselves not driven by an objective desire to carry out research but are politically motivated to identify and question issues of inequality. To many this is highly problematic as it is not in the spirit of doing independent scientific research. Fairclough, however, argues the contrary: that such motivations are an excellent basis for 'a critical questioning of social life in moral and political terms, e.g. in terms of social justice and power' (2003: 15). He also argues, reasonably, that in fact all other research is equally socio-politically situated, selective, limited, partial and thereby biased. The difference is that this other research claims neutrality and objectivity.

Doing Critical Discourse Analysis

CDA is carried out either on selected examples of texts or speeches. These can either come from a larger corpus or a smaller sample. In each case a smaller number of texts will be closely analysed using the tools provided in this chapter. For example, a project may wish to look at the representation of students on current university websites. Typically ten websites would be selected and then two or three sample texts could be analysed that were representative of the broader sample. The analysis might show that there were certain naming strategies used that presented the students as customers rather than learners. Analysis may find that certain actions were always represented through nominalisation in order to conceal who is the agent. Analysis might present a table of who the social actors are and of what they do. The aim would be to reveal the discourses of education that the universities use to present the nature of being a student. Conclusions might point to the market model used, which emphasises value for money rather than education and self-betterment through knowledge.

Summary

- CDA is a loose set of tools used to describe the language and grammar choices in a text. Its power is that it can allow us to produce a more systematic analysis of texts. For example, we may have the feeling that a political speech appears very confident but seems to shy away from actually committing to something; CDA can show us exactly how this is achieved through language.

- CDA is an approach which seeks to draw out the ideology of a text by pointing to the details of language and grammar.
- The proponents of CDA believe that through this kind of critical analysis we can bring about social change. Therefore, this view of language analysis and research is a political project. Of course, this motivated view of research may sound 'unscientific' since it lacks the necessary objective stance to what we study that is normally required by academic ideals. This can be countered by the argument that most research simply hides its motivations, which are always ideological.
- CDA is a qualitative approach. The analyst points to linguistic and grammatical features that they feel are significant and then explains their meaning. Some argue that its tools are not systematic and that thus it is actually neither a method nor a concrete approach.
- Another criticism is that CDA places too much emphasis on texts and in the end makes many assumptions without actually consulting the readers about how they will understand these. Likewise it attributes ideology to texts which may be explainable through production factors.

CHAPTER 7

Analysing narratives and discourse schema

In this chapter we are interested in how we can research the narratives of texts. Here we look at how to research the narrative structure or underlying 'discourse schema' of texts or other media representations. Such analysis allows us to break down what appear to be quite complex stories and texts to reveal very basic messages about the kinds of values and identities, concerns and social boundaries that lie at their basic level. In the chapter we begin by looking at what we mean by narrative, distinguishing this from 'genre' and 'discourse' – showing that the same narrative structure discourse schema can be found across different genres. We then show how this form of analysis can be carried out, first to understand films and then women's lifestyle magazines. Analysis allows us to draw out the most basic cultural meanings in such media.

Social anthropologists, like Lévi-Strauss (1967), were fascinated with the nature of the stories told by people of different cultures. He believed that while such stories may have been intriguing and exciting, or even strange and at times rather complex, what was most interesting about them was the way they could be used to reveal the fundamental values of that particular society at that particular time. At the heart of these stories were basic underlying structures which could be identified and analysed. These social anthropologists showed how oppositions in a story could represent broader oppositions in cultural values in society. So left and right or culture and nature might represent good and evil. Analysis of such oppositions could point to the way a society made evaluations of kinds of identities and of how people should reasonably behave.

Scholars from other fields such as linguistics (Fowler, 1977; Rimmon-Kenan, 1983) and literary studies (Propp, 1968) showed how long and complex stories could be broken down into basic stages and components that allowed the analyst access to some of the underlying social assumptions and evaluations found in them. However, in literary studies and much of linguistics the aim was to show how individual stories work rather than to reveal deeper social and political values.

Of course, the oppositions and evaluations found in stories are not simply based on the broader concerns of people in that particular society but will tend to reflect certain interests – of those who have the power to have their stories heard and to influence the stories others tell. For example, in Western society crime stories found in novels, on television and in the news tend to represent crime, criminals and their victims in terms of an opposition of good versus evil. Yet sociological studies show that most of the people who come to be defined as criminals are from poorer sections of society, that those from certain ethnic groups will be more likely to find themselves in prison than those from other ethnic groups. An analysis of these stories would therefore point to basic values in our society that seek to exclude the role of social context in criminal behaviour. In such stories criminal behaviour is more about personal choices and morality as opposed to life opportunities and social justice. Clearly, such values, such narratives, serve the interest of the wealthy and powerful. But nevertheless, analysis of some of the basic structures found in these stories can help to reveal something about the dominant social values held in the societies who create them. This chapter looks at the procedures through which researchers can break down narratives, isolating their stages and reveal their underlying values. The methods we consider in this chapter can be applied to many genres of communication such as movies, computer games, plays and news items.

What is a narrative?

To begin with we need to think a little more about what we mean by narrative. In fact, narrative has been defined and treated very differently both across and within different academic disciplines. Narrative is often confused with 'story'. Or it is used in a sense of 'personal narratives' where people talk about themselves and their lives. Or it can be used in a broader sense such as 'The American Narrative'. Here we point to a specific meaning of narrative best illustrated through examples. In this chapter we describe how a number of scholars have shown how complex stories and other texts can be analysed in terms of narrative structure and how this helps reveal deeper meanings. We then explain how we need to think about this not so much as narrative structure but as 'discourse activity schema'. This view better serves, as we show, the aims of media text analysis, which is not to simply describe texts but to connect them to socially constructed ideas about the world, people and events. The discourse activity schema that can be found within texts, we show, points at the basic underlying 'practices' that are the 'doing' of the ideas contained in discourses.

To begin to illustrate what we mean by narrative we first describe that it is not the same as 'story'. The following examples show how the same narrative can be contained in different genres. The first is a news headline, the second a limerick:

Two Israeli soldiers were killed by militants today in the Gaza strip. Israeli government pledges reprisals

> *There was a young terrorist called Bill*
> *Who didn't really ever want to kill*
> *But when they took all his land*
> *And his family died in the sand*
> *He found he just couldn't sit still*

Both of these examples have a narrative. For a linguist a definition of narrative is that it must contain a number of narrative clauses, which are clauses containing a verb. Thornborrow and Coates (2005) give the example from Sacks' (1995: Vol I, 236): 'The baby cried. The mommy picked it up.' Here we can see that the two verb clauses set up a sequence of events. Of course, in this case the meaning of the narrative would be changed were we to change the order of the sentences to 'The mommy picked the baby up. It cried.' Toolan (1988) argues that narrative is a sequence of events that are not random but which have a trajectory. So here we can see that in this definition it is a sequence of clauses containing a verb that sets up a sequence of events.

But what is important in this case is to point out that these two examples, the news headline and the limerick, are different genres of communication, yet both contain a narrative. Both describe a succession of events, where there is an attack and an aggressive response, but they are different types of communicative event. The same narrative could also be communicated through other genres such as personal letters, political speeches, legal testimony, dance, theatre, classical Hollywood movies or children's play.

Below we see a photograph of the son of one of the authors at play with a friend and holding a plastic toy machine gun (Figure 7.1). There was a great deal of imagination taking place in this play. When asked what was going on, it was clear that the son and his friend were playing as highly trained Special Forces soldiers dealing with a motley collection of attackers who threatened the social order of a locality to which they had been sent on their mission. The genre here is different to the news item and the limerick yet we can see that there is the same basic type of narrative where territory must be defended from an external threat. We can argue additionally that while the actors and possibly the settings and even the details of how the attack and defence were accomplished in each case are different in the news story, the limerick and the play, the narrative is the same.

Figure 7.1   The son of one of the authors at play

Narrative theorists have been interested in the infinite number of stories that can be generated from a small number of structures (Greimas, 1971). Of course, the structures can become obscured in more complex stories. But nevertheless they can still be discovered. In the three different genres we could say that while the actors are different, all have the same deeper structure. All three could be represented by the following:

1.   There was an attack on A by B
2.   A takes action against B

Of importance here is that this manner of presenting the narrative can exclude preceding events such as the occupation or exploitation of the territory of B by A in the first place. In the 'War Against Terror' that took place in the early years of the twenty-first century US President George W. Bush made a call for a move against the enemies of freedom which used just such a narrative sequence. Yet this glossed over the decades of political and economic activities on behalf of the US, and before that European colonialism, that played a part in the action of some of those societies or people then described as a threat by Bush.

To this sequence of events we can also add a third stage in terms of what is implied:

1.   There was an attack on A by B
2.   A takes action against B
3.   A is safe

It is implied in the above examples, although often overtly stated by the likes of politicians such as Bush, that it is not subtle diplomatic and humanitarian actions that will lead to safety but a like-for-like attack. That we find two young boys playing as Special Forces soldiers eliminating a chaotic, inferior, yet fanatical evil enemy, points to the way such stories can come to appear neutral. It is of note that Ronald Reagan initiated the promotion of Special Forces as a best possible solution in the 1980s when he presented them as a strong US response in the face of the preceding 'weak' diplomatic strategies of Jimmy Carter (McClintock, 2002).

This process of breaking stories down into basic components has a tradition originating in the work of Vladimir Propp (1968). Propp uses the idea of functions to look at the basic structure of narratives. He analyses 150 Russian folk tales showing that the same events kept being repeated. He argued that these were narrative functions and were necessary for narratives to take place. Breaking the stories down into their smallest irreducible units, he identified 31 functions, although not all of these need to be present at all times in stories. Examples of functions are: pursuit, villainy, lack, displacement, rescue, punishment, solution, difficult task, etc.

Importantly, through these functions, it is possible to identify the role played by characters. So, for example, at the beginning of a story a person might be displaced, which immediately allows us to recognise them as the hero. We find this in Disney's *Jungle Book* in the case of the character Mowgli (Simpson, 2004). He also has helpers, Baloo the bear and Bagheera the panther, who are identified as such by advising him of danger. Propp refers to this as the 'interdiction function', meaning that they prevent him from straying. There is also the villain, the tiger Shere Khan, who attempts to take possession of the hero, the sixth of Propp's functions. Finally, the hero battles with the villain using fire, Propp's twelfth function – the intercession of a magical agent.

Simpson (2004) shows how the very same functions are present in *Harry Potter and the Philosopher's Stone*. Here we find the hero, Harry, his helpers; we find the villain, the battle and the use of the magical agent. These functions do not have to take place in any particular order and can be found in very long or very short stories.

What was important for Propp was that in each story we will have descriptions of settings, such as houses, landscapes and costumes. But these are details which are draped over the basic narrative structure. It is these details that Barthes (1977: 92) called 'indices'. These enrich our experience of the environment of the story but are not necessary for the basic structure, although as Barthes argues indices too should be the subject of analysis to understand narratives. And subsequent theorists (Toolan, 1988) have also pointed to the importance of character for telling the reader what kind of narrative we are dealing with and how it should be experienced. For instance, in the example above where the two boys play it is clearly of importance to the narrative that they are highly trained Special Forces soldiers rather than regular army. Toolan points out that it is often character in narratives that readers find so engrossing. Later in the chapter we will come on to the importance of analysing character.

Drawing on Propp (1968) and also on Burke (1969) Wright (1975) also believed that characters in narratives should be viewed as representing social types acting out a drama in the social order where each character represents a set of social principles. This can be most easily done through stock characters. Wright thought that by reducing narratives, in his case specifically those of movie westerns, to their basic functions he could reveal the fundamental cultural values that form the driving force of the story and the way that characters are used to celebrate or challenge particular kinds of identities.

By analysing the basic narrative sequences of films from the 1930s and 1940s and comparing them to films of the 1950s and 1960s he was able to arrive at a number of important observations. The earlier westerns depicted lone heroes who had special powers (fast with a gun, shrewd). The hero would be different from the rest of society, which while basically good was also weak and in need of the hero to save them from a threat. In these films the hero is morally good. Often at the end the hero is unified with society.

In contrast the later westerns were different. The hero ceased to be a loner and began to work in teams, which Wright called the 'professional plot'. Society is no longer essentially good but has become petty, mercenary and amoral. Now the hero does not defend society but rather offers his specialist skills to the group of other specialists. By doing this the hero shows they are superior to the petty, mercenary, amoral society.

Wright connects these changes in narrative to changes in feelings towards a society becoming dominated by market capitalism. The hero lives out the contradictions in the values of individualism held in society and the difficulties of realising this in the rather cynical and mercenary market economy. Therefore the change in plot represents changes in attitudes to society, the self and our relationships with others.

In order to arrive at his observations Wright broke individual movies into their most basic narrative structure. He gives the following example of the structure for a typical romantic film:

A loves B
↓
B ignores A
↓
A dies
(Wright, 1975: 26)

The actual movie may contain many characters, events and minor issues, but this is what lies at its core. Like the examples given earlier of the news head-line, the limerick and the children's play, the movie can be broken down into its basic activity sequence. By doing this we can then ask what roles the char-acters play in the sequence and what kinds of social values are being tested out. In the case of the children's play, for example, the boys take the role of the heroes who work in a team using their special powers (training and high-tech equipment) to defeat the villain.

Wright suggests that in the case of the above activity sequence we can ask a number of questions to help us to establish the kinds of values being dealt with specifically. For example, in this particular sequence if A is a man and B is a woman then this is a story about love between different sexes and what this involves. But if A is also upper class and very wealthy and B working class and very poor then it can also be a story about class difference and the clashes that such interactions can involve. The appearance of such a narrative might also indicate a concern about a changing society where earlier fixed boundaries have become challenged. This too would be the conclusion of the likes of social anthropologists such as Lévi-Strauss (1967). He would want to look for some of the basic oppositions that were represented by characters or interactions and consider how these point to anxieties held in that particular society at that particular time.

In his summary of the kinds of values dealt with in westerns, Wright suggests that in earlier plots broadly felt cultural conflicts are dealt with by one individual, such as progress versus freedom, law versus morality. In the case of the social class difference above it could be the anxiety about break-down of social boundaries by social change.

As regards the *Harry Potter* movies, we also find a society under threat by evil. Harry is the hero, he is an outsider who possesses special powers and is also someone associated with the lower classes. But as with the later westerns Harry also works to some extent in a team along with his friends who also have special talents, although these often play the interdiction function of warning Harry. In the *Harry Potter* movies society is basically good, although sometimes lost in the bureaucracy of the magic community, unable to see its own problems within, blind to the evil that threatens.

In this case scholars such as Lévi-Strauss or Wright would want to ask what kinds of cultural concerns such a plot suggests. Do people now feel that society has become bureaucratically obscure and stilted, that there are impending dangers which our leaders appear either blind to or unwilling to address. Wright might want to connect this to contemporary concerns about rampant global corporate activity that seems to go unchecked amidst petty and irrelevant political debate, threatening the very nature of our social order. The very fabric of Western societies changes as all manufacturing shifts to Asia and public services are slyly privatised. At the same time we appear to be involved in wars for which the purpose is never really clear against enemies who are never really identified. As with Wright's later westerns there is a sense that there are anonymous forces affecting our lives. Society is basically good but has itself become largely misguided and amoral.

Discourses and discourse schema

The Proppian type analysis has been applied only to stories. What we are suggesting here is that narrative sequences can be found across genres of communication and also multimodally in and across language and images. But what we also want to stress here is the need to be able to draw out the narrative sequence of events, the deeper structure, in a way that shows how this is connected to broader social and political issues, issues that can be found in movies, news items, political speeches, toys, etc. This approach uses the term 'discourse schema' (Machin and van Leeuwen, 2007) to emphasise the way that narratives are not simply stories, but also draw on socially shared ideas about the world, people and events. It emphasises the way that narratives are socially produced ideas about what kinds of sequences of events are possible and necessary. Importantly the term 'discourse schema' links this kind of analysis to the kinds of knowledge disseminated and legitimised in society by media texts. 'A discourse schema' is the activity sequences associated with the knowledge or discourse that is disseminated.

The term discourse here is taken in a Foucaultian (1978) sense of 'socially constructed knowledge'. Discourses have generally been treated as the broader ideas communicated by a text (van Dijk, 1993; Fairclough, 2000; Meyer and Wodak, 2001). These discourses can be thought of as models of the world. One example of such a discourse is that 'immigrants are a threat to a national culture' (as discussed in Chapter 3). This is a model of events associated with the notion that there is a unified nation and an identifiable national identity and culture. Normally this discourse encompasses a mythical proud history and authentic traditions. We can often see such headlines in right-wing tabloid newspapers. For example in the editorial from the *Daily Mail* (25.10.07) mentioned above titled 'Britain will be scarcely recognisable in 50 years if the immigration deluge continues'. In the context of Britain's evolving multicultural make-up and the diversity of ways of life and cultural values that have long been present based around social class, regional and other groupings how can we pin such factors down? Other discourses might represent immigration as a good thing, as a contribution to diversity and a challenge to stagnant tradition, as would be the view of these authors.

However, in much discourse theory it is argued that much knowing is based on doing. Fairclough (2000) and van Leeuwen (1996) have argued the case for discourses being closely interwoven with social practice. There is room then for the study of what exactly is the basis of such social practice. What activity sequences does such a social practice comprise?

Van Leeuwen and Wodak (1999) suggest that discourses have associated sequences of activity as well as related identities, values, settings and times. These sequences of activity can be communicated by a range of texts, types, genres and modes of communication, such as language, images and even sounds. We see this in terms of language in our example from the *Daily Mail*. This discourse involves participants: real British people and immigrants. It involves values or an 'indigenous culture'. It specifies that 'we' must 'defend' this culture. In terms of sequence of activity we find a social order that is under threat by an intruder. The editorial wisely avoids presenting the case for what should be done, but what is implied is clear, that the social order should defend itself. It is this sequence of activity that leads us to the underlying socio-cognitive schema that we can think of as the discourse activity schema. It is not the details of the specific case but the basic underlying structure that is the focus of attention here.

The analysis we present here is essentially similar to the Proppian narrative analysis used by Wright in that it deals with the narrated events. But there is also a difference since this analysis not only applies to narratives but also to all genres. It is not an analysis of the form of the text but of the knowledge that underlies the text. And the analysis should seek to reconstitute links with the activities that the text recontextualises. In other words what is the sequence of events that is present as in the case of the *Daily Mail* editorial or the children's play above?

It is important to note that even in the case of highly abstract texts we are able to find a narrative. Fabb (1997) notes that listeners will make an assumption that elements have some kind of sequential relationship even when they are very difficult to find and certainly not placed there deliberately. Social psychologists have shown that humans are predisposed to seeing narrative, as is demonstrated where people can describe character and plot for randomly moving shapes (Bruner, 1990) – for example, a bigger shape bullies a smaller one. Barthes (1977) stresses that as listeners and readers we are trained to place clauses and even words into causal chains. Todorov

(1990) explains the process whereby humans appear able to find a narrative or discourse activity sequence where none is clearly present, what he calls an 'ideological narrative'. This is the process whereby actions may not be linked to each other, yet we are able to interpret a link. This is one way, we might argue, that we often hear and interpret the lyrics of pop songs. We don't know exactly what they are saying but we decide they are about a struggle or a journey for example. Here the perceived narrative may be built through the connotations of certain words or the way that they are delivered and in part it is for this reason that it is so essential that we also look carefully at the description of character, as we do so later in this chapter. As Toolan (1988) points out, one important aspect of perceiving narrative are the predispositions a reader brings with them to the text, which will include their knowledge of kinds of people and the types of events to which they might be linked.

In summary, it is discourses that are the building blocks of narratives. Discourses allow different kinds of narratives to be composed. We can therefore analyse the sequences of activity to reveal the discourse building blocks and we can think of these sequences as discourse schemas. This level of analysis has been recognised in many other approaches to narrative such as those of Lévi-Strauss (1963), Wright (1975) and Bettelheim (1976). In film studies it has been carried out by writers like Nichols (1981) and Bell (1982) to look at non-fiction films. What was not necessarily made clear in this excellent work was the fact that these activity sequences or discourse schemas can be applied to different genres which might have slightly different communicative aims. The model we present here is, we emphasise, only one possible form of narrative analysis which we believe suits the aims of media studies. Other forms of analysis include looking for expectation of audiences in narratives (Hyvarinen, 1998; Bamberg, 2004), examining the genres of oral narratives (Riessman, 1990; Labov and Waletsky, 1997), narrative in social psychology (Bruner, 1990) and the structures of stories and myths (Leach and Aycock, 1983). These too provide valuable tools for the analysis and understanding of narrative. These all inform the model we present here and should be considered for a fuller understanding of the field.

Applying discourse schema analysis to different genres and modes

Let's think about the discourse schema to the headline analysed earlier in this chapter:

Two Israeli soldiers were killed by militants today in the Gaza strip. Israeli government pledges reprisals

There is a social order
(setting – Gaza)
↓
There is a disruption of social order
(there is an unprovoked attack)
↓
Order is restored
(there is punishment or eradication of threat)

It is this discourse schema that can be applied to a range of other genres. And it could clearly be used to tell a story, or create a political speech, or to play at soldiers. This is the same discourse schema that US Presidents, from Kennedy to George Bush, have used to talk about world terrorism – these often being threats that come from populations whose worlds have been under radical threat through the actions of the US for many decades. In the case of the news story the setting is relegated to after the events to give more impact. In a story genre we might have 'Once upon a time in the Gaza strip'. In a political speech we might get 'The security of the Free World is being slowly nibbled away at the periphery by world terrorists'. Here setting, or social order, is established by the use of the rhetorical device 'Free World'.

At the peak of Bush's War on Terror the same discourse could be found in advertisements produced by the government. A one-page advert appeared in the US Oprah Winfrey magazine (September 2004). It comprised a close-up of a rack of neatly arranged used women's shoes as if in a regular closet. Across the middle of the page was written 'But do you have a whistle?' Beneath the shoes was written 'Ready.gov. You have the things that make you happy. Get the things that make you prepared. Make a plan. Get a kit. Brought to you by The America Prepared Campaign, Inc.'

Here we have a different genre but find the same discourse schema being drawn upon. But in the genre of the caution advertisement, we find that different moves are used. This is a warning genre. This can be used in adverts to sell things that can be marketed as safety products such as quality tyres, or cars themselves that have advanced braking systems, showed swerving gracefully past a deer on a deserted road through a forest, cutting back to the sleeping child seen through the back window. The same can go for insurance policies or 'healthy' foods for children. In each case problems, or dangers, are chosen, in order to help to sell a product or particular kind of preventative measure. In the same way the 'America Prepared' advert allows one kind of solution to be presented as naturally linked to setting and threat. Another solution to the attacks on the US could be to seriously address US foreign policy. The discourse schema again here is as follows:

There is a society
(indicated here by the shoes rather than a place)
↓
There is a threat to that society
(this remains unmentioned but implied)
↓
Solution
(here we are left with the question as to whether you are part of the solution, which is the absurd – having a whistle!)

The discourse schema underpinning a movie: the example of *Black Hawk Down*

Here we look for the discourse schema in the movie *Black Hawk Down*. This is a US film about a US military mission in Somalia in the 1990s. In fact, as we will shortly explain, the movie excludes a number of key contextual issues and basically inverts what actually took place in this country, for which the US was entirely responsible in the first place due to its foreign policy of supporting and arming sympathetic rulers. This lead to massive internal warfare and famine in Somalia. The film depicts US Special Forces entering Somalia to address this problem, which in fact, evidence shows, they only made worse. What is important in this case is how a certain discourse theme is used to recontextualise these oversights.

We begin with a synopsis of the film. In this kind of analysis it is always useful to first break the text down into a sequence of events, before then proceeding to isolate the most basic sequence of activity.

1) We are shown gangster types taking control of a Red Cross food delivery. They shoot ruthlessly into the crowd of desperate civilians. This is watched by US soldiers from a helicopter who are unable to engage for political reasons.
2) We meet the US soldiers in stereotypical soldier representations, writing home, telling jokes.
3) We are told about the mission, which is to capture a warlord (named Aidid) who is creating the problems.
4) The soldiers are taken to the location.
5) There are a series of difficulties.
6) The soldiers get back to base.
7) The soldiers talk about the meaning of soldiering.

At the deeper level we can find the same discourse schema as we have already seen above in several cases:

There is a threat to social order
(by a warlord, Aidid)
↓

There are some special individuals who could provide a solution
(the elite soldiers)
↓

They are special individuals
(we hear about the men's commitment to each other)

In this film there is no complete closure in terms of the threat. But we learn about the special qualities of the soldiers and their commitment. We are told at the end that 'When the shit hits the fan and the bullets start flying politics goes out the window. All that matters is that man standing next to you'.

As with the advert we do not have closure in the discourse schema and we have a kind of warning. In the advert we need to be ready, by having our whistle. In the film we need the Special Forces. While the politics might be complex – we are told at various points about the way that bureaucratic/political red tape often makes things overly complex where clearly matters are simple – we can rely on these soldiers. We are also told at the end that around 20 US soldiers died, but also that thousands of Somalis died. They are indeed effective soldiers. But like the advert we focus more on the solution than the nature of the problem.

The events as depicted in the movie are in fact a long way from what really happened. Since the early 1990s Somalia has been seen as one important way for the US to have military bases close to the Middle East before an agreement was later reached with Saudi Arabia. At the time the Soviet Union was in a similar situation in neighbouring Ethiopia. Both the US and Soviets fed massive amounts of arms into these countries to support friendly rulers and to keep each other a bay. The 6 million deaths in Somalia were as a direct consequence of arming violent warlords and the huge population displacements that followed. It was only when the US left and ceased to provide 'aid' that relative stability returned to the country. And in fact it has been argued that the US army did nothing to help during the famine but rather provoked further population displacement and fighting. It was the Red Cross who provided most constructive aid, working diplomatically with different clan leaders and advising the US military to leave. However, the film *Black Hawk Down* claims the opposite in that we need the military, as unlike politicians and bureaucrats it has a simply and easily comprehensible morality.

Importantly, the same kind of analysis can be applied to news items and to a range of genres such as children's play.

The problem–solution discourse schema

We have focused so far mainly on a discourse schema for war. We now move on to a different kind of schema found here in a women's lifestyle magazine: the 'problem–solution' schema. Here we find a discourse schema, like that of the conflict resolution found above, which can make a sequence of activity appear natural, reasonable and all-encompassing when in fact it is highly ideological and selective.

Here are two extracts from the problem page of *Cosmopolitan* magazine (November 2001). The first is a case story and the second comprises the views of the magazine's own psychologist:

Liesbet (30): My partner often works late, as he has a very demanding job. I myself work from home. I used to start looking at the clock at 5. At 6 he would be home. A minute too late and I would be furious. I would throw his dinner in the bin, lock the front door at 5 past 6, go to bed alone at 10 and throw his duvet down the stairs. After many angry outbursts I realised the true reason for my anger. It was always me who had to clean up the mess in the house. I am also busy. I felt he didn't take my work seriously. Now he helps clean up in the evenings. And when I start my day in a clean house, I don't mind so much if he's late.

Lillien: you mention two extremes, and as so often, the middle road is best. The solution is to express your anger immediately or as soon as possible. In that way you rid yourself of it and the message hits home. An example: you have a shared job and your colleague always leaves your shared desk in a mess. You don't say anything, but you are extremely irritated. Your anger mounts up. Suddenly, you can't repress it anymore and there is an enormous outburst. Result: the message does not hit home because your reaction is excessive. And afterwards you will feel even worse. If you had acted in time, your colleague would have understood you and you would have felt better.

There are many differences between these two sections of text, the case and the expert counselling. The first deals with a personal relationship, the second with a work relationship. Yet both are based on the same activity sequence: Something upsetting happens. The upset person represses their anger, which has bad consequences leading to more anger. Finally, communication leads to the outcome where the solution is found. It is this problem–solution schema that dominates stories, advertisements and letters in women's lifestyle magazines. As in advertisements these can work, through making solutions seem natural and simple, to ideologically define what the problem is in the first place. We will explain this further shortly. First the schema can be illustrated as follows (the asterisk signifies a 'wrong solution' leading to a 'problematic outcome'):

Initial problem
(various)
↓
*Solution
(suppress anger)
↓
Problematic outcome
(physical and/or mental well-being affected)
↓
*Solution
(excessive bursts of anger)
↓
Problematic outcome
(problems continued and aggravated)
↓
Solution
(self-expression and communication)
↓
Final outcome
(problem solved)

We can see that this schema could fit a range of genres and modes. It could be realised through a story, a game or an advertisement, for example where a woman finds the correct solution for skin problems. But what is important to note here is that the problem, for which the solution is provided, is itself ideological and engineered to fit the solution. Magazines like *Cosmopolitan* work in part by providing women with snippets of empowering advice and expertise. In the case of the skin problems we could argue that this is in itself ideological because cosmetics producers seek to create the kinds of problems their products can resolve. As Western magazines move into new global territories, new sets of readers are able to find out that they should be thinking about kinds of skin problems that they had never before considered.

In terms of the extracts above, we could argue that in both cases there may be many other factors that have caused the difficult situation to occur. Take the case of the desk sharing. One of the authors has a colleague, a university lecturer, who had to share a desk when they were moved to a new building which was open plan and required all lecturers/researchers to 'hot desk'. The old building was sold as part of a process of managing finances and rebranding. Both she and her colleague found it stressful to share the desk as it gave them something further to juggle in their daily routines along with the usual business of teaching, writing emails, seeing students and doing administration. Both colleagues switched some of their work to home, but both found sharing a desk difficult. Formerly they had their own office space where they could leave their things, marking and books, and could take tutorials with students.

This change to 'hot desking' was part of a broader set of changes faced by British universities that involved waves of financial cuts and deprofessionalisation of academics. But in the expert part of the extract above there is no mention of actual context, nor of the concrete situations nor disposition of those involved. This suppression of contextual matters allows the solution of 'communicating' to appear more feasible.

Cameron (2000) has given a thorough analysis of the way that communicating about our problems has become a replacement for actual concrete solutions. What was formerly simply 'talking', a commonplace activity, has become rather a technical skill in its own right with professional experts able to tell us how it should be done. Cameron connects this to changes in the economy and relates it to human resources and management trends where workers are not trained in subject/job-specific skills but in attitudes and styles of work practice. So talk is increasingly codified and communication is seen as an end in itself rather than as a means to bring about change.

Many employees will find themselves stressed when faced with heavy work loads and new increased demands being put on them as staff and resources are cut back. Due to financial constraints there is little they, or their employers, can do about this. However, they will most likely find that they have the right to counselling where they are able to talk about their problems and therefore, the theory goes, understand their own responses, learn to manage their time and their stress better. In this *Cosmopolitan* text, actual concrete issues of work loads and requirements, along with the personalities of the individuals, are omitted. The issue of the domestic task sharing is easily resolved through communication irrespective of how much things like work, family and other personal issues may be making crushing demands on those involved. Of course, it is clear that for organisations this is all an advantage as concrete issues can be more easily sidelined.

This problem–solution schema can be applied across genres and contexts and in particular non-specialist experts are able to provide the details of just what the problems and solutions are. In this next example, from *Marie Claire* (May 2010), we are able to draw this out further. The following extract is from a careers advice section of the women's lifestyle magazine. The text was preceded by a photograph of a woman dressed in casual clothing, sat informally holding a note book looking off to the left of the frame towards a large window as if musing. The setting here is comprised mainly of a large window.

Yes, it is still possible to scale the corporate ladder in spite of layoffs. Here, Bob Calandra, coauthor of *How to Keep Your Job in a Tough Competitive Market*, offers advice for gingerly negotiating a title bump:

- **Act like the boss.** If your manager gets canned, set up a meeting with her supervisor right away. Calandra's no-fail script: 'I'm not looking to be promoted, but I also recognize no one wants chaos. I know the ins and outs of my boss's job, so feel free to tap me for any of her work while we're in this transitional phase.' To come off a hero, you can't appear as if you're expecting anything in return.
- **Pollyanna gets the corner office.** Be a relentless cheerleader for the company, even if it means irking coworkers. Your manager is bound to pick up on your positive outlook and use you as a model.
- **Mind your alliances.** If watercooler gossip reveals your cubemate is on management's hit list, publicly align yourself with the office hotshot, even if it makes you feel like Tracy Flick. Appearances matter – and you can always commiserate with your axed colleague over cocktails later (your treat).

Again here we find advice from an expert that seeks to fit all cases. A woman is faced with a situation where there are redundancies in her workplace. She is not encouraged to engage in collective action by seeking out union advice but to act alone and strategically. Here is the discourse schema:

There is a society
(indicated by the setting shown in the image and the generic word 'company')
↓
Initial problem
(institutional obstacle to success)
↓
Solution
(acquire skills and take control)
↓
Final outcome
(success)

Of course, a woman may face many institutional obstacles in a male-dominated world. She may have difficulty accessing certain places or activities, getting promotions, etc. But this is in principle due to issues of social and gender inequalities. But in women's lifestyle magazines such as *Cosmopolitan* and *Marie Claire* this is usually formulated as a personal problem and the social and political issues behind it are rarely dealt with explicitly. And in this case, as is also usual, we find an absence of any kind of contextual personal issue such as life situation, personal dispositions and abilities. In the problem–solution schema one size fits all.

We can ask what is omitted in this schema, in the same way that we saw what was omitted earlier in the case of the movie *Black Hawk Down*. Here we have a situation where the woman's colleagues are losing their jobs yet this is represented not as a problem in itself for others or for the woman to deal with on their behalf. It is presented simply as an institutional obstacle to her own success. The solution is to acquire a new set of skills. Typically in these lifestyle stories these skills are related to manipulating others or to issues of self-presentation or superficial organisational skills.

We can see from the text that setting is also unclear. Here the setting is provided simply by an informal environment in the photograph that is used to connote or symbolise 'work'. In Proppian terms this provides the first stage of the discourse schema since it is the disruption of the regular social order in the workplace where promotions could be naturally gained that has triggered the sequence of events. In the text we also find lack of specificity with the mention of your 'company' and 'watercooler'. This is clearly a generic office environment. The woman is not told in specifics how she can up her work load or produce new methods of work with the reduced staffing. She improves her situation by alignments, self-promotion and by being positive.

One important question to ask here is how such texts appear as anything other than extremely callous and selfish. In order to answer this we need to take a step in the direction of Barthes' (1977) 'indices', in other words we need to think more about the details that make up the narrative, the characters and details of the action. In the case of *Black Hawk Down* it will be the way that US soldiers are represented as attractive and humane that will help to sell the narrative where thousands of local inhabitants of a town are killed. In this *Marie Claire* article too we can look closer at the participants. As Toolan (1988) points out, character too is key to the way that people grasp narratives. Narrative structure can be more of an idea that is created in the heads of the reader or viewer as they come across key elements. Toolan gives the example of readers coming across the introduction of a 'beggar' in a story about Victorian Britain (1988: 98). He points out that this in itself sets up a narrative sequence in that we are likely to assume that this person represents some kind of social injustice which at some point will become an issue.

When we wish to understand the role of characters in a narrative we can do two things. First we can simply list the characters. Second, we can then assess and classify them. In the example of the movie *Black Hawk Down* above, characters were the US soldiers, the enemy militia and civilians. The last two of these regularly blurred (where, for example, children were armed) in order to show the complexity of the world the soldiers need to deal with.

In the *Marie Claire* text the characters are: Boss, Manager, Management, Supervisor, Calandra, Office Hotshot, I, You, Her, We, Pollyanna, Cheerleader, Co-workers, Colleague, Tracy Flick, Cubemate. We can arrange these into four categories. The first are more formal work terms, the second more trendy language, the third fictional characters, and lastly personal

Table 7.1 Participants in the *Marie Claire* text

Boss	Office Hotshot	Calandra	I
Manager	Cheerleader	Pollyanna	You
Management	Cubemate	Tracy Flick	Her
Supervisor			We
Co-workers			
Colleague			

pronouns. Placing categories of participants in a table as in Table 7.1 can help to visualise them.

What we can now do is consider what kinds of character features each of these groups and individuals brings to the narrative, what is in linguistics called 'distinctive feature analysis' (Fowler, 1977; Bolinger and Sears, 1981). On the one hand we have a set of participants that we might expect when dealing with the work environment as in 'boss', 'management', 'supervisor' and 'colleague'. Although markedly absent here is any reference to trade unions. In this text the woman who is addressed acts alone and strategically. She is not concerned about the possibility of further redundancies or how she and her colleagues might work together to prevent further job losses.

These work-type characters place the events into a formal work environment, although we should note that there are no more specific terms to define exactly what kind of worker the woman is. We are not told what particular job is performed by these people, only that they are generic 'supervisors', etc.

On the other hand it is the second column of participants that play the role of lightening the topic. If characters were only of a formal workplace nature this may indeed have made the text too cynical. But this is changed on the one hand through the use of terms for participants such as 'office hotshot', 'cubemate' and 'cheerleader'. This use of the latest expressions plays an important part in indicating that this is an up-to-date way of seeing the world. This is a crucial part of lifestyle discourse, which is harnessed to the 'latest-thing' discourse of consumerism (Machin and van Leeuwen, 2007).

On the other hand the tone of the narrative is lightened since some of the characters are fictionalised as we find in the third column of the table. 'Tracy Flick' is a fictional character portrayed by actress Reese Witherspoon in a comedy movie called *Election*. In this movie Flick is largely unpopular as she is ambitious and self-focused but likeable and is played by a very attractive Hollywood actress. Pollyanna is a girl from children's fiction who is 'naughty' and assertive but in an endearing way. By drawing on these fictional characters the analysis offered by *Marie Claire* is able to sidestep the real concrete issues of industrial dispute but is able to draw on connotations of assertiveness, likeability and individuality.

We can imagine the effect were this kind of use of characters made in an actual case of an industrial dispute. It would appear bizarre if a news story of a strike at a manufacturing plant referred to workers as 'Pollyannas'. Yet in the world created by lifestyle magazines real-world terms and fiction blend seamlessly.

Finally, what is important in terms of character in this narrative is the use of 'I' and 'you' as found in the fourth column of the table. The use of personal pronouns is common in advertising and also in conversational language (Machin and van Leeuwen, 2007). This text claims to be neither but is drawing on both kinds of language. In advertising these pronouns help to personalise products and producers and their relationship with the consumer. For example, an advertisement for mortgages might read: 'We agree with your wife. You can afford a new house'. The conversational style of speaking to 'you' also prevents this from reading as authoritative knowledge, but rather as the language of an expert who speaks closer to the level of the addressee. This language therefore aims to inspire trust not on the basis of prescribed status as is the case in the professions, but in terms of its claim to personal experience, which is communicated partly through being on your level by means of personal pronouns and partly through the up-to-date language.

What is also interesting about the strategies found in this text is that while it contains personal address through the personal pronoun 'you', at the same time personal characteristics are suppressed. The text creates a world of generic types, the 'Tracy Flick', the 'Pollyanna', the 'office gossip', the generic 'boss'. Yet in reality how we experience our work lives depends on who we are, our dispositions, our appearance, our qualifications and also those of our boss and colleagues. In these texts, as we often find in advertising, the world is reduced to a simple problem–solution formula. None of this envisages personal issues. Everyone can use the problems and solutions offered and they are universally applicable. Everything is displaced to a set of strategies.

Doing a research project with discourse schema analysis

Discourse schema analysis can be carried out on a sample of texts as in the case of Wright's (1975) study of westerns. Wright compared films from two different periods of time in order to draw out the differences. This would follow usual sampling procedures. The sample could be defined as including texts from over a time period or that dealt with a particular topic. Machin and van Leeuwen (2007) collected international versions of the women's lifestyle magazine *Cosmopolitan* over two months. They then translated a sample from these and compared the discourse schemas.

Discourse schema analysis is a qualitative form of analysis since to some extent it involves interpretations of what can be viewed as the most basic sequences of activity in a text. It also involves a qualitative assessment of characters in the texts. But in the tradition of Critical Discourse Analysis it can be seen as one further way that we bring an analytical framework to texts that encourages us to ask a more systematic set of questions. But as a qualitative form of analysis the researcher need not seek high numbers for purposes of representativeness but only ensure that they have enough examples to feel satisfied that they have indeed identified a pattern in the manner stated by Wright. On the other hand a discourse schema analysis might be carried out alongside other methods where the aim is an in-depth analysis of one or several films, or other media such as computer games. Semiotic analysis and Critical Discourse Analysis could be carried out to look at the details of the text and discourse schema analysis used to reveal the basic activity sequences.

Summary

- Discourse schema analysis is largely interpretive but can draw our attention to the basic underlying structures of any media text.
- Discourse schema analysis is used in order to look for the basic activity schema that is the doing part of the knowledge part of discourse. As such it is used to reveal the basic sequences of events that frame how a particular practice should reasonably be carried out.
- Discourse schema analysis is not the same as story analysis. It draws on narrative theories that seek the underlying structures to look at activity sequences across different genres of communication and across different modes of communication. A stage in a sequence may be represented by a sentence, a sequence of a movie or an image.
- When carrying out discourse schema analysis we should first attempt to summarise the basic events that make up a text. We can then take this to the next stage of looking for the underlying schema.
- The sampling of data for this kind of narrative analysis, in the tradition of Critical Discourse Analysis, involves collecting a sample that will depend on the aims of the research. For example, a piece of research may seek to compare the schemas in representations of war reporting over two separate periods of time. The researcher would collect a sample of stories from each period and carry out analysis until they were certain that they had identified a pattern. It is common in Critical Discourse Analysis to collect a 'corpus' of texts, which may include all those available on a topic and then select a number for closer analysis that are presented as representative of the wider corpus.

- Discourse schema analysis may be carried out alongside other forms of discourse and semiotic analysis.

Further reading

Wright, W. (1975). *Sixguns and Society: A Structural Study of the Western*. Berkeley, CA: University of California Press.
Classic study of structural comparisons of movies.

Machin, D., and van Leeuwen, T. (2003). Global Schemas and Local Discourses in *Cosmopolitan, Journal of Sociolinguistics*, 7/4, 493–512.
A look at the various ways that a problem–solution schema can be used for different topics and genres.

Hyvarinen, M. (2008). Analysing Narratives and Story-Telling, in Aluutari, P., Bickman, L. and Brannen, J. (Eds.) *The SAGE Handbook of Social Research Methods*. London, Sage, pp.477–60.
An excellent overview and explanation of the different kinds of narrative research done in a variety of fields.

Hornig, S. (1990). Television's NOVA and the Construction of Scientific Truth, *Critical Studies in Mass Communication*, 7/1, 11–23.
Looks at the narratives and binary oppositions of science documentaries.

CHAPTER 8

Symbols, semiotics and spectacle: analysing photographs

While photographs form a major part of media communication there has, in comparison with other areas of media research, been a relative lack of attention to developing a strict methodology for their analysis. Even books whose titles suggest otherwise such as *Triumph of the Image* (Mowlana, Gerbner and Schiller, 1992) and *Visualising Deviance* (Ericson, Baranek and Chan, 1987) in fact provide little in the way of models for analysis. Other volumes such as *Visual Studies* (Elkins, 2003), *The Visual Culture Reader* (Mirzoeff, 1998) and *The Photography Reader* (Wells, 2002) contain excellent essays about the nature of looking at photographs and how historically we came to see them as offering factual information rather than simply offering one particular point of view at a particular moment. But again there is little sense of how to study them systematically. In fact most analysis of photographs has been in the area of cultural studies where 'close readings' are given, but they are very much a matter of open interpretation.

This chapter brings together a number of approaches from traditional semiotics and linguistics-based Multimodal Critical Discourse Analysis (Machin and Mayr, 2012) in order to show how we can produce much more systematic analyses of photographs. What follows are a set of guidelines for how in the first place we can *describe* what we see in photographs. Often this level of investigation is what is overlooked and the analyst jumps immediately to *interpretation*. This is because in academic culture we often value interpretation over description. We criticise student essays for being 'too descriptive'. But description is a vital level of analysis in the case of photographs. So this chapter is for the most part a guide in how to really be able to 'see' what we are looking at.

The methods described in this chapter are to some extent qualitative and are intended for detailed analysis of a smaller number of cases. Yet also, since they draw on linguistic forms of analysis, they have a quantitative aspect as we describe actual concrete features of photographs. So some of the tools in this chapter can lend themselves to quantitative research and can be aligned to content analysis as described in Chapter 5. At the end of the chapter we will discuss specifically what a research project using this approach would look like in terms of such aspects as sample size. But as with other chapters in this book it should become clear just how this approach should be used by the way the examples are dealt with and the models applied.

Here we draw on a number of key observations of Barthes (1977) as regards the simple contents of images and on a number of ideas from the Multimodal Analysis of Kress and van Leeuwen (1996), who look at viewer positioning, gaze, classification of participants, representation of action and how photographs and elements and features in photographs might be thought of as more real or less real. We also look at the way that we can apply Halliday's (1994) observation on documenting verb processes in language to think about what we see happening in photographs.

The semiotics of Barthes

Barthes offers a simple set of questions we can ask of an image. Simply, these allow us to think about what ideas and values, the people, the places and objects in images stand for. But he also points out that at one level we must describe carefully what we see in the photograph independent of our interpretation of it. In fact, this first level of analysis can be the most difficult.

Denotation

At Barthes' first level of analysis, often overlooked, we ask what an image depicts. Literally, what do we see? Or in his terminology, what does the image *denote*? Photographs of a family member or of a house simply depict or denote these things. They represent a particular person and a particular place respectively. A news photograph might document or *denote* a group of people in a particular place. Figure 8.1 denotes two women in a room. It also denotes particular colours, objects and a setting with a specific kind of lighting and different levels of focus. So asking what an image denotes is asking: who and/or what is depicted here? What follows in the rest of this chapter are tools for drawing our attention to this process of denotation. It is surprising how difficult we can find this activity. But it is through enhancing this skill that we can develop our ability to produce more accurate interpretations.

Of course, we never really see any image in this kind of innocent way as simply depicting something. Images usually mean something to us. Writers like Bal (2006) in fact take this idea of how images or any of their parts can trigger different meanings for us. But denotation, for Barthes (1977), is one way to think about the first level of meaning in a photograph and it can help to direct our observations. Even at the level of denotation a photograph can

Figure 8.1   Women in an office (Two women with a laptop. Per Magnus Persson/Johner Images/ Getty Images. © 2012 Getty Images. All rights reserved.)

define the subject. For example, whether we photograph a person alone or as part of a group can influence whether they are shown as an individual or as a type, whether we are encouraged to identify with an individual or just see them as an anonymous part of a crowd. Denoting people in particular places or in groups, from different angles, in distance or close-up, will have an effect on how we will see them. But all these too can be carefully described and classified as we will show later in this chapter.

Connotation

Here we ask, what ideas and values are communicated through what is represented, and through the way in which it is represented? Once we have identified what is depicted we can ask what it means, what are the cultural associations of elements, features in, or qualities of the image? Barthes (1973), in *Mythologies*, calls connotative meanings 'myths'. Myth is the concept used to express the condensed associations of what is represented in an image or element or feature in an image. Myth here is very much like the term 'discourse' used by Foucault (1972). He used this term to describe the kinds of taken-for-granted models of the world that are broadly shared in society to understand how things work. These models will generally be pretty much arbitrary and will generally reflect particular interests of groups and powerful individuals. So, for example, in a society we might have a broadly accepted discourse of crime and punishment where it is understood that bad people commit crimes and are appropriately punished by being placed in prison. However, in fact, it is for the most part the case that prisons are filled with a society's disadvantaged and those from lower socio-economic groups. In the USA, for example, there are a disproportionate amount of black men in prison. This problematises the discourse that frames crime as being committed by bad people who should be punished. This in turn raises questions about the nature of how we organise our societies and why some people end up committing acts that are defined as bad. Barthes would call these accepted models of the world 'myths' as they are taken-for-granted models of the world that are basically unfounded.

In Figure 8.1 therefore we can ask what meanings, myths or discourses are associated with the kind of women we find, the objects they carry and the colours we see? However, before we take this step of analysis we need to first begin to break the image down into its components and qualities in order to carry out more accurate observation. We need to take a step in the direction of more accurately describing what is denoted.

Barthes listed a number of key carriers of connotation. In turn we look at poses, gaze, objects and settings.

Carriers of Connotation

Poses

According to Barthes there exists a dictionary of poses in our heads. These poses often carry connotations drawn from association. For example, a soldier, at attention, stands straight, rigid and tense. The pose is regular and precise. But why is it that a particular posture can connote discipline and respect? There are in fact a number of what we can call 'metaphorical associations' taking place here. Arnheim (1969) has shown that metaphorical association is at the core of much visual communication. For example, we might make a small distance between our thumb and forefinger to represent how close we were to verbally berating someone. In fact, no physical proximity was involved in how close we felt at all, as it was simply a feeling of emotion. But the representation, the comparison, allows us to visualise this feel and the way we felt close to a particular action.

Another typical use of metaphorical association in visual communication is in the shape and form of letters used in advertising. We will normally find that an elegant product will use a taller, slimmer, lighter font than a product that wishes to communicate durability, which will use a wider, heavier-looking letter shape. Here the elegant product can use the association of height with status and slimness with lack of heaviness, which is important to signify elegance. In contrast the durable product will wish to avoid associations of lightness and elegance and emphasise stability. These associations come from our experiences of things in the real world. Wider, blockier objects are generally more stable and slimmer objects lighter, and possibly more agile.

Figure 8.2 Woman with attitude (Young business-woman standing on desk, portrait. Tim Robberts/The Image Bank/Getty Images. © 2012 Getty Images. All rights reserved.)

The same kinds of metaphorical associations can be found in poses and there are a number of qualities that we can look for. The first is rigidity versus looseness. In the case of a pose where we make our body very straight and rigid this emphasises us controlling it consciously. This can have the association of discipline, subjection to the confines and restraint of authority. This is why standing in this manner can suggest the machine-like nature of the army particularly where we find many people striking the same pose. In contrast we might find a young teenager standing very loosely with their shoulders drooping. This may be no less deliberate than the rigid pose, but can connote the opposite of control and rigidity.

Figure 8.2 was taken from an image archive where it was classified under the search terms 'women' and 'attitude'. A search of the archive under these terms or for 'women and confidence' throws up many images of women staring at the camera with their heads slightly to one side and hands on hips. In these images 'attitude' is depicted therefore not through a person's attitudes to a particular issue but rather by the pose that they strike.

Therefore what in fact is a mental process is represented by pose alone. The pose we find here is one that is rigid and controlled and designed to look deliberate. It is this which communicates 'attitude'. Were the same pose done but with loose shoulders and neck it would not convey the same level of determination.

Another question we can ask of a pose is the extent to which it involves the taking up of space. In the pose in Figure 8.2 we find the woman taking up space by placing her feet apart. We generally associate taking up of space with confidence and lack of inhibition, although of course it can have another meaning, of arrogance and insensitivity. In Figure 8.2 this taking up space, spreading oneself around, suggests lack of timidity. The woman indicates that she has the confidence to take up space. We can imagine the opposite effect if her feet were placed close together and her arms pulled in close to her chest. This would suggest timidity and vulnerability.

Figure 8.2 also depicts the woman as leaning slightly away from the viewer. A person depicted as moving into or out of our space can have metaphorical reference to physical proximity in the everyday world. Of course, this can either mean something positive or invasive. Imagine a picture of a policeman leaning over a desk towards you as opposed to one leaning away, which might mean them distancing themselves from you. A news reader would maintain a neutral position in order to suggest no personal involvement. Imagine if a news reader were to deliver the news leaning back away from us, or leaning right over towards us. Leaning back, as well as suggesting relaxation, might suggest lack of engagement with the viewer and therefore lack of trust. Leaning forwards would suggest excessive intimacy and excessive desire to persuade us of something.

Angularity and curvature can also communicate important meanings. In Figure 8.3 while the woman takes up space she also brings her hips slightly to one side. This creates curvature, which is associated with femininity rather than masculinity. Again in terms of metaphorical association we often find in the letter forms used for products in advertisements that those aimed at male consumers use more angular fonts whereas those targeting women use curved fonts. Curved fonts suggest something softer and more organic, whereas angular fonts suggest something more aggressive and mechanical. The pose of the woman in Figure 8.3 therefore suggests confidence along with femininity. There is also slightly less rigidity communicated because of this curvature.

Figure 8.4 draws on the meanings of poses that are open as opposed to closed. In the image archive from which this was taken this photograph was classified as 'women' and 'freedom'. A search under these terms throws up thousands of images of women jumping or whirling, with their arms or legs out wide. This pose, particularly the openness of the body, is used to connote

Figure 8.3 Woman and leadership/confidence (Portrait of an assertive female CEO standing with two businessmen. Rayman/ Digital Vision/Gerry Images. © 2012 Getty Images. All rights reserved.)

freedom. In contrast to the containment of the pose in Figure 8.2 we get a sense of joy and energy. The idea of freedom, which can mean many things – freedom from financial worry or oppression, concerns about job security, freedom of thought – is metaphorically represented through the freedom from restriction of physical movement. So images of women jumping in the air, or raising their hands, can be used for health products, insurance policies, etc., to connote freedom from worries. But it is not sufficient to see them only jumping. A photograph of a woman jumping but with her body otherwise closed, with arms pressed against her sides, will suggest that she is somehow closed to the outside world.

Also important in these images representing freedom is a sense of comfort. Freedom can also be communicated by a woman depicted relaxing on a beach. Here, of course, the pose will not be rigid, but rather relaxed, which will indicate lack of control and give a sense of inner comfort. In Figure 8.4 the pose communicates not only that the woman is relaxed but also that she is comfortable with herself.

In summary there are seven questions we can ask of a pose to help us to consider its meaning potential:

- To what extent do they take up space or not?
- Is the body open or closed?
- Is the body aligned and controlled or liberated?
- Is there an emphasis on relaxation or intensity?
- Is there a sense of comfort or discomfort?
- Is angularity or curvature emphasised?
- Do they appear to lean/move towards or away from the viewer?

Figure 8.4 Woman in meadow (Young woman in white dress dancing in meadow. Mike Timo/ Photographer's Choice/ Getty Images. © 2012 Getty Images. All rights reserved.)

Analysing gaze

One important feature of the photographs we have considered so far is whether or not the person/people depicted are looking out at us, or if not where they are looking exactly. In pictures, as in real life, the depicted people can *look* at the viewer, so that there is symbolic 'contact' or 'interaction' between the viewer and the people depicted. They can also be depicted as *not* looking at the viewer, so that this kind of 'contact' or 'direct address' is absent. Kress and van Leeuwen (1996: 127–8) offer a way to think more precisely about how these two kinds of images work for us by drawing on Halliday's (1985) notion of speech acts. Halliday claims that when we speak we do one of four basic things:

1) Offer information (e.g. 'I am busy today')
2) Offer services and goods (e.g. 'Do you want any help?')
3) Demand information (e.g. 'Is this broken?')
4) Demand goods and services (e.g. 'Could you help?')

In each of these cases the listener will be aware that there is an expected response.

Kress and van Leeuwen (1996: 129) do not think that photographs could realise all of these speech acts but suggest that we could think about the way they work in terms of two *image acts* – 'offer' and 'demand'. Image acts, like speech acts, are realised by what are called 'mood systems'. For example, in speech, commands are realised by the imperative mood as in, 'Don't be silly!' An offer of information can be realised by the indicative mood as in, 'You can't live off that amount of money.' In images we can find both acts of offer and demand. And also we can find different kinds of moods of address.

In Figure 8.2 the viewer is addressed by the gaze of the woman on the desk. This has two functions. On the one hand it creates a visual form of address. The viewer is acknowledged. On the other it produces an image act. So the image is used to do something to the viewer. This is what we can think of as a 'demand image'. It asks something of you in an imaginary relationship.

The kind of demand, or the mood of address, will be determined by other factors. In the case of Figure 8.2 we find a rigid posture that takes up space with the lower body, yet which is also closed at the top. The expression is serious. She clearly has an issue and is making some kind of stand. In this case we may relate with the woman in terms of associating with her issue, or as being the person who should respond to it. In contrast, she could have had a bodily posture that suggests welcome through, say, open arms, or more aggression through clenched fists being placed on their hips. All of these allow the image to define its relationship to the viewer.

In real life we know what happens when someone smiles at us or when someone strikes such a pose. We must smile back or take their anger seriously in each case. We understand the response in the case of images although we know of course that there will not be the same kind of immediate consequences if we do not respond. Of course, as in the case of speech acts, we may reject what is being demanded of us. But in this imaginary relationship we will recognise that there is a particular kind of demand.

Where the represented people do not look at the viewer there is a different kind of effect. Here there is no contact made with the viewer and no demand made of them. In this case the viewer can observe the people represented since they are not called upon for a response. Kress and van Leeuwen (1996: 124) call this kind image therefore an 'offer'. This is because the viewer is offered the images as information. In Figure 8.1 the woman with the laptop does not engage with us, nor invite us to share in her experiences. We are simply observers. We have no relationship with her.

In offer images it is important to consider where the person is looking. In Figure 8.1 the women look at the computer. But often people are depicted looking off frame. In such cases the viewer is invited to imagine their thoughts or mood. We are invited as an observer to imagine their thoughts, although if they do not look at us no response or action is expected. What that person is thinking about, whether in a news item, feature or advertisement will be shaped by the caption such as 'Worried about your pension?' Here off frame represents off world, or inner thoughts, even though, in fact, the image may be a cropped version of a scene where the person was actually looking at something specific.

When those represented do look off frame there is also meaning potential in terms of *where* they look. This can be based on the simple metaphorical association of up and down, where up is positive, powerful, high status and down is negative, low energy, low status. In Western culture up and down have strong metaphorical associations. We say 'I am feeling down' or that 'things are looking up'. We can say that a person 'has their head in the clouds', or is 'down to earth'. We have upper and lower classes and people with higher status are often seated higher than those with lower status. In images we often find politicians, when represented positively, looking off frame and slightly upwards. In images in women's magazines in contrast we often find women looking slightly downwards, alongside captions like 'Can you trust your boyfriend?', although where the woman is looking upwards the same topic can be made more upbeat. The politician looks upwards to lofty ideals and to high status whereas the woman in the magazine is worried that things are bad and requires the advice of the magazine to work things out.

Where people in images look directly outwards, although not directly at the viewer, this can communicate a sense of dealing with issues straight on. Again these meanings will depend on other features like facial expression and pose.

Objects

Our second carrier of connotation is objects. In the first place, as with poses, we need to describe what we see in the photograph. We can then think about the meaning potential of this object. Figure 8.1 was also sourced from an image archive, this time using a search for 'women' and 'office'. It is an image that could typically be found in the careers section of a women's lifestyle magazine. In this image the objects are the laptop, the sleek clothing and hair and also the lack of other objects that normally make up the everyday clutter of a work environment. While we know nothing about these women, these objects tell us something about them due to their associations. We have no idea where these women are, yet these props suggest a particular kind of work and therefore create specific identities for the women. These identities would have been different had the objects been a desk-based PC rather than a laptop, had their desks been cluttered with files, had there been a landline telephone sat on the desk. An image such as that in Figure 8.1 is more likely to depict women holding mobile phones rather than landline phones. Both the laptop and the mobile telephone suggest a kind of work that is independent and not based solely in an office, or which does not tie a person to one particular desk. Even if this image were to be used in a promotion or advert to reference work in general, it is able to connote something of independence and mobility. This also suggests other values such as work being a challenge, creative and dynamic. A PC and a landline telephone would tend to suggest a more mundane job where there was less mobility and less independence. Figure 8.2 has a slightly different meaning because of the presence of the desk, which does have a landline telephone. This suggests a more static role for the person who works there. Often in women's lifestyle magazines about 'issues in the workplace' there will be no concrete reference to any actual kind of job. But images will show women with mobile phones and laptop computers who may be dressed in high fashion.

Pose too is important in Figure 8.1 in the context of the work setting. The women do not appear to be slumped over the machine carrying out repetitive work. Both appear loose and relaxed and are sat in a manner that does not suggest they will be positioned there for long, as if this may have been spontaneous sharing of ideas. Along with the laptop, this too also suggests a workplace where these women have freedom and control. There is no one watching over them and regulating how they work. This will be in contrast to the work experiences of the majority of the readers of the lifestyle magazines.

Important too, in Figure 8.2, are the objects that are missing – such as files, pens, papers. Imagine if an administrator in a university were to stand on her desk full of her ongoing work. This would give a very different meaning. It would appear silly and give the impression even of mental instability. Here the lack of other objects serves to decontextualise the image and therefore increases its symbolic role.

In Figure 8.3 the shoes worn by the woman are important, as well, of course, as the suits worn by her and the two men. The suits obviously tell us that they are professional business people. But the shoes have particular salience. We will look more at how we judge the relative importance of objects in photographs shortly. But for now we can say that objects that either seem out of place or have particular cultural resonance should be considered as salient in any image. The shoes have very high heels and the woman wears her trousers short to emphasise them. This photograph emphasises power through the suit but at the same time shows the woman as seductive and sexual. This is different to Figure 8.2, in which the woman is not seductive. In Figure 8.3 we can see that the shoes work in a similar way to the pose. The woman strikes a confident pose but one where she curves her hips. She wears a suit but with shoes ready for seduction. Here power is not independent from her sexuality. Again in women's lifestyle magazines it is common to find women carrying objects that connote independence and agency yet which at the same time signify traditional feminine seduction through make-up, clothing and posture. Of course in such lifestyle magazines these are the ways that readers can themselves align alongside the core values of the magazine.

In photographs composed for advertisements we find objects chosen very carefully for the connotations that they carry. In an advert for a refrigerator in a women's magazine, for example, we find a chrome refrigerator in an empty room. In front of it are two transparent plastic shopping bags containing coloured peppers. We see a well-dressed attractive man carrying another of the same kind of bag, also containing bright vegetables, bringing them to the refrigerator. We can think of the meaning of these objects.

We can ask why is the refrigerator chrome? At the time of writing this look was currently fashionable but also due to its lack of paint finish therefore openly presents its metal-ness. The use of chrome was fashionable in expensive shops and restaurants in London usually combined with larger luxurious empty spaces, connoting modernity, clean simple lines and surfaces. The peppers add colour to the composition and the plastic bags allow them to be seen, although since only half full they connote light, easy to carry shopping. This allows us to imagine that this fridge is not hard work to fill with heavy shopping. And the man is not stacking it with beer or ready-made meals but crisp, vibrant vegetables. For a British audience peppers rather than carrots and peas would connote a more cosmopolitan and sophisticated cuisine.

One way to work out the meaning carried by objects is through the 'commutation test'. This means simply replacing the object with something else and then imagining how the meaning is changed. If it is radically changed then this is an indication that the object carries important meanings. So we can imagine the change of meaning were the fridge in the previous example black and dull rather than chrome and shiny, if the bags had been filled with alcohol, had the space been cluttered with other household objects and there was a woman carrying the bags. In the images described above we could imagine the differences in meaning if we were to replace a pose with a more relaxed one or remove a feature such as the window in Figure 8.1. This would help us to think more clearly about the meaning that such an object brings.

Settings

Barthes also pointed to the important connotations carried by the settings we see in images. In Figure 8.4 the woman is depicted in an area of grass and flowers with trees in the background. Here nature is depicted. But we can ask what kind of nature this is and what this connotes. Would the effect be the same had the setting been a rocky mountainside, farmland or were it a bleak overcast day or were she in the middle of bushes or trees? First of all, this is a kind of nature associated with leisure and strolling, perhaps a park. It is a space free of other objects in nature such as bushes and rocks. The open space itself is used to connote freedom from physical restriction. This can be used in advertising, promotional and lifestyle images to connote freedom from psychological restrictions such as work and financial pressures as noted above.

Other promotional photographs might contain different images of nature. For example, we might see a car travelling on a road through rocky terrain or a desert. Here nature can mean power and adventure. Rather than metaphorical association the meaning in this case comes from provenance, in other words the established cultural associations of adventure in the context of such landscapes. Hansen (2002) described the way that advertisements draw on a rather predictable repertoire of depictions of nature. He shows that nature is never presented as a threat or dangerous but is used to connote a number of themes such as freedom, the authentic, nature as a challenge (manhood/sport/endurance), nature as intrinsically good (healthy, fresh). In other words different kinds of nature settings can be used to bring different kinds of associations.

In Figure 8.3 we find an interior setting where there are a number of important features. The first is the size of the space in which the participants are positioned. We can ask how this image would be different were the three participants placed in front of a very small entrance hall. Space means luxury and of course wealth and power. Were this woman, striking this particular pose, with her heels and slightly short trousers, positioned in the entrance to a small shop her meaning would be changed. The glass and shiny surfaces are also important in this image. In universities throughout the UK business and management studies departments are now being rebuilt with glass buildings or glass wall partitions. On the one hand in Western thought there is a metaphorical association of knowledge and truth with transparency, and lack of knowledge with obscurity. In language we say 'it is becoming clear to me now'. The association here is with vision. On the other hand glass and shiny surfaces are associated with modernism, itself aligned with truth in Western thought. So business often wishes to associate itself with clarity of vision and with modernity.

There is one other kind of setting that is increasingly important in the photographs that we see in magazines and newspapers. Figure 8.1 is an example of this. Here there is no actual identifiable setting so to speak. We might easily assume these women are seen in a work environment were it to be used in a 'careers' feature in a magazine. But apart from the laptop there is no concrete indicator of where they are. We can refer to such settings as 'decontextualised'. In such cases the attention of the viewer is drawn to the role played by the participants and the props. Were these women in a real work environment with piles of papers, files and personal items this would not have been the case. The role of such decontextualised images tends to be more symbolic than documentary. They record not a particular moment in time, nor a particular event, but are used to symbolise an idea or a concept. The more an image is decontextualised the greater its symbolic role.

In Figure 8.1 the setting is partly provided by the window. This window suggests transparency, light and optimism and is one way to include a scene of a bright sunny sky. The window itself is of a kind not characteristic of new office spaces but those converted from older buildings. This loft or ex storage/factory space itself has connotations of renewal and modernisation but also importantly the exclusive inner city.

Also important in images such as Figure 8.1 is the role of colour coordination, which serves to create links between the elements and adds to the stylised look of the image. So there will be harmony between the colours worn by the participants and with objects and the setting. Often in magazine pages where such images are used colours will be taken from the image and used for fonts and borders on the page. This adds a feeling of cleanness, order and simplicity.

Generally in these kinds of images, such as in Figures 8.1 and 8.3, the colours themselves will have also been flattened and saturated digitally. Flattened colours are simplified by taking out the normal play of light on them created through the way it falls on folds in material and different shapes. You will see this if you look at how the light falls on your own clothing. This simplification creates a clean, tidy, uncluttered look. This effect has become a standard feature of the feel-good world presented in advertising, promotional material and lifestyle magazines. Often the modulation of colours, that is the way that light brings out the details on surfaces, is exaggerated in order to give images a gritty or documentary feel.

Saturated colours are where the colour itself has been enriched, so that it appears fuller and deeper. Saturated colours are associated with emotional intensity whereas more muted colours with reserve and moderation. Often these kinds of promotional photographs contain mainly muted colours with one exciting saturated colour placed in several places in the image. It is not uncommon to find this practice now in news feature photographs.

Of course people themselves can constitute the setting. In Figure 8.3 the two men in the background could be identified as part of the setting in which the woman appears. Standing in front of them we might imagine them to be subordinate to her in some way. We can identify people in the image who can be classified as part of the setting as these will not be interacting with the main actor. The main actor will be identified through salience. Of course in a photograph it might be that an object itself is most salient as in adverts and promotions. To work out exactly what is the most important element in a photograph or visual composition such as an advertisement we can consult a number of principles of salience.

Salience: identifying the subject of the images

In this next section we look at some basic principles of salience taken from van Leeuwen (2005) and Machin (2007a). These are ways that we can identify what is the central or most important element in a photograph or composition.

Potent cultural symbols

The first way to identify what might be the salient element in an image is to look for potent cultural symbols. These are often central in telling the viewer how to read an image. In Figure 8.1 the laptop has salience as it is a potent cultural symbol. The laptop and loft-type window help to connote mobility, independence and therefore a high-powered business environment. In Figure 8.3 the woman is salient due to her exaggerated posture, where she flaunts her sexuality. However, while these potent cultural symbols might be important criteria for salience they will always interact with the others as we will see in the following. The analyst has to work out which one, or which combination, is in operation in each particular case.

Foregrounding

We can identify the most salient element as that which is foregrounded. In Figure 8.3 we can simply say that the woman wearing the heels is the most salient element in the image as she is placed in the foreground. However, it is the potent cultural symbols that clearly have the higher salience in this image. We must always take other criteria for salience into consideration before arriving at our conclusions.

Overlapping

The principle of overlapping is like foregrounding since it has the effect of placing elements in front of others. In Figure 8.3 we can see that the woman overlaps the outlines of the two men. Often in adverts the product overlaps the participants. There can be a hierarchy of overlapping of elements or persons. On film posters we can often identify how central characters are through such a hierarchy.

Size

This can simply be the element that is the biggest in the composition ranging to the smallest. It is important to note here that in advertisements it is common to find that products take up much less space in the composition than other elements. An advert in a magazine may contain a large picture of a model smiling at the viewer and a smaller picture of the product below. In older advertisements we would most likely find a product shown much larger with a smaller illustration. What is emphasised in the newer advert is not so much the use value of the product but the lifestyle association, connoted through the photograph of the model or other potent cultural symbol. Often in promotional literature for banks the lifestyle photograph, say of a handsome professional woman staring confidently out at the viewer, a typical potent cultural symbol, will be bigger than the information given for the account itself, at least on the cover of a pamphlet. From all this we can conclude that these compositions tell us that lifestyle and branding are now more salient than the actual nature of the products and services themselves.

Colour

Colour is often used to give salience. The main element may carry a particular saturated or vibrant colour.

Tone

This can be simply the use of brightness to attract the eye. In Figure 8.3 we can see that the faces have received extra lighting, drawing our attention to their expressions, particularly that of the woman, who is salient due to foregrounding and overlapping. In Figure 8.1 the whole scene is very well lit. In this sense we might assume that it is the scene as a whole that is to be viewed as meaningful rather than any specific element. In the scene as a whole there is nothing drawn out in terms of colour or particularly through size. Only the objects and the window are potent cultural symbols.

The use of tone can often be seen in advertisements where one particular element is highlighted through directional lighting. Often in promotional photographs the photographer will direct light specifically onto the product itself. While the rest of the elements and set might be well lit, this may create a very slight aura on the product itself.

Focus

In Figure 8.1 the focus is clearest in the participants. This would not have been the same were it an advertisement for laptops or furniture design. Often in such images of workplaces the setting becomes almost a blur. Here a single object such as a briefcase, laptop or mobile phone should do all the work of signification.

In Figure 8.3 the setting is out of focus. Our attention is drawn not to the setting, therefore, although it is sufficiently in focus to distinguish what kind of setting it in fact is. Our attention is drawn to the experience of the woman and to her posture.

Positioning the viewer in relation to the image

In this section we look at two aspects of the alignment of the viewer with the participants: angle of interaction and proximity. Both of these influence the way we relate to them, relative power relations and degree of association.

Angle of interaction

The angle from which a photograph is taken can suggest different relations between the people represented and the viewer. These are based on physical associations of experiences such as of height and power and how we view scenes.

Vertical angle

This is to do with power and the association of height and superiority/inferiority or with strength/vulnerability. If you look up at someone this has the metaphorical association of them having higher status than you or of them being physically in a stronger position than you. We associate size with power and status. In social life we might stoop down to speak to small children if we do not wish to intimidate them. Yet when we look down at someone this can give us a sense of power. These kinds of associations influence the way we assess the relative power of a person depicted in a photograph. Imagine the different effects of two photographs of dirty-faced children shown with neutral facial expressions. One looks down on them, the other up at them. In the first they appear vulnerable, whereas in the second the same children appear threatening. A photographer might stoop or even lie on the ground to take shots that look up at children to make them appear imposing or intimidating, for example if they wish to emphasise children out of control in a society.

If someone is depicted at the same level in a photograph then equality is implied. But once our viewing position is raised or lowered our status relationship is changed. In Figure 8.1 we are positioned just slightly below the height of the women. Our viewing position is on a similar level and to some extent equality is implied. In Figure 8.3, in contrast, the camera position is much lower and we look slightly up at the woman, giving her power. Of course all of these are only meaning potentials and must be used in combination with other factors described in this chapter. And in the case of Figure 8.1 it is important to note that slightly lowered viewing position is often used to suggest intimacy with the subject. For example, we might look slightly upwards from below at a politician who carries a worried expression. Here looking upwards suggests not lack of power but closeness to a more personal or intimate moment.

The communicative potential of power in angle of interaction can be used to change the meaning of elements in an image. For example, a cover of a women's lifestyle magazine can carry an image of a woman wearing very little clothing. But a low-angle shot looking up at the woman will prevent her from appearing vulnerable, or objectified as a sex object. To achieve this effect the camera position may be around her waist level. Of course as well as giving power a low angle can be used to create a sense of the person being overbearing. A newspaper might depict a politician from such an angle to connote oppression and arrogance.

Horizontal angles
While the vertical axis influences power relations to those we view in photographs, the horizontal axis can influence involvement/detachment. On the horizontal axis we can see participants from the front as they face us. This gives the viewer a sense of involvement. If we view the scene from the side, in contrast, we simply observe it. Consider the difference in effect if we view a photograph of a group of men in ski-masks, holding guns, looking towards the frame, directly at us, compared to if we view the same scene from the side. The first is threatening as it suggests involvement. The second is detached and creates objectivity. Just as the vertical axis was based on real-life associations of height and power, so the horizontal axis is based on our association with real-world experiences of being involved in situations in which we are required to act, or we are onlookers where the people we watch have business with others.

Once we move on the horizontal plane to go behind the person represented, when we see their backs as they look on to a scene, there is a different effect. This can have two kinds of meaning. First it can have the effect of aligning the viewer with the represented person since we stand with them, viewing the world as they do. Imagine a photograph showing the back of a person as if we were standing behind them. Beyond them we can see that they are being held at gunpoint by another rather dangerous-looking person. Second, seeing the back of a person can also mean anonymity or them having turned their back on us.

Oblique angles

These are where the camera will be tilted, or 'cantered', so that the person appears at an angle, rather than being positioned vertically in the frame. These are used to give an unsettling effect, to suggest tension, or to give a sense of playfulness and energy through movement. The use of cantered images is increasing in news and features to give just this sense of surprise, and creativity, and can also therefore connote a more sophisticated design style.

Proximity and interaction

Distance

This is the association of physical proximity and intimacy. In images as in real life, distance signifies social relations. We 'keep our distance' from some people we do not like and 'get close to' people we see as part of our circle of friends or intimates. This varies between cultures, but generally we feel uncomfortable if strangers get too close. In pictures, distance translates as 'size of frame' (Close Shot, Medium Shot, Long Shot, etc.). This is simply how close to the viewer a person is represented as being in an image. So a closer shot suggests intimacy, whereas a longer shot is much more impersonal. In Figure 8.2 the woman on the desk is seen in medium shot. The way we associate with her would differ were we close up, seeing only her face, or were she in the distance. In any photograph we can ask which participants are depicted as being close to our social space and which are kept at a distance. A photograph in a newspaper report on a war zone might show a close shot of a child in order to generate empathy. On the other hand, angry, dirty civilians might be kept in long shot.

Close shots can also suggest claustrophobia or a threat. For example, if we imagine the photograph of the hooded gunmen staring at us in close shot, or a close shot of the faces of a crowd during a riot. In this second case this takes us too close to the energy of the moment and suggests the need to pull back from the madness of the situation.

Analysing participants in images

There are also a number of simple questions we can ask that help to draw our attention to how participants are depicted. This draws on the work of Machin and van Leeuwen (2005b) and tells us more specifically what kinds of people are represented and how the viewer is therefore encouraged to relate to them.

Individuals and groups

In images people can be shown as individuals or *en groupe*. This can make a massive difference to the way that the people and the events in which they are involved are represented.

'Individualisation' is realised through language by singularity, for example 'a woman' as opposed to the plural 'women'. This has the effect of drawing us close to specific people therefore humanising them. All tabloid journalists know that a story telling the experiences of one person will be far more compelling than statistics that speak of many. Visually, individualisation is realised by shots that show only one person. The woman in Figure 8.4 is individualised. Visual individualisation is a matter of degree. It can be reduced by increasing distance, making individual traits less easy to observe.

In language, 'collectivisation' can be realised by plurality or by means of mass nouns or nouns denoting a group of people (e.g. clan, militia, terrorists). We can immediately see the ideological effect of this where instead of individuals who might have specific motivations we are dealing with anonymous groups. Visually, collectivisation is realised by images that show groups or crowds. The members of the groups or crowds can be 'homogenised' to different degrees. They can all be shown wearing the same clothes, performing the same actions or striking the same poses. In Figure 8.3 we can see that the two men are collectivised through clothing and posture.

Collectivisation can also be achieved by focus on the generic features of a group of people so that they are turned into types. For example, a news photograph of Muslim people in London might foreground those individuals wearing traditional clothing.

Individualisation and collectivisation can occur at the same time for the people depicted. In Figure 8.3 the woman is individualised through foregrounding yet also collectivised as a business person. We find such combinations in promotional photographs for pop bands. Some bands will show themselves as individuals by being depicted as standing apart and striking different poses, even though they might all wear the same clothing and be otherwise homogenised. Other bands might only wish to emphasise their sameness.

Categorisation

Visual representations of people can also *categorise* them, regardless of whether they are also 'individualised' or 'collectivised'. Visual categorisation is either 'cultural' or 'biological' or a combination of the two.

Cultural categorisation is realised through standard attributes of dress, hairstyle, body adornment, etc. The woman in Figure 8.3 is categorised by her business clothing and her posture as are the men behind her. In news photographs Muslim people are often culturally categorised through wearing clothing that Western viewers have come to associate with more traditional looks, even Islamic fundamentalists. So we will see a woman wearing a veil to represent all Muslim women. These people will always be used in news photographs simply because they easily connote familiar news frames for audiences.

Biological categorisation is achieved through stereotyped physical characteristics. Such categorisation may be used to invoke both positive and negative connotations. Images might depict soldiers as 'Action Man' stereotypes or women appear as 'Barbie' stereotypes of female attractiveness. Often in photographs of soldiers that appear in the press 'our boys' might be shown with square jaws and muscular build. This is to emphasise strength and security. Soldiers shown writing home in the classic war photograph style, on the other hand, may be more youthful and slimmer built to emphasise vulnerability.

Biological categorisation can also lead to racist stereotypes. In political cartoons, biological categorisation is used to represent ethnic stereotypes. Van Leeuwen (2001) shows examples of the representation of black people with exaggerated lips. During Bush's 'war against terrorism' pro-Bush cartoonists would represent Middle Eastern people with large noses and long thin faces.

Non-representation

Finally, it is crucially important if someone is not represented in an image. For example, a caption for a photograph might read 'Attacks on villages lead to 100s dead today'. Yet in the image we see no corpses, only a soldier patrolling. A caption might read 'Banks responsible for economic downturn', whereas in the photograph we see an image of houses with 'For Sale' signs in front of them. In both these examples, we can ask why certain participants are not represented. Why in the first case do we not see images of destroyed villages and dead people and in the second images of banks? Wherever there is such exclusion we should always consider the political and ideological motivations and how these contribute to concealing responsibilities or specific details.

In summary there are three questions we can ask in order to help us think about the representation of participants in images. We can ask if they are represented as individuals or as a group. This is important in connecting the viewer to the interests and experiences of the participants. We can look at the kind of categorisation resources used. These inform the viewer of what kinds of participants are involved. And we can ask if any participants are absent from the representation. This can be a way of concealing responsibility for actions, or can remove the role of some participants.

Analysing what is happening in an image

Of course in photographs we find not just people, objects and settings represented but also actions and behaviours. Many photographs depict people doing things. In the analysis of written texts linguists have shown that a more careful and systematic analysis of what people are depicted as doing can reveal less obvious messages about who has agency, what kind of agency they have, and who does not. These same kinds of observations can be adapted to the analysis of agency in images. This is an approach that draws on the functional semiotic theory of Halliday (1985). Applying this to images gives us a more precise tool kit for thinking about action (what gets done) and agency (who does what).

Halliday was interested in the ways that action and transaction (acting in a way that has a result) were linguistically communicated. Through his approach, texts could be analysed to show how people were represented as behaving, in other words who was shown as being active and who as passive.

In order to be specific about analysing this process of agency and action, Halliday uses the terms 'actor', 'goal', 'process' and 'circumstance'. For example, in a news item we might find the following sentence:

The man cared for the children in the garden

The actor in this case is the man who carries out the process of caring. The goal is the children, who are to be cared for and protected, and the circumstance is the garden. In this sentence it is the man who has the agency, or power. The children are the goal and have no agency. As we will see, we can also use these same concepts to think about the *visual* representation of what people are shown doing or who is the goal or recipient.

Halliday also distinguished different kinds of processes (see also Chapter 6 above). Just because someone is depicted as being an actor involved in processes, it does not follow that they are active agents, even when they are not the goal. This is very important both in language and in images as processes can give the impression of agency where there is none. So we must ask what kind of process it is and what kind of role the participants must play in that process.

Here are Halliday's six processes glossed for visual analysis:

1) *Material*: This is simply doing something in the world that has a material result or consequence. We can see this in the sentence 'The woman built the house'. We can call this *transactional* action.
2) *Behavioural*: This is where we act without material outcome. For example, 'The boy jumped'. Here the boy acts but with no end result.
3) *Mental*: This is where a person thinks, evaluates or senses. For example, 'The boy saw them' or 'The girl thought about her family'.
4) *Verbal*: This is where a person is represented as simply saying something. For example, 'The boy talked about football'.
5) *Relational*: This is where people are represented as being like, or different to, something else. Simply, 'The boy was taller'.
6) *Existential*: This is where people are represented simply in a state of existing, appearing. For example, 'He was in London', or 'He sat in the chair'.

Using these different processes as an analytical tool we can reveal the level of agency and power or the lack of it. A person can be represented as being very active or busy, but in fact achieving very little. For example, a heroine in a romantic novel might be engaged in a great deal of action, but this may involve a lot of *existential* processes, such as being in different places, *mental* processes, such as wishing, missing, hoping, and *behavioural* processes, such as watching and listening. All this produces no outcome in the world. She is not an active agent and is not depicted as having power over the world. In women's magazines we often find many photographs of women leaping around, throwing their arms into the air, or twisting their bodies, as in Figure 8.4 above. This brings a feeling of energy and agency to the magazine. Yet the women are not represented acting out material processes.

In women's magazines we also often find women depicted as the agents of mental processes. We find them looking thoughtfully off frame in images accompanied by captions such as 'How to seduce a man' or 'Do you get yourself heard at work?' We could compare such representations of action with representations of men in a magazine such as *Men's Health*. Do we find men depicted in the same way or not?

In fact association of agents with mental processes can suggest not only passivity but also sensitivity and thoughtfulness. Mental processes give the impression that we have access to thoughts and feelings of a person. This will usually humanise them, or allow us to empathise with them. In a women's magazine such a technique could therefore be used to align the readers to the world of fashion consumption depicted within its pages. It might also be used to align us to a particular protagonist in a news story to allow us to associate with their inner experiences.

In an analysis of agency in war photographs Machin (2007b) showed that images depicting the occupation of Iraq represented US soldiers mainly as searching and guarding, whereas in photographs from Vietnam they were shown as carrying out material processes destroying things, killing and bombing, dropping napalm on villages. In Vietnam photographs they were also shown as 'goals', as the recipients of processes having been themselves shot; carrying out behavioural processes, as simply suffering, running, lost, through woodlands; or in existential processes lying in fields bewildered or exhausted. Many photographs show mental states thus emphasising the chaos and lack of purpose of the war as soldiers were represented as confused, afraid, bewildered. Also in photographs from this war civilians are shown as goals, having been burned, thrown out of their villages and suffering and dying. The photographs from Iraq show the US soldiers mainly as engaged in behavioural processes of observing and searching. Poses also suggest mental processes of calmness and considera-tion. The cool but thoughtful concentration shows that the soldier keeps guard, vigilant but peaceful and disciplined. Civilians are represented as the goals of the act of the protection or appear to wander aimlessly suggesting lack of coordinated and purposeful action. We can see that these verb processes are used to present very different views of war when the activities and results will have been exactly the same. These processes represent the actions of soldiers in Iraq to emphasise that the US forces are peacekeep-ers. They are not shown acting aggressively, nor as the victims of aggression in any kind of process. Occasionally they are shown in shooting poses, but not actually firing. Mainly they wait and watch. These are the civilised actions of the peacekeeper rather than acts of destruction. An analysis of action in the photographs in the press of the occupation of Iraq allows to us identify what roles participants are given and how they are acting and there-fore what is the meaning of the occupation. The same kind of analysis can be carried out on any topic.

Of course in photographs there might be two or more actions being carried out. In an advertisement a woman might be dancing while a man looks at her. In this case both carry out behavioural processes whereas the man's also has the goal of the woman. It would be possible to carry out an analysis of the depiction of the actions of men and women in advertisements, particularly where they are found together, or compare them across genres of magazines, in children's storybooks, or anywhere else where there are visual representations of social action. Machin (2007b) collected photographs from the press over a given time period and then analysed a small sample of these in depth in order to draw out the main themes. The same could be done for any topic.

Modality: measuring truth and concealment in images

Many photographs that we now see have been modified. While such alterations are as old as the medium itself digital technology has made the process cheap and very easy. It is useful therefore that we have a tool kit or procedure that can help us to draw our attention to exactly what has been changed and therefore to think about the effect of these changes. This allows us to more accurately identify and understand what has been enhanced and what has been 'silenced' or concealed in an image.

Modality refers to the way that we communicate how true or how real a representation should be taken as being (see also Chapter 6 for a discussion of modals). In linguistics, Halliday (1985) told us that language provides us with resources to express and also to conceal kinds and levels of truth. These are called 'modals' and are verbs such as 'will', 'can' and 'must' and adjectives such as 'certain', 'possible' and 'impossible'. Consider the two following statements.

It is possible he is in the house

It is certain he is in the house

The first of these statements has lower modality than the second. There is less certainty. Therefore high modality claims to represent closely what we would expect to find in the real world. One use of this observation is that it allows us to look at what aspects of a written or spoken representation are offered to us as certain and which are distanced from the real world, avoided or edited out. Modality can also be expressed by attitudes. We can see this in a comment of the kind made by a politician.

Some think that globalisation is a bad thing, we know it is an opportunity

Here the speaker uses 'think' to reduce the certainty of a particular point of view and 'know' to increase the modality of their own.

Looking at what is reduced in modality, taken out, left in or emphasised, therefore, allows us to reveal something about the ideology of that representation. According to Hodge and Kress (1988) the same can be said for photographs or any visual representation. Hodge and Kress (1988) and Kress and van Leeuwen (1996) later showed that in place of words such as 'possible' or 'might', there are visual modals whereby visual truth can be reduced or enhanced. They did this by considering how qualities of an image might be different than had we been at a scene to witness it ourselves. So we compare what we see in the photograph to the standard of what Kress and van Leeuwen (1996: 176) call 'naturalistic modality'. These authors provide a tick list of visual modality cues that we can use to carefully examine an image.

Articulation of detail of the main participants or objects

Here we consider the extent to which the subject of the photograph appears different from how they would have been had we actually been there to see them in terms of articulation of detail. This can be illustrated by the difference in articulation of detail between a photograph and a rough line drawing of a person. Much more articulation of detail can be found on the photograph. Of course this would depend on the kind of photograph. Many photographs we now see of people in the media and even on their own webpages have been digitally manipulated in order to remove blemishes or wrinkles on skin or to whiten the colour of teeth and eyes. In this case we see less of the articulation of detail than we would have seen had we been there. Modality is therefore lowered and the visual truth is therefore also lowered. The person appears 'less real'. In men's lifestyle magazines women models often appear heavily digitally manipulated in this manner so that they look almost cartoon-like. Where detail is reduced in this way the person or object becomes idealised and simplified.

This measurement of modality should be seen as a continuum. Even lower down the scale of articulation of detail are cartoons and stick drawings. At the other end of the scale details can be enhanced by the use of close shots, lighting and contrast. This is often used to create a documentary effect, a sense of gritty realism or personal connection as opposed to the idealised models appearing in the men's magazines. Where modality is increased in this way images become 'more than real'. Kress and van Leeuwen say that in such cases we can call this a 'sensory modality' rather than a modality of truth (1996: 170).

In Figure 8.1 the women are represented through a different level of modality than the background. The women appear to be slightly out of focus or overexposed whereas the background is much more out of focus. In this image, meant for promotional uses, or in editorial work, the women are therefore simplified and idealised whereas the blurring of the background shifts it into the realm of the symbolic.

Articulation of detail of the background

Here we ask the same questions as above but of the background. Again we have a continuum where in the middle we find things represented as we would have seen them had we been there and with lowered and increased modality levels either end. In Figure 8.3 we can see that the background is out of focus, so reducing the detail. Again this has the effect of idealising. It also means that we see this as a generic setting rather than a specific one. Images that are intended to symbolise a particular event, kind of person or concept often use this level of focus. Where the background is shot with naturalistic if increased modality we tend to assume that it is the setting that is being documented, that it is not just the participants that are important but also time and place.

As with the subject of the photograph the details of the setting can be enhanced to give sensory effect, or can be reduced to the level of a sketch. What is interesting is when we find reduced modality backgrounds in news photographs. For example, in a local newspaper we have a caption that says 'Police report a reduction in racially motivated attacks against local shopkeepers'. The photograph shows two policemen and, seen from behind only, an Asian man. We take his point of view as he speaks to them. They are shown standing in a street of British late nineteenth-century terraced houses. Only the police officers are completely in focus. The street is out of focus as is the Asian man. This indicates that this photograph is not intended to document a particular instance nor a particular victim of racially motivated attacks. In fact this image could in reality represent nothing of the kind. It is intended to symbolise police vigilance and protection in the inner city. The street through reduced modality represents a generic street and the Asian man a generic person protected from racial attacks by the police.

In photographs and visual compositions such as graphics and advertisements in newspapers and television news it is interesting to look where modality has been reduced and enhanced. Often in advertisements we find idealised men, women and children in simplified settings but with the product shown in large size in enhanced detail and sensory modality.

Lighting and shadow

We can also ask the extent to which the lighting and shadow appear as if we had been present at a scene. We might find that shadows are missing as there are multiple sources of light. This is often not difficult to establish, simply by looking at the highlights on objects in the image. If we look at Figure 8.3 we can see that there are two main sources of light to either side of the three people. This has the effect of creating a shadow down the middle of their faces and bodies. This makes them appear more dramatic. The background in this image also contains more shadows, as compared to Figure 8.2 where there is backlighting, which normally indicates 'nothing hidden' and 'truth'. In Figure 8.1 we can see that there are at least several sources of light. If we look at the woman to the left she carries no shadow. Of course these are all highly posed photographs and we would expect there to be manipulation of light. But it is important to draw our attention to this as it helps us to identify levels of reduction in modality in all kinds of photographs.

We might also find that tone has been changed in order to reduce contrasts of light and dark or to increase them. Figure 8.1 appears to have reduced levels of contrast where there are few shadows. Much advertising photography is of this order. This is a brightly lit optimistic world. We have metaphorical associations of light with knowing and truth and also with optimism and brighter outlooks, whereas darkness and shadow are associated with mystery and bleaker moods. Where light and shadow are exaggerated we have the effect of high contrast between truth and mystery, optimism and pessimism.

Colour quality and range

In many of the images we now see in advertisements, promotional material and even newspapers, the colours have been modified. We have dealt with this in part already above when we described the connotations of settings. But to take this level of observation a little further, the colours in an image can be flattened in order to create a cleaner simplified look. This is what we called reduced modulation. This is the case in Figure 8.1. Modulation can also be increased to create a sensory effect where the play of light on a surface is exaggerated. Children's toys are often created using single flat, pure colours to suggest simplicity.

Colours can also be artificially saturated or muted. Saturated colours tend to be associated with emotional temperature and exuberance. Along with flatter colours they can be used by advertisers to create a mood of fun and vibrancy. More muted colours tend to be associated with more reserved and mellow moods.

We can also draw our attention to the way that the colour palette has been increased or decreased. This can encompass the whole range of colours to monochrome. If you look in any *National Geographic* magazine you will see that the photographs have a range of saturated colours added to them. This is used to indicate that the natural and human worlds are filled with colour, diversity and energy. Advertisements or promotional photographs will use reduced palette or monochrome to give a timeless or classical feel. Note how many pop artists use monochrome in publicity shots. Of course boy bands wishing to target a younger market will tend to use a wider palette of saturated colours.

Carrying out a research project

Many of the tools in this chapter, in the tradition of semiotic analysis, are to be used for qualitative observation. A study might compare, for example, how the participants of two sides of a conflict are represented in 20 photographs.

Or a study might compare the photographs used by online newspapers on their homepages. The researcher may decide to explain why the chosen examples are important and representative of a wider situation. In this case 20 photographs of a conflict might be taken that are considered by the researcher to be typical of representations of that conflict, or no more than six newspaper websites might be chosen. In such a case any relevant tool for observation and analysis would be applied where felt necessary. The point would not be to show statistically what the differences are, for example between different newspaper websites, but to point to some of the different strategies of representation used and the consequences of these in terms of ideologies. This would be in the fashion in which we attributed certain meanings relating to identity and discourse regarding images of women at work in this chapter.

Of course a much larger sample could be used and many of the observations made in this chapter, such as representation of participants, gaze, action and modality, could be used as the basis for a larger content analysis.

These methods, used qualitatively, can be best employed alongside other methods. For example, a content analysis of a sample of newspaper stories on a particular topic might also then carry out more detailed analysis of a smaller sample of these. This could be done using Critical Discourse Analysis and the visual methods described in this chapter.

The same criticisms would apply to these methods, if used interpretively, that would apply to Critical Discourse Analysis (see the end of Chapter 6 in this book). Such a form of analysis makes many assumptions about what is of importance in the image and how it should be understood. Visual analysts such as Bal (2006) and Elkins (2003) are highly critical of this reductive kind of analysis. Bal would argue that any single part of an image might trigger a whole set of associations for the viewer.

Summary

- In comparison to other research tools there has been less precision in terms of a tool kit for analysis as regards images.
- Many of the tools provided in this chapter involve some degree of interpretation. But what is important is that they encourage the analyst to describe what they see in images. The tools presented here push the analyst to ask a set of systematic questions rather than simply to provide an interpretation. We might see an image that is part of an advertisement and make an interpretation that it represents 'fun'. But asking a more careful set of questions requires that before we do this we ask who is represented, how, where and what precisely they do.

- Many of the tools presented in this chapter are drawn from linguistics. For this reason they tend towards greater levels of descriptive power. However, the point of such an approach, like that of Critical Discourse Analysis, is to reveal the broader discourses that are being represented. We aim to ask, what are the ideologies of these representations?
- These methods therefore are predominantly qualitative. They can thus be criticised for not being representative of any broader sample if we only carry out an in-depth analysis of a small number of images.

CHAPTER 9

Measuring audiences: survey research

If content analysis is perhaps the most frequently used method for analysing media content, then the survey is historically the most frequently used method for studying media audiences and people generally. Furthermore, the two methods have a great deal in common: they are quantitative methods, they both matured and came into their own as research methods during the first half of the twentieth century, they both use a coding schedule as their main research instrument, and – in media and communication research – they have frequently been used together, with considerable gain, to examine and explain communication processes and media influence.

While, as Babbie (2010: 254) reminds us with reference to ancient Egypt, the Bible and the Romans, 'Surveys are a very old research technique' and have been around for a very long time, it is to the beginning of the twentieth century that we need to look to find the origin of the uses of survey methodology in media and communications research. Around this time, prominent German sociologist Max Weber proposed that the systematic large-scale collection of data on people's opinions, beliefs and behaviour be combined with the systematic analysis of newspapers to provide indications of the role played by the news media in influencing trends and changes in public opinion. However, neither survey methodology nor content analysis methodology had been sufficiently developed at the time to get this project off the ground and it took another couple of decades for the appropriate resources, methods and tools to develop to a stage where Weber's suggestion could be realised.

Survey methodology is particularly interesting in the context of media and communications research because it has played – and continues to play – a central role for economic, organisational and policy purposes, as well as of course in relation to communication models and theories about the role and function of media and communication in society. Media organisations have for a long time relied heavily, both in relation to the setting of advertising fees and to programming policy, on the systematic, regular and continuous monitoring or measurement of audiences' media consumption habits and preferences. In the US this has traditionally been done by such survey organisations as Nielsen (http://en-us.nielsen.com) and Arbitron (http://www.arbitron.com/), while in the UK the Broadcasters' Audience Research Board (BARB – http://www.barb.co.uk/) and British Rate and Data (BRAD or Brad Insight http://www1.bradinsight.com/) provide media consumption figures and other detailed information on the media industry and media audiences.

Survey methodology has been one of several key methodologies used in major inquiries or commissions/committees set up to look into the state of broadcasting and media regulation and to provide policy guidance on changes and developments in the regulatory framework for both public service and private media. Examples include most of the UK's Royal Commissions on the press and on broadcasting, major US government-sponsored investigations into the relationship between media and violence, as well as such prominent and influential reports as the Kerner Commission report in the wake of civil/racial unrest and widespread rioting in the US in the 1960s. And survey methodology continues to be central to much of the research conducted or commissioned by key bodies such as Ofcom – the Office of Telecommunications – the body charged since 2003 with regulating the communications industries in the UK.

Survey methodology has played a prominent role in the history and development of media and communication research. Some of the major and most prominent models of media and communication, particularly agenda-setting research, cultivation research, uses and gratifications research, diffusion of innovations research, the two-step flow model of media influence, etc., have all relied centrally on survey methodology, often in combination – particularly in agenda-setting and cultivation research – with content analysis methodology. One of the earliest studies of media reporting and voting behaviour – by Lazarsfeld, Berelson and Gaudet (1944) of the American presidential election campaign of 1940 – paved the way for a much more nuanced perspective than had hitherto prevailed on media influence, introducing the notion of a 'two-step flow' of information and marking the beginning of the end of views of audiences as passive and the media as all-powerful. It also provided the panel-survey research model (see later in this chapter) and inspiration for the influential *Personal Influence* study by Katz and Lazarsfeld (1955), which further cemented the 'two-step flow' model of mass communications. Survey methodology also played a key role in studies of persuasive communication – the use of mass media campaigns for deliberately influencing or changing people's opinions, beliefs and behaviours in such diverse fields as health, politics, environment, science, business, international aid, etc. Early survey-based studies on media campaigns and persuasive communication in turn provided further strong evidence that media influence was anything but simple, direct or linear.

While much less prominent – compared with its uses in audience and media influence research – survey research has also been and continues to be an important tool in the study of media production, media organisations and particularly journalists and other media professionals. While classic studies of news production have predominantly been based on observation and news room ethnographies (see Chapter 4), several have also drawn on elements of survey methodology as a complementary method. By contrast major overviews of journalists and media professionals have been predominantly based on large-scale surveys (e.g. Weaver, 1998).

Definition

The word 'survey' comes, via French, from the Latin 'super+videre', that is approximately 'above/over' + 'look/see/view', and consequently to survey something means (amongst other meanings) essentially to create a comprehensive or commanding overview of something. *The Oxford English Dictionary* offers a more specific meaning relevant to the social sciences, namely 'A systematic collection and analysis of data relating to the attitudes, living conditions, opinions, etc., of a population, usually taken from a representative sample of the latter' (*Oxford English Dictionary Online*, 2010). In the social sciences literature – and as a social science method – we may consider the following prominent definitions:

> Surveys are information-collection methods used to describe, compare, or explain individual and societal knowledge, feelings, values, preferences, and behaviour. (Fink, 2009b: 1)

> Survey research is a method for collecting and analyzing social data via highly structured and often very detailed interviews or questionnaires in order to obtain information from large numbers of respondents presumed to be representative of a specific population. (Wiseman and Aron, 1970: 37; cited in Berger, 2011: 222)

> A *survey* is a study that collects information by asking people questions. The information collected – the data – is generally numerical and suitable for statistical analysis.... The vast majority of survey research projects are *sample surveys* in which data are collected from a subset of individuals in the population. Inferences about the larger population are made from the information gathered from those people in the sample. (Shoemaker and McCombs, 2009: 379)

These definitions then indicate the key features of the *survey* in social science research:

• It is a systematic and structured mode of collecting data, by asking people questions.

- It focuses – ideally – on a *representative* sample of a larger population.
- It uses, as its data collection instrument, an interview schedule, that is a list of questions to be asked of the interviewee/respondent by an interviewer, or a questionnaire to be completed by the interviewee/respondent.
- The data collected, that is the answers to the survey questions, are subjected to quantitative analysis to produce descriptive, comparative and inferential statistics that can be extrapolated from the sample studied to the larger population from which the sample was drawn.

Two types of survey

Adams suggests three different roles of surveys: *exploration, description* and *explanation* (1989: 19). He labels surveys which are undertaken to 'make an initial inquiry, simply to explore a domain to see if further study seems warranted' as exploratory surveys and notes that these are also often referred to as *pilot studies*. In general, however, communications and social science researchers (e.g. Berger, 2011; Giddens, 1989) have tended to simply distinguish between *descriptive surveys* and *analytical* (or *explanatory*, or '*puzzle-solving*' (Giddens, 1989)) *surveys*.

Descriptive surveys aim to collect information and describe patterns and trends relevant to a particular population. Their objective is to describe what is or what exists. Prime examples include the information routinely and regularly collected by broadcasting organisations on the size and socio-demographic breakdown of radio and television audiences (see Nielsen, Arbitron and BARB, mentioned earlier), but descriptive surveys also comprise research carried out to examine mobile phone ownership in different age groups, the number of homes with broadband access, the rate of uptake of new media technologies such as high-definition television or blu-ray DVD players.

Analytical surveys aim to analyse and describe the *why* and *how* of the opinions, beliefs or behaviours examined in a given population. Analytical surveys thus focus closely on the relationship between different dependent and independent variables in a study; such surveys are often – but not necessarily always – guided by specific hypotheses that stipulate particular relationships between variables, and the aim of the survey will be to examine and explain how, for example, certain demographic characteristics and beliefs are related – causally or otherwise – to certain types of behaviour trends, patterns. It is normally possible to determine from the abstract whether a survey is descriptive or analytical: if the abstract mentions relationships between variables or more particularly if reference is made to hypotheses and testing of hypotheses, then the survey is likely to be analytical rather than purely descriptive.

Why use surveys? Strengths and weaknesses

Surveys, like any other method, have both strengths and weaknesses. Awareness of these is important, not least at the very early stage of developing a research project, where decisions have to be made about which method or methods of data collection are most appropriate for the research objectives. In this respect it is always imperative to put a clear articulation of the objectives of the research first, and only then to decide on the most appropriate method or methods for collecting data that will enable the researcher to address the key research questions in a valid and reliable way. In the long history of research on media audiences, and on questions about the influence of the media and people's beliefs and behaviour, researchers have often been faced with choosing from laboratory experiments, focus group interviews, surveys or observational/ethnographic methods. Each of these methods has – as the audiences research literature is testimony to – features to commend it, but also drawbacks to be aware of. And the changing 'popularity' of each method over the history of audiences research also demonstrates a 'fashion' cycle in academic research that has parallels with fashion cycles in other areas of life. The strengths of survey research are often recounted with reference to laboratory experiments, whereas mentions of the weaknesses of survey research tend to centre on its shortcomings compared with more qualitative – and more flexible – types of research, such as focus group interviewing (see Chapter 10) or observation (see Chapter 4).

The key strengths of surveys can then be listed as follows:

- Surveys provide a more realistic/natural setting than the laboratory experiment. Respondents are approached in their natural environment, and are asked questions relating to their natural context and everyday beliefs and behaviours. They are not, as in the laboratory experiment, subjected to an artificially created and controlled situation or to artificially manipulated stimuli.
- Surveys are a highly structured mode of collecting information or data. As such they enable the collection of large amounts of data in an efficient, potentially highly reliable and often cost-effective way.
- Surveys – because of their highly structured format – allow or facilitate the examination of a broad range of variables.
- Surveys – as a quantitative and structured method of data collection – make it possible (although this relies also on the robustness of the sampling strategy used) to use powerful statistical analyses and tests to examine not just important trends in individual variables but more importantly relationships between variables.

Some of the important weaknesses or potential flaws of the survey method include the following:

- The most common form of survey – the cross-sectional survey (see below) – provides only a snapshot of people's beliefs, attitudes and behaviour, while telling us little about how people have arrived at these or indeed about how they might be changing in the future. This is perhaps particularly troublesome in relation to research which tries to understand the role played by the media in influencing people's beliefs and behaviour, because a snapshot offers little or no insight into the dynamic ways in which our opinions are formed, shaped, negotiated and developed through interaction – whether direct or mediated – with other people's opinions.

- The survey focuses on the individual respondent's beliefs, attitudes and behaviour and as such offers little that will help us understand how individual beliefs and behaviour are often formed and shaped in a social context. This is potentially troublesome if the aim of research is to understand how we – as media audiences and as consumers of media – develop and shape our views and opinions through conversation with others as well as perhaps in response to cues in our general symbolic environment, including of course our sense as media consumers and from the media of 'what everybody else thinks' about a particular issue.

- Answers to survey questions are easily 'framed', skewed or influenced by how they are worded and asked, that is by the choice of words and by the syntax or phrasing of questions. The importance of careful question construction cannot be overestimated in survey design, as results can literally to a large extent be a reflection not of some genuine trend or characteristic in the sample of respondents but of the way the questions have been asked.

- Surveys are excellent for demonstrating correlation between variables, but the cross-sectional survey in particular is poorly equipped to demonstrate causality. While two or more variables examined in a survey may thus appear to correlate or co-vary, it will often be difficult or impossible – depending on the nature of the survey design – to establish whether such co-variation is due to one variable's influence on the other variable or whether the co-variation is due to a third variable, which may or may not have been measured in the survey.

Before deciding to use the survey method, the researcher thus must consider the strengths and weaknesses of surveys when compared to other methods that may possibly be used to address the relevant research objectives. If it is clear that the survey offers the best approach to collecting data that will address the stated objectives of a given research project, the next steps are then to choose from a number of possible survey designs; to decide on the most appropriate mode of data collection (i.e. whether to conduct the survey as personal interviews or through self-administered questionnaires); and to define the population relevant to the survey and a strategy for drawing a representative sample from this population. We shall look at each of these three aspects in the following, and then proceed to introduce the core data collection instrument of the survey, namely the questionnaire. But first, it is worth noting that the choice of survey is guided essentially by considering:

- What is it that the survey aims to gather information on or to discover?
- Available resources (e.g. for distribution costs, travel, hiring and training of interviewers, printing of questionnaires).
- Type and accessibility of respondents (i.e. can a valid and reliable sample of relevant respondents be obtained?).

Main types of survey design

When considering types of survey design, we need to distinguish between the single one-off survey (properly called a 'cross-sectional' survey: respondents interviewed only once), on the one hand, and, on the other, longitudinal designs, which facilitate the examination of changes over time. Longitudinal designs comprise principally the trend study (repeated surveying/interviewing; a new sample drawn of a given population for every iteration of the survey) and the panel study (same sample of respondents interviewed repeatedly over a period of time). In the following we briefly consider the definition and characteristics of each of these designs.

The cross-sectional survey

The cross-sectional survey design is a one-off survey, where a (representative) sample of respondents is interviewed only once. It offers a comparatively cheap, potentially fast and efficient way of collecting information about, for example, people's media consumption habits or opinions about relevant issues. It can be used for identifying characteristics of the respondents at the time of the survey but it cannot tell us about change over time. It can help us identify associations between different variables (e.g. along the lines that preference for particular television programmes is associated with various demographic characteristics of the respondents, such as age, level of education, social class, gender, etc.), but it cannot tell us about the causal relationships, if any, between variables. In other words, the cross-sectional survey is not at all a useful instrument for examining how patterns of media consumption might relate to particular opinions or beliefs held by media audiences. Simply put, the cross-sectional survey cannot tell us whether people who watch a lot of violent programmes become more fearful, or whether an association between amount of violent programme viewing and level of fear might reflect simply that people with a fearful disposition tend to prefer violent programmes.

The trend study

The trend study is a longitudinal design for examining change over time in a population. The same set of questions is asked in a series of (in effect, cross-sectional) surveys conducted at different points in time. A new sample of a given population is drawn for every occurrence of the trend survey. This design thus facilitates the measurement of change over time in the set of variables examined, for example changes in internet access within a given population, changes in political opinions held by a given population (e.g. the electorate) and changes in what respondents regard as the most important issues facing society. A prime example of a trend survey is the Pew Research Center's (2010) tracking over a number of years of changes in Americans' understanding/perception of a range of issues relating to climate change. It is important to be clear that the trend study measures change in a given population's – not in the individual respondent's – behaviour, opinions, beliefs or perceptions. If it is change in the individual respondent that is of interest then a refined version of the trend study is required, namely the panel study.

The panel study

The panel study is a longitudinal design that enables the mapping of change in the individual respondent's behaviour, opinions, beliefs or perceptions. The same initial sample of respondents are surveyed or interviewed repeatedly at a given interval over a specified period of time. The same set of questions is thus asked of the same sample of respondents over this period. This design therefore facilitates the tracking of whether and how the individuals in the selected sample change their behaviour, opinions, beliefs or perceptions over time, and it further enables the researcher to investigate how any such changes correlate with external changes that might be thought to influence or interact with respondents' behaviour, views, etc.

In media and communication research, one of the first and most famous panel studies was that of political campaigning, media and voter intentions in the American presidential election campaign of 1940 by Lazarsfeld, Berelson and Gaudet (1944). Lowery and DeFleur describe this sophisticated study as 'one of the most imaginative uses of survey designs and techniques in the history of social science' and include it as one of the 'milestones' in their book *Milestones in Mass Communication Research* (1995: 72). Simply described, the same panel of respondents was interviewed every month starting in May and finishing with the last survey conducted just after the election in November.

While the principal objective of the researchers was to explore 'all those conditions which determine the political behaviour of people' or, in short, to 'discover how and why people decided to vote as they did', a sign of the sophistication of this research was the endeavour to also examine whether the sheer process of repeated interviewing might influence respondents' answers and voting intentions (Lazarsfeld et al., 1948 cited in Lowery and DeFleur, 1995: 72). In other words, this was a classic case of researchers being sensitive to the possibility that the mere fact of respondents' knowing that they are being studied might affect the results (a phenomenon commonly referred to in social science research as the Hawthorne effect, after the industrial sociology studies conducted in the early part of the twentieth century in the Hawthorne Works, a large factory complex outside Chicago, Illinois).

While the panel study is a powerful tool for examining how and why changes occur in a particular sample of respondents, its comparatively infrequent use – compared to trend studies and cross-sectional surveys – is symptomatic of the considerable difficulties of persuading respondents to agree to be interviewed repeatedly and of other types of attrition such as panel respondents moving away, disappearing or even dying during the planned survey period.

In media and communications, both trend and panel studies have been particularly important in agenda-setting research, where because time is a key independent variable their main strength is that they significantly enhance the possibility of plotting how changes in the media agenda (as measured through, for example, content analysis) may correlate with – and possibly 'cause' (at least the likelihood of showing cause-and-effect is considerably increased through the mapping of changes in the two agendas on a strict time-line) – changes in respondents' opinions, beliefs or behaviour.

Ethics in survey research

Survey research, like other approaches to studying people, involves collecting information from individuals about their beliefs and behaviour, and in this respect the success of surveys depends on the willingness of respondents to answer and to do so honestly. While good and decent researchers have long acknowledged the need to be truthful to their respondents, not to obtain information through deception, and the need to ensure that data are collected and used only for clearly and explicitly defined purposes, such requirements have increasingly been codified into formal professional and legal requirements in the form of 'ethics codes' or 'codes of practice'. Thus professional societies (e.g. the Market Research Society), academic and professional associations (e.g. the British Sociological Society; the Association of Internet Researchers), government funding bodies (e.g. the Economic and Social Research Council in the UK) and universities and other research institutions now have detailed codes of practice governing research in general and that involving human subjects in particular.

Key concepts – where human subjects are involved – are the requirements that 'informed consent' be given by the respondent prior to commencing the collection of information, and that assurances be given to the respondent regarding confidentiality and the use of any information given. University staff and students alike need to ensure that their research conforms to their institution's code of practice and associated ethics requirements, and that they have received the necessary ethics approval before embarking on research involving human subjects. This is imperative in all such research, but especially where children and younger subjects below 18 years of age are involved.

Modes of data collection in surveys

The central instrument of data collection in surveys is the questionnaire. A questionnaire is a list of – carefully worded (see later on the importance of wording) – questions either with a number of answer options (closed questions) or with space for respondents to enter answers using their own words (open-ended questions). Questionnaires are completed in one of two ways:

1) Through a *self-administered questionnaire*: the respondent fills in a questionnaire, which may be distributed by post or email, or – much less reliable in sampling terms – through a public venue or medium (e.g. a magazine, a website or similar).
2) Through an *interview*, in which the interviewer completes the survey questionnaire according to the answers given by the respondent. Interviews may be face to face, by telephone or (although not widely used as yet) by computer-mediated visual communication such as Skype.

A mode of data collection that combines features of these two principal forms is the 'group administration': a group of respondents – for example a school class – complete individual questionnaires under the general supervision/guidance of the researcher.

Table 9.1   Self-administered questionnaires and personal interviews: advantages and disadvantages (adapted from Berger, 2011: 226–7)

Self-administered questionnaires Advantages	Disadvantages
• Inexpensive • No interviewer bias to worry about • Highly personal questions can be asked • Complex questions or questions requiring detailed information (that the interviewer may have to look up) can be asked	• Potential for misinterpretation or misunderstanding of questions • Low response rates are the norm • Potentially difficult to verify who filled in the questionnaire

Personal interviews Advantages	Disadvantages
• Interviewer can explain questions • You know who is answering the questions • A higher likelihood of getting a response (than in the self-completion questionnaire)	• Can be intrusive (too personal) • Time-consuming and expensive • Difficult to optimise the matching of interviewer characteristics (social class, language, conversational style, mode of address, etc.) to respondent characteristics

The key advantages of the self-administered questionnaire are low cost and ease of distribution. The key disadvantage is an often very low response rate (the percentage of questionnaires completed and returned to the researcher). The key advantage of the personal interview is its interactive nature, that is the interviewer can explain difficult questions or instantly correct misunderstanding/misinterpretation of questions. The key disadvantages of the personal interview are cost and intrusiveness. Table 9.1 lists some of the major advantages and disadvantages in relation to each of the two principal forms of data collection.

Sampling and samples in surveys

While the census is an example of a survey that aims to interview every (adult) person in a given population, most surveys are – for practical reasons – not censuses, but focus instead on a small sample drawn from the population in question. Whether broadcasting organisations wishing to know about their audiences' media/programme preferences or political parties wishing to know about the electorate's voting intentions or opinions on controversial political issues, it would be extremely expensive and time-consuming, not to mention wholly unnecessary, to survey everybody in these two types of populations.

Instead, survey researchers or organisations draw a smaller sample, ideally but not always a 'representative' sample, from the population that they wish to study or obtain information about. A sample is essentially a smaller subset or miniature version of the population (Fink, 1995). Ideally, a sample should be 'representative', meaning that key characteristics (age, gender, social class, etc.) or variables relevant to the survey objectives are distributed similarly in the sample and in the larger population from which the sample is drawn. A sample is thus *not* a simple percentage of the larger population, nor is size per se a determining factor when deciding on how to draw a 'representative' sample – a sample of 4,000 people out of a population of 5 million is not necessarily any more representative than a sample of 2,000 respondents from the same population of 5 million. It depends, in very general terms, on the range and distribution of characteristics and variables relevant to the survey. A sample then ideally needs to: a) match the distribution of key characteristics – relevant to the survey – in the population, and b) be of sufficient size to enable the type of comparisons between variables that may be required in the analysis of the survey data (i.e. audience researchers may wish to break the audiences for a particular television programme down by gender, age, social status, level of education, etc. – the more variables included in this type of comparison, the smaller the numbers in each cell of a comparison table are likely to be, which then has implications for the kind of statistical conclusions that can be drawn).

There are two broad groups of sampling: probability sampling and non-probability sampling. All probability sampling deploys some kind of statistical randomness principle in the selection of respondents, whereas procedures to ensure randomness are not implemented in non-probability sampling. The choice of sampling strategy has implications for the kind and robustness or strength of statistical analyses/tests that can be applied to the data collected, and for the extent to which results can be generalised or extrapolated from the sample to the larger population examined. Probability sampling thus enables the use of much more sophisticated statistical tests and analyses – and ultimately much more confidence in the kind of conclusions that can be drawn from the sample data about the population examined in the survey. Within each of these two broad types of sampling, there are a number of specific approaches that are introduced briefly in the following.

Probability sampling

Simple random sampling
Each member of a given population has an equal chance of being selected. In practice, this approach involves assigning a number to each member of the chosen population. Then consult a 'random numbers table' (from a statistics

book, methods book or from survey websites) to select – from the individually numbered members of your population – as many of the numbers listed in the random numbers table as you require for your sample, for example the first 20 random numbers listed, or the first 30 random numbers listed, depending on the size of sample aimed for.

Systematic random sampling

The first respondent is chosen randomly – again using a random numbers table – from a numbered list of each member of the population. Starting with the randomly chosen first respondent, every n'th number in the population is chosen; for example if a sample of 20 respondents is required from a population of 100, then the sampling interval is (100/20=) 5, and if the first randomly selected number is 3, then the sample will consist of every fifth number starting from the first randomly selected number, that is the following numbers from the population: 3, 8, 13, 18, ... 93, 98.

Stratified random sampling

The population is first divided into a number of sub-groups/strata according to specified characteristics relevant to the survey, for example gender, age, ethnicity, etc. Respondents are then sampled using random sampling within each sub-group/stratum.

Cluster sampling and multistage sampling

It may be impossible or impractical to obtain a complete list of the full population to be studied; researchers therefore often first select particular naturally occurring sub-groups, such as electoral wards within a city, and then apply some form of random sampling to the selected sub-groups/areas. A form of cluster sampling is the *multistage sampling strategy*: for example for a nationwide survey of England, one might start by randomly selecting a number of shires; within each shire, we would then select – again using random sampling – a number of smaller administrative units, for example boroughs; from these we might select particular electoral wards, and, finally, within each electoral ward, we might randomly select – for example from the electoral register – a sample of individual respondents to be surveyed.

Non-probability sampling

Quota sampling

Bryman offers the following clear definition:

> The aim of quota sampling is to produce a sample that reflects a population in terms of the relative proportions of people in different categories, such as gender,

ethnicity, age groups, socio-economic groups, and region of residence, and in combinations of these categories. However, unlike a stratified sample, the sampling of individuals is not carried out randomly, since the final selection of people is left to the interviewer. (2008: 185)

The population is first divided into a number of sub-groups/strata according to specified characteristics relevant to the survey, for example gender, age, ethnicity. The required number or *quota* of respondents in each sub-group are then selected on the basis of whether they meet the criteria relevant to that sub-group (e.g. one sub-group could comprise 20 male television viewers aged 30–40 years).

Convenience sampling
Respondents are selected in terms of their relevance to the research objectives and on the basis of availability and willingness to be interviewed, for example a media researcher may survey fellow participants in an academic conference, a class of university students that they teach, cinema-goers as they enter or leave the cinema.

Snowball sampling
As in convenience sampling, a group of respondents is selected initially in terms of their relevance to the research objectives (e.g. that they use Facebook) and on the basis of availability and willingness to be interviewed. These respondents are then asked to identify other people – of similar relevance to the research objectives – who would be willing to participate in the survey.

Designing questionnaires and asking questions

As indicated previously, the core research instrument of a survey is the questionnaire, and designing the questionnaire is one of the most important tasks in the process of conducting survey research. Not so long ago, this task also used to be both arduous and time-consuming. Researchers using survey methodology have, however, been quick to realise the tremendous potential of the internet: in addition to the internet increasingly being used as a vehicle for conducting surveys and gathering survey data, there are now also a wealth of sites providing easy access to past surveys and/or excellent advice and guidance on how to design surveys and questionnaires. Rather than offering duplicate and generic examples of questionnaires here, we therefore refer you (at the end of this chapter) to selected sites, and we further emphasise (as in Chapter 2) the importance – in survey research as in any other kind of social science research – of starting by searching for, identifying and reviewing published research that has tackled comparable or similar research questions to those which you intend to investigate in your own research.

There is no need to spend valuable research time on 'reinventing the wheel', and, more often than not, already tested and tried survey instruments from previously published comparable studies can be a tremendous resource. This is true not only in terms of the format of the questionnaire and type of questions, but potentially also with regard to the wording of questions, where the process of designing new research and questionnaires can benefit from the testing, validity and reliability checks which have already been performed in relation to published survey research. With this preamble, we now turn to discussing some of the key considerations in relation to questionnaire design.

Question formats

A questionnaire is a list of questions, where each question offers either a set of responses from which the respondent can choose (closed questions), or a space for the respondent to record an answer in their own words (open-ended questions). Whether a question is asked in a closed or open-ended format may affect how respondents answer. The Pew Research Center, for instance, offers the following instructive example:

> in a poll conducted after the presidential election in 2008, people responded very differently to two versions of this question: 'What one issue mattered most to you in deciding how you voted for president?' One was closed-ended and the other open-ended. In the closed-ended version, respondents were provided five options (and could volunteer an option not on the list).
>
> When explicitly offered the economy as a response, more than half of respondents (58%) chose this answer; only 35% of those who responded to the open-ended version volunteered the economy. (Pew Research Center, no date)

One way to ensure that closed questions in a survey questionnaire contain answer options that reasonably reflect or match how respondents think about the issue addressed by the question is to conduct a few focus group discussions (see Chapter 10). Focus group discussions can often be instrumental in demonstrating what issues people are concerned with, how they view these and, not least, how they 'talk' about such issues, in other words the types of words/labels that they use when referring to the issues.

While the open-ended form of the question referred to above in the Pew Research Center example ('What one issue mattered most to you in deciding how you voted for president?') asks for just a single 'issue' to be mentioned, open-ended questions will more often invite a longer and more elaborate response. Closed questions come in principally three different formats: *multiple choice*, where the respondent ticks/circles one answer from a given list; *ranking scales*, where the respondent ranks a list of options – for example a list of television programmes – in order of preference: 1, 2, 3 ... etc.; or *agreement rating scales*, where the respondent indicates their choice on a preference scale such as 'strongly agree', 'agree', 'neither agree, nor disagree', 'disagree', 'strongly disagree'.

As respondents often, and rightly, see their time as precious, it is important to keep survey questionnaires as brief, clear and succinct as possible. There are three important considerations to engage with when starting out on the design of a questionnaire: which questions should be included? How should they be asked? And in which order should they appear?

Which questions?

There is no such thing as a 'standard set of questions' that must or should be included in a questionnaire, regardless of the objectives of the research. A questionnaire should include questions – and only such questions – that are relevant to the research objectives or envisaged as potentially important independent variables relative to the particular (dependent) variables examined in the research. Surveys should not in general include 'fishing-expedition' questions that may or may not yield some interesting information but where it is not clear how or whether they will be used in the analysis of the questionnaire data. There may, particularly in studies of a mainly exploratory nature, be exceptions to this general rule, but it is still important to have at least some idea about how such variables may illuminate or contribute to the research objectives at hand.

How asked?

Questions need to be intelligible and indeed possible for respondents to answer. 'Intelligible' refers both to the terms, concepts or phenomena referred to in individual questions (are they known or recognisable to the respondents?) and to the 'route' through the questionnaire (i.e. is it sufficiently clear when a particular answer to one question, for example, requires the respondent to skip ahead a few questions?). 'Possible' refers to whether the information asked for is something that the respondent can reasonably be expected to know or reliably estimate. A typical example in media research is a question about the amount of television viewing in the last week or the number of hours spent on the internet in the last week. Few, if any, carry this kind of information around in their heads, and it is therefore more sensible to ask respondents about 'yesterday' and perhaps the 'day before yesterday', or, alternatively, to ask respondents to keep a daily diary/log over a given period of the number of hours spent watching television or accessing the internet. 'Possible' also relates to the mode of data collection used, for example if filling out a self-completion questionnaire, respondents may have time to check relevant written records (e.g. bills, medical records) for some of the information required, whereas this would not normally be practical or feasible in a face-to-face or a telephone interview.

Word choice and question formulation can easily influence or skew the answers. Careful consideration therefore needs to be given to all of these dimensions and with the particular target sample audience in mind. The following is a checklist of some of the key considerations in questionnaire design:

- Questions should be clear (simple syntax and using words that will be understood by the target population; avoid specialist terminology, unless of course respondents are particularly familiar with the terminology), concise (getting straight to the core idea or point) and unambiguous.
- Avoid long questions, as respondents are likely to lose interest or concentration, not to mention get irritated.
- Avoid double-barrelled questions, that is questions that in effect ask about more than one thing. As Wimmer and Dominick (2006: 184) advise, beware if a question contains an 'and', as this is often an indication that respondents are being asked about more than one piece of information. The trouble with double-barrelled questions of course is that we don't know which part of the question the respondent's answer relates to: For example, 'politicians receive too much news coverage and are often ridiculed. Do you agree or disagree? A respondent answering 'agree' may agree that politicians receive too much news coverage, but disagree that they are often ridiculed, or vice versa.
- Avoid leading questions or questions which may make the respondent feel guilty, excluded, 'labelled' or similar.
- Avoid potentially sensitive questions, or questions which can be construed as offensive. If such questions are necessary, put them towards the end of the questionnaire (see also below on question order).
- Avoid asking for detailed information that the respondent can't reasonably be expected to have or which may be embarrassing to the respondent, for example illness or similar conditions.

In which order?

The order of questioning is important, as it may affect whether respondents complete the questionnaire and how honestly they answer the questions. In general the following principles apply:

- Always start with a full introduction of who you are, who's behind the survey, how/why the respondent was selected, what the purpose of the survey is, how the data will be used and by whom, and by assuring respondents of the confidentiality of the information provided.
- In general, survey questions should progress from simple to more complex questions, and from innocuous questions to those, if any, that may be potentially sensitive or may touch on issues that the respondent feels uncomfortable about discussing or answering, for example questions relating to the respondent's sexual behaviour or attitudes, religious beliefs and views, or even general political views. Sensitive or taboo-type questions are best put towards the end of the questionnaire, by which time the respondent's confidence and rapport may have been gained and the respondent is perhaps also more willing to disclose relevant views, opinions or information that they would have been reluctant to discuss at the beginning of the questionnaire or interview.

Piloting/pre-testing

Before 'going into the field' to conduct survey interviews or to administer self-completion questionnaires, it is essential to pilot the questionnaire. This is to make sure that everything 'works' before embarking on the resource-intensive task of conducting the full survey. As indicated above, answers are easily influenced by the way questions are worded and asked, so it is important to ensure – as far as is possible – that a) questions are understood as intended; b) interviewers and respondents know how to work their way through the questionnaire; c) respondents can answer the questions; d) questions are worded such that they will yield useable and appropriate – that is to the objectives of the research – data; e) answers are not unduly skewed by particular phrases or word choice.

One way of piloting a questionnaire is of course to simply try it out on a few colleagues and/or friends, but ideally piloting should be done on a 'genuine' sample, that is a small sub-sample of the sample that will actually be surveyed. The sub-sample should thus ideally have the same general characteristics as the respondents who will eventually be surveyed in the full survey sample. Piloting is not only a necessary step to enhance both the validity and reliability of the research; it is also a cheap and efficient way to improve the design and to iron out any problems or errors before commencing the full-scale survey. Once a mail-shot self-completion questionnaire has been sent out there is, for example, little or no chance to correct any problems in it, so it is clearly important that any such problems are picked up before embarking on the full-scale survey.

Recording, managing, analysing survey data

The traditional questionnaire, which is still widely used, is a printed document where answers are recorded by hand-writing in tick-boxes or in the form of hand-written words (in the case of open-ended questions). However, increasingly questionnaires are completed on computer or equivalent electronic devices. In personal interviews this takes the form of 'computer-assisted telephone interviewing' (CATI), or in the form of 'computer-assisted personal interviewing' (CAPI). In self-completion questionnaires, this takes the form of questionnaires embedded in or attached to emails, or questionnaires on a website.

Computer-formatted questionnaires have advantages both of speed and reliability over traditional printed questionnaires filled in by hand: computer-based questionnaires can be set up such that the data (answers) are automatically transferred to a data analysis program, and results can be generated almost immediately; complex questionnaires, which, for example, might have various filtering questions with associated branching routes, can be set up so that respondents are automatically transferred to the appropriate next question depending on their answer to the filtering question; data entry is more reliable, as answer categories can be restricted so that only valid answers can be entered, etc. Internet-based questionnaires can of course also make use of audio and visual prompts, instructions or input.

Whether using traditional printed questionnaires or computer/web-based electronic questionnaires, the recorded answers will eventually need to be transferred to a statistical analysis program suitable for the types of analysis to be performed on the collected data. For most analytical surveys, statistical analysis programs such as SPSS or SAS, capable of performing powerful statistical analyses and tests, should be used, while for less demanding descriptive surveys much can be done with readily available spreadsheet programs like Microsoft Excel or equivalent.

Readying survey data for analysis also involves coding open-ended text-answers in a numeric format that can be read and analysed by the relevant data analysis program, and it involves checking for error codes and missing data or missing answers.

Once the questionnaire data have been transferred and checked (e.g. for error codes and missing data), the researcher is ready to start analysing the data. Where to start and what kind of analyses to perform will of course depend on the objectives of the research, but generally it works well to start by familiarising yourself with relatively simple descriptive trends in the data, in other words by running simple frequencies analyses to show how many of this and how many of that, and how many said this and how many said that in relation to each question in the questionnaire. This will then be elaborated and followed by more complex analyses involving, usually, comparisons (crosstabulations) between two or more variables, as well as statistical tests for significance and strength of correlation, etc.

Summary

- The survey is historically one of the most frequently used methods for studying media audiences. It has played a prominent role in the history and development of media and communication research and models.
- Survey research is a method for collecting and analysing social data via highly structured and often very detailed interviews or questionnaires in order to obtain information from large numbers of respondents presumed to be representative of a specific population (Wiseman and Aron, 1970: 37; cited in Berger, 2011: 222).
- Definitions of survey research stipulate that:
  - It is a systematic and structured mode of collecting data, by asking people questions.
  - It focuses – ideally – on a *representative* sample of a larger population.
  - It uses, as its data collection instrument, an interview schedule, that is a list of questions to be asked of the interviewee/respondent by an interviewer, or a questionnaire to be completed by the interviewee/respondent.
  - The data collected, that is the answers to the survey questions, are subjected to quantitative analysis to produce descriptive, comparative and inferential statistics that can be extrapolated from the sample studied to the larger population from which the sample was drawn.
- Surveys have both strengths and weaknesses:
  - Strengths include: advantages of a more natural research situation than that of the laboratory experiment; a highly structured mode of collecting data, affording advantages of efficiency, reliability and cost-effectiveness; they enable the examination of a broad range of variables; as a quantitative and structured method of data collection they make it possible to use powerful statistical analyses and tests to examine relationships between variables.
  - Weaknesses include: the survey provides potentially only a snapshot of people's beliefs, attitudes or behaviour, while telling us little about the dynamic ways in which opinions are formed, negotiated or changed; the survey focuses on the individual's opinions, beliefs and behaviour and provides few clues to the social context circumscribing and impacting on these dimensions; answers to survey questions are easily framed, skewed or influenced by how they are worded and asked; surveys are

good at demonstrating correlation between variables, but generally not well equipped to demonstrate causality between variables.

- There are three main types of survey:
  o *The cross-sectional survey*: a one-off survey, where a sample of respondents is interviewed only once.
  o *The trend study*: a longitudinal design for examining change over time in a population. The same set of questions is asked in a series of surveys conducted at different points in time. A new sample of a given population is drawn for every occurrence of the trend survey.
  o *The panel study*: a longitudinal design for examining change over time in the individual respondent's behaviour, opinions, beliefs or perceptions. The same set of questions is asked of the same sample of respondents in a series of surveys conducted over a given period of time.
- Survey research must always meet standard ethical requirements regarding informed consent, confidentiality, data protection, etc.
- Most surveys rely on sampling and are carried out on a sample of respondents that are representative of the target population of the survey.
- The choice of sampling strategy depends on considerations regarding cost, resources, access to respondents, as well as the type and strength of statistical analysis envisaged.
- There are two principal types of sampling: *probability* and *non-probability* sampling. The former comprises the four types: simple, systematic, stratified and cluster sampling. The latter comprises quota, convenience and snowball sampling.
- The questionnaire is the core research instrument of the survey. Questionnaires can be self-administered or administered by an interviewer in face-to-face, telephone or computer-mediated interviewing. Questionnaires must be carefully designed to reflect the objectives of the research. Care and thought must go into deciding on question formats (closed or open-ended; multiple choice, ranking or rating scale questions, etc.), order of questioning, wording of questions (e.g. questions must be clear, brief and unambiguous; questions must not: be double-barrelled or leading; ask for complex, detailed or sensitive information that the respondent is unlikely to have to hand or may be embarrassed by).
- The questionnaire should be pilot-tested in order to iron out any problems (e.g. in relation to question wording, comprehension) and fine-tune question wording before embarking on the full-scale survey.
- Surveys are increasingly conducted with the help of computers and other digital media, affording significant advantages of speed and reliability in the collection, recording, processing, management and analysis of data.

Further reading and resources

As indicated earlier in this chapter, the process of searching for, identifying and locating previous relevant (to the focus and objectives of one's own study) and/or comparable survey research and associated sampling strategies and questionnaires has become infinitely faster (as well as potentially more reliable, comprehensive and systematic) since the rise of the internet in the 1990s. In addition to the results that can be gleaned from standard literature searches on key library databases, general searches on powerful search engines such as Google will help in quickly identifying potentially relevant publications or websites (which must of course be scrutinised carefully in terms of the quality of information and advice that they offer).

Below we offer a few web addresses selected for their relevance to survey and questionnaire design generally, and, in the case of some of them, for their relevance to media and communication research in particular. Following these, we then point you in the direction of books that provide excellently detailed and easy-to-follow guidance on how to design, conduct and report on surveys, including web-based surveys.

Selected web addresses/web resources

The Pew Research Center: http://pewresearch.org

The Pew Research Center in the US is an excellent resource for anybody interested in the news media and public/political attitudes and opinions, including in the interplay between news coverage and public interest. A sub-division, The Pew Research Center for the People and the Press (http://people-press.org/about/) conducts regular *monthly polls* on politics and major policy issues as well as the *News Interest Index*, a weekly survey aimed at gauging the public's interest in and reaction to major news events. Shorter *commentaries* are produced on a regular basis addressing the issues of the day from a public opinion perspective. In addition, the Center periodically fields major surveys on the news media, social issues and international affairs.

Particularly useful and detailed information and guidance on survey methodology is available under the sub-heading 'Methodology' at http://people-press.org/methodology/ including key topics such as 'Sampling', 'Collecting Survey Data' and 'Questionnaire Design'.

The Survey Resources Network: http://www.surveynet.ac.uk/srn/introduction.asp

Funded by the UK Economic and Social Research Council (ESRC), the Survey Resources Network's principal resource is its Survey Question Bank (http://www.surveynet.ac.uk/sqb/about/introduction.asp). This offers access to a range of – fully searchable – major UK and cross-national social surveys conducted mainly since the mid-1990s. It comprises guidelines/factsheets on survey methodology (including on sampling, questionnaire design and piloting) as well as links to other relevant sites.

There are many commercial websites offering interactive survey design, web surveys, survey analysis software and related services and products for a fee. Many of these also have extensive free guides and tutorials, which may be worth consulting. Examples include:

- Survey Monkey: http://www.surveymonkey.com/
- Creative Research Systems: http://www.surveysystem.com/sdesign.htm
- StatPac: http://www.statpac.com/surveys/

Further reading

Fink, A. (2009). *How to Conduct Surveys: A Step-by-Step Guide* (4th edn.). London: Sage.
Probably one of the best and most accessible introductions available, this guide covers all aspects of the survey process, from conceptualisation and design to analysis and presentation of the survey results. Each chapter is replete with illustrative examples (from question types and question wording to tables/charts and PowerPoint slides for presenting results). Each chapter ends with a concise and succinct summary of key points and practice exercises/questions.

Wimmer, R. D., and Dominick, J. R. (2011). *Mass Media Research: An Introduction (International Edition)* (9th revised edn.). Belmont, CA: Wadsworth.
Now in its ninth revised edition, *Mass Media Research* continues to provide an excellent introduction to the key considerations for media and communication researchers wishing to use survey methodology in their research.

Couper, M. P. (2008). *Designing Effective Web Surveys*. Cambridge: Cambridge University Press.
Leading scholarly guide to designing web surveys, covering both the scientific evidence and theory behind web-based surveys and the practical components of designing and using them.

CHAPTER 10

Interpreting audiences: focus group interviewing

Discovering *how* audiences make sense of media messages is not easily done through survey research. Survey research is good at providing a snapshot of audience beliefs, attitudes and behaviour – the *what* of audience/media relationships – but is much less suited for telling us about the *why* or *how* of such relationships. For examining the dynamics of what experiential knowledge and frames of interpretation audiences bring to bear in their use of media content, what role media use has in the everyday life of audiences, or how audiences use the media as a resource in their everyday lives, it is necessary to turn to more qualitative methods, to methods which allow us to observe in a more naturalistic setting than that of the survey or the laboratory experiment how audiences relate to media both as technologies and as content.

Observational and ethnographic approaches are methods that meet these requirements, but problems of access often rule out their extended use for the study of audiences in their 'natural' home environment (Silverstone, 1991). This is not to say that observation in the home setting is impossible: indeed, a number of media audience studies have successfully observed media use in a family setting, including Hobson's (1982) study of audiences for a popular British soap opera, Morley's (1986) study of family television in Britain, and several studies reported in *World Families Watch Television* (Lull, 1988), including a study of video and television in the American family by Lindlof and his colleagues (Lindlof, Shatzer and Wilkinson, 1988).

Semi-structured individual interviews or semi-structured group interviews are approaches which allow the researcher a potentially much richer and more sensitive type of data on the dynamics of audiences and their relations to media than the survey. At the same time, these approaches are comparatively cheap (although often time-consuming), and they are not burdened by the resources and lengthy access negotiations often needed for observational studies.

The phenomenal rise of the internet since the 1990s has brought with it exciting new opportunities for studying not only media audiences (as witnessed by numerous studies focusing for example on fan communities around popular television series, see e.g. Hine, 2011; Pullen, 2004) but also the increasingly interactive processes by which new media technologies are becoming an integral part of and being used for communication and 'meaning-making'. There are intriguing parallels between the kind of meaning-making that might take place in traditional focus group discussions, and that which can be witnessed – unobtrusively – in internet discussion forums, fan-sites, blogging or tweeting. There are also significant and important differences, however, and the rise of the internet as both an object and a tool for research has thus extended and enhanced rather than replaced more traditional approaches to the study of media audiences such as surveys, experiments and focus group interviewing.

In this chapter, we will introduce the focused group interview as a method for studying media audiences. While the individual in-depth interview and the focused group interview produce similar data in many respects, our reasons for focusing on the group interview are twofold: first and foremost, focused group interviews allow the researcher to observe how audiences make sense of mediated communication through conversation and interaction with each other in a way that is closer, although clearly not identical, to how we form opinions and understandings in our everyday lives. Second, group interviews are more cost-efficient than individual interviews – a wider range of people can be interviewed within the same limitations of time, resources and research money.

Brief history

The focused group interview has gained widespread popularity as a research method for studying media audiences. With the rise of 'reception studies' in media research during the 1980s, the focused group interview became a key component of the arsenal of approaches deployed by communications and media researchers. The history and origins of the method, however, extend much further back in time than the 1980s, as well as across to many other fields of study.

In a delightful account of personal history, Merton (1987), in his article on the focused interview and focus groups, traces the conception and development of the method back to the early 1940s. He refers to radio audience research at University of Columbia with Paul Lazarsfeld at the Columbia Office of Radio Research, and to research on film audiences, notably in Merton's own work on army morale boosting and training films for the Research Branch of the United States Army Information and Education Division. Merton and Kendall's article 'The Focused Interview', published in 1946, and the book-length treatment published a decade later (Merton,

Fiske and Kendall, 1956)[1] are generally reckoned to mark the birth of the method as a one for the study of media audiences and communication processes.

Despite the early origins in the social sciences, it was in commercial marketing research rather than in sociology and related disciplines that the method became widely used in the next few decades. Not until the late 1970s and early 1980s did the approach experience a renaissance in the social sciences, bringing with it renewed examination of its methodological merit and applications (Morgan and Spanish, 1984; Krueger, 1988; Morgan, 1988; Stewart and Shamdasani, 1990; Morgan, 1993), although, interestingly, some of the key discussions of the renewed interest in and use of the method in media and communications research did not appear until the 1990s (Liebes and Katz, 1990; Schlesinger et al., 1992; MacGregor and Morrison, 1995; Lunt and Livingstone, 1996; Morrison, 1998).

The renaissance since the 1980s of the focused group interview as a method for media and communication research relates to the turn away from the traditional effects paradigm, and variations thereof which include such predominantly survey-based approaches as cultivation analysis, agenda-setting, and uses and gratifications research. The turn in the media audience research of the 1980s and 1990s marked a move away from questions about media influence and 'effects' on audience behaviour and beliefs, and towards concerns with how audiences interpret, make sense of, use, interact with and create meaning out of media content and media technologies. In the words of one prominent media scholar:

> The form which 're-conceptualization' took here involved an attempt to carry over cultural studies' alertness to discursive and symbolic processes into an analysis of the organization and forms of viewing activities rather than those of media texts themselves. 'Influence', whatever its strength and direction, had to work through meaning, and it was to the formal and social complexity of meaning-production that the new research addressed itself. Meaning was seen as *intra-textual* (requiring analysis of textual structures), *inter-textual* (requiring analysis, among other things, of genres and relations between them) but also finally and decisively *inter-pretative* (requiring research into the situated practice of 'receptive' understanding). (Corner, 1991: 270)

For many of the audience 'reception' studies of the 1980s the choice of focus group discussions, participant observation and related ethnographic

---

1   The original 1956 book has long since been out of print, even when Merton wrote his historical article in 1987. A second edition was finally published in 1990 (Merton, Lowenthal and Kendall, 1990).

methods marked a deliberate and conscious rejection of traditional quantitative approaches. But as Schlesinger et al. have eloquently argued, while there are good reasons for adopting 'qualitative' approaches in the study of media audiences, there are no grounds for making the qualitative emphasis 'into an article of faith that excludes any attempt at quantification' (1992: 8). Schlesinger et al. advocate – and in this they reflect a more general trend in the new audience research (e.g. Schrøder, 1987; Höijer, 1990; Livingstone, 1991) – the use of quantitative methods *in combination with* qualitative approaches and techniques.

In this context, it is also instructive to remind ourselves that in the early formulations of focus group methodology in the first half of the twentieth century, focus groups were indeed seen as a useful complement to survey methodology, both as a way of generating better-focused and better-formulated questions for surveys and as a method for pursuing interesting trends identified in survey in a much more detailed way.

While media research of the 1980s may still have been characterised to a large extent by entrenched antagonism between quantitative and qualitative approaches, and their principal proponents, media and communications research since the early 1990s has been characterised by ever-increasing *convergence* between quantitative and qualitative research techniques and approaches (see our discussion in Chapter 1; see also e.g. Schrøder et al., 2003; Hansen, 2011; Philo and Berry, 2011). In the same period, the method of focus group interviewing itself has also been developed and applied in new and innovative ways, particularly – in relation to understanding how audiences 'deal' with and make sense of media content – through the use of editing tasks and active engagement with media content (MacGregor and Morrison, 1995; Philo and Berry, 2011).

When to use focus group interviews

As in all research, the choice of method should principally reflect the purposes and objectives of the study to be carried out, although other more pragmatic factors, such as convenience, available resources and time will often play a role in determining how to approach a particular problem.

Focus group interviews may be the single substantive mode of data collection in a piece of research; but more frequently the approach has been used in conjunction with other, complementary, types of data collection. In media research, it has notably been used together with questionnaires, observation (ethnography) and analyses of media content. Likewise, the use of focus groups may be appropriate at different points in the progression of a study: they may be used at a very early stage for exploratory purposes, to investigate which issues and topics people are concerned about within a particular domain/field, and how they talk about these issues. Such exploratory data will help in the construction of relevant questions for a larger survey study using questionnaires; in this respect, focus group interviews are invaluable both in terms of providing pointers to relevant issues, themes and concerns, but, much more specifically and crucially, in terms of ensuring that survey questions deploy vocabularies and reference frames which resonate with those of the respondents who are to be surveyed. Alternatively, a survey study or a content analysis of media may have drawn attention to a number of topics that require further and more detailed examination through the use of focus group discussions.

Discontent with the 'passive' audience view and with the stilted view of media influence seen as the defining characteristics of traditional approaches to the study of media audiences, the new 'reception' and ethnographic audience studies emerging since the 1980s have been keen to employ methods of investigation which allow for a more active and meaning-constructive role for audiences. To many of the qualitative audience studies of the 1980s and early 1990s, the choice of focus group interviews as a method of investigation has thus been governed by the desire to examine, through a more 'natural' setting and frame than that of the survey or experiment, how media audiences relate to, make sense of, use, negotiate and interpret media content:

> The first priority was to determine whether different sections of the audience shared, modified or rejected the ways in which topics had been encoded by the broadcasters. (Morley, 1980: 23)

> ... the aim was to discover how interpretations were collectively constructed through talk and the interchange between respondents in the group situation. (Morley, 1980: 33)

> Specifically, it is a study of patterns of *involvement* in an episode of the world-wide hit *Dallas*, focusing on how viewers discuss the programme in nearly natural settings. (Liebes and Katz, 1986: 152)

> ... we wished to include as a primary element of our study an investigation into how viewers made sense of, and evaluated, the programmes we chose for analysis. (Corner, Richardson and Fenton, 1990: 47)

While the qualitative depth sought by these studies could equally well have been obtained through in-depth individual interviews, there are at least two important reasons for choosing the focus group discussion over the individual interview as a method of investigation. The first reason concerns the argument that the generation of meanings and interpretations of media content are 'naturally' social activities, that is audiences form their interpretations of media content and their opinions about such content through conversations and social interaction. Liebes and Katz thus argue that by using the method of focus group interviews, they 'were, in effect, operationalizing the assumption that the small-group discussion following the broadcast is a key to understanding the mediating process via which a program such as this enters into the culture' (1990: 28).

The second reason for choosing focus group discussions over individual interviews is that focus group discussions offer dynamics and ways – not available in individual interviews – of eliciting, stimulating and elaborating audience interpretations. It is precisely the group dynamics and interaction found where several people are brought together to discuss a subject that are seen as the attraction of this mode of data collection over individual interviews (Morgan, 1988; Kitzinger, 1994). Interaction between participants in a focus group 'allows researchers to study how people respond to each other's perspectives and mobilize or resist media accounts in debate with one another' (Kitzinger, 2004: 174). Philo and Berry similarly note that the focus group discussion format often leads to participants 'opening up', that is as rapport is established within the group participants become 'less guarded and more prepared to say what they really believe', but, more significantly, as discussion develops and participants hear arguments and information that they may not previously have been aware of, it becomes possible for the researcher to see how participants' 'beliefs are modified and develop' (2011: 281).

> Focus groups impel participants to think about and stay with the subject being discussed in a way which is surely *not* natural. The analytic abilities revealed in some of these discussions is probably far beyond the level of everyday discussion of television and is probably inspired by the seriousness with which participants' opinions are solicited. Group members were asked to generalize about the themes, messages, and characters, as well as about the functions of such programs for the viewer, at levels of abstraction which are unusual in gossip. Thus, the focus group was a catalyst for the individual expression of latent opinion, for the generation of group consensus, for free-associating to life, and for analytic statements about art. But even these more formal discussions have an informal thrust; in fact, a major part of our analysis is devoted to the casual commuting in the focus groups between the story and real life, where the story serves as a basis for interpreting and evaluating life and vice versa. The group context induces the expression of such latent thoughts. Negotiation within the group then produces an awareness of others' thoughts. The result is an incremental input into the world view of the community. (Liebes and Katz, 1990: 28–9)

Gamson further spells out the advantages of focus groups over individual interviews and surveys as a method for understanding how people socially construct meaning about public issues:

1. To talk about issues with others, people search for a common basis of discourse....
2. Focus groups, compared to survey interviews, allow us to observe the natural vocabulary with which people formulate meaning about the issues....
3. Through challenges and alternative ways of framing an issue, participants are forced to become more consciously aware of their perspective. (Gamson, 1992: 191–2)

Of course, some of the reasons for choosing focus groups may also be used as arguments against this approach. Some individuals inevitably exert more influence than others in a group situation, to the extent that they may begin to dominate the discussion (although this can often be countered and minimised by a skillful moderator – see later on the role of the moderator). Group discussions also tend to work towards 'consensus' ground – dissenting views may be marginalised and disagreement amongst participants becomes less visible as the group pressure moves discussion towards a common frame. These are well-known processes. Both Gamson (1992) and Liebes and Katz (1990), however, argue that these processes make the group discussion a more 'natural' form of data generation:

> Group dynamics are such that opinion and participation are *not* equally weighted; some people have disproportionate influence. But real life is like that: opinions are not as much the property of individuals as public-opinion polling would have us think. Opinions arise out of interaction, and 'opinion leaders' have disproportionate influence. (Liebes and Katz, 1990: 29)

While the idea of getting groups of people together to 'talk about media content' may sound like a productive way of generating 'rich', 'natural', 'detailed' and 'complex' data about how people interpret, accommodate, negotiate and use media content, the reality is often less rosy. People do not 'naturally' volunteer elaborate interpretations of media content, nor do people necessarily consciously think about, let alone articulate, how they use media content in their daily lives:

> That television programmes are topics of conversation is obvious, but do we really elaborate our interpretations here? Relying on everyday experience it seems more realistic to suppose that we discuss television programmes very briefly and at a superficial level, as when we talk about the weather. In news viewing, for instance, Levy (1977) has shown that some viewers even use television news to provide

them with items for small talk or chit-chat, accordingly not elaborations of their interpretations. (Höijer, 1990: 34)

Focus group discussions, in order to produce 'useful' data, require active input and structuring on the part of the convenor or moderator (see below, for more detail about this role). Indeed, the 'focus' of the discussions needs to be set very clearly, and the framework within which participants are being asked to articulate their views and comments needs be clear. While focus group discussions will often work gradually from relatively general and unstructured talk towards the more specific areas of interest to the researcher, the success of focus groups as a method of data collection ultimately depends on the (moderator's) ability to focus the discussion around the processes and issues relevant to the overall objectives of the research.

Steps in focus group research

The steps involved in conceptualising, carrying out and analysing focus group discussions are at a general level very similar to those of survey research (see Chapter 9) or content analysis (see chapter 5). They involve definition of the research problem, creation of the research instrument (in this case an interview guide), sampling, pilot-testing, etc. A useful overview of the steps involved in focus group research is offered by Stewart, Shamdasani and Rook (2007); see Figure 10.1.

Here we will discuss some of these steps in more detail and with reference to and illustrations from media audience research which has used focus groups. Before doing so, however, we start with the all-important requirement for any research that involves human subjects, namely to ensure that

1. Problem definition/formulation of the research question
2. Identification of sampling frame
3. Identification of moderator
4. Generation and pre-testing of interview guide
5. Recruiting the sample
6. Conducting the group
7. Analysis and interpretation of data
8. Writing the report

Figure 10.1   Steps in the design and use of focus groups (adapted from Stewart, Shamdasani and Rook, 2007: 48)

the work is conducted in accordance with institutional and professional regulations regarding research involving human subjects.

Ethics: regulations and requirements for research involving human subjects

Unlike research on media content, any research involving human subjects must conform strictly to the relevant regulations and ethics requirements as set out by the researcher's university, professional or other institutional code for human subject research. In practice, this means that ethics approval must be obtained *prior* to any involvement of human subjects, even if this is only for the purpose of piloting the research instruments, from the university's or research organisation's ethics approval panel or equivalent committee. There are particularly strict requirements where children or young people are to be involved in the proposed research, but in all cases ethics regulations require that participants 'must be informed of the study's rewards and risks, told the study is voluntary and confidential, and told they can quit participating at any time' (Krueger and Casey, 2009: 29–30).

Sampling and recruitment of groups

> Focus groups are conducted to obtain specific types of information from a clearly identified set of individuals. This means that individuals who are invited to participate in a focus group must be both able and willing to provide the desired information and must be representative of the population of interest.... A focus group is not just a haphazard discussion or brainstorming among people who happen to be available; it is a well-planned research endeavor that requires the same care and attention that is associated with any other type of scientific research. (Stewart, Shamdasani and Rook, 2007: 51)

That 'individuals who are invited to participate in a focus group must be able and willing to provide the desired information and must be representative of the population of interest' may seem obvious enough, but it is important to note that, unlike in surveys, the total number of participants in a focus group study is comparatively small; it is therefore essential that the sampling of groups takes careful note of any particular demographic, occupational, ethnic, cultural or other dimensions expected or hypothesised to be of relevance to the subject under investigation.

Indeed, focus group studies in media research have rarely sought to obtain groups representative of the general population as such. Rather, they have selected groups according to specific dimensions thought to be of significance to the way in which people use and interpret media content.

Additionally, audience studies using focus group methodology have often aimed to draw participants from what Philo and Berry term ' "normally occurring" groups, that is, people who would meet and speak with each other in the normal course of their lives' (2011: 276). Indeed in some studies, focus group methodology is deployed specifically with a view to exploring how social interaction mediates audience understandings, and it therefore becomes important to 'work with pre-existing groups' (Kitzinger, 1993: 272), that is groups of people who live, work or socialise together.

Corner and his colleagues similarly anticipated that public views and understanding would be shaped by a range of demographic, political, professional and other dimensions and they thus chose their principal participant groups from 'pre-constituted' 'interest groups':

> We anticipated that the main political parties would have reason to be interested in this topic (even though nuclear energy is not a simple partisan issue). We accordingly obtained the participation of respondent groups from the local Labour, Conservative and SLD parties. The net was extended to groups from the local Rotary club, one from the Labour and Trade Union Resource Centre of unemployed people, a women's discussion group, a group of comprehensive school pupils, a group of medical students, some Friends of the Earth members and a set of workers at the Heysham nuclear power plant. (Corner et al., 1990: 48–9)

Burgess and Harrison (1993) in their research on the circulation of claims and the role of media in relation to a controversial environmental issue complemented a general household survey with a focus group study involving just two groups. However, each of these groups was convened not once but six times over a half-year period with a view to examining how claims developed during this period. Burgess and Harrison deliberately chose one group consisting of local people who were generally supportive of the development in question, and another group consisting of local people who were 'all paid-up members of nature conservation and environmental organizations' (1993: 202), and who were, by implication, against the controversial development examined in the study.

In a study of press coverage and public understanding of the new genetics, Durant and his colleagues (Durant, Hansen and Bauer, 1996) chose a combination of types of groups. In addition to a number of 'general population' groups, they chose groups consisting of participants who, through their interest group membership or occupation/profession, had 'specialist' knowledge or concerns (moral, legal, health and commercial) relevant to the subject under investigation.

Liebes and Katz were interested in examining why the American television serial *Dallas* was almost universally popular. More specifically, they wished to examine whether and how audience interpretations of and involvement with the serial varied depending on the cultural background of the viewers:

> Thus, we chose four widely different groups within Israeli society to compare with each other, with second-generation Americans in Los Angeles (as representatives of the audience for whom the original program was intended), and with Japanese in Japan (where the program failed). In the choice of the Israeli groups, in particular, we hoped to be able to demonstrate that the nature of involvement in the program, in spite of its universal popularity, nevertheless varies with the social and cultural background of the viewers. (Liebes and Katz, 1990: 21)

> All told, the sample consisted of sixty-six groups of (usually) six persons of like ethnicity, age, and education ... for a total of some 400 participants. The analysis involved ten groups of Israeli Arabs, sixteen groups of Israelis of Moroccan origin, ten groups of recent immigrants from Russia to Israel, six groups from kibbutzim, ten groups from the Los Angeles area, and eleven groups from greater Tokyo. (Liebes and Katz, 1990: 24)

Like Corner et al. (1990), Philo in his analysis of media coverage and public beliefs relating to the British miners' strike of 1984/5 also aimed for groups which were ' "natural" in the sense that they had some existence prior to the research project' (1990: 22), although at the same time 'the people did have to be selected such that they could highlight possible differences in perception caused by factors such as class and cultural background' (1990: 23). Philo brought together a total of 169 people in 16 groups, which fell into four main categories: 1) groups with a special knowledge or experience of the strike (e.g. miners, police); 2) occupational groups; 3) special interest groups; and 4) residential groups.

> This selection of groups made it possible to hold constant some key variables such as regional area, while varying others such as class/cultural background. Sometimes these variables could be compared in the same group. (Philo, 1990: 23)

If the objectives of the research allow that participants be recruited from already naturally existing groups or communities, this clearly makes the task of finding, contacting and engaging the desired types of participants a great deal easier than drawing participants completely at random. Constituencies where they can be drawn from already existing lists – provided access is granted – include, for example: local, regional or national pressure groups, consumer organisations, special interest groups or party political organisations who can be contacted through their administrative offices or headquarters, and who may provide access to their membership lists; large employers, companies, trade associations and trade unions, who, likewise, may allow access to directories of employees and members; public institutions, associations (e.g. viewers' and listeners' associations, fan clubs, parents' groups, women's associations, ethnic societies, religious societies, housing associations) and professional societies (e.g. of doctors, scientists, solicitors, accountants, journalists).

Where the types of participants sought do not belong to already existing groups or communities, or cannot be drawn from pre-existing directories or membership lists, it is necessary to resort to the same kinds of sampling/recruitment methods normally used in survey research. These include contacting people in shopping centres, 'on the street' or in other public places;[2] 'advertising' for participants on public notice boards in workplaces, community centres or shops – or even through advertisements in local/regional media outlets; or contacting people by post (perhaps by random sampling names and addresses from electoral registers) or by telephone.

Numbers of groups and participants

How many groups? How many participants in each group? There is no single right answer to either of these two questions. The number of groups will depend on the aims of the research and on available resources. If focus groups are used merely for exploratory purposes and/or for generating ideas for a larger – perhaps survey-based – study, then as few as two, three or four groups may be sufficient (Hedges, 1985; Morgan, 1988). Where focus groups form a central and more substantive part of the data collection of a study, it would generally be difficult to justify fewer than six groups. As indicated by Morgan, one approach is to vary 'the number of groups according to whether the additional discussions are producing new ideas' (1988: 42). This strategy was followed by Livingstone and Lunt in their study of audience interpretations of television talk show programmes: 'The number of focus groups was determined by continuing until comments and patterns began to repeat and little new material was generated' (1993: 181). Livingstone and Lunt thus conducted 12 focus group discussions with a total of 69 participants in groups of between 4 and 8 people.

The single main factor (cost and resources notwithstanding) in deciding

---

2　　Gamson (1992: 16):

> We chose public sites where a recruitment table for the project was not out of place, and where it was possible to carry on a conversation and establish some rapport with potential recruits. This led us to focus on neighborhood and community events of various sorts – festivals, picnics, fairs, and flea markets, for example. We also posted notices of the research, with a phone number to contact us at various neighborhood and work sites. We avoided recruiting at any event or any site associated with a political cause or tendency, since we were eager to avoid any kind of political atypicality.

on the number of groups must be the types of comparisons across different group or population characteristics specified by the objectives of the research. Thus, if the aim is to examine how audience interpretations of a television programme vary according to social class, sex, age or according to interest group membership, profession/occupation or lifestyle, then there must be sufficient groups to represent these dimensions/populations.

> One important determinant of the number of groups is the number of different population subgroups required. The more homogeneous your groups are in terms of both background and role-based perspectives, the fewer you need.... [I]f there are several distinct population segments in the groups that you are studying, you may want or need to run separate groups in each, e.g., groups composed entirely of men and run separately from groups composed entirely of women. Running a minimum of two groups in each distinct segment will obviously increase the total number of groups. (Morgan, 1988: 42)

The number of groups used in the media audience studies of the 1980s and 1990s has varied considerably. Morley (1980), in his classic study of audiences for the UK current affairs programme *Nationwide*, interviewed 29 groups (although 3 of these were omitted from his analysis due to faults in the tape-recording) of, mainly, between 5 and 10 people. Morley's later study, *Family Television* (1986), involved 18 families. Liebes and Katz's (1990) study of cultural differences in the interpretation of *Dallas* comprised 66 groups of, usually, 6 participants (3 married couples) in each group. Kitzinger's (1993) study of audience understandings of AIDS involved 52 groups with a total of 351 participants, and group sizes were generally in the region of 4–9 participants. In their study of women and television violence, Schlesinger et al. (1992) conducted 14 group discussions with a total of 91 women (with group sizes of between 5 and 9 participants). Durant et al. (1993) conducted 12 focus group discussions with groups of between 7 and 9 participants.

More recent studies have generally used fewer groups than the studies of the 1980s. Thus, Philo and Berry (2011) in their study of audience perceptions and understanding of the Israeli–Palestinian conflict used 14 focus groups (of on average 7–8 participants). Shepherd et al. (2007) in their study of media coverage and public attitudes regarding human cloning used 10 focus groups (with on average 10 participants in each group). Shaw, Whitehead and Giles (2010) in their study of media coverage of celebrity drug use and its influence on young people's perceptions of drugs conducted just 4 focus groups, with 4–6 participants in each group. Vicsek and Gergely (2011), in a study of 'Media Presentation and Public Understanding of Stem Cells and Stem Cell Research in Hungary', similarly used just a small number of focus groups, in this case 7 groups with, on average, 8 participants per group.

As indicated by the examples mentioned above, the number of participants in each group may vary considerably – from as few as 2 people to as
many as 25 (one group in Kitzinger's (1993) study of AIDS representations
and interpretations). There also, however, appears to be – at least in the studies mentioned above – a general consensus that the optimum group size for
focus group discussions is in the region of 5–10 people per group. Krueger
and Casey note that while the 'traditionally recommended size of the focus
group within marketing research is 10 to 12 people [this] is too large for most
noncommercial topics' (2009: 67). They go on to advise that the 'ideal size
of a focus group for most noncommercial topics is five to eight participants.
Don't plan focus groups with more than 10 participants because large groups
are difficult to control and they limit each person's opportunity to share
insights and observations' (Krueger and Casey, 2009: 67).

The cost advantage of using group discussions in preference to individual
interviews clearly deteriorates with very small groups. With fewer than six
participants in each group it may also be more difficult to generate and maintain a dynamic and lively discussion. Conversely, larger groups, while more
cost-efficient and less likely to be atypical, also have distinct disadvantages.
The larger the group, the more likely it is that less vocal and less confident
participants will be marginalised and will tend to 'hide' behind the more
articulate members. It becomes more difficult for the moderator to keep the
discussion focused, and to avoid participants speaking at the same time
(Hedges, 1985).

In summary, then, the trend in media and communication research using
this method appears to be moving in the direction of deploying fewer than 20
groups with a group size of, ideally, around 6–10 participants per group.

Arranging participation

Once the appropriate type of participants have been identified, these should
be contacted and if – possibly after additional screening questions – they are
indeed the type of participants looked for, they should be formally invited to
participate in a group discussion. At the point of invitation, prospective
participants should of course be told in general terms what the purpose of
the focus group discussion is, where it will take place, with whom, and who
the researchers are and what they represent.

Most people are rightly reluctant to give up what could easily be a whole
morning, afternoon or evening of their time, if travelling is included. Indeed
some studies require significantly more, in the case of Schlesinger et al.
(1992), for example, a whole day, and other studies have required participation in not just a one-off focus group interview but in two or more focus
groups spread out over a period of time (in a design similar to the panel

design often used in surveys, see Chapter 9). It is therefore common practice to offer an incentive, and the nature and form of any incentive should be made clear to participants at the point when they are invited or recruited. Incentives can take various forms, but will normally include, covering travel and other expenses (e.g. childcare arrangements) incurred in relation to participation in a focus group. In addition, participants are often offered a cash payment for their time. Amounts inevitably vary widely and change over time, but should ideally bear some kind of relationship to the hourly pay that participants could normally expect to command (Krueger and Casey, 2009: 77–80, offer a particularly helpful discussion of 'incentives').

If the participants who have been approached agree to take part, it is important to send a written confirmation of their agreement along with confirmation of the location, date and time of the focus group. It is normally advisable to contact participants again a few days prior to the date of the focus group interview to remind them and to give any final details about how to get to the location.[3]

Interview setting/location

The location chosen for focus group discussions will vary depending on the purpose of the research, convenience and practical feasibility. Liebes and Katz (1990) held their focus group discussions in people's homes – this being important both to the purposes of the research and in terms of bringing together families who knew each other. Gamson likewise stressed the need to involve people who knew each other for discussions on the 'participants' turf rather than in a bureaucratic setting' (1992: 193). Consequently, Gamson's focus group discussions were held in the homes of individual participants. Durant et al. (1996) held the focus group discussions in the private homes of people who for a fee specialised in making their homes available for such purposes. This approach had the advantage that a non-threatening, non-bureaucratic setting combined with a 'homely' atmosphere in which the host served light refreshments to the participants.

In contrast, Schlesinger et al. (1992) held the majority of their focus group discussions in a university setting. As their subject of study included domestic violence toward women and a large proportion of their focus group participants were women who had been at the receiving end of

---

3   A variation on the mode of recruitment is the two-stage approach where suitable participants are first identified and contacted by the researcher, and it is then left to each of these contact-participants to bring together a group (friends, colleagues, family). Gamson (1992) used this approach, as did Liebes and Katz (1990), who contacted individual couples, who in turn invited other couples to form focus groups.

domestic violence, a domestic setting would clearly not have been appropriate for the focus group discussions, let alone conducive to 'open' and 'frank' discussion.

While a domestic setting may be a more 'natural' location than an institutional setting (e.g. a university department, an office in the workplace of a professional group) for focus group discussions, the choice of setting always needs to be considered in relation to the nature of the topic/issue to be discussed as well as practicality, and it needs to be borne in mind that the setting – any setting – inevitably exerts a 'framing' influence on the nature of participants' responses and on the group discussion as a whole.

The moderator role

With the groups selected and convened we come to the core part of the process, the focus group discussion itself. There are two key components to be considered here: the moderator role and the interview guide. The role of the moderator will vary depending on the subject of analysis, the type of response which is sought and the nature of the participants. It is in the nature of focus group discussions that the role of the moderator or facilitator is essentially to 'facilitate', 'moderate' and 'stimulate' discussion amongst the participants, not to 'dominate', 'govern' or unduly 'lead' such discussion. In practice, however, the degree to which the moderator plays an active steering role is a sliding scale from continuous active intervention to a much less active, opaque background role.

Typically, the principal roles of the moderator are to ensure that the issues, topics and foci outlined in the interview guide are covered in the course of discussion (this task includes managing the time spent on each topic), that a reasonable balance of contributions is maintained (i.e. no single individual is allowed to commandeer and dominate the group), and that the discussion is kept on course and not allowed to drift off in directions of little or no relevance to the study. However, these roles can be fulfilled in either more or less active ways. Gamson, for example, was keen to minimise the facilitator's intervention:

> To encourage conversation rather than a facilitator-centered group interview, the facilitator was instructed to break off eye contact with the speaker as early as politeness allowed and to look to others rather than responding herself when someone finished a comment. (Gamson, 1992: 17)

Other scenarios, and other types of participants (e.g. children), may call for more active steering by the moderator.

In media and communications research it is often the researcher themself who acts as the moderator for group discussions. This has the distinct advantage that the moderator is fully aware of the nature of the research and its objectives, although it also carries with it the danger that the moderator may be tempted to steer responses in the directions which best fit the researcher's preconceived expectations of the research. If the moderator is someone other than the researcher(s), it is important that they be appraised fully of the aims of the research, the topics/issues to be covered, the extent of active steering and probing required. These requirements should be clearly stated in the interview guide (see below).

Depending on the nature of issues/topics to be discussed and on the type of participants, it may also be desirable to specify particular socio-demographic and other characteristics of the moderator. Thus, the gender and age of the moderator will be important where groups of teenagers are brought together to discuss their sexual behaviour. There may be types of issues and group constellations where it would be desirable to match the race, ethnicity or religion of the moderator with those of the participants in the groups. Social-class matching could also be important. Such specific requirements notwithstanding, the successful moderator will more generally be a person who has such difficult-to-define attributes as the ability to establish rapport with group participants, the ability to put participants at ease, the ability to stimulate discussion amongst participants rather than with the moderator themself, and the ability to gently keep the discussion on course without imposing an overly restrictive agenda or format on the participants.

The interview guide

While a major strength of the focus group discussion, compared with a survey questionnaire study, is precisely its openness and the flexibility it offers for participants to respond, at length, in their own 'language' and on their own terms, this characteristic should not be confused with a 'free-for-all' unstructured chaos. Focus group discussions must have a 'focus'. While it is the job of the moderator/facilitator to ensure that the discussion in a focus group stays on the subjects or issues relevant to the research, it is the job of the researcher to draw up – on the basis of the definition of the research problem and issues or phenomena to be investigated – a guide or manual for the moderator to work from and follow.

The focus group interview guide is principally a 'menu' of the topics, issues or areas of discussion to be covered, but, in addition to simply listing these, it should also give directions as to: a) the sequence of topics/issues to be covered; b) the nature and extent of prompting and probing; c) the nature and use of visual or verbal aids, and the points during the course of a group discussion where these should be introduced; d) the nature, format and timing of any exercises, such as the news writing/editing exercises used by Philo and Berry (2011: 279).

One of the main reasons why it is important to have a clear interview guide, and to ensure that it is followed consistently through all the focus groups involved in a study, is to enable comparisons between groups. Focus groups, as we have seen above, are often constituted with a view to examining variations relating to the particular socio-demographic, experiential, professional or other characteristics of the participants. Only if the topics/issues discussed across different groups are the same, and only if the way in which discussions progress and are conducted is consistent, is it possible to say with some confidence that whatever differences and variations occur are the product of factors and characteristics other than those of the prompting used or manner of moderator intervention.

Focus group discussions in communication research generally follow a 'funnel approach', that is they progress from the general to the more specific, from non-directive questions (which allow participants to choose their own frame of reference and articulate their thoughts) towards more focused questions, requiring participants to discuss particular specific aspects of 'the problem'. In studies of media audiences, the start of a group discussion would often consist of the group viewing a television programme (or an excerpt, or an edited compilation); this is then followed by asking the participants in very general and vague terms 'what they thought about the programme' or 'what the programme was about', thus giving the participants the chance to define not only the 'frame of reference' for discussion of media content, but also, of course, the types of issues seen as important *and* the language for discussion. The mode of progression followed by Schlesinger et al. is typical for research in this field:

> The format for programme discussions was broadly standardised, although where necessary, due allowance was made for specific issues raised within a given group. After filling in the short questionnaire on immediate reactions, the discussion of each programme opened with a request for initial reactions and responses. Group members were invited to offer judgements on specific aspects of the programme: for example, whether they liked or disliked the programme, regarded it as 'good' or 'bad', or found it entertaining. By permitting the initial reaction to remain open, we sought to elicit the themes and issues which were most salient for group members. Initial reactions were followed by more focused discussions guided by a series of questions posed by the researcher, who acted as moderator … Although group members were free to raise any topic they wished, the researcher raised a standardised set of issues in each session, thus ensuring a degree of comparability across groups. (1992: 28)

The sequence typically followed in media audience research using focus group interviews is that of, first, exposure to selected media material (a television programme, a film, selected newspaper coverage, etc.), followed by, second, undirected general discussion, moving gradually – under the moderator's direction – towards more specific foci, issues, topics and questions. This, however, need not be the sequence. In particular, it will not be the sequence in studies which aim in the first instance to establish how different groups of people talk and think generally about particular issues before introducing specific media content into the discussion. Press (1991), for example, aimed to first establish how working-class and middle-class women talk about morality and abortion, and, second, to examine how the viewing of a television programme with an abortion storyline influenced the language and mode of discussion employed by the groups.

Similarly, Durant et al. (1993) were keen to explore general public thinking and meanings regarding genetics before introducing particular media 'stimuli' into the group discussions. Thus initial discussion about genetics, stimulated only by a three-dimensional model of the DNA double helix, was followed, some way into the group discussions, by a second stimulus consisting of two newspaper articles (one negative in its coverage of genetic research, the other positive), and, later still, by a third stimulus, a controversial documentary programme dealing with advances in genetic engineering. As in the case of the study by Press (1991), a major objective of the research was to examine how far group sentiments, vocabulary and mode of discussion were influenced by exposure to the media material. In cases such as these it is clearly essential therefore that the 'script' – that is the sequence of discussion and introduction of stimuli – is laid out clearly in the interview guide, and strictly adhered to by the moderator.

The focus group schedule and interview guide used by Hughes, Kitzinger and Murdock (2008) in their research on media discourses and public framing of risk is exemplary, and may serve as a model. It details (see Figure 10.2) general introductory comments to be used, formal requirements such as explaining the 'ethics sheet', the progression of questioning and the types of questions/issues to be addressed, as well as the place and questioning relating to the 'picture exercise' and the progression from there.

As with other types of research instrument, it is always important to pilot-test the interview guide for focus group discussions by conducting one, two or sometimes more pilot group discussions. Pilot-testing will throw up potential problems with the type of stimuli used, with sequencing, with the framing and wording of questions, etc.

What are the data produced by focus group discussions? The principal data produced by focus groups are the verbal responses, statements, opinions, arguments and interactions of the participants. Additional data may include observational accounts of facial expressions, gestures and body language more generally, although it is not often that such observations – if

Appendix 2: Example of focus group schedule

[2 hours session focussing primarily on stem cell research]

Welcome and introduction

Thank-you for attending [help yourself to sandwiches – it's a long session so I'll give you a break in the middle]

Distribute name stickers [explain – makes it easier for me to remember everyone's names as well and for you to address each other]

Check approval for taping, read out and explain ethics sheet.

Explain modes of discussion e.g. You do not have to know lots to take part, no right or wrongs, I'm just interested in what you have to say. What I really want is for us to have a conversation and to explore the issue and what you think individually and as a group. Try to hear from everyone in the group, talk to each other – not just to me

Go round circle asking people to introduce themselves

Discussion

Has anyone heard of stem cell research? – you don't have to know much about them but I want to check that at least the phrase is familiar to you. What do you think it is?

What's the first thing that comes to mind when I say 'stem cell research' – what do you immediately associate with those words? [Prompt afterwards: any visual images?]

Can you remember how you first learnt about stem cell research ['cloning' if that is only word they can associate with] – one particular event?

What do you think are the benefits of stem cell research?

What do you think are the risks?

What do you think *might* happen in the future? What has *already* happened?

Where do you think you have got most of your info on stem cell research from? If you wanted to find out more about stem cell research where would you go for that info?

Picture Exercise [Invite them to use set of photographs to construct a 'typical' television news bulletin about stem cell research. Followed by questions such as: Do you think your bulletins were typical of a news bulletin? Does this bulletin reflect your own views on stem cell research? What would you do differently if you were constructing a news bulletin? What did you think of each other's bulletins?]

Do you have an opinion about how the media has covered stem cell research?

Any other comments on stem cell research?

Repeat questions for GM – why similar/different?

Repeat questions for nanotechnology – why similar/different?

Figure 10.2 Focus group schedule and interview guide (from Hughes, Kitzinger and Murdock, 2008)

recorded at all – have been used to any great extent in focus group-based media and communications research.

Focus group discussions should as a minimum be audio-recorded on a good-quality digital recording device. Participants should always be made aware at the outset that the discussion will be recorded, and reassured of the confidential and anonymous use of the material. Generally, it will be the responses of the group as such, rather than individual contributions, which are of relevance to the research, but where the research aims are such that individual contributions need to be identifiable, it is important to keep a record of who is who in the group – and on the audio-recording. A good starting point for the group discussion is therefore an introductory round where each participant is asked to briefly introduce themself (e.g. name, interests) – if this is recorded the researcher then has a 'voice-identification' for each participant for the remainder of the recorded discussion. The voice-identification is often matched with a standard questionnaire (sex, age, occupation, media consumption, special interests and/or relevant experience, etc.) filled in by each participant prior to the discussion.

Video-recording of interview discussions offers the advantage that the contributions of individual participants can be identified more easily, and gestures and body language observed directly. Video-recording is, however, also considerably more complicated (e.g. changing camera angles) than audio-recording, and it is potentially rather more intrusive.

The principal record of a focus group discussion then normally consists of an audio-recording and additional observational notes jotted down by the moderator or an observer during the discussion. While it is possible to commence analysis directly from listening to the recording, it is more often the case – and there are strong practical and methodological reasons for this – that audio-recordings are first transcribed before starting analysis. A written transcript is easy to browse through, to annotate and, indeed, to share with colleagues, where the research is a team effort. An electronic transcript also opens up possibilities for computerised textual analysis with significant scope for faster, more systematic, more reliable and more in-depth analysis than is feasible or practical by conventional 'manual' annotation and analysis. And this brings us to the final step in the focused group interview: the analysis and write-up.

Analysing and reporting focus group discussions

Focus group interviews produce a large amount of textual data. Even a relatively small number of focus group interviews can result in several hundred pages of transcription. How to analyse this material? One dilemma facing the

researcher is between, on the one hand, reading through the interview transcripts to select 'striking' or 'typical' quotes which illustrate, confirm and
enhance the researcher's (preconceived) ideas of the processes and phenomena which are being investigated, and, on the other hand, to remain open to
new ideas, unanticipated responses, unexpected conflicts in the statements of
participants, etc. In the words of Höijer:

> When analysing reception interviews you certainly need sensibility and intuition,
> but you also have to be methodical, because you cannot grasp the totality of an
> interview and even less the totality of a set of interviews. Whether you are gener-
> ous with citations or not, you will be influenced by your hypothesis and expecta-
> tions as well as the very natural phenomenon that some individuals' statements
> will have a greater impact on you than others. (Höijer, 1990: 40)

Schlesinger et al. likewise caution against the subjective selection of quotes
sometimes seen in presentations of qualitative data:

> Qualitative results arising from interpretative methods, such as participant obser-
> vation, in-depth interviews and group discussions, present researchers with a
> series of dilemmas regarding analysis and presentation. Various strategies, such as
> case studies and the presentation of verbatim accounts, are often employed. These
> have the benefit of 'fleshing out' and illustrating the significant themes and
> patterns identified by the researcher(s). Often, however, it is difficult for readers
> to understand *how* certain materials are chosen over others and *why* certain quotes
> take precedence over those which never appear. In this study we have attempted a
> systematic approach to the development of significant themes and illustrative
> quotes arising from group interviews. (1992: 31)

While focus group discussions will almost inevitably generate some topics,
frames, references and argumentative angles which are new and unanticipated, it is also of course in the nature of such discussions that they are
focused around the topics and phenomena determined by the researcher. One
task for the analysis then is to examine, categorise and analyse the types of
responses generated in relation to the 'headings' and specific 'foci' determined by the research framework and set out in the interview guide. The
need to do this in a systematic fashion was emphasised above.

The way to commence the analysis task then is to start by developing a
scheme for categorising and labelling the responses, statements, arguments
and exchanges recorded in the interview transcripts. The 'categories' may be
the 'headings' used in the interview guide, or, more often, they will be a modified version of these combined with any additional categories which may have
presented themselves, unexpectedly, in the course of the group discussions.
As in content analysis (see Chapter 5), a prerequisite for developing good

categories is to 'soak oneself in the material', that is to read through the interview transcripts several times to become familiar with the spread of arguments, topics and issues covered. Additional observational notes taken during the interviews may also contribute to the development of analytical categories.[4]

The categories which are used for classifying the contents of interview transcripts will of course vary entirely depending on the foci, purposes and objectives of the research. Additionally, it will often be necessary to systematically classify and analyse the contents of interview transcripts along both different *types* and different *levels* of categories. Thus, one coding sweep through the material may be concerned with coding statements and arguments in terms of the principal frames (Gamson, 1992), themes and subthemes (see Höijer, 1990, and Durant et al., 1993). A second coding sweep, at a more detailed level, may be concerned with classifying 'causes, motives, and justifications' (Schlesinger et al., 1992), anchors, metaphors and positive/negative evaluations (Durant et al., 1993), etc.

The coding and analysis of interview transcripts is now (in sharp contrast to the situation only a few decades ago at the start of the resurgence of focus group interviewing in media and communication research) most powerfully done with the help of electronic text analysis software. A wide variety of software is available for the coding, analysis and retrieval of qualitative data, such as the open-ended, unstructured text produced by focus group discussions. Text analysis software ranges widely: from basic index and retrieval programs which enable you to go directly to any word or string of words in the entire body of interview transcripts, to examine specified words in their immediate context, to list the entire vocabulary (in alphabetical order, or in order of word frequency) of the group interview transcripts; to more complex and elaborate programs which enable you to attach 'codes', 'tags', 'labels' to words, sentences, arguments, statements – any string of text – and to perform quantitative analyses of the coded units, as well as analyses of 'networks' of arguments and 'associations' between related types of statements, subjects, contributor characteristics, etc. A more detailed discussion of ways of managing and analysing the data generated by qualitative methods such as focus group discussions and participant observation is given in Chapter 11.

Reporting the results of focus group interviews is, like all data analysis, an act of synthesising, summarising and the reduction of an unstructured mass of textual data to its 'essentials', key trends and representative examples. While it is tempting – with the 'rich' qualitative textual data produced by

---

4   Indeed, the analytical categories may derive from the reading of, not only the interview transcripts, but also a much broader set of documents, publications and media, see for example Gamson (1992).

focus group interviews – to quote comprehensively from the transcripts, to, as it were, 'let the data speak for themselves', this approach to reporting does not achieve the task of summarising, let alone 'analysing' the material. Verbatim quotes to illustrate key points, modes of discussion, vocabularies, frames, etc. should indeed be used in the reporting of results. Not to do this would negate one of the major reasons for using focus group discussions: to capture the way in which participants 'naturally' talk about, make sense of, reason about and generate meaning in relation to specified issues, topics and phenomena. But verbatim quotes should be limited to 'representative' illustrations. Any quantitative coding which has been done on the transcripts is helpful when reporting the results both in terms of finding and selecting (this is where text-retrieval programs come into their own) representative verbatim quotes relating to particular dimensions of analysis, and in terms of justifying that the quotes presented in the report are indeed representative of some larger body or trend in the data.

Reporting the results of focus group interviews is also an act of relating the textual data to the 'research problem/objective' as it was articulated before commencing the research (and before the decision that 'focus group methodology' would be the most appropriate method for studying the research problem) and to the wider theoretical framework of the study. Faced with the large and rich body of textual data generated by focus group discussions, it may often seem difficult to decide which aspects to report on and which to leave out. Essentially, the analysis and reporting should proceed along the lines of the 'headings' outlined in the interview guide – these were drawn up in relation to the problems, objectives, issues and hypotheses articulated as part of the theoretical framework for the study and the 'statement of the research problem'. Additional 'headings' (that is concepts, issues, frames, phenomena) may, and most often do, present themselves in the process of reading through the material and 'soaking oneself' in the textual data – these 'headings' and their associated results are added to the write-up.

The report of focus group research – again like the report on any other kind of empirical research – should not simply present the reader with results/findings, but must also enable the reader to understand the process of the research, that is what was done, how it was done, with what subjects it was done, where and by whom it was done. It is particularly important to remember to include in the report a full account of: who the participants were (and what they represent); how they were recruited; where and by whom they were interviewed; the nature and format of the group discussions; the use of stimuli; the nature of probing; and the ways in which interviews were recorded and analysed. Much of this information should be presented in a 'design, sample, and methods' chapter, sandwiched between introductory chapters (outlining the research problem, theoretical framework and reviews of related research) *and* the presentation of results and findings. In order to maintain a reasonable 'flow' and in order not to burden the reader unnecessarily with technical detail, it may well, however, be preferable to relegate some of the more detailed methodological descriptions and accounts to an appendix. Most of the media audience studies referred to in this chapter offer exemplary models in terms of detailed accounts of their methodology, but perhaps one of the clearest and most concise expositions of methodology is that offered by Schlesinger and his colleagues in their study of *Women Viewing Violence* (1992).

Summary

- Focus group interviewing generates a potentially much richer and more sensitive type of data on the dynamics of audiences and their relations to media than the survey.
- Focus group interviews may be the single substantive mode of data collection in a piece of research; but more frequently the approach has been used in conjunction with other, complementary, types of data collection. In media research, it has notably been used together with questionnaires, observation (ethnography) and analyses of media content.
- Unlike individual interviews, focus group interviews more closely approximate the 'naturally' social activity of generating meanings and interpretations in relation to media use and content. Through group dynamics they also offer ways – not available in the individual interview – of eliciting, stimulating and elaborating audience interpretations, and they can provide insight into how participants' beliefs and opinions take shape as they encounter, resist, assimilate and/or negotiate new information and arguments.
- It is rarely the case that people will 'naturally' volunteer elaborate interpretations of media content. Focus group discussions therefore require active input and structuring on the part of the moderator. Indeed, the 'focus' of the discussions needs to be clear, although the structuring and focusing will often progress from the loose and open-ended to the more disciplined during the course of a focus group interview.
- Focus group methodology entails research involving human beings, and must therefore always be circumscribed by clear and explicit ethical considerations. In practical terms, researchers must ensure that the proposed research conforms with the ethical regulations and requirements of their university, organisation or professional association, and that appropriate ethics approval has been obtained prior to the commencement of focus group discussions.

- The steps in focus group interviewing can be summarised as follows (adapted from Stewart, Shamdasani and Rook, 2007: 48): 1) problem definition/formulation of the research question; 2) identification of sampling frame; 3) identification of moderator; 4) generation and pre-testing of interview guide; 5) recruiting the sample; 6) conducting the group; 7) analysis and interpretation of data; 8) writing the report.
- The sampling and constitution of focus groups are important, particularly where comparisons between groups are envisaged and where group answers and arguments will be related to 'independent variables' such as demographic and other characteristics. A case is often made for selecting groups from 'naturally existing' constituencies, for example pressure groups, political organisations, professional associations, religious communities or simply groups of people who normally work or socialise together.
- The number of groups in a study will depend on the aims of the research and on available resources. If used for exploratory purposes, as few as two, three or four groups may suffice. If this method constitutes a more substantive part of a study, a larger number of groups would be desirable, although it is relatively rare for media and communication studies to use more than 20 groups and often the number of groups has been in the region of 6 to 12.
- There is a general consensus that focus groups should be no larger than 10–12 participants, and that the ideal group size is between 6 and 10.
- The choice of a location or setting for focus group interviews is important. The setting inevitably exerts a 'framing' influence on the nature of participants' responses and on the group discussion as a whole. The choice of setting needs to be considered in relation to the nature of the topic/issue to be discussed and, of course, in relation to practical feasibility.
- The role of the moderator will vary depending on the subject of analysis, the type of response which is sought and the nature of the participants. It is in the nature of focus group discussions that the role of the moderator is to 'facilitate', 'moderate' and 'stimulate' discussion amongst the participants, but there is considerable flexibility as to how forcefully this is done. The role of the moderator must be clearly defined in the interview guide.
- The focus group interview schedule or guide is principally a 'menu' of the topics, issues or areas of discussion to be covered, but, in addition to simply listing these, it should also give directions as to: a) the sequence of topics/issues to be covered; b) the nature and extent of prompting and probing; c) the nature and use of visual or verbal aids, and the points during the course of a group discussion where these should be introduced; d) the nature, format and timing of any exercises to be performed by the participants.

- While focus group discussions will almost inevitably generate some topics, frames, references and argumentative angles which are new and unanticipated, it is also in the nature of such discussions that they are *focused* around the topics and phenomena determined by the researcher. One task for the analysis then is to examine, categorise and analyse the types of responses generated in relation to the 'headings' and specific 'foci' determined by the research framework and set out in the interview guide.

Further reading

Stewart, D. W., Shamdasani, P. N., and Rook, D. W. (2007). *Focus Groups: Theory and Practice* (2nd edn.). London: Sage.
Well-structured, detailed and accessible introduction to focus group methodology.

For exemplary accounts of the use of focus group methodology in media and communication research, we particularly recommend the following two:

Hughes, E., Kitzinger, J., and Murdock, G. (2008). Media Discourses and Framing of Risk. *Social Contexts and Responses to Risk Network (SCARR) Working Paper 27.* Available at http://www.cardiff.ac.uk/jomec/resources/KitzingerWkPaper27.pdf
Schlesinger, P., Dobash, R. E., Dobash, R. P., and Weaver, C. K. (1992). *Women Viewing Violence.* London: BFI Publishing.

CHAPTER 11

Dealing with data: computer and analysis software

Media and communication research tends to produce large volumes of data. This is so, practically regardless of the method or approach adopted, and regardless of whether the research and data are principally qualitative or principally quantitative. While in the distant past much of the planning, design, execution (including the collection of data), analysis and writing up of research would have been done with 'pen and paper', most or all of these tasks are now done 'electronically' with the use of computers for the simple reasons of advantages of speed, organisation, retrievability, documentation, collaborative potential, power of analysis, etc. We have already seen in previous chapters how important computing technology, software, the internet, etc. are in relation to retrieving information and data, reviewing literature, managing bibliographies and references, conducting content analyses or surveys.

In this chapter, we introduce ways and tools for managing and analysing quantitative and qualitative communications research data. In the first section, we introduce the analysis of quantitative data using one of the most powerful and widely used statistical analysis programs in the social sciences, namely SPSS (Statistical analysis Program for the Social Sciences).[1] In the second part, we consider computer-assisted management and analysis of qualitative data, and we introduce some of the ways of using qualitative analysis programs in the analysis of qualitative communication research data.

The chapter outlines the steps involved in preparing quantitative data – whether from a survey or a content analysis – for computer analysis, and it discusses the use of SPSS for the statistical examination of data. The chapter further discusses the organisation, management and analysis of 'qualitative' textual data, be they in the form of participant observation field-notes,

---

[1] At the time of writing SPSS – now IBM SPSS Statistics – was marketed as PASW (Predictive Analytics SoftWare) Statistics. The screenshots used in this chapter thus carry the label 'PASW Statistics' and refer to version 18 of SPSS.

interview transcripts or electronic newspaper text. While seeking to avoid the detailed description of individual computer programs for these purposes, we introduce readers to the significant gains of flexibility, efficiency and reliability which computer-assisted handling of qualitative data offers over more traditional 'manual' or card index-based methods, and we outline some of the types of analysis which can productively be used in research on qualitative 'textual' data.

The analysis of quantitative data using SPSS

Computer tools, programs or software for analysing social science data have progressed in leaps and bounds in the last few decades, and have become increasingly accessible and user-friendly. The media and communication researcher of today can choose from a wide variety of powerful or less powerful computer programs ranging from databases and spreadsheets with some (again, more or less powerful) statistical calculation facilities to statistical programs or packages designed specifically for the full range of statistical analysis used in not just social science research but also in natural science and medical research.

Here, we wish to introduce the reader to the very basics of a powerful computer program developed, as its name suggests, for the analysis of social science data, namely SPSS – Statistical Package for the Social Sciences. When SPSS was first designed in the late 1960s, data were 'stored' in the form of punch cards – so called because 'values' were indicated by holes punched on index-type cards – and users had to know a large array of general computing commands as well as commands and syntax specific to SPSS. All in all, a very different scenario from today's user-interface where most, if not all, data entry and analysis can be done by choosing from and clicking on windows and menu buttons on a computer screen.

Our objective in the first section of this chapter is to introduce the reader to: a) how to enter data (e.g. from a content analysis or a survey) into an SPSS data file; and b) how to do relatively simple, but useful, types of analysis with SPSS. Our introduction to SPSS will refer specifically to the Windows version of SPSS, but note that SPSS is also available for other operating systems or platforms.

Three types of variables: continuous, categorical and string

Content analyses, surveys and potentially other kinds of approaches use research instruments such as content analysis schedules and questionnaires on which answers are circled, ticked or recorded in the form of numbers or codes. The main reasons for using numbers or codes are speed and the need to standardise the way in which answers are recorded so that they can be subjected to quantitative analysis.

There are two different types of numeric codes used for the kinds of variables that you will find on a survey questionnaire or a content analysis coding schedule: *continuous* and *categorical* variables. In addition, it is also possible to record information in a non-numeric format, namely as text or 'string'. The reason why we need to know the difference between these types of codes is that the type of code determines what kind of analysis can be done in a program such as SPSS. Continuous variables thus lend themselves to more powerful statistical analysis than categorical variables, while text or string variables can only be subjected to relatively limited statistical analysis. The three types of codes or variables can be defined as follows:

1) *Continuous* variables ('real' number variables): Answers are recorded in terms of 'real' numbers, where the number recorded on the questionnaire means just that – for example a person's age might be recorded as '28', meaning that the person is 28 years of age, or a respondent's height might be recorded as '165', meaning that the respondent is 165 centimetres tall.

2) *Categorical* variables: Answers are recorded in terms of arbitrary or nominal 'codes', where the code or number refers to particular dimensions of a variable, that is for the variable 'sex', the code '1' might be used to mean 'female' and the code '2' to indicate that the respondent is 'male', or for the variable 'newspaper' on a content analysis schedule, the code '1' might be used to indicate the *'Daily Telegraph'*, '2' for *'The Times'*, '3' for the *'Independent'*, etc. These are just arbitrary codes of convenience – we could equally well have used the codes '1' for 'male' and '2' for 'female', or the codes '6' for 'male' and '8' for 'female'. Thus, these codes have none of the numeric properties associated with real numbers. In other words, although possible to do, it would not make sense to calculate the 'difference' between 'male' and 'female' respondents in a survey by subtracting '1' from '2', nor would it make sense to perform any other arithmetical calculations such as finding the average of '2's and '1's (males and females).

3) *String* variables (text variables): data are entered as 'natural' textual information, that is in non-coded form. For a content analysis of newspapers, it would often be desirable to write down the headlines of individual articles in full on the schedule, as this makes identifying cases much easier. Survey questionnaires will often have open-ended questions, where respondents are invited to write their answers or comments in their own words. Such 'textual' answers can be entered in full, with a

view to later coding or categorisation, or with a view to statistical analysis of the frequency and distribution of individual words or phrases.

From coding sheets or questionnaires to SPSS

While it is possible to manually record data, writing by hand on a content analysis coding schedule or a questionnaire, content analysis and survey data are increasingly recorded (and we would certainly recommend this for reasons of speed, reliability, efficiency and convenience) electronically. The first step towards using a program such as SPSS for data management and analysis is to get the data into the SPSS program. There are two principal ways in which this can be done:

1) Manually typing the data directly into an SPSS data file. As indicated in Chapter 5 on content analysis, we recommend that content analysis data be entered directly into SPSS, but if the data are first recorded on a content analysis coding sheet (or in the case of a survey, on a questionnaire), then this process is a matter of transferring, by typing, the data from the coding sheet/questionnaire to the SPSS file.

2) Transferring/importing the data from another program. The data may have been recorded in a spreadsheet such as Microsoft Excel or similar, including online programs or formats, or they may have been recorded in comma/tab-delimited form in a wordprocessing file. In such cases, data can be transferred or imported either through the 'import' options available in SPSS or by simple copying and pasting from another program into SPSS.

Open SPSS and create and name a new data file

SPSS opens, by default, with an empty data-entry window (Figure 11.1), called 'Data View' (see the bottom left corner of Figure 11.1). The data-entry or Data View window is divided into rows and columns, and is of course empty because we have not yet typed in any data, hence the name 'Untitled1 [DataSet0]' in the title bar at the top of the screen. As soon as some information has been entered, the file should be given an appropriate name and saved (using 'Save' or 'Save As' from the File menu).

Case, variable, values

Each row in the Data View window represents a *case*. In a content analysis, a 'case' may be an individual newspaper article, an individual news item in a news programme, an individual blog entry or a webpage. In a survey, a 'case' would normally be the individual respondent/person interviewed, although there are other possibilities, for example 'a household'.

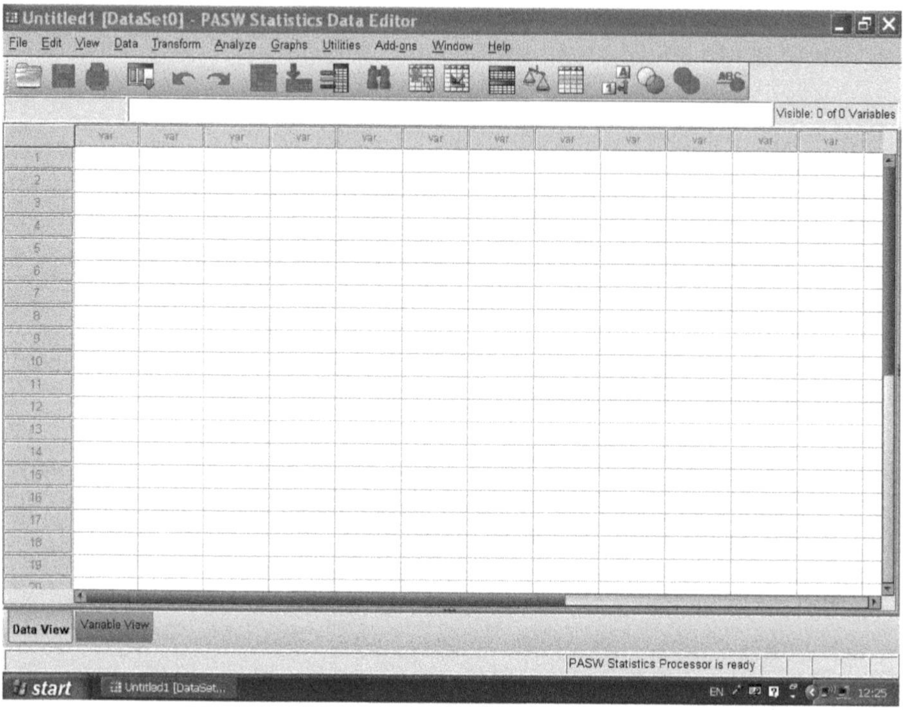

Figure 11.1　The SPSS Data View window

Each column represents a *variable*. A variable is an individual dimension or characteristic analysed, such as, in a content analysis of newspaper articles, the 'date', 'which newspaper the article appeared in', 'the number of words in the article', 'the topic of the article', etc. In a survey, a 'variable' would be such dimensions as 'the age of the respondent', 'annual income of the respondent', 'newspapers read by the respondent', 'weekly amount of television viewing', etc.

Each variable in a content analysis or survey can take on a number of *values*. Thus, a survey may record the *variable* 'respondent's sex' using the *values* '1' for male and '2' for female. Or a content analysis of television news may record the variable 'news channel' using the values '1' for 'BBC World News', '2' for 'Al-Jazeera', '3' for 'CNN', etc. The relevant values are typed into each cell of the Data View window: each cell then represents a *single value* of the particular *variable* in question, relating to the single *case* recorded in the particular row in question.

Defining variables and entering data
The first task, before entering or importing data, is to define the variables and the values associated with each variable. We do this by changing from the

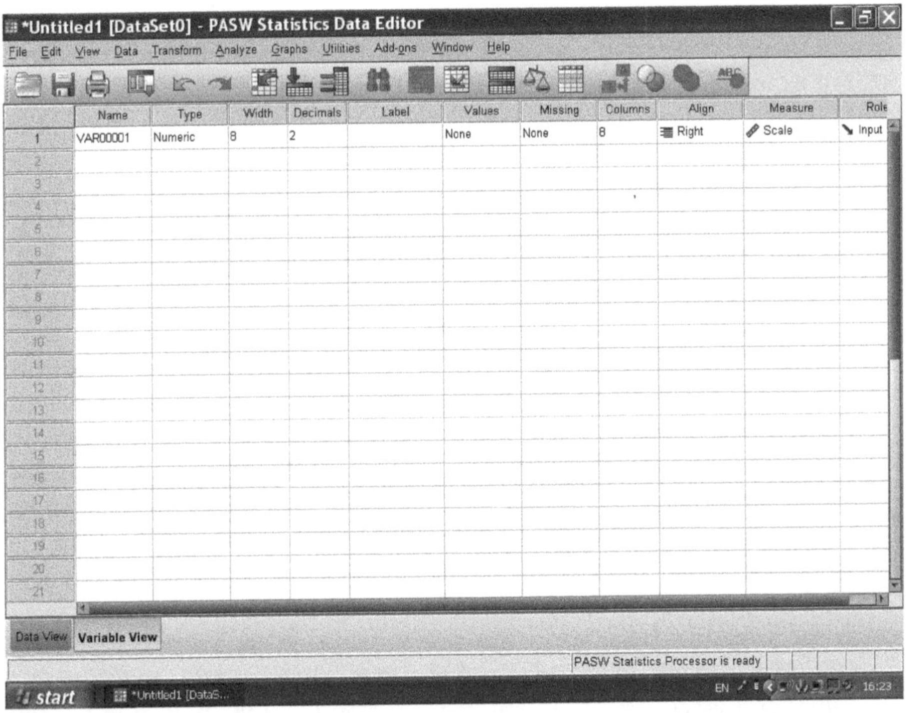

Figure 11.2 The SPSS Variable View window

present 'Data View' to 'Variable View', by clicking on the 'Variable View' button in the bottom left corner of the screen. This brings up the screen shown in Figure 11.2.

The 'Variable View' screen shows, in each row, the detailed definitions relating to each variable, as follows (here we describe just the first six characteristics listed):

1) Name (column 1): here we enter a short name describing the first variable in our data set.
2) Type (column 2): click in the right-hand side of the cell and a dialogue box crops up, allowing us to choose from a set of types, including Numeric (the default choice), Date, String, etc.
3) Width (column 3): refers to the width of the data column; in most cases this can be left as is.
4) Decimals (column 4): most variables in content analyses or surveys are likely to be coded using integers, that is whole numbers, so for clarity the default of 2 Decimals should be changed to '0'. Click in the cell, and use the up/down arrow that appears to choose 0 (zero) instead of the default 2.

5) Label (column 5): this allows us to enter a longer label than the single brief name entered in column 1, to describe what the variable refers to. For example, a variable name such as 'Programme' can be labelled 'Title of news programme' to clarify that this refers to the title or name of the news programme analysed.

6) Values (column 6): this is of key importance, as it is here that we define what each of the numbers/codes associated with a (categorical) variable refers to. If the variable consists of *continuous* data/real numbers then it is of course not necessary to define labels, as each number represents its own numeric value, '1' means '1', '2' means '2', etc. (an example would be the Duration variable in our example data set, where each number represents the duration in seconds of the news item). For *categorical* data, however, the numbers represent codes and we therefore need to indicate what each number or code means or refers to. Clicking in the right-hand side of the Values cell brings up a dialogue box that allows us to do this by defining a Label for each Value. Start by typing in the first value/code, 1, in the Value box. Then click in the Label box and type in the label, for example BBC1. Then click on the Add button, and the value and label will appear in the large box. Then enter the next value, 2, in the Value box and the label, for example BBC2, in the Label box, click on Add, etc. When all values and labels have been entered, click on the 'OK' button in the top right corner of the dialogue box. In the example shown in Figure 11.3, we have defined, for the Channel variable, the codes 1, 2 and 3 as referring to the following three television channels BBC1, BBC2 and Channel 4.

When all variables in your study have been named and defined (in the example shown in Figure 11.3 we have defined five variables for a content analysis of a sample of British television news coverage of the 2009 Environment summit) you are ready to start entering data. Change back to the Data View screen (by clicking Data View in the bottom left corner of the screen), which now shows each of the variables (just defined in the Variable View screen) as column headings, that is each column corresponds to a single variable. To enter the data for the first case (row 1), click in the top left cell to type in the value for the first variable. Then click in the second cell along this row to type in the value for the second variable, etc. continuing until all values for the first case have been entered. Then move to the second case (row 2) and repeat the process.

As we have indicated above, it is also possible to enter data by copying and pasting from another program or by using SPSS's Read Text Data (see the File menu) import feature. However, for content analyses we recommend coding data directly into SPSS on a case-by-case basis, as described above, as the most efficient way to code content analysis data.

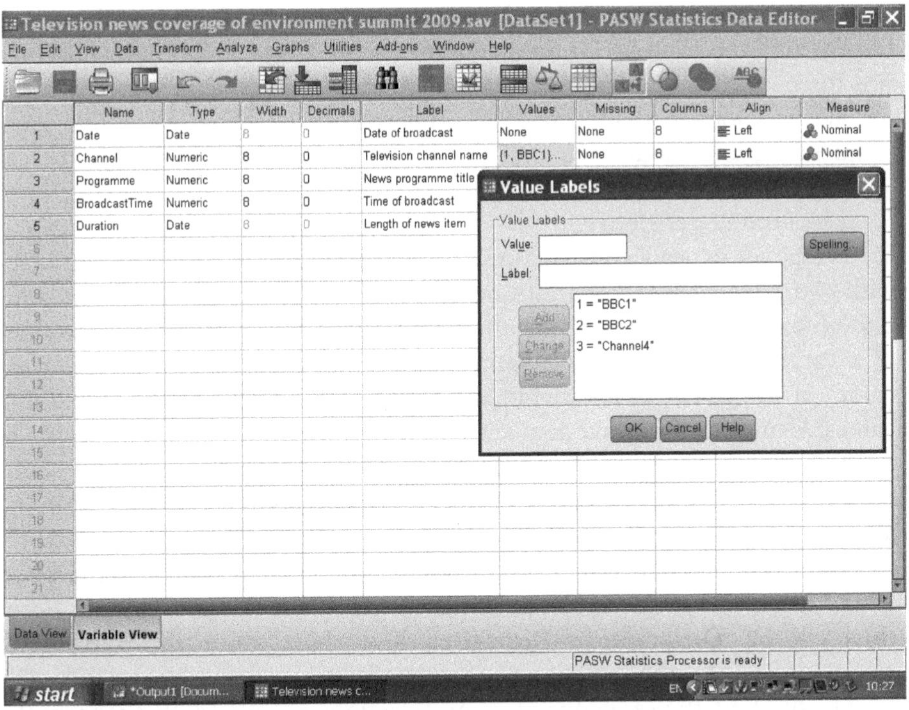

Figure 11.3 The SPSS Value Labels dialogue box showing three values relating to the variable Channel

As with all computing work, but particularly work that involves the meticulous and time-consuming entry of numeric data, it is important to Save (see the File menu) your SPSS file at short regular intervals while in the process of entering data. It is also worth backing up your SPSS file on a separate medium, for example a memory stick, at regular intervals.

Analysing data with SPSS

Once the variables have been defined and the data entered into the SPSS data file, we can then proceed to the interesting and exciting part of the research, namely the analysis of the data. Here we wish to introduce four basic types of analysis which are useful for describing and summarising the results of the data collected, regardless of whether the data come from a content analysis, a survey or other types of research data collection.

Thus the first thing one would often want to do is to get a general 'feel' for what the data show – a general 'feel' for the distribution of different variables in the data set; for example: How many men and how many women were there in the survey? What was their average age (and the minimum and maximum ages of respondents)? What percentages of men and women respectively use Twitter? Or, in a content analysis, how much news coverage was there on each television channel? Were the news items on some channels on average longer than those of other channels? Who were the most frequently quoted sources/actors? Etc. etc.

Frequencies and descriptives

We can begin to get a good picture of the distribution of individual variables with two types of SPSS analysis: one for analysing the *frequencies* of individual values in a variable, and the other for a *descriptive* summary of the values of a variable in terms of calculating the average (also known as the mean value) of the values of a variable and showing its minimum and maximum values. Using our example data set of selected variables from an analysis of television news coverage of the 2009 Environment summit, we start by examining the distribution (frequency) of the three television channels analysed and the distribution (frequency) of the four news programmes analysed.

From the menu bar (File, Edit, View, etc.) shown near the top of the SPSS Data View screen (see Figure 11.1 above), select the **Analyze** menu. From this, choose **Descriptive Statistics** and then, from the sub-menu, **Frequencies**. In the remainder of this chapter we will, for clarity and simplicity, show the sequence of menu selections as follows, that is from the top-bar menu through to sub-menus:

Analyze > Descriptive Statistics > Frequencies

This brings up the Frequencies dialogue box shown in Figure 11.4. The left side of the dialogue box shows the five variables in our example data set. Click (to highlight it) on the variable showing as 'Television channel ...', then click on the arrow between the two boxes in the dialogue box to move the selected variable into the right side box. Repeat this process for the variable 'News programme ...'. With these two variables transferred into the right-side box, click on the OK button showing at the bottom of the dialogue box.

Having clicked OK in the Frequencies dialogue box, SPSS proceeds to calculate the frequencies for the two variables which we have specified. The results of this calculation appear in a new window called 'Output 1' (see Figure 11.5). In the output window, SPSS shows a table for each of the two variables used in this analysis.

The two variables analysed above with the Frequencies command are both categorical variables, that is they consist of arbitrary code numbers indicating a limited set of unique characteristics or values. As indicated at the beginning of this chapter, it would not make much sense to carry out arithmetic calculations on these types of numbers, which are simply numeric codes, but

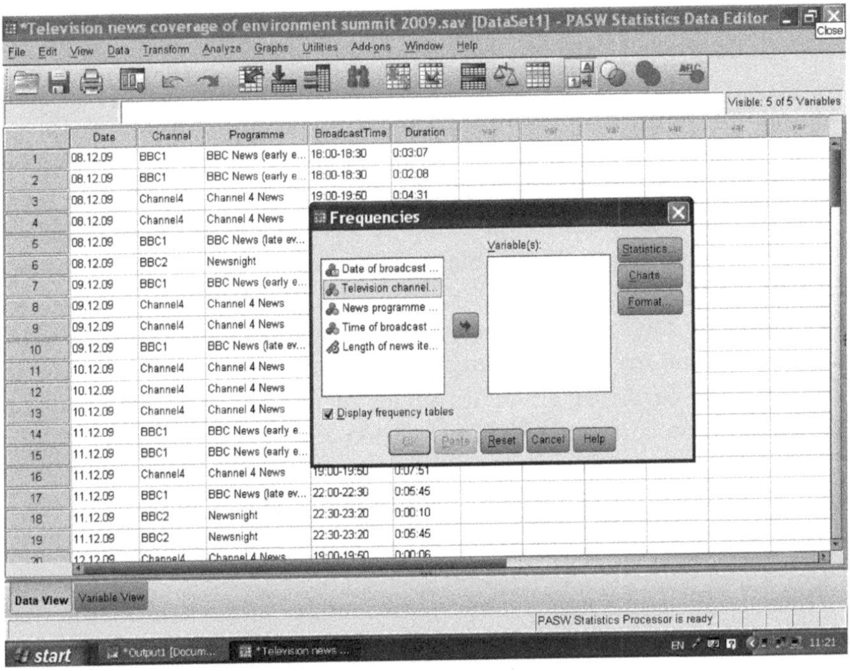

Figure 11.4   The SPSS Frequencies dialogue box

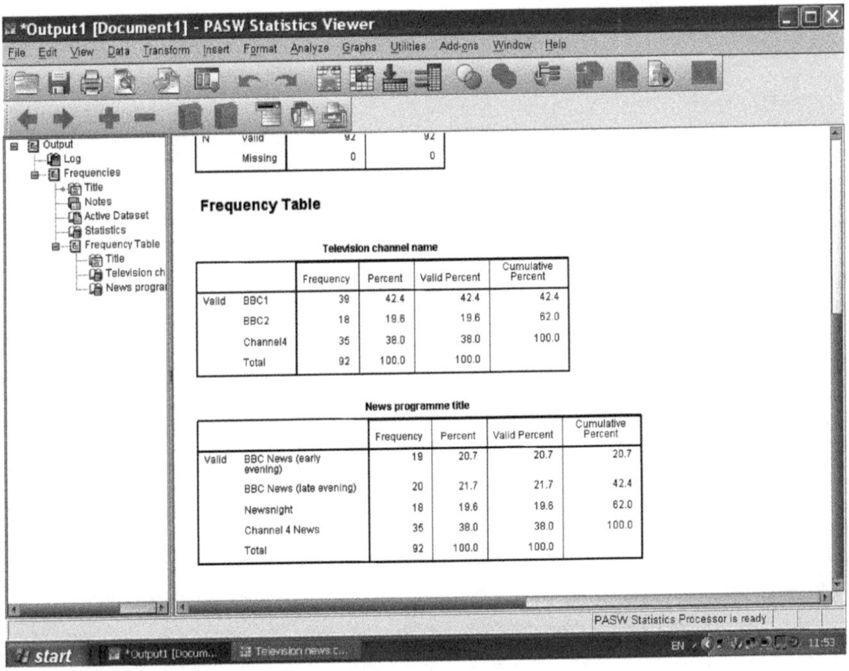

Figure 11.5   The SPSS Output screen showing Frequency Tables for two variables

have none of the properties of 'real' numbers. In other words, it would not make sense to try and calculate such arithmetic measures as the sum or the average (mean) of the values used as codes for these variables.

One variable in the data example used here which is not a categorical variable, but consists of 'real' numbers, is the 'Duration' variable, which records the length in seconds of the individual news item. For this variable then it *does* make sense to summarise the data in terms of such measures as the average length of news items or the total length of time devoted to this type of coverage.

To summarise the information coded regarding the duration of each news item (or indeed of any other variable consisting of 'real' numbers – e.g. in a survey this may be the age, height, weight of respondents), we choose the **Descriptives** procedure in SPSS, as follows:

Analyze > Descriptive Statistics > Descriptives

In the resulting Descriptives dialogue box (Figure 11.6), we click on the variable 'Length of news item' in the left rectangle, then click on the arrow button between the two rectangles to transfer the variable to the rectangular

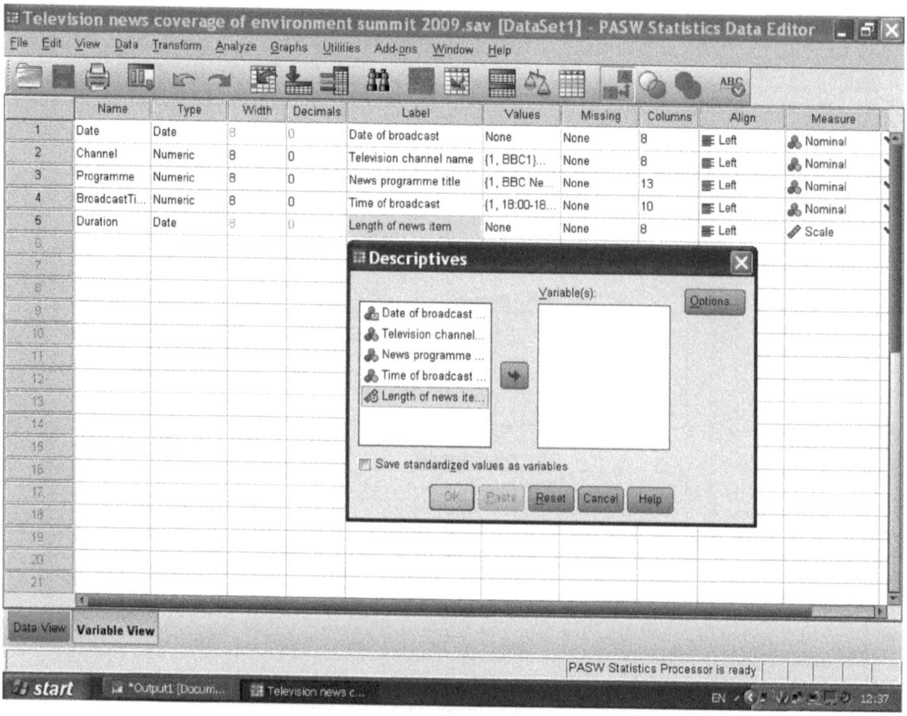

Figure 11.6　The SPSS Descriptives dialogue box

box on the right. We then click on the OK button at the bottom of the dialogue box.

SPSS proceeds to produce, in the Output window, a single table that summarises the distribution of the Duration variable by showing, for the 92 items in our sample, the minimum and maximum duration, the mean (or average) duration, as well as a statistical measure called the Standard Deviation (which is a measure of how much variation or dispersion there is in the data set in relation to the average, in other words how close or far from the average the values recorded are).

Crosstabs and means

So far we have used two SPSS commands – frequencies and descriptives – for describing and summarising individual variables. But what if we wanted to know how much coverage each television channel (the Channel variable) devoted on different dates (the Date variable), or if we wanted to know whether the news items on one television channel (the Channel variable) were on average longer or shorter (the Duration variable) than those on another television channel, then we would need a command that could compare two or more variables with each other. In SPSS these commands are **Crosstabs** (for comparing categorical variables) and **Means** (for comparing a continuous variable – such as the Duration variable in our example data set – across a categorical variable).

To examine the number of news items across television channels by dates of coverage, a comparison of the two categorical variables 'Channel' and 'Date', we use the SPSS Crosstabs command as follows:

Analyze > Descriptive Statistics > Crosstabs

This brings up the Crosstabs dialogue box shown in Figure 11.7. Now click on the 'Date of broadcast' variable to highlight it, then click on the arrow next to the box labelled 'Row(s):' to transfer the Date variable to the Row(s) box. Next select the 'Television channel name' variable and transfer it, by clicking on the second arrow down, to the box labelled 'Column(s)'.

Then click on OK at the bottom of the dialogue box. SPSS produces the output table illustrated in Table 11.1, which shows the number of news items broken down by each of the three channels (the columns) by each of the dates (the rows of the table) analysed.

Table 11.1 shows only, in each of its cells, the actual number of news items by each date and each channel (and the row totals in the right-side column, and the column totals in the bottom row). Often, however, it would be desirable to have considerably more information per cell, for example column and row percentages, as well as perhaps some statistical tests to see whether the

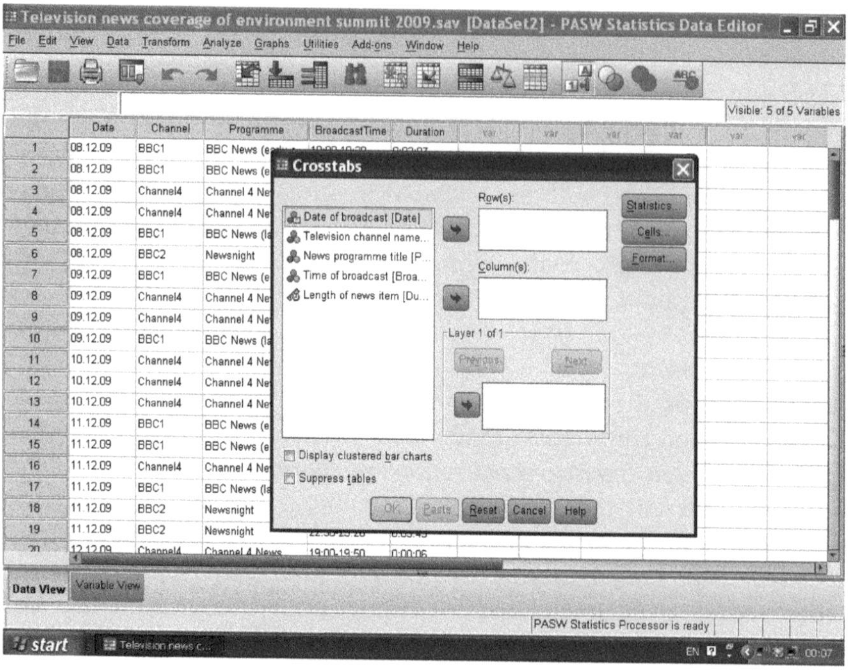

Figure 11.7   The SPSS Crosstabs dialogue box

Table 11.1   Crosstabs table of Date by Channel

Date of broadcast by Television channel name Crosstabulation

Count

		Television channel name			Total
		BBC1	BBC2	Channel4	
Date of broadcast	08.12.09	3	1	2	6
	09.12.09	2	0	2	4
	10.12.09	0	0	3	3
	11.12.09	3	2	1	6
	12.12.09	2	0	3	5
	14.12.09	6	2	3	11
	15.12.09	3	3	3	9
	16.12.09	4	6	6	16
	17.12.09	4	1	4	9
	18.12.09	7	3	4	14
	19.12.09	4	0	3	7
	20.12.09	1	0	0	1
	21.12.09	0	0	1	1
Total		39	18	35	92

differences observed are statistically significant (as opposed to being potentially chance occurrences). Such information could easily be included in the table by selecting from the sub-menus shown on the right side of the Crosstabs dialogue in Figure 11.7. Thus, to include column and row percentages in the cells of the output table, click on the 'Cells' button in the Crosstabs dialogue box. This brings up the 'Crosstabs: Cell Display' dialogue box. Now click in the box next to 'Row' and the box next to 'Column' in the area labelled 'Percentages' to put a tick in each of these boxes. The dialogue box now looks like Figure 11.8. Then click on 'Continue', which closes the 'Crosstabs: Cell Display' dialogue box to reveal again the Crosstabs dialogue box. Then click on OK to close the Crosstabs dialogue box and to produce an output table of Date by Channel, with each cell showing the number of items and the row and column percentages.

Let us finally introduce an analysis command for comparing a continuous variable (Duration) across a categorical variable (News programme). As one of the variables (the Duration variable, which measures the length in seconds of the news item) consists of real continuous numbers, we need an analytical procedure which will calculate the average duration of news items for each of the news programmes analysed. The SPSS procedure for

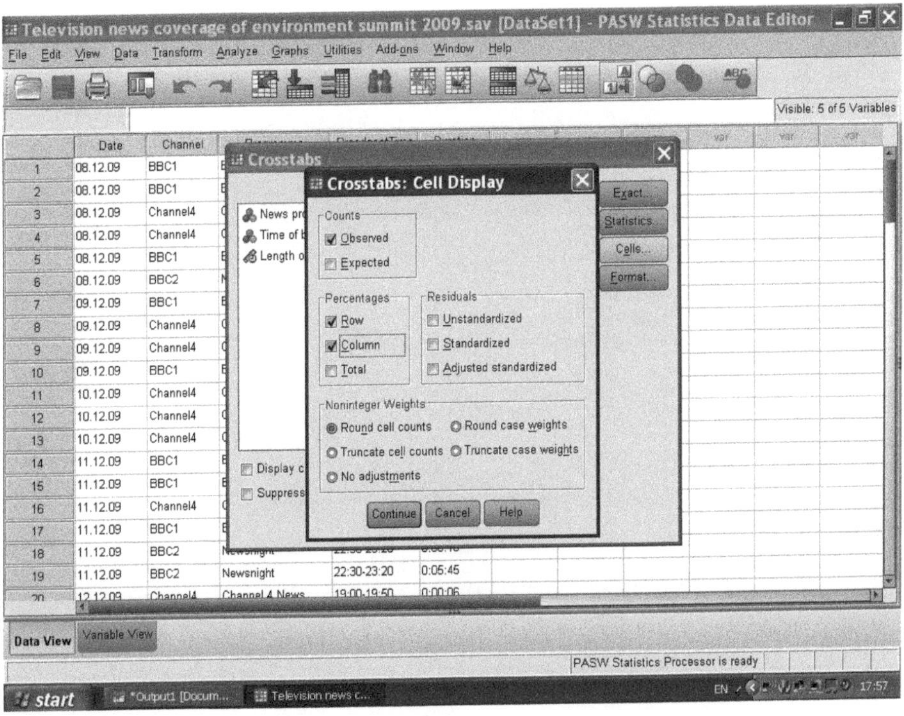

Figure 11.8 The Crosstabs: Cell Display dialogue box

this is called **Means** and we find this command in the **Analyze** menu, as follows:

Analyze > Compare Means > Means

This brings up the Means dialogue box (Figure 11.9). Click on the 'Length of news item' variable and transfer it, using the top arrow, to the 'Dependent List' box. Then select the 'News programme' variable and transfer this, using the bottom arrow, to the 'Independent List' box. Now press OK. SPSS produces the table shown here as Table 11.2, which shows (in the columns) the average duration, number of news items, and standard deviation for each of the news programmes in the sample (the rows of the table). From this, we can, for example, instantly see that the *Newsnight* items were the longest (at, on average, 4 minutes 48 seconds) and the items appearing on the *BBC News* in the early evening were the shortest (at, on average, 1 minute 57 seconds).

We have introduced four basic analytical procedures in SPSS: Frequencies and Descriptives for analysing individual variables; Crosstabs and Means for comparing two (or more) variables. As we said at the beginning, it is important to know whether the variables to be analysed are continuous/real

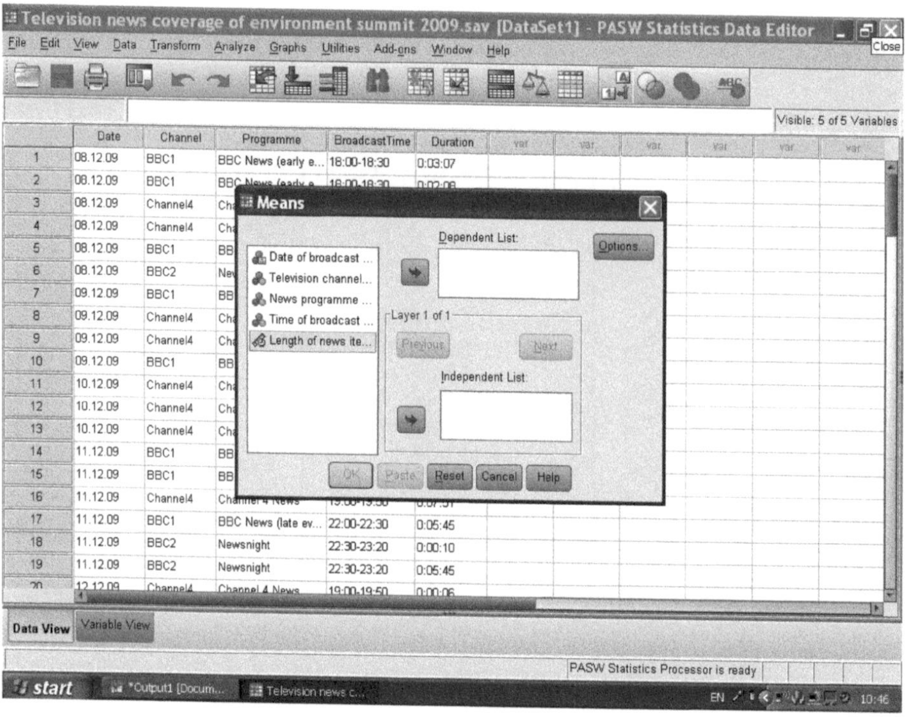

Figure 11.9   The SPSS Means dialogue box

Table 11.2 Mean duration of news items by news programme

Report			
Length of news item			
News programme title	*Mean*	*N*	*Std. Deviation*
BBC News (early evening)	00:01:57	19	00:01:27.433
BBC News (late evening)	00:02:15	20	00:01:53.221
Newsnight	00:04:48	18	00:05:51.838
Channel 4 News	00:03:53	35	00:05:28.153
Total	00:03:19	92	00:04:28.097

number variables or coded as categorical variables, because this determines what kind of SPSS analysis commands are appropriate: thus we use Frequencies and Crosstabs for analysing categorical variables, and we use Descriptives and Means when continuous (real number) variables are involved.

Selecting and transforming data with SPSS

Before ending this section, we wish to draw attention to three additional procedures or commands within SPSS, procedures which are useful for manipulating or transforming data in ways that will further facilitate particular types of analyses. Unlike the analysis commands just introduced, these procedures do not produce output tables, but are used for transforming, selecting or rearranging the data in ways that will facilitate further analysis with the analysis commands:

- **Data > Select Cases**. The Select Cases command in the Data menu enables the user to select a sub-set of the full data set for analysis; in our data set, we might, for example, for some purposes, wish to exclude the BBC *Newsnight* programme and to perform analysis only on the mainstream news programmes. This can be specified through the Select Cases dialogue box. Note that the Select Cases command does not change or affect the basic data set, but only specifies what cases should be included in any given analysis. Any selection can be 'reset' at any time to revert back to the full data set.
- **Transform > Recode into Different Variables**. The Recode command in the Transform menu is useful for regrouping the values of a variable. In our data set, we might, for example, wish to rearrange the current four programmes into just three groups by grouping the early evening *BBC News* together with the late evening *BBC News* into just a single category called *BBC News*, while retaining *Newsnight* and *Channel 4 News* as

distinct categories. Similarly, in an analysis of a selection of individual newspapers, it may often be desirable – in addition to analysing the characteristics of individual newspapers – to group the papers into such groups as Popular and Quality newspapers.

- **Transform > Compute Variable**. The Compute Variable command in the Transform menu is used for combining or computing two or more variables into a single expression. This may, for example, be necessary where information – for instance a person's length of time at their current address – has been recorded as years and additional months. In this case, it would be desirable for ease of analysis to express the length of time in either whole months (i.e. by multiplying the 'years' by 12 and adding this figure to the 'months') or in years with decimal points (i.e. by dividing the 'years' information by 12 and then adding the additional 'months').

Conclusion

As we have already glimpsed in the various dialogue boxes, there are many more formatting, information, data manipulation and analytical options available than we have covered here. SPSS is, as we have indicated, a powerful and highly flexible program for managing and analysing media and communication research data. Our modest aim here has been to provide the basics to get started on using SPSS for data management and to introduce basic analytical procedures that will go a long way towards describing/analysing the kind of data that are frequently collected in media and communication research, whether through content analysis, survey methodology or other approaches.

For further exploration of these and other more sophisticated types of analysis, we refer the reader to the SPSS program itself – experiment with it, and use the online help functions as well as the online tutorials which come with it. The program itself offers advanced and sophisticated help menus and guidance. In addition, we list at the end of this chapter a few selected reference books and guides which provide excellent and much more detailed introductions to SPSS and to statistical analysis of social science/communication research data generally.

Handling, organising and analysing qualitative data

Qualitative data in mass communication research come in a number of different shapes and forms. We can use a 'negative' definition and refer to as 'qualitative' any data which are not primarily numerically coded, quantified or consisting of numbers. We say 'not primarily' because the distinction between qualitative and quantitative data and analysis has become increasingly less marked and indeed we would argue that the best type of sociological analysis often moves seamlessly between the two types, taking advantage of the significant potential gains of exploiting complementarity and convergence between quantitative and qualitative analysis. Thus, many of the computer programs created for the management and analysis of qualitative data have sophisticated facilities for subjecting qualitative data to quantitative analysis.

Typical examples of qualitative data in media and communication research include: transcripts of focus group interviews or in-depth individual interviews; field-notes from observational or ethnographic research; newspaper articles; transcripts of television or radio programmes; online text from blogs, websites, social media, etc. Of course, qualitative data need not necessarily be 'text', but would increasingly include audio or visual material such as audio-recordings/sound-bites, photographs, images, drawings or video-recordings posted on websites and other media. Of course, all of these forms could also be subjected to quantitative analysis.

Just as communications media themselves have evolved dramatically since the early 1990s, so too have computer programs for handling and analysing audio and visual data. While early advances in the development of programs for handling qualitative data were very much focused on translating traditional manual approaches (e.g. card indexing and organisation of analysis notes in relation to interview transcripts) into computer-based approaches, much work in the most recent decade has been focused on developing tools for handling and analysing the enormous amount of multi-media information (text and images) facilitated by the exponential growth in internet, mobile and other digital communications. We shall refer briefly to some of these developments towards the end of this chapter but our primary objective here is to offer a brief introduction to programs for handling and analysing primarily electronic text, such as news text, blogs or interview transcripts.

The computer-assisted management, organisation and analysis of textual qualitative data can be broken down into three distinct steps: 1) entering or capturing text, 2) organising and preparing text for analysis and 3) analysing text. These three steps still predominantly apply in relation to the handling, management and analysis of historical media content that was not initially produced for the internet or other digital/electronic dissemination and for qualitative data such as the recordings of individual or focus group interviews. However, as electronic media and media content such as websites, online communication, social media, etc. themselves become the principal object of analysis, steps 1 and 2 are increasingly eliminated as analysis software is applied directly to the digital media content itself without the need to first capture, download or organise the data on a personal computer.

Entering or capturing text

Analysis of digital/electronic media and forms of communication notwithstanding, the first step for much computer-assisted analysis of qualitative data still revolves around the need to store and organise such data on a personal computer. In the past, this was very much a case of laboriously typing handwritten notes, questionnaire answers or text which existed in print-only form into a computer file. While typing or scanning may still be the only option available in much historical research on media text, many kinds of media and communications text is of course now – thankfully – readily available in electronic form, and this first task then becomes mainly a question of sampling and capturing electronic data for analysis. As we have seen in Chapter 9 on survey research, questionnaire data – including in relation to open-ended questions/answers – are also increasingly recorded straight to electronic format, bypassing the need for typing or scanning. Likewise (although advances here may have been rather slower), media and communication researchers who conduct participant observation or ethnographic research would increasingly be recording field-notes directly onto electronic media (e.g. notebooks, laptops, iPads or their equivalents). If the data exist only in audio format – such as radio-recordings or interview-recordings – it is necessary to transcribe these into computer text files. If the data exist in printed-text form only – for example older newspaper text, policy documents, annual reports, historical documents – these will need scanning or typing into a computer.

While there are still then many cases where the first task for the researcher is that of transcribing, typing or scanning qualitative data into a computer, the exponential growth in the last two decades in the digitisation and electronic availability of all types of media, documentation and text means that the nature of this first step in the management and analysis of qualitative data has changed. As the variety and range of media and communications data are increasingly available electronically, the key considerations for the communication researcher for this step revolve around questions to do with navigating the wealth of qualitative data available and questions about sampling, that is how to obtain samples that will accurately reflect the medium, subject or population that the research focuses on.

Thus, while a wealth of global news text is now available from the websites of news organisations themselves or from large commercial databases such as Nexis®, the researcher who is interested in analysing printed newspapers needs to be aware that the electronically available formats may not be simple, complete or accurate 'copies' of the newspapers that can be bought from a news stand. However, it is also the case that increasingly the core object of research is indeed that which is available electronically (and increasingly consumed in this form by media users/consumers) and therefore the potential differences between printed media formats and their electronic equivalents are of less, or indeed no, significance.

Organising and preparing text for analysis

Qualitative data, such as interview transcripts or news text, are stored and organised in the form of individual computer 'files', which are located within 'folders', which may, in turn, be organised hierarchically, that is a top folder or master folder with a tree structure of sub-folders and folders within sub-folders. While computer programs for the analysis of qualitative data can increasingly handle a variety of file/text formats, a simple text file format (ASCII files) will ensure the widest compatibility. Key considerations in the organisation of qualitative data are deciding on what 'unit' of analysis each file should represent and deciding on the most sensible hierarchy of files and folders. 'Units' of analysis are often more or less 'given', for example an individual interview, an individual open-ended question, a newspaper article, a research memo or a day's participant observation notes.

There is no single best way of hierarchically organising individual units into folders (groups of files) and sub-folders; it all depends on what will work best for the researcher in terms of keeping track of the data/information, and in terms of achieving the analytical goals set for the research. Thus, files may be divided into folders on the basis of 'kind' – for example for a participant observation study in a newsroom, daily write-ups of observational notes may be in one folder, formal interviews with news professionals in another folder, policy documents extracted from the news organisation in a third folder, research memos and emerging ideas in a fourth folder. Alternatively, folders may be organised on a chronological basis: a new folder for each day; or it may be that some combination of 'kind' and 'chronology' classification will work best.

For a study of newspaper text, a useful set-up would normally consist of a folder for each newspaper, with sub-folders arranged chronologically, for example separate folders for each month, year or other timespan best suited to the study in question. This set-up immediately facilitates comparisons between different newspapers and comparisons of changes over time in the nature of coverage (e.g. changes in the vocabulary and terminology used for characterising certain phenomena). Textual data from a survey or from focus group interviews could sensibly be grouped in folders according to the main controlling or independent variables used in the study, for example sex, social status, age, occupation, geographical location or education.

Qualitative data analysis

The analysis of qualitative data is very much a matter of discovering what occurs where, in which context, discussed in which terms, using which vocabulary or terminologies, and it is a matter of discovering trends, relationships and differences. A large part of the task facing the qualitative researcher then is one of 'keeping track' of what came from where in the body of data, what was related to what, which terms were used by whom, which ideas arose in relation to what observations, etc. These are precisely the kind of tasks that computers are good at. They offer fast, reliable and powerful ways of managing, manipulating and searching large bodies of textual data, although Tesch's admonishing at the dawn of computer-assisted analysis of qualitative data is as true now as it was then in the early 1990s:

> The thinking, judging, deciding, interpreting, etc., are still done by the researcher. The computer does not make conceptual decisions, such as which words or themes are important to focus on, or which analytical step to take next. These intellectual tasks are still left entirely to the researcher ... Thus all the computer does is follow instructions regarding words, phrases or text segments previously designated by the researcher as analysis units. (1991: 25–6)

The types of software or computer programs available for managing, manipulating, searching, coding and analysing qualitative textual data are many and varied. Furthermore, they are – like computer technology itself – in continuous development. Our modest objective here is to introduce two principal categories of computer programs for the management and analysis of qualitative data, and to give a brief indication of what they can do and how they can be useful in media and communication research.

The first category consists of programs (primarily) for indexing and searching text, for retrieving segments of text and for examining word use/vocabulary. The second category consists of programs (primarily) for coding text, examining relationships between (coded) segments of text and for building theory. We say 'primarily', because, as with so much in computer programming, there is continuous enhancement and increasing convergence in terms of what programs can do.

Text indexing and retrieval

Identifying occurrence, location and context
As a starting point for analysis of qualitative textual data, it is necessary to be able to identify the occurrence and location of specific words, terms, references and mentions across the different and multiple documents or files which make up the body of data. In much the same way as the index at the

back of a book provides a shortcut for the reader who wishes to look up a particular concept or issue, computer indexing programs enable the researcher to go straight to the particular places in the body of data where a certain word or reference is used. Rather than flicking or browsing through what could easily be hundreds of pages of interview transcripts to find, say, all the times that interviewees had mentioned a particular soap-opera character, this type of computer program enables the researcher to either jump from one occurrence of the character's name to the next, or alternatively to produce a list of all occurrences of the character's name, complete with identifiers showing the location (folder name, file name, page number) of each occurrence.

Often it will not be sufficient to simply identify the location of specific words or terms – you would want to see these 'in context' in order to determine the meaning and use of a specified term or word. Such a listing is known as a 'key-word-in-context' list, or KWIC for short. A key-word-in-context list shows a line of text for each occurrence of the specified word – that is the specified search word in the middle of the line with a specified number of words of context on either side.

Keyword searching can include the specification of synonyms (e.g. find all occurrences of 'car' or 'automobile' or 'vehicle'); the use of 'wildcards' (i.e. find any word that begins (or ends) with a specified string of letters regardless of what the ending (or beginning) letters are (e.g. 'scient*' would find all occurrences of 'scientist', 'scientists', 'scientific', 'scientifically', 'scientology')); and the use of Boolean operators ('and', 'or', 'not') with or without proximity conditions (e.g. find all occurrences of the words 'nuclear' or 'atomic' within ten words of 'weapons' or 'arms', but not within ten words of 'energy').

Examining vocabulary and word frequency

Almost regardless of the nature of textual data (newspaper articles, interview transcripts, policy documents), a useful starting point for the qualitative researcher is to examine the vocabulary used for discussing, talking about, writing about the topics, themes and issues concerned. What words, terms, slang expressions, etc. are used? What differences exist in the vocabulary used by some respondents or media compared with that of other types of respondents or media? What are the most frequently used words, and, perhaps equally revealing, which words or terms are used very infrequently (or not at all, as the case may be)? Which new terms or concepts are added over time? Computer programs of this kind (known generally as concordance programs) can provide vocabulary lists detailing each individual word used in a body of text as well as concordances, that is show all occurrences of each individual word in its context. Vocabulary lists can be ordered by frequency of occurrence or alphabetically (in ascending or descending order) to instantly provide an overview of which words are most, and which least, frequent or common in a body of text.

Examining co-occurrence and associated words

Perhaps one of the most powerful and productive uses of programs in this category is for examining the co-occurrence of words, that is for examining which words are associated with or tend to occur in the context of which terms. Co-occurrence and word association provide important clues and pointers to the 'framing', 'thinking behind', the perspective or the ideology of a text. As a prominent linguist noted long ago, 'You shall know a lot about a word from the company it keeps' (Firth, 1957). Moreover, while crucially important in itself, this insight extends – as we shall see in the example below – beyond the meaning associations of individual words to wider discourse analytic concerns with syntax, grammar and agency.

At the immediate level of word associations, it clearly, for example, makes a difference whether, say, 'alcoholism' or 'drug-abuse' are discussed in terms of 'treatment', 'health', 'victims', 'patients', 'social skills' or, alternatively, in terms of 'deviance', 'crime', 'law enforcement', 'punishment'. Similarly, the analysis of co-occurrence may help reveal not just the general ways in which key actors are described – their characteristics and attributes – but also the legitimacy and authority with which they are, differentially, invested by the text: some sources and actors, for example, may be quoted as 'saying', 'testifying', 'stating', 'declaring', 'arguing', 'explaining', while others may be quoted as 'alleging', 'asserting', 'speculating', 'claiming' – two sets of associated words which invest the quoted actors or sources with different degrees of authority or legitimacy.

Concordance programs have the dual advantage of being geared towards and able (like content analysis) to cope with extraordinarily large quantities or bodies of text. By providing almost instant summaries of the type and frequency of words used in a text, and by enabling the researcher to see all occurrences of selected individual keywords in their immediate context, these programs and analytical procedures allow 'researchers to objectively identify widespread patterns of naturally occurring language and rare but telling examples, both of which may be over-looked by a small-scale analysis. Such language patterns can help to illuminate the existence of discourses that may otherwise be unobserved' (Baker and McEnery, 2005).

Using a concordance program, and drawing principally on keyword (in this case 'teacher' and 'teachers') in context analysis combined with collocation analysis, Hansen (2009) – in an analysis of the changing portrayal of teachers in UK newspapers between 1991 and 2005 – found that the types of words most closely associated with the keywords 'teacher'/'teachers' changed from a relatively singular emphasis on a lexicon of crisis, confrontation, conflict and problems to a much more nuanced lexicon emphasising both the challenges and achievements of the teaching profession. But possibly more significant was the finding – based on close scrutiny of the key-word-in-context-list for the two keywords teacher and teachers – that the syntactic position of teacher(s) changed dramatically between the earlier and the later part of the period examined: thus the position of teacher(s) in news headlines changed 'from an almost exclusive position as object/target of government and other actions to a much more active position as the subject/agent of various actions' (Hansen, 2009: 340). Figure 11.10 shows an excerpt of a key-word-in-context listing from the study just referred to using the program Concordance (described further below and at the end of this chapter). One of the key features of Concordance is the ability to arrange/order the concordance or key-word-in-context listing alphabetically (ascending or descending) by either the word immediately to the left, or immediately to the right, of the (centred) keyword.

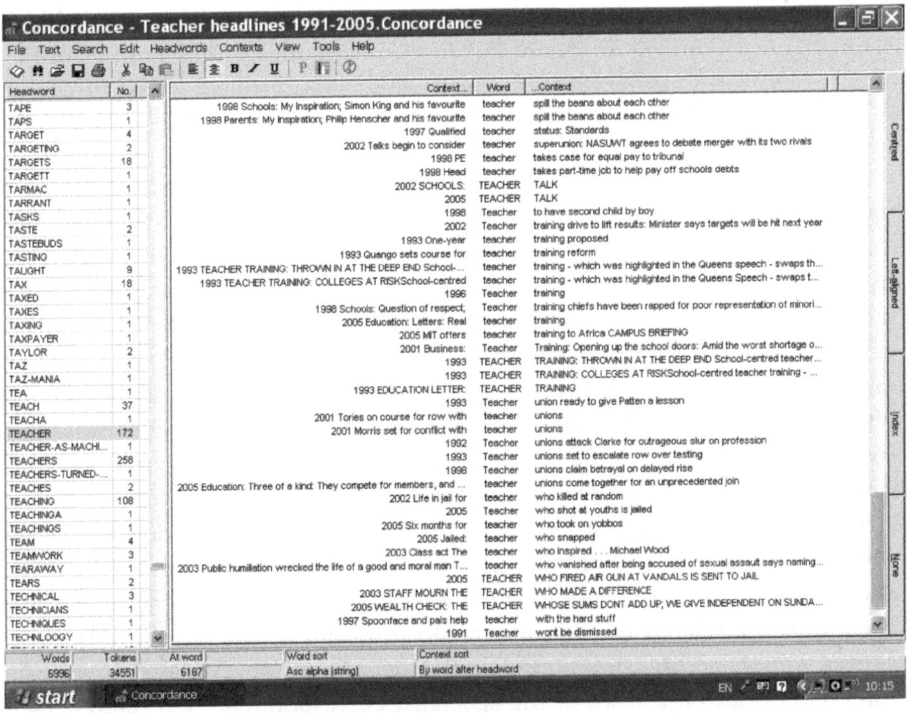

Figure 11.10 Excerpt of word frequency list (left side) and key-word-in-context list (right side) arranged alphabetically by the first word to the right of the keyword 'teacher' in Concordance

Two programs that handle the above procedures well and powerfully, while at the same time being both accessible and straightforward to use are the one just mentioned, Concordance, and WordSmith Tools (for details, see the resources section at the end of this chapter). But perhaps the single most important virtue of these types of programs is that they enable the qualitative researcher to 'stay close' to the data. That is the programs are used primarily for identifying what appears where, how frequently, in which context, associated with what, etc. and searches and analyses are not based on complex assumptions or formulae about proximity, etc. The programs lend themselves well to examining key linguistic patterns, which can then be explored in the light of linguistic theory, discourse theory and other relevant theoretical frameworks.

Text coding, relationships and model-building

The second category of computer programs are those designed for electronic coding or tagging of text segments, for examining relationships between coded segments of text, and, on the basis of such relationships, for building and graphically representing models of relationships in texts. A 'segment' can be a word, a sentence, a paragraph – in fact, almost any length of text. In the same way as programs in category one, described above, enable the retrieval of all occurrences (with location identifiers) of a word or group of words, programs in this category allow the researcher to retrieve and list all segments of text with a specified code.

Thus, the researcher analysing a series of interviews with specialist journalists may have coded all references to or mentions of source agenda-setting – situations where the agenda for news coverage is set by sources rather than by media professionals – and would be able to retrieve these and compare what different journalists say about this aspect. The point is that the concept of source agenda-setting may be talked about and referred to in many different ways, indirectly and directly, and indeed in ways which do not deploy either the word 'source' or the word 'agenda-setting'. Unlike the word-based searches of programs in the previous category, coding or tagging thus is not dependent on the particular vocabulary or words used in the textual data.

Once the textual data have been coded, it would often be desirable to go further than simply examining and comparing text under each of the codes used, and to start exploring whether and how different topics, themes and categories are related to each other. Do those interviewees who talk about source agenda-setting, for example, also tend to emphasise strong editorial intervention into the work of the specialist correspondent? Do references to concept X always co-occur with references to concept Y? Is the presence of concept Y conditional upon concept X? etc. Qualitative data analysis programs of this kind thus not only facilitate complex coding of textual segments and fast and flexible retrieval of coded segments – itself a major advantage over traditional paper/index card-based approaches to working with qualitative data – but, more importantly, they enable the examination and modelling of complex relationships, links, co-occurrences and perspectives in qualitative textual data.

Increasingly, qualitative data analysis programs – whether of the concordance type or the coding/tagging type – are also capable of performing quantitative statistical analyses of their own or they have facilities for exporting the codes attached to segments of text to statistical analysis programs such as SPSS or Excel, so that further quantitative analysis can be carried out in these.

Two of the most prominent and useful programs in this category are ATLAS.ti and QSR NVivo (for details, see the resources section at the end of this chapter), both of which provide a powerful framework for organising, managing, coding and analysing textual and visual information in a variety of formats.

Summary

- Whether dealing with quantitative or qualitative (textual) data, computer-assisted analysis involves three major steps or areas of consideration: 1) the transfer of 'raw' data from their original form/medium (e.g. coding schedules, questionnaires, handwritten notes, printed text) to the computer medium; 2) the organisation of data (e.g. in data files, text files, folders) on the computer medium; 3) analysis of data, using appropriate computer applications or programs.
- SPSS is a powerful and flexible program for the statistical analysis of social science data, including communications research data. Coded data from, for example, content analysis coding schedules or survey questionnaires are entered into an SPSS data file, where each column represents a variable (e.g. sex, age, occupation) and each row represents a case (e.g. a survey respondent, a newspaper article). 'Data' may take the form of one or more of three principal types of variables: categorical variables, continuous variables and 'string' variables (e.g. words, text).
- The choice of analytical procedures in SPSS will depend in large measure on the types of variables to be analysed, as well as, of course, on the aims of the research. We have introduced four fundamental analytical procedures in SPSS: two for examining the distribution of individual variables in a data set (Frequencies and Descriptives), and two for examining relationships between two or more variables (Crosstabs and Means).

- When dealing with qualitative textual data, careful consideration should be given to the question of how best to organise the data in terms of files and folders (including master folders and hierarchies of sub-folders).
- We see computer programs for the management and analysis of qualitative textual data as falling into two major groups: 1) concordance-type programs for indexing and the analysis of vocabulary, context and collocations; and 2) programs for the coding and code-based analysis of text (qualitative text analysis programs).
  - Concordance-type programs enable the researcher to examine and analyse keywords, vocabulary, word frequencies, key-words-in-context, co-occurrences and words associated with specified keywords. These programs allow the researcher to move quickly and reliably to relevant occurrences and references in a potentially very large body of texts, and to retrieve identified relevant occurrences/segments of text, for further analysis and comparison, or for inclusion as 'examples' in research reports.
  - Qualitative text analysis programs facilitate coding and analysis of coded text. The researcher attaches (electronic) codes, 'tags', labels to segments of text (e.g. words, sentence, paragraph, which refer to or express the idea, phenomenon, concept, theme, issue or topic denoted by the particular code). Coded segments can then be retrieved and examined, and further analysis can be carried out to establish how different coded segments interact and relate to each other.

Further reading and resources

SPSS

Since 2010 SPSS has been formally known as IBM SPSS Statistics. The IBM SPSS Statistics website offers details of SPSS products, example uses/application and selected software trial downloads:

> www.ibm.com/software/analytics/spss/products/statistics/

Book resources

Bryman, A. (2008). *Social Research Methods* (3rd edn.). Oxford: Oxford University Press, Chapters 14 and 15.
   A very accessible and clear introduction to SPSS.

Field, A. (2009). *Discovering Statistics Using SPSS* (3rd edn.). London: Sage.
   A comprehensive, detailed and yet accessible introduction to statistical analysis with SPSS.

Qualitative data management and analysis: programs and resources

Concordance

Concordance by R. J. C. Watt (http://www.concordancesoftware.co.uk/) is a flexible and easy-to-use program for indexing textual data, producing word lists, examining vocabulary, producing key-word-in-context lists, examining collocations and word associations, etc. It offers an efficient and powerful way of analysing text that makes few assumptions and always stays 'close' to the original source text in the sense that no (potentially subjective) coding or tagging is involved. For examples of its use in media and communication research, see:

Hansen, A. (2006). Tampering With Nature: 'Nature' and the 'Natural' in Media Coverage of Genetics and Biotechnology, *Media, Culture & Society, 28/6,* 811–34.

Hansen, A. (2009). Researching 'Teachers in the News': The Portrayal of Teachers and Education Issues in the British National and Regional Press, *Education 3–13: International Journal of Primary, Elementary and Early Years Education, 37/4,* 335–47.

WordSmith Tools

Mike Scott's WordSmith Tools (http://www.lexically.net/wordsmith/) offers a suite of tools for producing word lists, analysing word frequencies, producing concordances, collocations and examining textual patterns. The following are key introductions to the use of WordSmith and to the variety of powerful analyses drawing from corpus linguistics, linguistic theory and discourse analysis:

Scott, M., and Tribble, C. (2006). *Textual Patterns: Key Words and Corpus Analysis in Language Education* (Vol. 22). Amsterdam: John Benjamins Publishing Company.

Baker, P. (2006). *Using Corpora in Discourse Analysis.* London: Continuum International Publishing Group Ltd.

For a considered and instructive discussion of the combination of Critical Discourse Analysis with corpus linguistics, see also:

Baker, P., Gabrielatos, C., Khosravinik, M., Krzyzanowski, M., McEnery, T., and Wodak, R. (2008). A Useful Methodological Synergy? Combining Critical Discourse Analysis and Corpus Linguistics to Examine Discourses of Refugees and Asylum Seekers in the UK Press, *Discourse & Society, 19/3,* 273–306.

ATLAS.ti and NVivo

ATLAS.ti (http://www.atlasti.com/) and NVivo (http://www.qsrinternational.com/) have evolved since the 1990s to become two of the most versatile and powerful programs for managing, organising, coding, analysing and visualising qualitative data such as interview transcripts, audio data, textual and visual media content and research notes.

For a comprehensive introduction to the steps involved in computer-assisted qualitative research – with particular reference to, amongst others, these two programs mentioned – see:

Lewins, A., and Silver, C. (2007). *Using Software in Qualitative Research: A Step-by-Step Guide*. London: Sage.

See also Lyn Richard's (one of the original developers of NVivo and its predecessor NUDIST) introduction to qualitative data analysis:

Richards, L. (2009). *Handling Qualitative Data: A Practical Guide*. London: Sage.

And:

Friese, S. (2012). *Qualitative Data Analysis With ATLAS.ti*. London: Sage.

The Web and beyond

As we have indicated, computer programs and analysis are increasingly being developed for the direct analysis of online or web-based information, bypassing the need for retrieving/downloading and organising data on personal computers. Search engines such as Google offer a number of ways of tracking or mapping key trends in web traffic and web-based information. Research organisations such as the Pew use automated analysis programs for monitoring what the news media as well as bloggers and social media users are most focused on in any one week. For a general introduction to these types of programs, see:

Thelwall, M. A. (2009). *Introduction to Webometrics: Quantitative Web Research for the Social Sciences*. San Rafael, CA: Morgan & Claypool Publishers.

Glossary

Agenda-setting	Term referring, in communication research, to the power of the news media to set or influence the hierarchy of issues, events and actors/agencies perceived by the public or considered/addressed by social and political fora, including other media. The classic reference on agenda-setting in communication research is McCombs and Shaw, 1972.
Analytical survey	See: Survey.
Angle of interaction	A photographer might capture a subject by looking up or down at them, looking straight at them, from the side or behind. These decisions, these angles of interaction, will influence the way that the subject is represented in relation to the viewer in terms of power and in terms of engagement. Looking up at a subject makes them appear more powerful; looking down at them makes them appear less powerful. If we look straight at them there is a greater degree of involvement than if we look side on. If we are positioned behind them we tend to take their point of view.
Anthropology	This is the broad academic field that studies human cultures and societies. While associated with studying more primitive societies it was the early anthropologists that challenged the view that these societies were somehow primitive in terms of the way they think. It was shown that belief systems of contemporary Western societies were no more rational and that those of smaller-scale societies were just as rich and complex and often served much the same purposes. Anthropology can equally be the study of contemporary societies. Its main research method is ethnography.
Binary oppositions	The concept of binary oppositions is, in semiotics, based on the notion that signs derive their meaning from relationships with other signs, and, consequently, the meaning of a sign is defined principally by its position within the system of signs (e.g. language) and by what it 'is not', i.e. by its companion opposite: we know what 'good' is because it contrasts with 'evil'. Semiotics takes this principle further

283

to note that all texts are organised around a core set of binary opposites, which are key to how texts communicate meaning and ideology. Binary oppositions should not be confused with simple negations.

Categorical variable

A variable consisting of arbitrary codes assigned to indicate the range of values that the variable can take. In content analysis, for example, the names of the newspapers being analysed may be coded as: 1. *The Daily Mail*, 2. *The Daily Mirror*; 3. *The Daily Telegraph*; etc. In a survey, for example, a variable such as the social class of the respondent may be coded as: 1. Lower class; 2. Middle class; 3. Upper class. Categorical codes may have some of the properties of the numerical scale, e.g. they may be rank ordered and/or they may be equidistant, but mostly they tend to have none of these properties, which in turn limits the type of statistical analysis that can be done. See also: continuous variable.

Census

A survey of all members of a population.

Closed-ended question

A survey question that offers the respondent a limited set of pre-formulated answers, from which one or more – as specified in the questionnaire – must be selected. See also: question formats.

Coding

The act of classifying by assigning values or tags to images or text-segments in analysis of media content or to respondents' statements/answers in surveys, interviews or observational studies.

Coding protocol/ code-book/coding frame

The content analysis protocol (also frequently referred to as the 'code-book' or 'coding frame') is the coding instruction manual that coders refer to when they code. It sets out not only what variables are to be coded, and their associated values, but equally importantly it gives clear instructions about how the coding is to be done. It thus provides definitions, where appropriate, of the variables and their values, and it helps ensure that most fundamental aspect of content analysis, namely that it must be 'replicable'.

Coding schedule

Like the questionnaire in a survey, the coding schedule is the core research instrument in content analysis. It is a list specifying the variables (and their associated values) or dimensions that are to be coded in the selected sample of content. Instructions about how to code each variable are normally given separately in the code-book or coding protocol, but are sometimes included on the actual coding schedule.

Collocation analysis	The study of word co-occurrences to see whether/how selected keywords routinely appear together with specific other words.
Concordance	A list (ordered alphabetically or by frequency) of all individual words in a body of text, with each word shown in its immediate context.
Connotation	Images and other representations can be said to denote or depict something. So a photograph can be said to denote, or depict, a woman with long hair. But images and other representations can also communicate or connote broader meanings. So a photograph of a woman can connote beauty, romance and desire, for example.
Content analysis	'Quantitative content analysis is the systematic and replicable examination of symbols of communication, which have been assigned numeric values according to valid measurement rules and the analysis of relationships involving those values using statistical methods, to describe the communication, draw inferences about its meaning, or infer from the communication to its context, both of production and consumption' (Riffe, Lacy and Fico, 2005: 25).
Continuous variable	A variable consisting of 'real' numbers with the properties of the numerical scale (i.e. ordered, equidistant and with an absolute zero), as opposed to arbitrary 'codes', which may have some or none of these properties. Continuous variables in content analysis may be, for example, the length of newspaper articles measured in terms of number of words or the length of broadcast news items measured in number of seconds. A typical continuous variable in a survey is the respondent's age in years. See also: categorical variable.
Corpus linguistics	The study of linguistic patterns in a selected corpus of text, e.g. all national newspaper articles published over a specified time-period. Corpus linguistic analysis examines vocabulary, selected keywords in their context, patterns of co-occurrence in selected keywords, etc. It combines the strengths and advantages of quantitative analysis with inquiry guided by linguistic and discourse theory.
Critical Discourse Analysis	A broad approach to the study of language which seeks to point to the linguistic and grammatical features of texts that allow the analyst to reveal the discourses buried in the them that may not be so readily apparent to the casual reader. This process seeks to make explicit the ideology and interests promoted by the text.

Cross-sectional survey	A survey design in which the selected sample of respondents is interviewed once only.
Crosstabulation analysis (crosstabs)	A procedure in SPSS and other statistical analysis programs that compares two or more variables, e.g. a crosstabulation of *sex of respondent* by *age* in a survey would produce a table showing the number of male and female respondents in each age category.
Cultivation analysis	Cultivation analysis, originally introduced by American communication scholar George Gerbner, posits that the more time that is spent watching television (or other media), the more likely it is that viewers/audiences form a view of the world which is consistent with dominant media/mediated representations of reality.
Cultural symbols	In any image, photograph or other kind of representation we can ask which are the important cultural symbols and think about the role that they play. In an advertisement, for example, we might say that red lips are a potent symbol since they are used in our culture to communicate sensuality and beauty. In a photograph a woman in an office might speak on a mobile phone. This is a cultural symbol for mobility and independence as opposed to the meanings communicated by a woman speaking on a landline in an office.
Denotation	This is what an image or other representation simply depicts. So a photograph may depict or denote a house. There is an implied assumption that this is a neutral judgement. But when we look at any image we will of course always assume what kind of house it is, if it is where wealthier people live, for example. There is no neutral denotation. The term is used to distinguish between what is depicted and what its associated meanings are.
Dependent variable	The variable under study or observation to see how or whether it is influenced by one or more independent variables.
Descriptive statistics	Statistical analysis summarising the distribution and frequencies of variables, but without drawing statistical inferences from the relationship between variables (inferential statistics).
Descriptive survey	See: Survey.
Descriptives	A procedure in SPSS for summarising the distribution of a continuous variable, by showing the mean or average value of the variable as well as the minimum and maximum values of the variable.

Discourse	Discourses are the broader chunks of knowledge we share about how the world works. A society may favour a discourse about crime and punishment – that crime is committed by bad people who deserve to be punished in prison. However, discourses always reflect certain interests. In terms of crime, prisons tend to be filled with poor, less privileged people and powerless ethnic minorities. This suggests that the dominant discourse of crime and punishment reflects the interest of powerful groups.
Discourse schema	Discourses have associated identities, values and ideas. They also have associated sequences of activity. So we tend to have particular scenarios, particular sequences of activity associated, for example, with crime and punishment. Only one part of a discourse need be established in order to connote the whole. Therefore only one aspect of a discourse schema need be present for the whole to be understood.
Ethnography	This is the research approach associated in the first place with anthropology. Ethnography can consist in obtaining any kind of data to get a picture of how a culture works. But for the most part ethnography involves observation and participation in social life.
Focus group/focus group research	A group interview or discussion, conducted by a moderator, and involving – usually – between 5 and 12 respondents.
Framing	Framing in communication research refers to the way in which *selection* (i.e. of events, actors, attributes, issues, but also of lexis and linguistic paradigms) and *emphasis* (i.e. the relative prominence given within a text to events, actors, issues, etc.) shape the messages that are communicated and the way in which they are (likely to be) received. The classic reference in communication research is Entman, 1993.
Frequency analysis (frequencies)	A procedure in SPSS and other statistical analysis programs for summarising the frequency distribution of the values of an individual variable (normally a categorical variable). A frequency analysis of the variable *sex of respondent* in a survey produces a table showing the number of male and female respondents in the survey.
Genre	Genre is a term often used to refer to different genres of film or television format, e.g. comedy or drama, although it is frequently noted that the boundaries of such genres are always blurred. In linguistics it is used more specifically to consider the way that different forms of communication

rely on certain assumptions and expectations. So we have different expectations from a lecture than a conversation. We must have expectations if we are to accomplish communication. This assumption allows us to look at the way that different media texts follow certain genre principles or moves. What is important is that genres can be shapers of information – something that is often easy to overlook.

Globalisation versus localisation	As regards media studies there has been an interest in the way that transnational corporations have spread their products around the planet. This is part of a perceived process of globalisation. Of interest, however, is the extent to which these products transmit values, ideas and discourses that reflect dominant cultures, or the extent to which these products must be localised and adapted for the new markets. Often this is difficult to identify since the 'global' is located in the formats and genres whereas the 'local' is that which can be a useful tool for the global to operate and may be no more than a gloss over these formats and genres.
Hypothesis	A statement or prediction, subject to testing, about the relationship between two or more variables; used to guide the formulation of types of analysis/tests to be conducted in a study.
Ideology	Ideologies are ways of thinking about the world, a set of ideas and beliefs, which claim to be the truth. These reflect the needs and concerns of individuals or groups. For example, capitalist ideology embodies the belief that all of society should be based around making money, around profit and business. So schools and universities should equally, in this view, not have a role primarily of making the lives of students better, of making society a more creative and open place, but of providing business with suitable workers.
Independent variable(s)	The variable(s) analysed and presumed to influence the dependent variable. Statistical comparison/testing is used to test whether or how variation in selected independent variables causes or influences variation in the dependent variable.
In-depth interview	These are carried out with individuals who are chosen because they can provide detailed insights into our research topic. Each interview may be based around prepared questions but will take the form of open discussions as it may be assumed that the interviewee can provide unexpected, as

	yet unknown, information. This information can be used to develop and target subsequent interviews.
Inter-coder reliability	A statistical measure or test used in content analysis to establish the extent of agreement between those involved in coding. The higher the inter-coder reliability, the more consistent or reliable – and hence replicable – the content analysis. See also: intra-coder reliability.
Interview guide	The set of instructions that tells interviewers how to conduct the interview and record the answers, i.e. how to introduce and ask questions, which prompts to use – if any – which explanations/elaborations are permitted in relation to each question, how to end the interview, etc.
Interview schedule	See: questionnaire.
Intra-coder reliability	A statistical measure or test used in content analysis to establish the extent to which a single individual coder remains consistent over time in their coding. The higher the intra-coder reliability, the more consistent or reliable the content analysis. See also: inter-coder reliability.
KWIC (key-word-in-context)	A list of selected key words in their immediate context, i.e. the key word is centred on the page and is shown in the context of the 5–8 words appearing either side of the key word.
Lexis/lexical choice/vocabulary analysis	The study of the types of individual words that are used and are characteristic of the text or communication content under investigation.
Lifestyle	This term is used to refer to a newer kind of identity that is associated with late capitalism and consumerism. Formerly people had more stable identities based around gender, social class, occupation and location. In contemporary society, it is thought, we can modify our identities through products, fashion items and leisure activities. One criticism of this process is that the way we are now encouraged to realise who we are is always closely aligned to acts of consumption.
Mean or mean value	Same as average value, i.e. the sum of values divided by the number of cases.
Means	A procedure in SPSS that summarises the values of two or more continuous variables across a categorical variable, e.g. a means analysis of *age* by *sex of respondent* in a survey produces a table showing the mean/average, minimum and maximum age of respectively male and female respondents in the survey.
Media de/regulation	We cannot understand media content unless we know something about the way the media are owned and run.

And we must place this in the context of how the media are regulated, what they are permitted and not permitted to do. Crucial to understanding the nature of commercial radio and newspapers, for example, are the changing number of stations and titles that companies are entitled to own. Media regulation documents for different countries may be available online from relevant government departments.

Metaphor

Metaphor is of importance in Critical Discourse Analysis. Metaphor should not be thought of only in the literary and poetical sense. Metaphors underpin the way we think and involve a process where we try to understand one thing, process or event through another. 'Our country is flooded with immigrants' is one such use of metaphor. Flooding has a number of properties: it is out of control; can wash existing things away; it can be a natural disaster. These properties can be transferred to the new domain in order to shape understanding of it. In this case it has been used to represent immigration not as a process of enrichment but of damage.

Multimodality

In linguistics in the 1990s there was a concern that analysis had been focused on one mode – language – whereas much of the meaning-making in many of the texts analysed was done so by images and visual communication. Theorists began to apply linguistic models to visual communication in order to provide some kind of equivalent systematic analysis. This analysis was therefore 'multimodal' rather than 'monomodal'. However, what constitutes a 'mode' is difficult to establish. Visual communication, in itself, cannot be reduced to one single mode, for example – is the way a traffic light communicates the same mode as a person communicating through hand gestures?

Narrative

This is the basic sequence of events that underpin any story or can be found in other genres of communication. When we carry out narrative analysis we seek out the basic stages of the story or other genres that may be either concealed by details or which may be only partly overtly apparent in the text.

Nominalisation

This is when verbs are transformed into nouns in language in order to conceal agency, temporality and causality. So the noun phrase 'The changed economy' contains the noun 'changed'. This is one way that specifically who has changed the economy, when and how it has been changed, can be glossed over.

Observational methods	These methods simply involve observing people. We may observe people as they watch television to see how they interact with it. We may observe a person in different contexts in order to understand how their identity relates to certain media definitions. We may also observe processes of media production. For example, we might observe the way a photographer prepares images for a newspaper or website. We may observe them in editorial meetings, at a photo shoot and in the editing process. In both cases observation will throw up insights that would not have been available had we simply asked the participant. It also allows us to study people over time and in different contexts where they may behave slightly differently.
Offer and demand images	Drawing from linguistics this is one way by which we categorise whether persons in images engage with the viewer, therefore demanding a reaction from us, or whether they do not, in which case they are offered to the viewer, like the rest of the contents of the image, as information.
Open-ended question	A survey question that allows the respondent to answer in their own words, with no prompting or restrictions. See also: question formats.
Panel study/panel survey	A longitudinal survey design in which the same sample of respondents is interviewed at two or more different points in time. See also: cross-sectional survey.
Participant observation	An ethnographic study design in which the researcher observes work routines, behaviours and practices of fellow workers, while themself working/engaging in these. A type of research much used in the study of journalism/ journalists, news production and news rooms.
Pilot study/piloting	A test or trial run of a study, conducted on a small sub-sample to test whether the research design and research instruments, questions or coding categories 'work' as intended, i.e. capture what they are supposed to capture.
Political economic analysis	This is where we study ownership, control and financing of media. Here we might study a particular magazine title. We look at who owns it, how this has changed over the years and ask how this might relate to content. We will also look at the way the magazine is financed. Is it through advertising, or state funding or cover price? All of these answers help us to build up a picture of why content may be the way it is. Underpinning this kind of analysis is the idea that there may be unfair and uneven distribution of control over media content.

Population

The entire group or universe of people, media, programmes, objects or cases that the researcher/study is aiming to find out about and to be able to say something about with regard to the dimensions being studied. As it is rarely feasible or indeed necessary to study the entire population, a representative sample is drawn and this then forms the basis for the research and extrapolation – depending on how representative the sample is – to the population.

Presupposition

This term points to what is assumed as the taken-for-granted in a text. For example, the sentence: 'We must take this opportunity to move forward' makes the presupposition that the event in particular is an opportunity and not in fact a problem. This is one rhetorical device through which speakers, such as politicians, can lay claim to what is widely thought or already established when it is in fact contestable.

Primary definers/
sources/actors

Interchangeable terms used in media and communication research to refer to the people, agencies or sources who are quoted or referred to in news reporting. A variable often included in content analysis of news.

Qualitative research

Qualitative research – from Latin 'qualitas' = 'of what kind' – is perhaps best described by contrast to quantitative research in the sense that qualitative research is *not* concerned with counting the number of times different dimensions appear, but rather with examining and understanding *what* appears and what it *means*. Qualitative methods include focus group research, in-depth interviews, observation, ethnography, discourse analysis, semiotic analysis, narrative analysis, genre analysis, etc. Due to its intrinsically interpretive and more subjective nature, it is often difficult to obtain high reliability or replicability, while, on the other hand, qualitative research tends to benefit from a high degree of validity.

Quantitative research

Quantitative research focuses on counting and quantifying relevant dimensions according to clearly specified rules. Consequently, it lends itself to a broad variety of statistical ways of describing data and testing relationships between dimensions/variables. Key quantitative methods include the survey for studying people and content analysis for studying text/documents/media content. Due to its rule-governed and transparent nature, quantitative research has the potential to be highly reliable and replicable, while it is frequently more difficult to obtain a high degree of validity.

Question formats	Question formats can be divided into two principal groups: closed and open-ended questions. Closed questions in turn may take a number of formats: e.g. selection of single answer from a restricted list of answers; multiple choice: selecting one, two or more – as specified – from a restricted list of answers; rank ordering by preference of a restricted range of answers; agreement scale, i.e. the respondent indicates the extent to which they agree or disagree with selected statements on a predefined scale.
Questionnaire	An ordered list of questions forming the key research instrument in a survey and, where necessary, including instructions about how to ask/answer the questions and how to navigate through the sections of the questionnaire.
Reliability	A measure of the extent to which research and research procedures are replicable and consistent over time and across different researchers.
Replicable/replicability	Replicable means that other researchers or coders applying the same rules and procedures to the same communications content should arrive at the same or very similar results. If they do, then the content analysis is not only replicable, but also its results meet the scientific criterion of reliability.
Representative/ reasonably representative	A sample is said to be representative of the population from which it is drawn, when key variables and dimensions (e.g. demographic characteristics such as sex, age, social status) appear in the same proportions in the sample as in the population. 'Reasonably representative' here is taken to mean a sample which is not skewed or biased by the personal preferences or hunches of the researcher, the desire to 'prove' a particular preconceived point, or by insufficient knowledge of the media and their social context.
Research	We define media and communication research as the planned, critical, systematic and transparent investigation into or gathering of information about media and/or communication processes.
Research instrument(s)	In practical terms, the research instrument and definition of variables for data collection will differ depending on the method used, but in very general terms the research instrument is the researcher's menu of questions/variables and manual of how to collect the information. In a content analysis, this is the code-book that specifies what content dimensions are to be coded and how; in a survey, it is the questionnaire and any associated instructions to

interviewers/respondents; in a focus group study, it is the script indicating the moderator's role, speech and menu of questions/topics to be discussed, as well as directions for any prompts or stimuli that are to be used; in an observational study, it is the plan for who will be observed where, what dimensions will be observed, what questions will be asked, how answers and observations will be recorded, etc.

Rhetoric | This describes language that is used for purposes of persuasion. The study of rhetoric involves documenting and classifying the different strategies that can be used by speakers and authors in this process.

Rolling week sampling/composite week sampling | A simple sampling strategy often used in content analysis. It consists of sampling media content from Monday of the first week, Tuesday of the second week, Wednesday of the third week, etc. continuing until a full week (or more, if required) has been sampled.

Salience in images | This refers to the way that elements and features of images can be made to stand out above others. There is a range of ways that this can be accomplished and this can create a hierarchy of elements. For example, an element can be placed in the foreground, it can overlap others, carry a particular colour or tone.

Sample (noun) | A sub-group of respondents, objects or cases selected for analysis or study from a larger population or universe. The general and ideal aim is for a sample to be representative in the sense that the key characteristics under study are approximately equally distributed in the sample and the population from which the sample is drawn.

Sample/sampling (verb) | The act of selecting a – preferably – representative sub-group for study and analysis from a larger population. There are two principal types of sampling: probability sampling (including various types of random sampling) and non-probability sampling (including quota sampling, convenience sampling, snowball sampling).

Sampling interval | The interval or gap between sampled units in systematic sampling, e.g. a population of newspaper articles may be sampled by systematically selecting every fifth article – i.e. a sampling interval of 5 – from a chronological and number-ordered list of the articles in the population under study.

Semiotics/semiology | Literally, 'the science of signs'. Drawing on the linguistic theories of Swiss linguist Ferdinand de Saussure and American philosopher Charles Sanders Peirce, semiotics is the study of how signs (words, icons, images, sounds, etc.)

derive their meaning and are made to mean through their position within systems of signs and their relationships with other signs in the system (e.g. the language system). In communication research, the work of French semiologist Roland Barthes has been particularly influential.

Social actor analysis
This is the systematic study of the language or visual techniques used to describe and represent the participants in texts and images. We look for whether they are represented as individuals or collectivised, as generic or particular persons, etc. As part of the project of Critical Discourse Analysis the idea is that we look for the kinds of discourses that are signified through these patterns of representation, which may not be overtly stated. For example, in a sequence of texts we might find that one set of participants are regularly collectivised, whereas another set are individualised. We can ask then what broader message about the events in which they are involved is being communicated to us.

Social construction
We live not so much in an objective reality but one which is filtered, or even constructed, appearing as simply objective, through the beliefs of our cultures. Anthropologists are interested in the ways that different societies and cultures construct reality, or see the world, in different ways. So the kinds of identities that we play out, the kinds of knowledge that we hold at different times as important, are a result not of anything inherent in the world but due to the ways particular groups of people have come to define and accept them as such. Of course the media can play a large part in this process of social construction.

SPSS
Statistical Program for the Social Sciences. A powerful program for the management and statistical analysis of social science data, such as – but not limited to – the data generated by surveys or content analyses. At the time of writing SPSS was marketed as PASW (Predictive Analytics SoftWare) Statistics. It is now formally known as IBM SPSS Statistics.

Stance
A content analysis variable designed to code/measure the attitude/perspective or stance of news content to establish whether this conveys a primarily negative or primarily positive representation of the actors, topics or issues under investigation.

String variable
A variable consisting of text, e.g. answers to an open-ended question in a survey questionnaire, or the headline or the name of the reporter in a content analysis of

newspaper articles. String or text variables contrast with numerical variables, and – not being numerical – do not lend themselves to the kind of statistical analysis that can be performed on numerical variables.

Survey

Literally, 'over-view', but in communication and social science research specifically referring to the quantitative method of collecting data from and about people. A distinction is sometimes made between 'descriptive surveys', which simply or mainly aim to collect (descriptive) information, the 'what' of a research scenario, and 'analytical surveys', which aim to collect information on a specified number of variables and then to analyse the relationship between variables, i.e. the 'what-causes-or-relates-to-what' of a research scenario. Surveys can further be classified into the cross-sectional survey, the trend survey and the panel study.

Systematic random sampling

A sampling design that starts by randomly selecting a first item from a numbered list and then proceeds to select every n'th item in the list, where 'n' is the sampling interval. E.g. a population of newspaper articles are arranged in chronological numbered order; it has been decided that a 20% sample should be drawn from the population of newspaper articles. A first number is chosen randomly from the first five articles, e.g. article number 2, and the sampling then proceeds by selecting every fifth article, i.e. articles 7, 12, 17, 22, etc.

Theme/topic/issue

Interchangeable labels often used for a content analysis variable designed to measure broadly what topics or issues are addressed in the content under study.

Trend survey

The trend study is a longitudinal design for examining change over time in a population. The same set of questions is asked in a series of surveys conducted at different points in time. A new sample of a given population is drawn for every occurrence of the trend survey.

Unit of analysis

The 'unit of analysis', that which is counted, can be the individual word, the sentence, the paragraph, the article, the news programme, the news item, an individual character/actor/source, the series episode, the scene, the 'incident' (e.g. a violent incident, the consumption of alcohol), etc.

Validity

The degree to which a study does indeed examine or measure what it claims to be examining or measuring.

Value

See: variables and values.

Variables and values   'Variable' refers to the specific individual dimensions under study, e.g. in a survey variables would often include the age, sex and social status of respondents, while in a content analysis variables would often include medium, type of programme, actors quoted or referred to, theme, etc. Each variable can take a number of 'values', e.g. the *sex* variable in a survey may be coded as the value '1' to signify 'female' and the value '2' to signify 'male'. In a content analysis of newspapers, the *newspaper* variable may be coded using the following values: '1' *The Daily Mirror*, '2' *The Daily Mail*, '3' *The Times*, '4' *The Guardian*.

References

Achugar, M. (2007). Between Remembering and Forgetting: Uruguayan Military Discourse about Human Rights [1976–2004], *Discourse and Society*, 18/3, 521–47

Adams, R. C. (1989). *Social Survey Research Methods for Mass Media Research.* Hillsdale, NJ: Lawrence Erlbaum Associates

Altheide, D. L. (2002). *Creating Fear: News and the Construction of Crisis.* New York: Aldine de Gruyter

Altheide, D. L., and Snow, R. P. (1979). *Media Logic.* London: Sage

Andsager, J. L. (2000). How Interest Groups Attempt to Shape Public Opinion with Competing News Frames, *Journalism and Mass Communication Quarterly*, 77/3, 577–92

Arnheim, R. (1944). The World of the Daytime Serial, in Lazarsfeld, P. F. and Stanton, F. N. (Eds.) *Radio Research 1942–43.* New York: Duell, Sloan and Pearce, pp.38–45

Arnheim, R. (1969). *Visual Thinking.* Berkeley, CA: University of California Press

Asad, T. (1986). The Concept of Cultural Translation in British Social Anthropology, in Clifford, J. and Marcus, G. E. (Eds.) *Writing Culture: The Poetics and Politics of Ethnography.* Berkeley: University of California Press, pp.141–64

Babbie, E. (2010). *The Practice of Social Research* (12th edn.). Belmont, CA: Wadsworth

Baker, P. (2006). *Using Corpora in Discourse Analysis.* London: Continuum International Publishing Group Ltd

Baker, P., and McEnery, T. (2005). A Corpus-based Approach to Discourses of Refugees and Asylum Seekers in UN and Newspaper Texts, *Journal of Language and Politics*, 4/2, 197–226

Baker, P., Gabrielatos, C., Khosravinik, M., Krzyzanowski, M., McEnery, T., and Wodak, R. (2008). A Useful Methodological Synergy? Combining Critical Discourse Analysis and Corpus Linguistics to Examine Discourses of Refugees and Asylum Seekers in the UK Press, *Discourse and Society*, 19/3, 273–306.

Bal, M. (2006). *Reading Rembrandt.* Amsterdam: University of Amsterdam Press

Bamberg, M. (2004). Positioning with Davie Hogan: Stories, Tellings and Identities, in Daiute, C. and Lightfoot, C. (Eds.) *Narrative Analysis: Studying the Development of Individuals in Society.* Thousand Oaks, CA: Sage

Barthes, R. (1973). *Mythologies.* London: Paladin

Barthes, R. (1977). *Image, Music, Text: Essays Selected and Translated by Stephen Heath.* London: Fontana

Bauman, R. (1986). *Story, Performance and Event: Contextual Studies of Narrative.* Cambridge: Cambridge University Press

Bell, P. (1982). *Headlining Drugs: An Analysis of Newspaper Reports of Drug Related Issues in the NSW Press, 1980–1981*. Sydney: NSW Drug and Alcohol Education and Information Centre

Bengston, D. N., Fan, D. P., Reed, P. and Goldhor-Wilcock, A. (2009). Rapid Issue Tracking: A Method for Taking the Pulse of the Public Discussion of Environmental Policy, *Environmental Communication: A Journal of Nature and Culture*, 3/3, 367–85

Beniger, J. R. (1978). Media Content as Social Indicators: The Greenfield Index of Agenda Setting, *Communication Research*, 5/4, 437–53

Berelson, B. (1952). *Content Analysis in Communication Research*. Glencoe, IL: Free Press

Berger, A. A. (2011). *Media and Communication Research: An Introduction to Qualitative and Quantitative Approaches* (2nd edn.). London: Sage

Bettelheim, B. (1976). *The Uses of Enchantment: The Meaning and Importance of Fairy Tales*. New York: Knopf

Bird, E. (2003). The Audience in Everyday Life. London: Routledge

Bjorkvall, A., and Engblom, C. (2010). Young Children's Exploration of Semiotic Resources During Unofficial Computer Activities in the Classroom, *Journal of Early Childhood Literacy*, 10/3, 271–93

Boas, F. (1921). Ethnology of the Kwakiutl Based on Data Collected by George Hunt, 35th Annual Report of American Ethnology, Pt 2, 795–1481

Bolinger, D., and Sears, D. A. (1981). *Aspects of Language*. New York: Harcourt Brace Jovanovich, Inc

Bourdieu, P. (1998). *On Television*, trans. Parkhurst Ferguson, P. New York: The New Press

Boyd-Barrett, O. (2002). Theory in Media Research, in Newbold, C., Boyd-Barrett, O. and Bulck, H. v. d. (Eds.) *The Media Book*. London: Arnold, pp.1–54

Boykoff, M. T., and Boykoff, J. M. (2004). Balance as Bias: Global Warming and the US Prestige Press, *Global Environmental Change: Human and Policy Dimensions*, 14/2, 125–36

Bruner, J. (1990). *Acts of Meaning*. London: Harvard University Press

Bryman, A. (2008). *Social Research Methods* (3rd edn.). Oxford: Oxford University Press

Burgelin, O. (1972). Structural Analysis and Mass Communication, in McQuail, D. (Ed.) *Sociology of Mass Communications*. Harmondsworth: Penguin Books, pp.313–28

Burgess, J., and Harrison, C. M. (1993). The Circulation of Claims in the Cultural Politics of Environmental Change, in Hansen, A. (Ed.) *The Mass Media and Environmental Issues*. Leicester: Leicester University Press, pp.198–221

Burke, K. (1969). *A Rhetoric of Motives*. Berkeley: University of California Press

Caldas Coulthard, C. (1994). On Reporting Reporting: The Representation of Speech in Factual and Factional Narratives, in Coulthard, M. *Advances in Written Text Analysis*. London: Routledge, pp.295–308

Caldas Coulthard, C. (1997). *News as Social Practice: A Study in Critical Discourse Analysis*. Florianopolis, Brazil: Federal University of Santa Catarina Press

Caldas Coulthard, C. R. (1996), 'Women who Pay for Sex and Enjoy It': Transgression versus Morality in Women's Magazines, in Caldas Coulthard, C. R. and Coulthard, M. (Eds.) *Texts and Practices: Readings in Critical Discourse Analysis*. London: Routledge, pp.250–70

Cameron, D. (2000). *Good to Talk? Living and Working in a Communication Culture*. London: Sage

Carrithers, M. (1992). *Why Humans Have Cultures*. Oxford, Oxford University Press

Chiapello, E., and Fairclough, N. (2002). Understanding the New Management Ideology: A Transdisciplinary Contribution from Critical Discourse Analysis and New Sociology of Capitalism, *Discourse and Society*, 13/2, 185–208

Christopherson, N., Janning, M., and McConnell, E. D. (2002). Two Kicks Forward, One Kick Back: A Content Analysis of Media Discourses on the 1999 Women's World Cup Soccer Championship, *Sociology of Sport Journal*, 19/2, 170–88

Clayton, A., Hancock-Beaulieu, M., and Meadows, J. (1993). Change and Continuity in the Reporting of Science and Technology: A Study of *The Times* and the *Guardian, Public Understanding of Science*, 2/3, 225–34

Clifford, J., and Marcus, G. (1986). *Writing Culture: The Poetics and Politics of Ethnography*. Berkeley: University of California Press

Corner, J. (1991). Meaning, Genre and Context: The Problematics of 'Public Knowledge' in the New Audience Studies, in Curran, J. and Gurevitch, M. (Eds.) *Mass Media and Society*. London: Edward Arnold, pp.267–84

Corner, J., Richardson, K., and Fenton, N. (1990). *Nuclear Reactions: Form and Response in Public Issue Television*. London: John Libbey

Cottle, S. (1993). *TV News, Urban Conflict and the Inner City*. Leicester: Leicester University Press

Couper, M. P. (2008). *Designing Effective Web Surveys*. Cambridge: Cambridge University Press

Curran, J., and Seaton, J. (1977). *Power Without Responsibility*. London. Routledge

Curran, J., Gurevitch, M., and Woollacott, J. (1987). The Study of the Media: Theoretical Approaches, in Boyd-Barrett, O. and Graham, P. (Eds.) *Media, Knowledge, Power*. London: Croom Helm

Danielson, W. A., and Lasorsa, D. L. (1997). Perceptions of Social Change: 100 Years of Front-page Content in *The New York Times* and *The Los Angeles Times*, in Roberts, C. W. (Ed.) *Text Analysis for the Social Sciences*. Mahwah, NJ: Lawrence Erlbaum Associates, pp.103–15

Davis, S. N. (2003). Sex Stereotypes in Commercials Targeted Toward Children: A Content Analysis, *Sociological Spectrum*, 23/4, 407–24

Dearing, J. W., and Rogers, E. M. (1996). *Agenda-Setting* (Vol. 6). London: Sage

DeFleur, M. L. (1964). Occupational Roles as Portrayed on Television, *Public Opinion Quarterly*, 28, 57–74

Druschel, B. E. (1991). Sensationalism or Sensitivity: Use of Words in Stories on Acquired Immune Deficiency Syndrome by Associated Press Videotex, in Wolf, M. A. and Kielwasser, A. R. (Eds.) *Gay People, Sex and the Media*. Binghamton, NY: Haworth Press, pp.47–62

Dunmire, P. (2005). Preempting the Future: Rhetoric and Ideology of the Future in Political Discourse, *Discourse and Society*, 16, 481–513

Durant, J., Hansen, A., and Bauer, M. (1996). Public Understanding of the New Genetics, in Marteau, M. and Richards, J. (Eds.) *The Troubled Helix*. Cambridge: Cambridge University Press

Durant, J., Hansen, A., Bauer, M., and Gosling, A. (1993). *The Human Genome Project and the British Public: A Report to the European Commission*. London: The Science Museum

Einsiedel, E., and Coughlan, E. (1993). The Canadian Press and the Environment: Reconstructing a Social Reality, in Hansen, A. (Ed.) *The Mass Media and Environmental Issues*. Leicester: Leicester University Press, pp.134–49

Einsiedel, E. F. (1992). Framing Science and Technology in the Canadian Press, *Public Understanding of Science*, 1/1, 89–101

Elkins, J. (2003). *Visual Studies: A Skeptical Introduction*. London: Routledge

Entman, R. (2010). Framing Media Power, in D'Angelo, P. and Kuypers, J. A. (Eds.) *Doing News Framing Analysis: Empirical and Theoretical Perspectives*. London: Routledge, pp.331–55

Entman, R. M. (1993). Framing: Toward Clarification of a Fractured Paradigm, *Journal of Communication*, 43/4, 51–8

Entwistle, V., and Hancock-Beaulieu, M. (1992). Health and Medical Coverage in the UK National Press, *Public Understanding of Science*, 1/4, 367–82

Ericson, R. V., Baranek, P. M., and Chan, J. B. L. (1987). *Visualizing Deviance: A Study of News Organizations*. Milton Keynes: Open University Press

Ericson, R. V., Baranek, P. M., and Chan, J. B. L. (1989). *Negotiating Control: A Study of News Sources*. Milton Keynes: Open University Press

Ericson, R. V., Baranek, P. M., and Chan, J. B. L. (1991). *Representing Order: Crime, Law, and Justice in the News Media*. Milton Keynes: Open University Press

Evans-Pritchard, E. E. (1937). *Witchcraft, Oracles and Magic among the Azande*. Oxford: Clarendon Press

Fabb, N. (1997). *Linguistics and Literature: Language in the Verbal Arts of the World*. Oxford: Blackwell

Faber, B. (2003). Creating Rhetorical Stability in Corporate University Discourse, *Written Communication* 20/4, 391–426

Fairclough, N. (1989). *Language and Power*. London: Longman

Fairclough, N. (1995). *Media Discourse*. London: Arnold

Fairclough, N. (2000). *New Labour, New Language*. London: Routledge

Fairclough, N. (2003). *Analysing Discourse: Textual Analysis for Social Research*. London: Routledge

Fairclough, N., and Wodak, R. (1997), Critical Discourse Analysis, in van Dijk, T. (Ed.) *Discourse as Social Interaction*. London: Sage, pp.258–85

Fan, D. P. (1988). *Predictions of Public Opinion from the Mass Media: Computer Content Analysis and Mathematical Modelling*. New York: Greenwood Press

Fenton, N. (Ed.) (2009). *New Media, Old News: Journalism and Democracy in the Digital Age*. London: Sage

Fernhout, J. (2004). The Dutch Cosmopolitan – The Place of a Glamorous Magazine in A Calvinistic Society, unpublished research report, Centre for Language and Communication Research, Cardiff University

Field, A. (2009). *Discovering Statistics Using SPSS* (3rd edn.). London: Sage

Fink, A. (1995). *How to Design Surveys* (Vol. 5). London: Sage

Fink, A. (2009a). *Conducting Research Literature Reviews: From the Internet to Paper* (3rd edn.). London: Sage

Fink, A. (2009b). *How to Conduct Surveys: A Step-by-Step Guide* (4th edn.). London: Sage

Firth, J. R. (1957). *Papers in Linguistics 1934–1951*. London: Oxford University Press

Fishman, M. (1980). *Manufacturing the News*. Austin: University of Texas Press

Fishman, M. (1988). *Manufacturing the News* (trade paperback), Austin: University of Texas Press

Foucault, M. (1972). *The Archaeology of Knowledge*. London: Routledge

Foucault, M. (1978). *The Archaeology of Knowledge*. London: Tavistock

Foucault, M. (1980). *Power/Knowledge: Selected Interviews and Other Writings 1972–1977*. New York: Pantheon

Foucault, M. (1994). What is Enlightenment?, in Rabinow, P. (Ed.) *Michel Foucault, Essential Works Volume 1 (Ethics)*. Harmondsworth: Penguin

Fowler, R. (1977). *Linguistics and the Novel*. London: Methuen

Fowler, R. (1987). Notes on Critical Linguistics, in Steele, R. and Theadgold, T. (Eds.) *Language Topics: Essays in Honour of Michael Halliday* (Vol 2). Amsterdam: John Benjamins

Fowler, R. (1991). *Language in the News*. London Routledge

Franzosi, R. (Ed.) (2007). *Content Analysis*. London: Sage

Frazer, J. (1922). *The Golden Bough: A Study in Magic and Religion*. New York: The Macmillan Co

Friese, S. (2012). *Qualitative Data Analysis with ATLAS.ti*. London: Sage

Galtung, J., and Ruge, M. H. (1965). The Structure of Foreign News, *Journal of International Peace Research*, 1, 64–90

Gamson, W. A. (1992). *Talking Politics*. New York: Cambridge University Press

Gans, H. J. (1979). *Deciding What's News*. New York: Vintage

Geertz, C. (1973). *The Interpretation of Cultures*. New York: Basic Books

Gellner, E. (1983). *Nations and Nationalism*. London: Blackwell

Gerbner, G. (1972). Violence in Television Drama: Trends and Symbolic Functions, in Comstock, G. A. and Rubinstein, E. A. (Eds.) *Media Content and Control: Television and Social Behavior* (Vol. 1). Washington, DC: U.S. Government Printing Office, pp.28–187

Gerbner, G. (1995). Toward 'Cultural Indicators': The Analysis of Mass Mediated Public Message Systems, in Boyd-Barrett, O. and Newbold, C. (Eds.) *Approaches to Media: A Reader*. London: Arnold, pp.144–52

Gerbner, G., Gross, L., Morgan, M., and Signorielli, N. (1994). Growing Up with Television: The Cultivation Perspective, in Bryant, J. and Zimmerman, D. (Eds.) *Media Effects: Advances in Theory and Research*. Hillsdale, NJ: Lawrence Erlbaum Associates, pp.17–41

Giddens, A. (1989). *Sociology*. Cambridge: Polity

Gillespie, M. (1995). *Television, Ethnicity and Cultural Change*. London: Routledge

Gitlin, T. (1978). Media Sociology: The Dominant Paradigm, *Theory and Society*, 6/2, 205–53

Golding, P., and Murdock, G. (2000). Culture, Communications and Political Economy, in Curran, J. and Gurevitch, M. (Eds.) *Mass Media and Society*. London: Arnold

Gramsci, A. (1971a). *Selections from the Prison Notebooks*, ed. and trans. Greimas, A. London: Lawrence & Wishart

Gramsci, A. (1971b). *Selections from the Prison Notebooks*, eds. and trans. Hoare, Q. and Nowell Smith, G. London: Lawrence & Wishart

Greimas, A. (1971). Narrative Grammar: Units and Levels, *Modern Language Notes*, 86, 7793–806

Gunter, B., Hansen, A., and Touri, M. (2010). *Alcohol Advertising and Young People's Drinking: Representation, Reception and Regulation*. Basingstoke: Palgrave Macmillan

Hacking, I. (1983). *Representation and Intervening: Introductory Topics in the Philosophy of Natural Science*. Cambridge: Cambridge University Press

Hall, S., Critcher, C., Jefferson, T., Clarke, J., and Roberts, B. (1978). *Policing the Crisis*. London: Macmillan

Halliday, M. A. K. (1978). *Language as Social Semiotic: The Social Interpretation of Language and Meaning*. London: Edward Arnold

Halliday, M. A. K. (1985). *An Introduction to Functional Grammar*. London: Arnold

Halliday, M. A. K. (1994). *An Introduction to Functional Grammar*. London: Arnold

Hallin, D. C. (1996). Commercialism and Professionalism in the American News Media, in Curran, J. and Gurevitch, M. (Eds.) *Mass Media and Society*. London: Arnold

Halloran, J. D. (1998). Asking the Right Questions, in Hansen, A., Cottle, S., Negrine, R. and Newbold, C. (Eds.) *Mass Communication Research Methods*. London: Macmillan, pp. 9–34

Halloran, J. D., Elliott, P., and Murdock, G. (1970). *Demonstrations and Communication*. Harmondsworth: Penguin

Hansen, A. (1991). The Media and the Social Construction of the Environment, *Media Culture and Society*, 13/4, 443–58

Hansen, A. (1995). Using Information Technology to Analyze Newspaper Content, in Lee, R. M. (Ed.) *Information Technology for the Social Scientist*. London: UCL Press, pp. 147–68

Hansen, A. (2002). Discourses of Nature in Advertising, *Communications*, 27, 499–511

Hansen, A. (2006). Tampering With Nature: 'Nature' and the 'Natural' in Media Coverage of Genetics and Biotechnology, *Media, Culture and Society*, 28/6, 811–34

Hansen, A. (2009). Researching 'Teachers in the News': The Portrayal of Teachers and Education Issues in the British National and Regional Press, *Education 3–13: International Journal of Primary, Elementary and Early Years Education*, 37/4, 335–47

Hansen, A. (2010). *Environment, Media and Communication*. London: Routledge

Hansen, A. (2011). Communication, Media and Environment: Towards Reconnecting Research on the Production, Content and Social Implications of Environmental Communication, *International Communication Gazette*, 73/1–2, 7–25

Hansen, A., and Dickinson, R. (1992). Science Coverage in the British Mass Media: Media Output and Source Input, *Communications*, 17/3, 365–77

Hart, R. P. (2000). *Campaign Talk: Why Elections are Good for Us*. Princeton, NJ: Princeton University Press

Hartmann, P., Husband, C., and Clark, J. (1974). Race as News, in Halloran, J. D. (Ed.) *Race as News*. Paris: The Unesco Press, pp.90–173

Hasty, J. 2006. Performing Power, Composing Culture: The State Press in Ghana, *Ethnography*, 7, 69–98

Hedges, A. (1985). Group Interviewing, in Walker, R. (Ed.) *Applied Qualitative Research*. Aldershot: Gower, pp.71–91

Herman, E. S. (1985). Diversity of News: 'Marginalising' the Opposition, *Journal of Communication*, 35/3, 135–46

Herman, E. S. and Chomsky, N. (1988). *Manufacturing Consent: The Political Economy of the Mass Media*. New York: Pantheon Books

Hermes, J. (1995). *Reading Women's Magazines: An Analysis of Everyday Media Use*. Cambridge: Polity

Hether, H. J., and Murphy, S. T. (2010). Sex Roles in Health Storylines on Prime Time Television: A Content Analysis, *Sex Roles*, 62/11–12, 810–21

Hills, M. (2002). *Fan Cultures*. London: Routledge

Hine, C. (2011). Towards Ethnography of Television on the Internet: A Mobile Strategy for Exploring Mundane Interpretive Activities, *Media Culture and Society*, 33/4, 567–82

Hobson, D. (1982). *Crossroads: The Drama of a Soap Opera*. London: Methuen

Hodge, R., and Kress, G. (1988). *Social Semiotics*. Ithaca, NY: Cornell University Press

Hodge, R., and Kress, G. (1993). *Language as Ideology* (2nd edn.), London: Routledge

Höijer, B. (1990). Studying Viewers' Reception of Television Programmes: Theoretical and Methodological Considerations, *European Journal of Communication*, 5/1, 29–56

Hollingsworth, M. (1986). *The Press and Political Dissent*. London: Pluto

Holsti, O. R. (1969). *Content Analysis for the Social Sciences and Humanities*. Reading, MA: Addison-Wesley

Hornig, S. (1990). Television's NOVA and the Construction of Scientific Truth, *Critical Studies in Mass Communication*, 7/1, 11–23

Hughes, E., Kitzinger, J., and Murdock, G. (2008). Media Discourses and Framing of Risk, Social Contexts and Responses to Risk Network (SCARR) Working Paper 27. Available at http://www.cardiff.ac.uk/jomec/resources/Kitzinger WkPaper27.pdf

Hyvarinen, N. (1998). Thick and Thin Narratives: Thickness of Description, Expectation and Causality, in Denzin, N. (Ed.) *Cultural Studies: A Research Volume* (Vol. 3). London: Jai Press, pp.49–174

Hyvarinen, M. (2008). Analysing Narratives and Story-Telling, in Aluutari, P., Bickman, L. and Brannen, J. (Eds.) *The SAGE Handbook of Social Research Methods*. London, Sage, pp.477–60

Irigaray, L. (1985). *This Sex Which Is Not One*. Ithaca: Cornell University Press

Jahner, E. A., Walker, J. R., and De Mallie, R. J. (Eds.) (1991). *Lakota Belief and Ritual*. Lincoln: University of Nebraska Press

Janowitz, M. (1976). Content Analysis and the Study of Sociopolitical Change, *Journal of Communication*, 26/4, 10–21

Jensen, K. B. (2002). The Complementarity of Qualitative and Quantitative Methodologies in Media and Communication Research, in Jensen, K. B. (Ed.) *A Handbook of Media and Communication Research: Qualitative and Quantitative Methodologies*. London: Routledge, pp.254–72

Jesson, J., and Matheson, L. (2011). *Doing Your Literature Review*. London: Sage

Katz, E., and Lazarsfeld, P. F. (1955). *Personal Influence*. New York: The Free Press

Kellner, D. (1990). *Television and the Crisis of Democracy*. Boulder, CO: Westview Press

Kitzinger, J. (1993). Understanding AIDS: Researching Audience Perceptions of Acquired Immune Deficiency Syndrome, in Eldridge, J. (Ed.) *Getting the Message: News, Truth and Power*. London: Routledge, pp.271–304

Kitzinger, J. (1994). The Methodology of Focus Groups – the Importance of Interaction Between Research Participants, *Sociology of Health and Illness*, 16/1, 103–21

Kitzinger, J. (2004). Audience and Readership Research, in Downing, J., McQuail, D., Schlesinger, P. and Wartella, E. (Eds.) *The SAGE Handbook of Media Studies*. London: Sage, pp.167–81

Kress, G. (1985). *Linguistic Processes in Sociocultural Practice*. Geelong: Deakin University Press

Kress, G. (1989). *Linguistic Processes in Sociocultural Practice*. Oxford: Oxford University Press

Kress, G., and van Leeuwen, T. (1996). *Reading Images: The Grammar of Visual Design*. London: Routledge

Krippendorff, K. (2004). *Content Analysis: An Introduction to its Methodology* (2nd edn.). London: Sage

Krippendorff, K., and Bock, M. A. (Eds.) (2008). *The Content Analysis Reader*. London: Sage

Krueger, R. A. (1988). *Focus Groups: A Practical Guide for Applied Research*. London: Sage

Krueger, R. A., and Casey, M. A. (2009). *Focus Groups: A Practical Guide for Applied Research* (4th edn.). London: Sage

Labov, W. (1997). Narrative Analysis: Oral Versions of Personal Experience, in *Journal of Narrative and Life History*, 7/1–4, 3–38

Labov, W., and Waletsky, J. (1997). Narrative Analysis, in Helm, J. and Martin. J. (Eds.) *English Text: System and Structure*. Philadelphia: John Benjamins

Lazarsfeld, P. F. (1941). Remarks on Administrative and Critical Communications Research, *Studies in Philosophy and Science*, 9, 3–16

Lazarsfeld, P. F., Berelson, B., and Gaudet, H. (1944). *The People's Choice: How the Voter Makes Up His Mind in a Presidential Election*. New York: Duell, Sloan and Pearce

Lazarsfeld, P. F., Berelson, B., and Gaudet, H. (1948). *The People's Choice: How the Voter Makes Up His Mind in a Presidential Election*. New York: Columbia University Press

Leach, E. E., and Aycock, A. D. (1983). *Structuralist Interpretations of Biblical Myth*. Cambridge: Cambridge University Press

Lévi-Strauss, C. (1963). *Structural Anthropology*. New York Basic Books

Lévi-Strauss, C. (1967). The Story of Asdiwal, in Leach, E. (Ed.) *The Structural Study of Myth and Totemism*. London: Tavistock, pp.1–47

Levitas, R. (2005). *The Inclusive Society: Social Exclusion and New Labour*. London: MacMillan

Levy, M. R. (1977). Experiencing Television News, *Journal of Communication*, 27/4, 112–17

Lewins, A., and Silver, C. (2007). *Using Software in Qualitative Research: A Step-by-Step Guide*. London: Sage

Liebes, T., and Katz, E. (1986). Patterns of Involvement in Television Fiction: A Comparative Analysis, *European Journal of Communication*, 1/2, 151–71

Liebes, T., and Katz, E. (1990). *The Export of Meaning: Cross-cultural Readings of 'Dallas'*. New York: Oxford University Press

Lindlof, T. R., Shatzer, M. J., and Wilkinson, D. (1988). Accommodation of Video and Television in the American Family, in Lull, J. (Ed.) *World Families Watch Television*. London: Sage, pp.158–92

Livingstone, S., and Lunt, P. (1993). *Talk on Television: Audience Participation and Public Debate*. London: Routledge

Livingstone, S. M. (1991). Audience Reception: The Role of the Viewer in Retelling Romantic Drama, in Curran, J. and Gurevitch, M. (Eds.) *Mass Media and Society*. London: Edward Arnold, pp.285–306

Logan, R. A., Zengjun, P., and Wilson, N. F. (2000). Science and Medical Coverage in the *Los Angeles Times* and *The Washington Post*: A Six-year Perspective, *Science Communication*, 22/1, 5–26

Lowery, S., and DeFleur, M. (1995). *Milestones in Mass Communication Research: Media Effects* (3rd edn.). White Plains, NY: Longman

Lull, J. (1978). Choosing Television Programs by Family Vote, *Communication Quarterly*, 26/1, 53–7

Lull, J. (Ed.) (1988). *World Families Watch Television*. London: Sage

Lunt, P., and Livingstone, S. (1996). Rethinking the Focus Group in Media and Communications Research, *Journal of Communication*, 46/2, 79–98

MacGregor, B., and Morrison, D. E. (1995). From Focus Groups to Editing Groups: A New Method of Reception Analysis, *Media Culture and Society*, 17/1, 141–50

Machin, D. (2002). *Ethnographic Research for Media Studies*. London: Arnold

Machin, D. (2007a). *Introduction to Multimodal Analysis*. London: Arnold

Machin, D. (2007b). Visual Discourses of War: A Multimodal Analysis of the Iraq Occupation, in Hodges, A. and Nilep, C. (Eds.) *Discourse, War and Terrorism*. Amsterdam: John Benjamins, pp.123–42

Machin, D., and Mayr, A. (2006). Antiracism in the British Government's Model Regional Newspaper: The 'Talking Cure', *Discourse and Society*, 18/4, 453–78

Machin, D., and Mayr, A. (2012). *How to do Critical Discourse Analysis: A Multimodal Approach*. London: Sage

Machin, D., and Niblock, S. (2007). *News Production: Theory and Practice*. London: Routledge.

Machin, D. and Thornborrow, J. (2003) Branding and Discourse: The Case of Cosmopolitan, *Discourse and Society*, 14/4, 453–73

Machin, D., and Thornborrow, J. (2006). Lifestyle and the Depoliticisation of Agency: Sex as Power in Women's Magazines, *Social Semiotics*, 16/1, 173–88

Machin, D., and van Leeuwen, T. (2003). Global Schemas and Local Discourses in Cosmopolitan, *Journal of Sociolinguistics*, 7/4, 493–512

Machin, D., and van Leeuwen T. (2005a). Computer Games as Political Discourse: The Case of Black Hawk Down, *Journal of Language and Politics*, 4/1, 119–43

Machin, D., and van Leeuwen, T. (2005b). Language Style and Lifestyle: The Case of a Global Magazine, *Media Culture and Society*, 27, 577–600

Machin, D., and van Leeuwen, T. J. (2007). *Global Media Discourse: A Critical Introduction*. Routledge, London

Malinowski, B. (1922). *Argonauts of the Western Pacific*. New York, E. P. Dutton and Co Inc

Matthes, J., and Kohring, M. (2008). The Content Analysis of Media Frames: Toward Improving Reliability and Validity, *Journal of Communication*, 58/2, 258–79

Mayer, V. (2005). Research Beyond the Pale: Whiteness in Audience Studies and Media Ethnography, *Communication Theory*, 15/2, 148–67

McChesney, R. (2004). *The Problem of the Media: U.S. Communication Politics in the 21st Century*. New York: Monthly Review Press

McChesney, R. W. (2003). The Problem of Journalism: A Political Economic Contribution to an Explanation of the Crisis in Contemporary US Journalism, *Journalism Studies*, 4/3, 299–329

McClintock, M. (2002). *Instruments of Statecraft: US Guerrilla Warfare, Counterinsurgency and Counterterrorism 1940–1990*, New York: Pantheon

McCombs, M. (2004). *Setting the Agenda: The Mass Media and Public Opinion*. Cambridge: Polity

McCombs, M., and Reynolds, A. (2009). How the News Shapes Our Civic Agenda, in Bryant, J. and Oliver, M. B. (Eds.) *Media Effects: Advances in Theory and Research* (3rd edn.). London: Taylor and Francis, pp.1–15

McCombs, M. E., and Shaw, D. L. (1972). The Agenda-setting Function of Mass Media, *Public Opinion Quarterly*, 36, 176–87

McCormack, T. (1982). Content Analysis: The Social History of a Method, in McCormack, T. (Ed.) *Studies in Communications: Culture, Code and Content Analysis* (Vol. 2). Greenwich, CT: JAI Press Inc, pp.143–78

McQuail, D. (1994). Theory of Media and Theory of Society, in McQuail, D. *Mass Communication Theory: An Introduction*. London: Sage

McQuail, D. (2004). Overview of the Handbook, in Downing, J., McQuail, D., Schlesinger, P. and Wartella, E. (Eds.) *The SAGE Handbook of Media Studies*. London: Sage, pp.1–16

Mead, G. H. (1934). *Mind, Self and Society*. Chicago: University of Chicago Press

Merton, R. K. (1987). The Focussed Interview and Focus Groups: Continuities and Discontinuities, *Public Opinion Quarterly*, 51/4, 550–66

Merton, R. K., and Kendall, P. L. (1946). The Focused Interview, *American Journal of Sociology*, 51, 541–57

Merton, R. K., Fiske, M., and Kendall, P. L. (1956). *The Focused Interview: A Manual of Problems and Procedures*. Glencoe, IL: The Free Press

Merton, R. K., Lowenthal, M. F., and Kendall, P. L. (1990). *The Focused Interview: A Manual of Problems and Procedures*. (2nd edn.). New York: Collier Macmillan

Miller, D., and Slater, D. (2000). *The Internet: An Ethnographic Approach*. Oxford: Berg

Mirzoeff, N. (1998). *The Visual Culture Reader*. London: Routledge

Mody, B. (2010). *The Geopolitics of Representation in Foreign News: Explaining Darfur*. Lanham, MD: Lexington Books

Molotch, H., and Lester, M. (1975). Accidental News: The Great Oil Spill, *American Journal of Sociology*, 81/2, 235–60

Morgan, D. L. (1988). *Focus Groups as Qualitative Research*. Newbury Park, CA: Sage

Morgan, D. L. (Ed.) (1993). *Successful Focus Groups: Advancing the State of the Art*. Newbury Park: Sage

Morgan, M., and Shanahan, J. (2010). The State of Cultivation, *Journal of Broadcasting and Electronic Media*, 54/2, 337–55

Morgan, D. L., and Spanish, M. T. (1984). Focus Groups: A New Tool for Qualitative Research, *Qualitative Sociology*, 7, 253–70

Morley, D. (1980). *The 'Nationwide' Audience*. London: British Film Institute

Morley, D. (1986). *Family Television*. London: Comedia

Morrison, D. E. (1998). *The Search for a Method: Focus Groups and the Development of Mass Communication Research*. Luton: University of Luton Press

Mowlana, H., Gerbner, G., and Schiller, H. (Eds.) (1992). Triumph of the Image: The Media's War in the Persian Gulf – A Global Perspective. Boulder: Westview Press

Murdock, G. (2002). Media, Culture and Modern Times, in Jensen, K. B. (Ed.) *A Handbook of Media and Communication Research: Qualitative and Quantitative Methodologies*. London: Routledge, pp.40–57

Neuendorf, K. A. (2002a). *The Content Analysis Guidebook*. London: Sage

Neuendorf, K. A. (2002b). *The Content Analysis Guidebook Online*. Retrieved 17 November 2011, from http://academic.csuohio.edu/kneuendorf/content/

Neuman, W. R. (1989). Parallel Content Analysis: Old Paradigms and New Proposals, in Comstock, G. (Ed.) *Public Communication and Behavior* (Vol. 2). San Diego, CA: Academic Press, pp.205–89

Nichols, B. (1981). *Ideology and the Image*, Bloomington, IN: Indiana University Press

Nimmo, D., and Combs, J. E. (1985). *Nightly Horrors: Crisis Coverage in Television Network News*. Knoxville, TN: University of Tennessee Press

Nisbet, M. C., and Lewenstein, B. V. (2002). Biotechnology and the American Media: The Policy Process and the Elite Press, 1970 to 1999, *Science Communication*, 23/4, 359–91

Okeley, J. (1992). Anthropology and Autobiography: Participatory Experience and Embodied Knowledge, in Okeley, J. and Callaway, H. (Eds.) *Anthropology and Autobiography*. London and New York: Routledge

Oxford English Dictionary Online (2010). Survey, n. Retrieved 21 June 2011, from http://www.oed.com/view/Entry/195089?rskey=pKTxV9andamp;result=1 andamp;isAdvanced=false

Oxford English Dictionary Online (2011). Research, n.1. Retrieved 16 August 2011, from http://www.oed.com/view/Entry/163432?rskey=y7cMnZandresult=1andis Advanced=false

Paek, H. J., Nelson, M. R., and Vilela, A. M. (2011). Examination of Gender-role Portrayals in Television Advertising across Seven Countries, *Sex Roles*, 64/3–4, 192–207

Paterson, C., and Domingo, D. (Eds.) (2008). *Making Online News: The Ethnography of New Media Production*. London: Peter Lang

Peter, J., Semetko, H. A., and de Vreese, C. H. (2003). EU Politics on Television News: A Cross-national Comparative Study, *European Union Politics*, 4/3, 305–27

Pew Research Center (2010). Little Change in Opinions about Global Warming. Retrieved 21 June 2011, from http://people-press.org/2010/10/27/little-change-in-opinions-about-global-warming/#overview

Pew Research Center (no date). Open and Closed-ended Questions. Retrieved 22 June 2011, from http://people-press.org/methodology/questionnaire-design/open-and-closed-ended-questions/

Pew Research Center's Project for Excellence in Journalism (2011a). News Index: Our Weekly Content Analysis. Retrieved 22 June 2011, from http://www.journal-ism.org/news_index/99

Pew Research Center's Project for Excellence in Journalism (2011b). The State of the News Media 2011: An Annual Report on American Journalism. Retrieved 17 November 2011, from http://stateofthemedia.org/2011/methodologies/#a-year-in-the-news

Philo, G. (1990). *Seeing and Believing: The Influence of Television*. London: Routledge

Philo, G. (2007). Can Discourse Analysis Successfully Explain the Content of Media and Journalistic Practice?, *Journalism Studies*, 8/2, April, 175–96

Philo, G., and Berry, M. (2011). *More Bad News from Israel*. London: Pluto

Philo, G., and Miller, D. (2000). Cultural Compliance and Critical Media Studies, *Media Culture and Society*, 22/6, 831–9

Picard, R. G., and Adams, P. D. (1991). Characterizations of Acts and Perpetrators of Political Violence in Three Elite U.S. Daily Newspapers, in Alali, A. O. and Eke, K. K. (Eds.) *Media Coverage of Terrorism: Methods of Diffusion*. London: Sage, pp.12–22

Polanyi, M. (1958). *Personal Knowledge: Towards a Post-Critical Philosophy*. London: Routledge

Poole, E., and Richardson, J. E. (2006). *Muslims and the Media*. London: I. B. Tauris

Press, A. L. (1991). Working-class Women in a Middle-class World: The Impact of Television on Modes of Reasoning about Abortion, *Critical Studies in Mass Communication*, 8/4, 421–41

Propp, V. (1968). *Morphology of the Folk Tale*. Austin: University of Texas Press

Pullen, K. (2004). Everybody's Gotta Love Somebody, Sometime: Online Fan Community, in Gauntlett, D. and Horsley, R. (Eds.) *Web.Studies* (2nd edn.). London: Arnold, pp.80–91

Reese, S. D., Gandy, O. H., and Grant, A. E. (Eds.) (2001). *Framing Public Life: Perspectives on Media and Our Understanding of the Social World*. Mahwah, NJ: Lawrence Erlbaum Associates

Resche, C. (2004). Investigating 'Greenspanese': From Hedging to 'Fuzzy Transparency', *Discourse and Society*, 15/6, 723–44

Richards, L. (2009). *Handling Qualitative Data: A Practical Guide*. London: Sage

Richardson, J. E. (2007). *Analysing Newspapers*. London Macmillan

Riessman, C. K. (1990). Strategic Uses of Narrative in the Presentation of Self and Illness, *Social Science and Medicine*, 30, 1195–200

Riffe, D., Aust, C. F., and Lacy, S. R. (1993). The Effectiveness of Random, Consecutive Day and Constructed Week Sampling in Newspaper Content Analysis, *Journalism Quarterly*, 70/1, 133–9

Riffe, D., Lacy, S., and Fico, F. (2005). *Analyzing Media Messages: Using Quantitative Content Analysis in Research* (2nd edn.). Mahwah, NJ: Lawrence Erlbaum

Rimmon-Kenan, S. (1983). *Narrative Fiction: Contemporary Poetics*. London: Methuen

Rosengren, K. E. (1983). Communication Research: One Paradigm, or Four?, *Journal of Communication*, 33/3, 185–207

Rothman, S., and Lichter, S. R. (1987). Elite Ideology and Risk Perception in Nuclear Energy Policy, *American Political Science Review*, 81/2, 383–404

Royal Commission on the Press (1949). *The Royal Commission on the Press, 1947–1949*. London: HMSO

Russell, C. A., and Russell, D. W. (2009). Alcohol Messages in Prime-Time Television Series, *Journal Of Consumer Affairs*, 43/1, 108–28

Schlesinger, P. (1978). *Putting Reality Together: BBC News*. London: Constable

Schlesinger, P., and Tumber, H. (1994). *Reporting Crime: The Media Politics of Criminal Justice*. Oxford: Clarendon Press

Schlesinger, P., Dobash, R. E., Dobash, R. P., and Weaver, C. K. (1992). *Women Viewing Violence*. London: BFI Publishing

Schrøder, K. C. (1987). Convergence of Antagonistic Traditions? The Case of Audience Research, *European Journal of Communication*, 2/1, 7–31

Schrøder, K., Drotner, K., Kline, S., and Murray, C. (2003). *Researching Audiences*. London: Arnold

Schwenkel, C. (2009). 'The Camera Was My Weapon': Reporting and Representing War in Socialist Vietnam, in Bird, E. (Ed.) *The Anthropology of News and Journalism: Global Perspectives*. Bloomington: Indiana University Press, pp.86–99

Scott, M. (2009). Marginalized, Negative or Trivial? Coverage of Africa in the UK Press, *Media Culture and Society*, 31/4, 533–57

Scott, M., and Tribble, C. (2006). *Textual Patterns: Key Words and Corpus Analysis in Language Education* (Vol. 22). Amsterdam: John Benjamins Publishing Company

Scott, W. A. (1955). Reliability of Content Analysis: The Case of Nominal Scale Coding, *Public Opinion Quarterly*, Fall, 321–5

Semetko, H. A. (1989). Television News and the 'Third Force' in British Politics: A Case Study of Election Communication, *European Journal of Communication*, 4/4, 453–79

Semetko, H. A., and Valkenburg, P. M. (2000). Framing European Politics: A Content Analysis of Press and Television News, *Journal of Communication*, 50/2, 93–109

Shanahan, J., and McComas, K. (1999). *Nature Stories: Depictions of the Environment and their Effects*. Cresskill, NJ: Hampton Press

Shanahan, J., and Morgan, M. (1999). *Television and Its Viewers: Cultivation Theory and Research*. Cambridge: Cambridge University Press

Shaw, R. L., Whitehead, C., and Giles, D. C. (2010). 'Crack Down on the Celebrity Junkies': Does Media Coverage of Celebrity Drug Use Pose a Risk to Young People?, *Health Risk and Society*, 12/6, 575–89

Shepherd, R., Barnett, J., Cooper, H., Coyle, A., Moran-Ellis, J., Senior, V., et al. (2007). Towards an Understanding of British Public Attitudes Concerning Human Cloning, *Social Science and Medicine*, 65/2, 377–92

Shoemaker, P. J., and McCombs, M. E. (2009). Survey Research, in Hansen, A. (Ed.) *Mass Communication Research Methods* (Vol. 3). London: Sage, pp.378–401

Silverstone, R. (1991). From Audiences to Consumers: The Household and the Consumption of Communication and Information Technologies, *European Journal of Communication*, 6/2, 135–54

Simpson, P. (2004). *Stylistics: A Resource Book for Students*. London: Routledge

Smith, L. J. (1994). A Content-Analysis Of Gender Differences In Children's Advertising, *Journal Of Broadcasting and Electronic Media*, 38/3, 323–37

Stahl, W. A. (1995). Venerating the Black-Box: Magic in Media Discourse on Technology, *Science Technology and Human Values*, 20/2, 234–58

Stevenson, R. (1995). Project Proposal: Corporate Study of Foreign News and International News Flow in the 1990s, Retrieved 10 January 2005, from http://www.ibiblio.org/newsflow/

Stewart, D. W., and Shamdasani, P. N. (1990). *Focus Groups: Theory and Practice*. Newbury Park: Sage

Stewart, D. W., Shamdasani, P. N., and Rook, D. W. (2007). *Focus Groups: Theory and Practice* (2nd edn.). London: Sage

Stone, P. J., Dunphy, D. C., Smith, M. S., and Ogilvie, D. M. (1966). *The General Inquirer: A Computer Approach to Content Analysis*. Cambridge, MA: MIT Press

Sumner, C. (1979). *Reading Ideologies: An Investigation into the Marxist Theory of Ideology and Law*. London: Academic Press

Sunoo, B. P. (1998). Corporate Universities – More and Better, *Workforce*, 77/5, 16–17.

Tankard, J. W. (2001). The Empirical Approach to the Study of Media Framing, in Reese, S. D, Gandy, O. H. and Grant, A. E. (Eds.) *Framing Public Life: Perspectives on Media and Our Understanding of the Social World*. Mahwah, NJ: Lawrence Erlbaum Associates, pp.95–106

Teo, P. (2000). Racism in the News: A Critical Discourse Analysis of News Reporting in Two Australian Newspapers, *Discourse and Society*, 11, 7–49

Tesch, R. (1991). Software for Qualitative Researchers: Analysis Needs and Program Capabilities, in Fielding, N. G. and Lee, R. M. (Eds.) *Using Computers in Qualitative Research*. London: Sage, pp.16–37

Tewksbury, D., and Reynolds, A. (2009). News Framing Theory and Research, in Bryant, J. and Oliver, M. B. (Eds.) *Media Effects: Advances in Theory and Research* (3rd edn.). London: Taylor and Francis, pp.17–33

Thelwall, M. A. (2009). *Introduction to Webometrics: Quantitative Web Research for the Social Sciences*. San Rafael, CA: Morgan and Claypool Publishers

Thomas, S. (1994). Artifactual Study in the Analysis Of Culture: A Defense of Content-Analysis in a Postmodern Age., *Communication Research*, 21/6, 683–97

Thornborrow, J., and Coates, J. (Eds.) (2005). *The Sociolinguistics of Narrative*. Amsterdam: John Benjamins

Thrasher, F. M. (1927). *The Gang: A Study of 1.313 Gangs in Chicago*. Chicago: Chicago University Press

Todorov, T. (1990). *Genres in Discourse*. Oxford: Blackwell

Toolan, M. (1988). *Narrative: A Critical Linguistic Approach*. London: Routledge

Trinity Mirror plc (2007). Annual Report and Accounts 2007. Retrieved 10 October 2012, from www.trinitymirror.com/pdf/Trinity_Mirror_web_07.pdf

Tuchman, G. (1978). *Making News: A Study in the Construction of Reality*. New York: The Free Press

Tufte, T. (2000). *Living with the Rubbish Queen: Telenovelas, Culture and Modernity in Brazil*. Luton: University of Luton Press

Tunstall, J., and Machin, D. (1999). *The Anglo-American Media Connection*. Oxford, Oxford University Press

Tunstall, J., and Palmer, M. (1991). *Media Moguls*. London: Routledge

Tusting, K., Crawshaw, R., and Callen, B. (2002). 'I Know, 'cos I Was There': How Residence Abroad Students Use Personal Experience to Legitimate Cultural Generalizations, *Discourse and Society*, Sep. 13, 651–72

Van Dijk, T. A. (1990). Discourse and Society: A New Journal for a New Research Focus, *Discourse and Society*, 1, 5–16

Van Dijk, T. A. (1991). *Racism and the Press*. London: Routledge

Van Dijk, T. A. (1993). *Discourse and Elite Racism*. London: Sage

Van Hout, T., and Jacobs, G. (2008). News Production Theory and Practice: Fieldnotes on Power, Interaction and Agency, *Pragmatics* 18/1, 59–85

Van Leeuwen, T. (1995). Representing Social Action, *Discourse Society*, 6/6, 81–106

Van Leeuwen, T. (1996). The Representations of Social Actors, In Caldas Coulthard, C. R. and Coulthard, M. (Eds.) *Texts and Practices*. London: Routledge, pp.32–70

Van Leeuwen, T. (2001). Semiotics and Iconography, in van Leeuwen, T. and Jewitt, C. (Eds.) *Handbook of Visual Analysis*. London: Sage, pp.92–118

Van Leeuwen, T. (2005). *Introducing Social Semiotics*. London: Routledge

Van Leeuwen, T., and Wodak, R. (1999). Legitimizing Immigration Control: A Discourse-historical Analysis, *Discourse Studies*, 1/1, 83–118

Vicsek, L., and Gergely, J. (2011). Media Presentation and Public Understanding of Stem Cells and Stem Cell Research in Hungary, *New Genetics and Society*, 30/1, 1–26

Wahl-Jorgensen, K. (2007). *Journalists and the Public: Newsroom Culture, Letters to the Editor, and Democracy*. Creskill, NJ: Hampton Press

Wallis, C. (2011). Performing Gender: A Content Analysis of Gender Display in Music Videos, *Sex Roles*, 64/3–4, 160–72

Wanta, W., Golan, G., and Lee, C. (2004). Agenda Setting and International News: Media Influence on Public Perceptions of Foreign Nations, *Journalism and Mass Communication Quarterly*, 81/2, 364–77

Warner, M. (1973). Decision-making in Network Television News, in Tunstall, J. (Ed.) *Media Sociology: A Reader*. Chicago: University of Illinois Press, pp.158–67

Wasko, J. (1982). *Movie and Money: Financing the American Film Industry*. Hillsdale, NJ: Ablex

Weaver, D. H. (Ed.) (1998). *The Global Journalist: News People Around the World*. Cresskill, NJ: Hampton Press

Weigel, R. H., Kim, E. L., and Frost, J. L. (1995). Race-Relations On Prime-Time Television Reconsidered: Patterns Of Continuity and Change, *Journal Of Applied Social Psychology*, 25/3, 223–36

Weitkamp, E. (2003). British Newspapers Privilege Health and Medicine Topics over Other Science News, *Public Relations Review*, 29/3, 321–33

Wells, L. (2002). *The Photography Reader*. London: Routledge

Widdowson, H. G. (1998). The Theory and Practice of Critical Discourse Analysis, *Applied Linguistics*, 19/1, 136–51

Wimmer, R. D., and Dominick, J. R. (2006). *Mass Media Research: An Introduction* (8th edn.). Belmont: Wadsworth

Wimmer, R. D., and Dominick, J. R. (2011). *Mass Media Research: An Introduction (International Edition)* (9th revised edn.). Belmont: Wadsworth

Wiseman, J. P., and Aron, M. S. (1970). *Field Projects for Sociology Students*. Cambridge, MA: Schenkman

Wodak, R. (1989). *Language, Power and Ideology: Studies in Political Discourse*. Amsterdam: John Benjamins

Wolfsfeld, G. (1997). *Media and Political Conflict: News from the Middle East*. Cambridge: Cambridge University Press

Wood, L. A., Kroger, R.O. (2000). *Doing Discourse Analysis: Methods for Studying Action in Talk and Text*. Thousand Oaks: Sage Publications

Wright, W. (1975). *Sixguns and Society: A Structural Study of the Western*. Berkeley: University of California Press

Ziman, J. (1978). *Reliable Knowledge: An Exploration of the Grounds for Belief in Science*. Cambridge: Cambridge University Press

Subject index

Author/name index

Printed and bound in Great Britain by
CPI Antony Rowe, Chippenham and Eastbourne